THE

ALMANAC OF

VIRGINIA POLITICS

2005

**The State Senators and Delegates
Their records and districts
2004 Legislation, Key Votes, Elections**

Flora Crater

Toni –Michelle C. Travis

A WOMEN ACTIVIST BOOK

The Woman Activist Fund, Inc.

The Woman Activist Fund, Inc.

Dedicated to the Women of Virginia

Copyright ©2003 by Flora Crater
All rights reserved.
Printed by Hammond Printing Co.
Seventeenth Edition

Published by The Woman Activist Fund, Inc.
16480 Trimmers Road, Orange, VA 22960
540-672-9210; info@almanacvapolitics.org
http://www.almanacvapolitics.org
ISBN 0917560-39-6
Library of Congress Catalog Card Number: 81-644203

ACKNOWLEDGMENTS

Special recognition and thanks are extended to **Flora Crater** and to Anne Morrow Donley for the founding of The Woman Activist Fund, Inc., and *The Almanac of Virginia Politics*. Their strength of example and shining inspiration to both women and men, that an informed public is both necessary and possible. Anne Donley's contribution to the publication is exemplary. We will miss her very fine contribution during the past production years.

The authors gratefully acknowledge the help of all who have assisted in the creation and production of this edition. The bills and resolutions themselves;, including the text, summary, and main votes are on the web at http://legis.state.va.us; as well as in hard copy in the 2004 Final *Cumulative Index of Bills, Resolutions, Joint Resolutions and Documents* and the *Summary* available from the Department of Legislative Services 804-698-1500. Election statistics are from the State Board of Elections at 804-786-6551 or 800-552-9745 or on the web at http://www.sbe.state.va.us. Federal and state outlays of money are accessed through the Auditor of Public Accounts at http://www.apa.state.va.us or in hard copy. Economic interest forms filed annually, but not electronically as yet, are at the Offices of the Clerk of the House (804-698-1619); the Clerk of the Senate (804-698-7400)p; and the Secretary of the Commonwealth (804-786-2441). Media accounts are credited in the text of the book/web edition. Photos are in part reduced from those provided by the officials, and in part photo credits are given to Virginia Legislative Directory published by Verizon, and available at http://legis.state.va.us, along with contact information, biographical material, room numbers, and committees. A general web address for the Virginia state government is http://www.state.va.us.

The writing, editing, and production of *The Almanac of Virginia Politics* was a cooperative effort. This includes The Woman Activist Fund, Inc., and its Board of Directors: **Flora Crater,** President; Vice President/Secretary; **Vivian Albertina Gray;** Treasurer; **Sandra Larson.** The editors for this edition were **Flora Crater**, who also selected and compiled the Key Votes of the session, The writers for this edition were Flora Crater and Toni-Michelle C. Travis. **Martha Boyle**, now deceased, first designed the wreath of flowers which has encircled each edition of this publication since 1977.

We especially thank Josette Smith, our production manager. The production of this edition would not have been possible without her knowledge and help. Also, a special thanks to Jean Gere for her help.

We also extend our thanks to past editors and writers. **Flora Crater** along with **Carolyn Weston Brickey, Elizabeth Vantrease, Meg Williams, Elizabeth Muriel Smith, Cathy Danford, Joanna Rubin, and Pat Fishback.** wrote and compiled the very first edition in 1977. **Carolyn Brickey and Elizabeth Vantrease,** with **Flora Crater,** defined the format and standards of the first edition. **Joanna Rubin** and **Jayne Conrad** provided organizational support. Other major authors and editors of the past were **Elizabeth Muriel Smith, Cathy Danford, Pat Fishback,** Anne Donley, Jeanne O'Hara, and Jeere Gibber.

TABLE OF CONTENTS
The 2005 Almanac of Virginia Politics

Senate and House members are listed according to their congressional districts.

FIRST CONGRESSIONAL DISTRICT

Senate District One   M.E. "MARTY" WILLIAMS (R)
      Part of County of York; part of Cities of Hampton and Newport News, Poquoson

Senate District Three   THOMAS K. NORMENT, JR (R)
      Counties of Accomack, Gloucester, James City, Northampton, and York; Part of Newport
      News, Williamsburg

Senate District Four   WILLIAM T. BOLLING (R)
      Counties of Caroline, Essex, Hanover, King and Queen, King William, Mathews,
      Middlesex, New Kent, Richmond, and Part of Gloucester

Senate District Seventeen   R. EDWARD "EDD" HOUCK (D)
      Fluvanna, Louisa, Spotsylvania Counties, City of Fredericksburg,
      Part of Counties of Orange, Goochland, Buckingham, Cumberland

Senate District Twenty-Eight   JOHN M. CHICHESTER (R)
      Counties of King George, Lancaster, Northumberland,
      Westmoreland, Part of Prince William, Stafford Counties

House District Twenty-Eight   WILLIAM J. HOWELL (R)
      Part of counties of Culpeper and Stafford

House District Fifty-Four   ROBERT D. "BOBBY" ORROCK (R)
      Part of County of Spotsylvania, City of Fredericksburg

House District Fifty-Five   FRANK D. HARGROVE (R)
      County of Hanover

House District Ninety-One   THOMAS "TOM" GEAR (R)
      Part of Cities of Hampton and Poquoson

House District Ninety-three   PHILLIP A. HAMILTON (R)
      Part of the City of Newport News

House District Ninety-four   GEORGE GLENN ODER (R)
      Part of the City of Newport News

House District Ninety-Six   MELANIE L. RAPP (R)
      King and Queen, King William Counties; Part of Counties Gloucester, York

House District Ninety-Seven   RYAN T. MCDOUGLE (R)
      Counties of James City, New Kent, Kent City, Williamsburg, part of Henrico County

House District Ninety-Eight   HARVEY B. MORGAN (R)
      Caroline County, Part of Counties of Essex, Gloucester, Middlesex, York, City of
Poquoson

House District Ninety-Nine   ALBERT C. POLLARD (D)
      Counties of King George, Lancaster, Northumberland, Richmond, Westmoreland, Part of
      Essex and Stafford

House District One Hundred   LYNWOOD W. LEWIS (D)

FIRST CONGRESSIONAL DISTRICT

Accomack, Mathews, Northampton Counties; Part of Gloucester County

SECOND CONGRESSIONAL DISTRICT

Senate District Six
    Part of Cities of Norfolk
    and Virginia Beach

NICK RERRAS (R)

Senate District Seven
    Western part of Virginia Beach

FRANK W. WAGNER (R)

Senate District Eight
    Eastern part of Virginia Beach

KENNETH W. "KEN" STOLLE (R)

House District Twenty-One
    Part of Virginia Beach

JOHN J. WELCH, III (R)

House District Eighty-One
    Part of Virginia Beach

TERRIE L. SUIT (R)

House District Eighty-Two
    Part of Virginia Beach

HARRY R. "BOB" PURKEY (R)

House District Eighty-Three
    Part of Virginia Beach

LEO C. WARDRUP, JR. (R)

House District Eighty-Four
    Part of Virginia Beach

ROBERT F. MCDONNEL (R)

House District Eighty-Five
    Part of Virginia Beach

ROBERT "BOB" TATA (R)

House District Eighty-Six
    Part of Norfolk

THOMAS D. RUST (D)

House District Eighty-Seven
    Part of Norfolk

PAULA MILLER (R)

House District Eighty-Eight
    Part of Norfolk

MARK L. COLE (R)

House District Ninety
    Part of Cities of Chesapeake,
    Norfolk, and Virginia Beach

ALGIE E. HOWELL, JR. (D)

SECOND CONGRESSIONAL DISTRICT

THIRD CONGRESSIONAL DISTRICT

Senate District Two   MAMIE E. LOCKE (D)
     Part of Cities of Hampton
     and Newport News

Senate District Five   YVONNE B. MILLER (D)
     Part of Cities of Chesapeake
     and Norfolk

Senate District Nine   BENJAMIN L. LAMBERT (D)
     Eastern part of Richmond City;
     Part of Henrico County

Senate District Sixteen   HENRY L. MARSH, III (D)
     City of Petersburg, Charles City,
     County, parts of counties of Chesterfield,
     Dinwiddie, Henrico, Prince George;
     Part of Cities of Hopewell, Richmond

House District Seventy   DWIGHT C. JONES (D)
     Part of City of Richmond,
     Part of eastern Henrico county

House District Seventy-One   VIOLA OSBORNE BASKERVILLE (D)
     Part of City of Richmond;
     Part of Henrico county

House District Seventy-Four   FLOYD H. MILES, SR. (D)
     Part of counties of Charles City,
     and Henrico, Part of City of Richmond

House District Eighty   KENNETH R. MELVIN (D)
     Part of Cities of Chesapeake
     and Portsmouth

House District Eighty-Nine   KENNETH C. ALEXANDER (D)
     Part of Cities of Chesapeake
     and Norfolk

House District Ninety-Two   JEION A. WARD (D)
     Part of City of Hampton

House District Ninety-Five   MAMYE E. BACOTE (D)
     Part of Cities of Hampton
     and Newport News

THIRD CONGRESSIONAL DISTRICT

FOURTH CONGRESSIONAL DISTRICT

Senate District Thirteen   FREDERICK M. QUAYLE (R)
Surry County, Part of Counties of Isle of Wight, Prince George, Part of Cities of
Chesapeake, Hopewell, Portsmouth, and Suffolk

Senate District Fourteen   HARRY BLEVINS (R)
Parts of the Cities of Chesapeake and Virginia Beach

Senate District Fifteen   FRANK M. RUFF (R)
Parts of Cities of Chesapeake and Virginia Beach, Counties of Appomattox, Charlotte,
Lunenburg, Nottoway, Prince Edward, and Suffolk; Part of Counties of Dinwiddie,
Greensville, Isle of Wight, Mecklenburg, Prince George and Southampton; Part of Cities of
Emporia, Franklin, and Suffolk

Senate District Eighteen   L. LOUISE LUCAS (D)
Counties of Brunswick and Halifax; Part of Counties of Greensville, Isle of Wight,
Mecklenburg, Southampton, City of South Boston; Part of Cities of Chesapeake, Emporia,
Franklin, and Suffolk

House District Fifty-Six   WILLIAM R. "BILL" JANIS (R)
Counties of Fluvanna, Goochland, and Louisa; Part of County of Spotsylvania

House District Sixty-Two   RILEY E. INGRAM (R)
City of Hopewell; Part of Counties of Amelia, Chesterfield, Dinwiddie, Nottoway,
Powhattan and Prince George

House District Sixty-Three   FENTON LEE BLAND (D)
City of Petersburg, Part of Counties of Chesterfield and Dinwiddie

House District Sixty-Four   WILLIAM K. BARLOW (D)
Part of Counties of Charles City, Henrico, Isle of Wight, Prince George, Southampton,
And Surry; Part of Cities of Franklin and Newport News

House District Sixty-Six   M. KIRKLAND "KIRK" COX (R)
Part of Chesterfield County and Colonial Heights

House District Seventy-Five   J. PAUL COUNCILL (D)
Counties of Greensville and Sussex;
Part of Counties of Brunswick, Dinwiddie,
Isle of Wight, Lunenburg, Southampton, and Surry;
City of Emporia; Part of City of Franklin

House District Seventy-Six   S.C. "CHRIS" JONES (R)
Part of County of Isle of Wight;
Part of Cities of Chesapeake and Suffolk

House District Seventy-Seven   LIONELL SPRUILL (D)
Part of Cities of Chesapeake
and Suffolk

House District Seventy-Eight   JOHN A. "COS" COSGROVE (R)
101 – 102; Part of City of Chesapeake,
One City of Norfolk precinct

FOURTH CONGRESSIONAL DISTRICT

House District Seventy-Nine   JOHNNY S. JOANNOU (D)
Part of Cities of Chesapeake and Portsmouth, one city of Suffolk precinct

FIFTH CONGRESSIONAL DISTRICT

Senate District Nineteen   CHARLES R. HAWKINS (R)
         Counties of Pittsylvania,
         Part of County of Campbell,
         City of Danville

Senate District Twenty   WILLIAM ROSCOE REYNOLDS (D)
         Counties of Floyd, Franklin, Henry, and Patrick;
         Part of County of Carroll,
         City of Martinsville

House District Nine   ALLEN W. DUDLEY (R)
         County of Floyd; Part of Counties of Bedford,
         Franklin, and Pittsylvania

House District Ten   WARD L. ARMSTRONG (D)
         County of Patrick, Part of Counties of Carroll,
         Henry and Pittsylvania

House District Eleven   ONZLEE WARE (D)
         Part of Counties of Franklin, Henry, and Pittsylvania,
         City of Martinsville

House District Nineteen   LACY E. PUTNEY (I)
         Part of Counties of Bedford, Botetourt,
         and Rockbridge; Cities of Bedford and Buena Vista

House District Twenty   CHRISTOPHER "CHIP" B. SAXMAN (R)
         Part of County of Pittsylvania;
         City of Danville

House District Fifty-Seven   MITCHELL VAN YAHRES (D)
         City of Charlottesville;
         Part of Albemarle County

House District Fifty-Eight   ROBERT "BOB" B. BELL (R)
         Part of Counties of Albemarle,
         Greene, and Rockingham

House District Fifty-Nine   WATKINS M. ABBITT, JR. (D)
         Counties of Appomattox, Buckingham,
         Cumberland and Nelson;
         Part of Prince Edward County

House District Sixty   CLARK N. HOGAN (R)
         Counties of Charlotte and Halifax;
         Part of Counties of Campbell and Pittsylvania;
         City of South Boston

House District Sixty-One   THOMAS "TOMMY" WRIGHT (R)
         County of Mecklenburg; Part of Counties of Amelia,
         Brunswick, Lunenburg, Nottoway,
         And Prince Edward

SIXTH CONGRESSIONAL DISTRICT

Senate District Twenty- One   JOHN S. EDWARDS (D)
Part of County of Roanoke, City of Roanoke

Senate District Twenty-Two   J. BRANDON BELL (R)
       Counties of Alleghany, Bath, Botetourt, Craig, Giles;
       Cities of Clinton, Forge, Covington, Radford, Salem;
       Part of Counties of Pulaski, Roanoke

Senate District Twenty-Three   STEPHEN D. NEWMAN (R)
       Counties of Amherst and Bedford;
       Part of County of Campbell,
       Cities of Bedford and Lynchburg

Senate District Twenty-Four   EMMETT W. HANGER (R)
       Counties of Augusta, Highland, and Rockbridge;
       Part of County of Rockingham;
       Cities of Buena Vista, Lexington,
       Staunton, and Waynesboro

House District Eight   H. MORGAN GRIFFITH (R)
       Part of Counties of Montgomery and Roanoke;
       City of Salem

House District Fourteen   DANNY W. MARSHALL (R)
       County of Craig; Part of Counties of Bedford,
       Botetourt, and Roanoke

House District Sixteen   ROBERT HURT (R)
       Part of Roanoke County;
       Part of Roanoke City

House District Seventeen   WILLIAM H. FRALIN (R)
       Part of Roanoke County;
       Part of Roanoke City

House District Eighteen   CLIFFORD L. "CLAY" ATHEY (R)
       Counties of Alleghany, Bath and Highland

House District Twenty-Two   KATHY J. BYRON (R)
       Part of Counties of Campbell and Pittsylvania;
       Part of City of Lynchburg

House District Twenty-Three   L. PRESTON BRYANT, JR. (R)
       Part of County of Amherst;
       Part of City of Lynchburg

House District Twenty-Four   BENJAMIN L. CLINE (R)
       Part of County of Amherst, Augusta, and Rockbridge;
       City of Staunton

House District Twenty-Five   R. STEVEN "STEVE" LANDES (R)
       Part of Counties of Augusta and Rockingham;
       City of Waynesboro

SIXTH CONGRESSIONAL DISTRICT

SEVENTH CONGRESSIONAL DISTRICT

Senate District Ten   JOHN C. WATKINS (R)
>Powhatan County; Part of Counties of Chesterfield and Henrico;
>Part of City of Richmond

Senate District Eleven   STEPHEN H. MARTIN (R)
>Amelia County; Part of Counties of Chesterfield and Dinwiddie;
>City of Colonial Heights

Senate District Twelve   WALTER A. STOSCH (R)
>Part of Counties of Goochland and Henrico

Senate District Twenty-Five   R. CRAIG DEED (D)
>Counties of Albemarle, Greene, Madison and Nelson;
>Part of Counties of Orange and
>Rappahannock; City of Charlottesville

Senate District Twenty-Six   MARK OBENSHAIN (R)
>Counties of Culpeper and Page;
>Part of Counties of Fauquier,
>Rappahannock, Rockingham,
>And Stafford; City of Harrisonburg

House District Twenty-Seven   SAMUEL A. NIXON, JR. (R)
>Part of Chesterfield County

House District Thirty   EDWARD T. "ED" SCOTT (R)
>Counties of Madison and Orange;
>Part of Counties of Culpeper and Greene

House District Sixty-Five   R. LEE WARE, JR. (R)
>Part of Counties of Chesterfield
>and Powhatan

House District Sixty-Eight   BRADLEY P. "BRAD" MARRS (R)
>Part of City of Richmond,
>Part of County of Henrico

House District Sixty-Nine   FRANKLIN P. "FRANK" HALL (D)
>Part of City of Richmond

House District Seventy-Two   JOHN S. "JACK" REID (R)
>Part of Counties of Chesterfield
>and Henrico

House District Seventy-Three   JOHN M. O'BANNON (R)
>Part of County of Henrico;
>Part of City of Richmond

SEVENTH CONGRESSIONAL DISTRICT

Senate District Thirty   PATRICIA S. "PATSY" TICER (D)
Part of Counties of Arlington and Fairfax;
City of Alexandria

Senate District Thirty-One   MARY MARGARET WHIPPLE (D)
Part of County of Arlington;
City of Falls Church

Senate District Thirty-Six   LINDA T. "TODDY" PULLER (D)
South-Eastern part of Fairfax County

House District Thirty-Four   VINCENT F. CALLAHAN (R)
Part of Fairfax County

House District Forty-Two   DAVID B. ALBO (R)
Part of Fairfax County

House District Forty-Three   MARK D. SICKLES (D)
Part of Fairfax County

House District Forty-Four   KRISTEN J. "KRIS" AMUNDSON (D)
Part of Fairfax County

House District Forty-Five   MARION A. VAN LANDINGHAM (D)
Part of Fairfax County;
Part of City of Alexandria

House District Forty-Six   BRIAN J. MORAN (D)
Part of City of Alexandria

House District Forty-Seven   ALBERT C. EISENBERG (D)
Part of Counties of Fairfax
and Arlington

House District Forty-Eight   ROBERT H. BRINK (D)
Part of Counties of Arlington
and Fairfax

House District Forty-Nine   ADAM P. EBBIN (D)
Part of Arlington County

EIGHTH CONGRESSIONAL DISTRICT

NINTH CONGRESSIONAL DISTRICT

Senate District Thirty-Eight   PHILLIP P. PUCKET (D)
        Counties of Bland, Buchanan, Russell, Tazewell, and Wythe;
        Part of County of Washington

Senate District Thirty-Nine   JAY O'BRIEN (R)
        Counties of Grayson, Montgomery, and Smyth;
        Part of Counties of Carroll and Pulaski;
        City of Galax

Senate District Forty   WILLIAM C. WAMPLER, JR (R)
        Counties of Dickenson, Lee, Scott, and Wise;
        Part of County of Washington;
        Cities of Bristol and Norton

House District One   TERRY G. KILGORE (R)
        Counties of Lee and Scott;
        Part of County of Wise

House District Two   CLARENCE E. "BUD" PHILLIPS (D)
        County of Dickenson;
        Part of Counties of Russell and Wise;
        City of Norton

House District Three   JACKIE T. STUMP (D)
        County of Buchanan;
        Part of Counties of Russell and Tazewell

House District Four   JOSEPH P. JOHNSON, JR. (D)
        Washington County, City of Bristol

House District Five   C. WILLIAM "BILL" CARRICO, SR. (D)
        County of Smyth;
        Part of Counties of Grayson and Tazewell

House District Six   W.B. KEISTER (D)
        Counties of Bland and Wythe;
        Part of Counties of Carroll and Grayson;
        City of Galax

House District Seven   DAVID A. "DAVE" NUTTER (R)
        County of Pulaski;
        Part of County of Giles;
        City of Radford

House District Twelve   JAMES M. SHULER (D)
        Part of Counties of Giles and Montgomery

TENTH CONGRESSIONAL DISTRICT

Senate District Twenty-Seven   H.R. "RUSS" POTTS, JR. (R)
     Counties of Clark, Frederick,
     Shenandoah, and Warren;
     Part of County of Winchester

Senate District Twenty-Nine   CHARLES J. COLGAN (D)
     Manassas, Manassas Park,
     Part of Prince William County

Senate District Thirty-Three   WILLIAM C. "BILL" MIMS (R)
     Loudoun County;
     North-Western Part of Fairfax County

Senate District Thirty-Seven   KENNETH D.CUCCINELLI II (R)
     Part of Counties of Fairfax and Prince William;
     City of Fairfax

House District Thirteen   ROBERT G. "BOB" MARSHALL (R)
     Part of County of Prince William

House District Fifteen   ALLEN J. LOUDERBACK (R)
     Page County;
     Part of Counties of Frederick, Rockingham, Shenandoah;
     City of Harrisonburg

House District Twenty-Six   GLENN M. WEATHERHOLTZ (R)
     Part of Counties of Rockingham and Shenandoah;
     City of Winchester

House District Twenty-Nine   BEVERLY J. SHERWOOD (R)
     Part of County of Frederick;
     City of Winchester

House District Thirty-One   LEE SCOTT LINGAMFELTER (R)
     County of Rappahannock;
     Part of Counties of Fauquier and Loudon

House District Thirty-Two   R.H. "DICK" BLACK (R)
     Part of Counties of Fairfax And Loudoun

House District Thirty-Three   JOE T. MAY (R)
     Clark County;
     Part of Counties of Fairfax, Fauquier, and Loudoun

House District Forty   TIMOTHY D. HUGO (R)
     Part of County of Fairfax

House District Fifty   HARRY J. PARRISH (R)
     Manassas and Manassas Park;
     Part of Prince William County

House District Sixty-Seven   GARY REESE (R)

TENTH CONGRESSIONAL DISTRICT
 Part of Fairfax County

ELEVENTH CONGRESSIONAL DISTRICT

Senate District Thirty-Two
    Part of Counties of Arlington and Fairfax

JANET D. HOWELL (D)

Senate District Thirty-Four
    Part of County of Fairfax;
    Part of City of Fairfax

JEANNEMARIE A. DEVOLITES (R)

Senate District Thirty-Five
    South-Central Part of Fairfax County

RICHARD L. SASLAW (D)

House District Thirty-Five
    Part of Fairfax County;
    Part of City of Fairfax

STEPHEN G. SHANNON

House District Thirty-Six
    Part of Fairfax County

KENNETH R. PLUM (D)

House District Thirty-Seven
    Part of Fairfax County;
    Part of City of Fairfax

J. CHAPMAN "CHAP" PETERSON (D)

House District Thirty-Eight
    Part of Fairfax County;
    City of Falls Church

ROBERT D. "BOB" HULL (D)

House District Thirty-Nine
    Part of Fairfax County

VIVIAN E. WATTS (D)

House District Forty-One
    Part of Fairfax County

JAMES H. "JIM" DILLARD II (R)

House District Fifty-One
    Part of Prince William County

MICHELE B. MCQUIGG (R)

House District Fifty-Two
    Part of Prince William County

JEFFREY M. FREDERICK (R)

House District Fifty-Three
    Part of Fairfax County

JAMES M. SCOTT (D)

ELEVENTH CONGRESSIONAL DISTRICT

INTRODUCTION

The Women Activist Fund, Inc.
16480 Trimmers Road, Orange, VA 22960
(540) 672-9210

PHONES, WEB ACCESS:

The bills and resolutions themselves, including the text, summary, and main votes are on the web at http://legis.state.va.us, as well as in hard copy in the *2004 Final Cumulative Indexes of Bills, Resolutions, Joint Resolutions, and Documents, and the Summary*, available from the Department of Legislative Services (804- 698-1500).

Election statistics are from the State Board of Elections at 804-786-6551 or (800-552-9745) or on the web at http:// www.sbe.state.va.us.

Federal and state outlays of money are accessed through the Auditor of Public Accounts at http://www.apa.state.va.us or in hard copy.

Campaign contributions and expenditures are filed with the State Board of Elections, and available though the Virginia Public Access Project (VPAP) at http://www.vpap.org.

Economic interest forms are filed annually, but are both electronically as yet, are the Offices of the Clerk of the House (804-786-2441).

The general web address for the Virginia state government is http://www.state.va.us.

The Women Activist Fund, Inc. is a non-profit research and educational corporation, founded by Flora Crater. In 1977, the Fund began publishing *The Almanac of Virginia Politics*. This annual publication examines the legislative agendas of the 140 member of the Virginia General Assembly, the work of the governor, lt. governor, and attorney general, and includes financial information, votes on selected key issues, election data, maps, and more.

We are building a record, providing the raw material for innovative political analyses so desperately called for when government decries injustice, yet tolerates racism, sexism, and other aberrations of our political system in general and in Virginia. Events continue to challenge the ingenuity of government and the Virginia people. Each year's addition unites in one volume information about each legislator and state official which would take considerable time, effort, and cost for an individual to access through other channels.   This makes a library of the volumes of The Almanac of Virginia Politics unique publications, providing in one place pertinent information for those seeking to get a handle on the components of political power in Virginia at the legislative level.

INTRODUCTION

2004 Overview

Budget Debate

Republican, Senator Russ Potts, Thomas Norment and John Chichester find their action and legislation challenged by anti-tax Republicans.

Issues of general assembly. Education, public safety, driving under the influence (DUI), abortion, taxes and spending were the three issues regarding abortion passed by the house would require parental consent before a minor can get a morning after pill, bars health centers at colleges from distributing such a pill and a requirement that fetuses be given anesthetic during most abortions performed after the first trimester.

The budget is generally the fulcrum around which legislative discourse or contention surrounds. This year was no exception. Budget discussion of a proposed $60 billion would raise the sales tax and taxes on income and cigarettes by Senators. The House would not take up tax increase with a budget of 58.3 billion basing their budget on projected revenue growth and element of sales tax on some businesses. Janet Howell (D-Reston) said, "Virginia is at a crossroads. We have to decide whether we will face up to our responsibilities or whether we will drift downward." She said that government demands are increasing "while revenue remains flat adding that by the end of the decade there will be in the state "41,000 more students in public school and 73,000 more people on Medicare".

In the matter of the budget, the Governor and legislature are bearing in mind when approving the budget such as Warner proposed of $1 billion tax increase and a balanced budget.

Examination by the legislature is grounded in the desire meaningly of protecting the states triple A bond rating.

Delegate Vincent Callahan (R-34) will disclose House Budget (Feb 22), which he says protects public education, health care and public safety.

Regarding the budget, press accounts say Warner's plan for taxes, "would generate more than $1 billion during the 2004-06 budgets to take effect July 1 reflecting primarily increase in education, health care, transportation and public safety.

On the broad issue of child care, the Virginia Child Care Council weighing consideration brought out by public debate called for adopting rules for the states 2,511 licensed day care centers calling for "more activity space, smaller classes, better qualified directors and more teacher staff training. The Department of Social Services will plan to reallocate money for changes during the next two or three years.

As expected by its past record contraception has been a subject of debate by the mostly male legislatures. In the debate, the House voted 51-48, passed a bill which lets schools teach "in the event of such sexual assault how to get controversial medication after rape or incest". This legislation was sponsored by Delegate James H. Dillard, II Republican from Fairfax. After passage in the House, Dillard informed the legislatures that one out of four women are sexually assaulted and the average age when victimized for the first time is at the age of 14. He also said many women do not report the attack.

INTRODUCTION

On the issue of abortion on February 2nd, a federal judge found that Virginias 2003 law which banned partial abortion to be unconstitutional. Virginia Attorney General Jerry Kilgore said the ruling would be appealed.

Unusual for the Capitol, doctors in their white coat marching down Gray street, nearly 2,000, to get the attention of lawmakers to explain why Lynchburg and other communities are losing access to medical care. The group came to the Capitol for a public meeting on malpractice reform bills. No legislative action was taken.

Regarding the budget, press accounts say Warner's plan for taxes, "would generate more than $1 billion during the 2004-06 budgets to take effect July 1 reflecting primarily increase in education, health care, transportation and public safety.

Of note politically, the Democrats in their primary action in 2004 held their second presidential primary
vote in Virginia history. The state held one other Democratic presidential primary in 1985. Since Virginia does not register by party anyone, who registers can participate. However, in practice, mostly only Democrats vote. Observers say that their primary is a very good thing for Democrats who will garner political information for future elections.

And let's not forget our Indians. According to Carrol Marello, staff reports for the Washington Post: In Virginia, Native Americans also endured a unique form of discrimination that largely erased bureaucratic evidence of their existence. The Racial Integrity Act of 1924 required that state records list a person's race as either white or Negro. By the time the law was struck down by the U.S. Supreme Court more than four decades later, it had excised all records of Indian heritage from state birth, marriage and death certificates.

Though generally, recognized as the descendants of Virginia's indigenous tribes, they have not gained federal recognition like that granted to 562 tribes across the country. Such recognition is important not only to get a slice of federal dollars received for Indians but as a matter of principle, tribal leaders say. Last year, the Smithsonian national Museum of natural History denied a request for the repatriation of their ancestors' remains because the tribes lack federal recognition.

Reports of the 2004 session, note that legislation to put abortion clinics out of business, limiting student access to contraception and exempting law makers

Note was made in the press about the action of Senator Mary Margaret Whipple (D-Arlington) who worried that when they retired there would be no women in line to fill their spots. There are now in the year 2004, 20 women in the legislature. Lately there has been "little unity among Democrats and Republican women".

Whipple from Arlington is the first women to hold a leadership position in the Senate. This is her fifth year as Democratic Caucus Chair. Democratic female senators formed last year Voice for Women, a political action committee to educate women about politics and elect more of them.

Men summarized the 2004 session of the Virginia General Assembly the Washington Post said: These are hardly breathtaking reforms but a bipartisan coalition overcame great odds to recognize that someone has to pay for Virginia's schools, universities, health care and other services. The accomplishments in Richmond raised Virginia's awareness of state and local needs of challenges remaining for the longer run. The bipartisan coalition that acted in Richmond could provide a model for politicians who failed a similar test in Annapolis this winter. Mr. Warner, Mr. Chichester and a large number of legislators who cast courageous votes deserve public support for their leadership.

INTRODUCTION

Also of note Winchester attorney Elizabeth Keller was appointed judge of the 26th Judicial District Juvenile –Domestic Relations Court for the next six years. Keller said she plans to use her judging to help the children of Virginia.

KEY VOTES OF THE 2004 SESSION

Constituent representative ness is the key factor in this review. Therefore, the *votes selected for the voting record are, to the extent possible, those affecting major voting blocs in the population.* Given the complex nature of legislative debate, the way in which the legislator votes on particular issues is just one of several methods to measure performance. The bill selected is followed by the date on which it was approved. **A total of 10 key votes were chosen from this 2004 session. Eight of the bills are the same for the House list as well as the Senate list.**

Some bills have more than one vote during the session, depending on amendments to the bill, and conference committee reports to settle differences between the bill as passed in the House and the Senate.

For a full picture on the voting, the reader may wish to ask for a copy of all the votes on that bill from the Legislative Services Information number (804-698-1500) or access it on the Internet: http://legis.state.va.us. However, not every committee vote is recorded at this web site. While a defining vote on the merits of the bill may be taken, it will not always be recorded if another vote is taken later, such as a vote to "lay it on the table" or to "pass by indefinitely." Thus, a legislator might vote on that same bill to the final vote, unless otherwise noted.

Each description of the vote is represented as follows: FOR , Yea; AGN, Nay, Against; NE, Not Elected; NV Not Voting; and ABS, Abstain. Legislators may be listed as Not Voting because they were absent, or out of the room or because they chose not to vote on this issue. Abstentions refer to Senate Rule 36 and House Rule 69 which provide that legislators who have *"an immediate, private or personal interest in the result of a question shall neither vote nor be counted upon it..."* The headings of the votes are necessarily abbreviated. Other abbreviations used are as follows: HB= House Bill; SB= Senate Bill, HJR– House Joint Resolution; D – Democrat; R– Republican; I– Independent; numbers following the political party refer to the Senate District or the House District.

KEY VOTES OF THE SESSION - The legislation selected for 1, 2, 3, 5, 6, 7, 8, and 10 is the same for both Senators and Delegates. Votes 4 and 9 differ for the Senate and for the House.

1) **Budget Bill SB 30** sponsored by Senator John H. Chichester (R-28), provided for the appropriation of the 2004-2006 biennium. There are many votes and discussion of various parts of the Budget. The vote taken for the Senate was on its passage March 2, 2004, 31 Y- 8 N-1A. Passed House February 26, 2004, 65 Y- 35 N.

2) **Penalty for Feticide (destruction of fetal life) HB 1** sponsored by Delegate John A. Cosgrove (R-78) provides that any person who unlawfully, willfully, deliberately and maliciously kills the fetus of another is guilty of a felony punished by confinement in a correctional facility for not less than five or more than 40 years. Passed House, February 6, 2004, 74 Y -25 N-1 NV. Passed Senate February 25, 2004, 33 Y- 7 N.

3) **Defended Marriage SB 91**, sponsored by Senator JeanMarie Devolites (R-34) urges Congress to prepare a constitutional amendment to protect marriage as a union between a man and a women and uniting similar relationship for such a marriage shall not be valid. Passed Senate February 27, 2004, 29 Y- 11N. Passed House February 1,2004, 74Y- 23N-3 NV.

xxvii

INTRODUCTION

4) **Abortion Procedure HB 315**, sponsored by R.H. "Dick" Black (R-32) requires in an abortion performed after the first trimester that the unborn child be anesthetized. A doctor who does not anesthetize the fetus is guilty of a Class 1 misdemeanor. Passed House February 11, 2004, 65 Y- 33 N.

5) **Family Life Education, HB 1015** sponsored by James Dillard (R-41) adds steps taken to avoid sexual assault and makes available counseling and legal resources, passed the House April 3, 2004, 72 Y, 27 N- 1 A. Passed Senate April 4, 2004, 40 Y -0 N.

6) **Fire Arms Control, HB 530** sponsored by Delegate Charles N. Hogan (D-60) Removes grandfather clause allowing localities to enforce gun laws passed before 1987 and declares all local ordinances adopted before 1987 are invalid. Change necessary because bill invalidate any local ordinance. Passed February 4, 2004. 82 Y– 18 N- 0. Passed Senate March 3, 2004, 31 Y– 9 N.

7) **Open Space Preservation, HB549**, sponsored by Delegate Joe T. May (R-33), imposes a fee for every deed recorded admitted to record in the jurisdiction where open space easements are held by the Virginia Ordinance Foundation. This bill requires the revenue from the fee to promote the preservation of open space land and to encourage private gifts from such preservation. This bill passed the House on February 16,2004. 80 Y – 19 N – 1 NV. Passed Senate on March 3, 2004, 32 Y – 8 N.

8) **Home Schooling, HB 675**, sponsored by Delegate Robert Hurt (R-16), requires those providing home instruction to hold a High School diploma. Under current law a baccalaureate degree is required. Passed the House on February 3, 2004. 60 Y – 40 N and the Senate on March 1, 2004, 25 Y – 15 N.

9) **Charter School Excellence and Accountability Act, HB 380**, sponsored by Delegate Lee Scott Lingamfelter (R-31), amends the Charter School Excellence and Accountability Act to allow charter schools to contract with private institutions of high education for school facilities, services, and including construction, evidence of support by school district residents. Passed the Senate March 9, 2004. 32 Y – 7 N – 1 NV. Passed House March 10, 2004., 79 Y – 21 N.

10) **Legal Aid Bill HB 1172**, sponsored by Delegate Terri Kilgore (R-1) increased by one dollar court fees in law and chancery cases and in each civil action in general district court paid into the Legal Aid Services Fund. Passed House March 1, 2004, 75 Y – 24 N – 1 NV. Passed Senate March 4, 2004, 37 Y– 3 N.

SENATE ONLY VOTES

4) **Child Abuse, SB 314**, sponsored by Senator Janet Howell (D-32) mandatory reporting of child abuse and neglect required that any minister, rabbi, priest or accredited practitioner report suspected child abuse or neglect to local social services. Passed Senate January 24, 2004. 22Y– 17 N-1 NV

9) **Charter School Excellence and Accountability Act, HB 380**, sponsored by Delegate Lee Scott Lingamfelter (R-31), amends the Charter School Excellence and Accountability Act to allow charter schools to contract with private institutions of high education for school facilities, services, and including construction, evidence of support by school district

INTRODUCTION

residents. Passed the Senate March 9, 2004. 32 Y – 7 N – 1 NV. Passed House March 10, 2004., 79 Y – 21 N.

CAMPAIGN CONTRIBUTIONS

The campaign contributions for members of the House are for 2004.

The State Board of Elections, 804-786-6551 or (800-552-9745), is the ultimate source for the information, although The Almanac has utilized the very excellent and valuable Virginia Public Access Project (VPAP) web site, developed by David Poole, at http://www.vpap.org. the Almanac has broken down the information into as defined a form as possible. This saves the reader infinite time in pursuing research on all 140 legislators and the three statewide officers.

Some legislators maintain that it is the vote, not the money that counts, and that if you can't eat their food, drink their wine and still vote against them, you are not independent. However, some legislators not only bristle, but brutally retaliate when ordinary voters reflect upon the possible connections between their votes and their money source. This frequent scenario, not always witnessed by the press, was reported during the 2001 session by *The Virginian-Pilot*. Delegate Leo Wardrup (R-83) became "enraged" when he was questioned by a citizen attending a public hearing, as to whether his "campaign contributions from real estate developers had influenced his support to reduce the $10 toll. And Wardrup struck back. The bills were first watered down. Then killed."

ECONOMIC INTERESTS

Keeping tract of the money, the gifts, and the business interests of each official is important for defining that official. More and more legislators, for example, are either involved directly with real estate, or have vast holdings in real estate, or represent real estate developers before state agencies. As laws change for "economic development", this has an impact on both the real estate business and the way of life of the citizens in urban and rural areas. How much influence may be placed upon legislator and state official in making laws related to these factors is an interesting question.

The financial disclosure forms were amended by the Assembly in 1997 and again in 1998. this section digests the financial disclosure forms required by law for each candidate for legislator and statewide official, using the forms filed in 2003 covering 2004. the complete statements may be viewed or purchased at the **Offices of the Clerk of the House**, 804-698-1619; the **Clerk of the Senate** 804-698-7400; and the **Secretary of the Commonwealth** 804-786-2441; Capitol Square, Richmond, Virginia 23219. These are not yet available on the Internet.

Nine categories: *Salary and Wages; Offices and Directorships; Personal Liabilities, securities, Payments for Talks, meetings and Publications, Gifts, Business Interests; Payments for Representation, Real Estate, and Real Estate Contracts with Government Agencies.* Under *Payments for Representation* there are three categories: *Payments for Representation By You*, payments for representing a business before any state governmental agency excluding courts, or judges, for compensation divided into five monetary categories: $1,001 - $10,000, $10,001 - $50,000, $50,001 - $100,00, $100,001 - $250,00, $250,001+; *Payments for Representation by Associates*: the same category but applicable to associates who represented businesses before state agencies in excess of Services Generally; representation by persons of a close financial association furnishing services to business in Virginia with compensation divided into five monetary categories: $1,001 - $10,000, $10,001 - $50,000, $50,001-$100,000, $100,001-$250,000, $250,001+.

The financial disclosure includes the individual and members of the immediate family. Under *Salary and Wages* the legislator must list salary or wages, other than legislator's salary, received personally or by a member of the immediate family in excess of $10,000 annually. We have not listed salaries received as legislators, since they are essentially the same. *Offices and Directorships* lists those which are paid but does not ask for a financial category. *Personal Liabilities* are those owned by the

INTRODUCTION

member and/or the immediate family in excess of $10,000. In *Securities* those owed by the member and/or the immediate family in excess of $10,000. In Securities those listed are as $10,000-$50,000, and in excess of $50,001.

Payments for Talks, Meetings, and Publications, to be reported are those in excess of $200 for travel, lodging, or honorariums for a single talk, meeting, or published work in their capacity as a legislator. Under *Gifts*, they must report any gifts exceeding $50 including business entertainment not directly related to the private profession. Under *Real Estate*, there is a listing of property, not listed elsewhere, valued in excess of $10,000. Summaries under each legislator are for those categories filed.

BILLS AND RESOLUTIONS – HOW THE PROCESS WORKS IN VIRGINIA

Bills and resolutions propose changes to the legal Code of Virginia, urge studies, or ask for other agreements from the legislature. **The person who presents the legislation is the "sponsor"** of the bill or resolution, and the other members of either house may sign on as "co-sponsors." The Governor, Lt. Governor, and Attorney General may enter legislation by requesting a legislator to carry it for them. Any citizen may request their Delegate to carry legislation.

The Virginia Constitution outlines some of the rules pertaining to legislation. Work on legislation is formally done in committees and their subcommittees and on "the floor" of the House and Senate. **"The Floor"** refers to the meeting of the full body of either the House or the Senate. Bills that to the floor can then be debated, or set into what is called **"the block"** where non-controversial bills and resolutions await quick passage, all at the same time.

In Virginia, unlike many other states, the legislature does not meet all year. The General Assembly convenes in January. The session lasts 30 days, and by the Virginia Constitution it may be extended an additional 30 days, but is usually extended 15 or 16 days for a total of 45 or 46 days and is called a **"short session."** In even years, the session is extended to 60 days and termed a **"long session."** Occasionally, when there is a tough bill that must be completed before the end of the session, the legislators have **"stopped the clock"** and continued until finished. Thus far, television coverage of the floor sessions is only available at the Capitol and General Assembly buildings.

There may be committee meetings at various times during the year to work on studies, to hear **"continued bills"**, or to carry out other legislative business. Bills may not be continued to the next year in an election year. Bills that are carried to the next year's session must be decided upon in the committees by December 20, so that when the next session convenes, the few surviving bills are ready to be voted upon by the full body.

Resolutions that are called "joint resolutions" must be voted on by both the House and the Senate. Resolutions that are simply termed a House Resolution or a Senate Resolution are voted on only by that particular body. Often the votes on resolutions are voice votes and not recorded votes for each legislator. **Commendations** are resolutions which "commend" or "celebrate the life" or "honor" individuals, organizations, teams, localities, or other entities. In the legislative summary section given each legislator, the number of commending resolutions is mentioned, so the reader may understand that the rest of the resolutions pertained to studies or constitutional amendments.

Bills must be introduced by an agreed upon deadline, and they are then assigned to a committee. House bills are assigned by the Speaker of the House; Senate bills are generally assigned by the Clerk of the Senate. Resolutions often go to the Rules Committee of either body. A bill or resolution that passes the committee is often considered by the full body.

Bills and Joint Resolutions which pass the House committee, go to the floor of the House to be voted on, and if they pass, must then proceed to the Senate side. There they must go to a Senate committee and the ones that survive there must be voted on by the full Senate. The same holds true for Senate

INTRODUCTION

bills. After being heard in a Senate committee, the passing bills are then before the full Senate. The ones that pass go to the House, through the committee process, and passed bills go to the full House.

If a bill passes the House and the Senate in different forms, with different amendments for example, it must have the two houses agree on the final language of the bill or go to a conference committee to reconcile the two versions. This differing in the bills can occur naturally in the process of things, or be another method to kill a bill.

Bills are listed in the *Final Cumulative Index* and the web site http://legis.state.va.us of the legislative services department as Passed, Failed, and Continued. **Bills can be killed in a number of ways with a variety of language** confusing to newcomers to the process. Motions and substitute motions on a bill can be to "PBS" (Pass By Indefinitely= kill it), **"lay it on the table"** (kill it)," **vote it up or down** "(vote for it or against it), ignore it completely and let it die that way and in a year that is not an election year to **continue** it (hold it over for a committee to vote on it before the end of the year). Efforts to **"message a bill"** (kill it or gut it with amendments), to kill it or sometimes to try to salvage it may result in an attempt to send it to another committee before the bill even reaches the floor, or to send it from the floor of the House or the Senate back to the same or a different committee. This is sometimes done when it is obvious that the committee will not be meeting again and thus the bill will die. Any bill can be reconsidered for another vote in committee or on the floor within specific deadlines. If legislators want to amend someone's bill, but not to **"gut"**it or defeat it, they may say that this is a **"friendly amendment."** But when a bill "has a fever" it may be given many harmful amendments so it is **"loaded up like a Christmas tree".**

The Speaker of the House presides over the House floor debates, ruling, usually on when requested, as to whether amendments are "germane" or not, and votes on the legislation. **The Lt. Governor** presides over the Senate, ruling on amendments and points of order, but only votes to break a tie vote. **The governor has the power to enter bills at almost any time,** and to lobby for and against bills, often using the power of the office to achieve results.

Sometimes a legislator will "strike" her/his own bill, for a variety of reasons, and it is listed as "stricken" or "stricken from the calendar." There has been a" courtesy" in the past to allow this striking of the bill by the sponsor to happen at any point in the process, but when a very controversial bill is being considered, the members of the Senate and House have argued, successfully, that the bills now **"belongs to the body"** and no longer to the legislator.

Bills that survive the legislative process are signed by the top officials of the House and Senate, and the "communicated," to the governor, who has a prescribed time, approximately 30 days, to sign bills, amend, or veto them. A **veto session,** held in early April, considers the governor's amendments and vetoes. If the governor's amendments are defeated, the governor has another chance to veto or sign the bills. To override the governor's veto, there must be a **2/3 vote of the members present to override the veto** in the house where the bill originated. If they override the bill, it goes to the house, where a 2/3 vote of the members present is complete the overturning of the governor's veto. If this occurs in both houses, the bill passes.

Information on bills and resolutions front he current and recent sessions may be accessed at the Legislative Information link from http://legis.state.va.us. **However, not every committee vote is recorded at this web site.** While a defining vote on the merits of the bill may be taken, it will not always be recorded if another vote was taken later, such as a vote to "lay it on the table" or to "pass by indefinitely." **Thus, a legislator might vote in favor of or against a bill in its final form, but have held an even more significant vote on that same bill when certain amendments were being considered to that bill.** The votes reported in the *Almanac Key Votes* refers to the final vote, unless otherwise noted.

CONGRESSIONAL ELECTED OFFICIALS

U.S. Senator **John W. Warner (R)** 225 Russell Bldg, Washington, D.C. 20510-4601; 202-224-2023; FAX 202-224-6295; senator@warner.senate.gov; Richmond 804-771-2579; Norfolk 757-441-3079; Abingdon 276-628-8158; Roanoke 540-857-2676, 2677.

U.S. Senator **George F. Allen (R)** 204 Russell Bldg., Washington, D.C. 20510; 202-224-4024; FAX 202-224-5432; senator_allen@allen.senate.gov; Richmond 804-771-2221.

1st Congressional District, Representative **Jo Ann Davis (R)** 1123 Longworth House Office Bldg, Washington, D.C. 20515-4601; 202-225-4261; FAX 202-225-4382; www.house.gov/writerep.

2nd, Thelma Drake **(R)** 322 Cannon House Office Bldg, Washington, D.C. 20515; 202-225-4215; FAX 202-225-4218; www.house.gov/writerep.

3rd, **Robert "Bobby" C. Scott (D)** 2464 Rayburn House Office Bldg., Washington, D.C. 20515-4603; 202-225-8351; FAX 202-225-8354; bobby.scott@mail.house.gov; Newport News 757-380-1000; Richmond 804-644-4845.

4th, **J. Randy Forbes (R)** 307 Cannon House Office Bldg., Washington, D.C. 20515; 202-225-6365; FAX 202-226-1170; www.house.gov/writerep.

5th, **Virgil H. Goode, Jr. (I)** 1520 Longworth House Office Bldg., Washington, D.C. 20515-4605; 202-225-4711; FAX 202-225-5681; 540-484-1254; www.house.gov/writerep.

6th, **Robert "Bob" Goodlatte (R)** 2240 Rayburn House Office Bldg., Washington, D.C. 20515; 202-225-5431; FAX 202-225-9681; Roanoke 540-857-2672; talk2bob@mail.house.gov; or www.house.gov/writerep.

7th, **Eric Cantor (R)** 329 Cannon House Office Bldg., Washington, D.C. 20515-4607; 202-225-2815; FAX 202-225-0011; http://cantor.house.gov or www.house.gov/writerep.

CONGRESSIONAL ELECTED OFFICIALS

8th, **James P. "Jim" Moran, Jr. (D)** 2239 Rayburn House Office Bldg., Washington, D.C. 20515-4608; 202-225-4376; FAX 202-225-0017; www.house.gov/writerep; Alexandria 703-971-4700.

9th, **Frederick C. "Rick" Boucher (D)** 2187 Rayburn Bldg., Washington, D.C. 20515; 202-225-3861; FAX 202-225-0442; ninthnet@mail.house.gov; Abingdon 276-628-1145; Big Stone Gap 276-523-5450; Pulaski 540-980-4310.

10th, **Frank R. Wolf (R)** 241 Cannon House Office Bldg., Washington, D.C. 20515-4610; 202-225-5136; FAX 202-225-0437; www.house.gov/writerep; Herndon 703-709-5800.

11th, **Thomas M. Davis, III (R)** 2348 Rayburn Bldg., Washington, D.C. 20515-0911; 202-225-1492; FAX 202-225-3071; tom.davis@mail.house.gov or www.house.gov/writerep; Annandale 703-916-9610; Herndon 703-437-1726; Woodbridge 703-590-4599.

3

STATEWIDE ELECTED OFFICIALS

GOVERNOR MARK WARNER

The administrative and appointive authority given to the Governor of Virginia makes the Governor one of the strongest state officers in the nation. To be eligible to serve, candidates must be citizens of the United States, at least 30 years old, and residents and registered voters of Virginia for five years preceding the election. The Governor is elected for a four-year term and may not serve an immediately consecutive term. The salary is $124,855.

POLITICAL BACKGROUND

2002 in totality was a challenging year for the new governor. *Washington Post* reporter R. H. Melton wrote, "Virginia's 69th governor endured crisis upon crisis. Legislators defeated his major education initiative in March, sniper shootings terrorized the Washington suburbs in October, and on November 5, voters crushed a transportation tax he championed. It was also Warner who, by his own admission, endured a year-long crash course in Virginia politics, both as the Democratic chief executive of a state trending conservative Republican and as a newcomer to elective office confronting Virginia's worst budget in its modern history."

In an interview with *The Washington Post*, Warner admitted that he found the first year overwhelming. But he asserted that he found his sea legs making structural changes in Virginia government so future budget problems could be averted. He said, "There have been other points where maybe I've been politically outfoxed or politically outmanned, where I say this isn't my strong suit. But this stuff now! This is my strong suit."

Warner spent his first year dealing with the wreckage of the state budget, which had been exacerbated by the Gilmore administration. Gilmore, who had been swept in to office four years before with his signature "no car tax" pledge, had virtually plundered the state budget to make good on that campaign promise. A recession reduced tax revenue just as his tax cuts were enacted. During the final year of Gilmore's administration, Republican and Democratic lawmakers grew concerned about the state's financial health, but the full depth of the fiscal crisis was not revealed until Warner was inaugurated.

Warner vetoed only one bill in 2002, and it was Delegate Robert Marshall's (R-13) "partial birth abortion" bill, to prohibit physicians from performing a certain rare late term abortion procedure. Warner wrote in his veto explanation that while he found this abortion procedure "deeply troubling," that "in some cases, HB 1154 would not allow a doctor to perform the procedure banned by HB 1154 when it would be safer than other procedures. Any health exception consistent with constitutional requirements must permit women to have access to the safest medical procedures." Referring to former court decisions, Warner wrote, "A federal court in Ohio recently struck down a statute with language similar to HB 1154 precisely because the so-called health exception was drawn too narrowly. As the court explained, 'logic dictates that when a physical health problem requires a woman to undergo a post-viability abortion, she must be permitted to use the least risky procedure ...'" The veto was sustained.

As Mark Warner nears the end of his four year term as Governor of Virginia, there is a sense of amazement from would-be conservative critics. He has been a successful governor in salvaging the partisanship of the former Republican George Gilmore.

He entered the governor's office as a successful business man who did not forget his modest beginning and brought an actual self-efficient but determined thrust to be a noteworthy Virginia governor and hopefully to put the rest the opprobrium of being not only from Northern Virginia but a newcomer.

To some observers Warner governed so sensibly and surely successfully that the establishment of conservative die-hards opened up with due consideration of this earnest practioner of politics.

4

In his final year as governor, Warner can be assessed by his skillful handling of his final budget as he proposed it and with the legislative process. In February at the half-way point newspaper accounts summarized the issues as education, public safety, driving under the influence (DUI), policy issues, and abortion.

The always contentious issue of abortion concerned Warner can give a sigh of relief for the failed issue of ending abortion clinics and putting limits on contraceptives by students. In education there was a new program sponsored by Delegate James Dillard (R-Fairfax) that provided better funding for school district with at-risk students to improve the scores of learning and decrease the drop-out ratio. DUI gets its share of attention killing legislature that allows the courts to take the car of DUI offender convicted for the third time. Also incurred was the time DUI offender must serve in jail.

Governor

Mark Warner (D)   b. Dec. 15, 1954 Indianapolis; educ. George Washington Univ. (BA), Harvard Law Sch. (JD); married, Lisa Collis; Presbyterian.

Formerly CEO Columbia Capital Corp.; founding chair VA Health Care Fndn.; SeniorNavigator.com; TechRiders; Virginia High-Tech Partnership; co-chair with Sen. George Allen, Virginia's Communities in Schools Foundation; served on boards of: VA Union Univ., GW Univ., Appalachian Sch. Law, VA Fndn. Ind. Colleges, VA Math & Science Coalition.

Offices   State Capitol, Third Floor, Richmond 23219; 804-786-2211.

Election Results

2001 general	Mark Warner	(D)	984,177	52.2%	$19,881,944
	Mark Earley	(R)	887,234	47.0%	$11,468,273
	W. B. Redpath	(L)	14,497	0.8%	$ 24,050

Campaign Contributions Political $7,788,739 (Repub. $1,500); Tech./Comm. $2,863,969; Finance $2,354,639; Realty/Constr. $1,761,661; Law $920,095; Misc. Individ./Co. $849,834; Health Care $431,300; Pub. Empl. $193,044; Electric $155,192 (Dominion $131,000, Duke $2,500, VA Pacific $1,000, Indep. Electric $12,025); Insurance/HMO $147,504; Beer/Wine/Dist. Spirits $141,940; Consultants $125,382; Auto Dealers/Rep. $99,610; Labor Miscellaneous $90,595 (AFL CIO $31,200); Advertising $87,679; Tobacco $84,734 (Philip Morris $53,584, Lorillard $10,000, Univ. Leaf $10,000, Conc. Friends $1,500); Security/Detective $81,950; Coal $80,296; Retail/Computer/Furn. $68,650; Gen. Retail $64,235; Food Proc. $54,050; Restaurants $48,531; Hotel/Tourism $45,600; Recreation/Amuse. Pk. $39,950; RR $39,250; Fishing $35,125; Misc. Energy $33,750; Personnel $26,991; Shipbuilding $26,700 (NN Shipbldg. $25,000); Grocery $25,275; Firefighters $25,000; Trash $24,750; Lumber $23,075; Clothing $21,718; Serv. Stat./Conv. St. $21,643; Gen. Farming/Vineyards/Equip. $21,405; Nat. Gas $20,750; Defense $17,660; Env. Eng. $17,060; Trucking $16,000; Manuf. $15,200; Metals $12,669; Hwy. Co. $12,000; Oil $11,100; Quarries $11,035; Pro-Business Trade Groups $10,585 (VA Greater Wash. Bd. Trade $6,000); Misc. Transp. $10,231; Services $10,100; Shipping $10,100; Paper $9,900; Schools $8,890; Travel Agents $8,075; Misc. Business $7,600; Chem./Plastics $7,575; Textiles $6,000; Billboards $5,000; Soft Drink $5,000; United Mine Wk. $5,000; Air Transport $4,825; Priv. Prison $3,700; Furniture $3,500;

Gardens $3,135; Misc. Issue $2,110; Funeral $1,635; Moving $1,500; Sales Rep. $1,300; Pest Cont. $1,000; Recycling $1,000; Envir. $900; Day Care $450; Boats $450; Veterin. $100.

Virginians for Warner Realty/Constr. $344,425; Finance $100,295; Tech./Comm. $52,910; Individuals $48,118; Medical $46,000; Attys. $39,600; Grocery (Ukrop) $26,631; Earle Williams $26,000; Coal $25,000; Insurance/HMOs $17,296; Rec./Amuse. Pk. $15,000; VMS Inc. $10,000; Misc. Defense $10,000; RR $8,250; Farmers $7,300; Lumber $7,000; Trucks $5,250; Quarries $5,000; Tobacco (Universal Leaf) $5,000; Chem./Plastics (Gottwald) $5,000); Pub. Empl. $4,600; Horses $4,500; Political $3,000; Paper $2,750; Sec./Detective $2,500; Tamaroff $2,000; Beer/Wine $2,000; Auto Dealers $1,950; Consult. $1,750; Electric $1,250; Restaurants $1,000; Envir. Eng. $1,000; Boats $750; Advertising $600; Misc. Manuf. $500; Tourism $500; Recruit. Ag. $500; Misc. Energy $500; Environmental $500; Moving $250; Ports/Shipping $250; Misc. Retail $200.

Economic Interests, 2002 *Sal. & Wages* $10,000+ MRW Enterprises, LLC; *Off. & Dir.*, Friedman, Billings, Ramsey Group, Dir. (resigned effective 12/31/01); *Pers. Liabil.*, $50,000+ ea.: banks (self), (family); $10,001-$50,000 stock co.; *Sec.*, **$50,000+ ea.:** 79 govt. bonds; 13 mutual funds; 65 ltd partnerships interest in (investors, tech., realty); bank mortgage fd., stocks in: ADC Tel/Comm., Akzo Nobel, Amersham PLC, Astrazeneca, AT&T, Autoliv, Aventis, Axa, BAE Systems, Bank Ireland, Barclays, Capital Cellular, Cheung Kong Holdings, Cisco, DBS Group, Deutsche Telecom, E ON AG ADR, Eni Spa ADR, Foreningssparbanken, Global SantaFe, Hanson, HSBC Holdings, Impac Mtge., Imperial Chem., ING Gr. ADR, Ishares (2), Istar Fin., Kaneb Serv., Komatsu, Koninklijke, Legg Mason, Lloyds ADR, McDonalds, Nasdaq, NEC, Nextel, Nippon Tel., Nokia ADR, Norfolk Southern, Pegasus, Presence Wks., Provox Tech., Repsol, Rolls Royce, San Paolo-IMI, Sony New, Swiss Reinsur., Telecom. Brasilei, Telefonica, Tele. Mexico, Tel. & Data, Telular, Thornburg Mtge., Total Fina (2), TPG ADR, Transcanada Pipeline, US Cellular, Unilever (2), United Business Media, Univ. Health Realty, Volkswagon, Volvo, Wolters, Worldcom MCI (2), XL Capital; **$10,001-$50,000 ea.:** 4 govt. bonds; 4 mutual funds; 7 ltd. partnerships; invest. trust; stocks in: Aegon NV, Aglient Tech., Aktiebolaget Electrolux, Alcatel, Allianz, AllTel, Alstom, An. Busch, AOL Time Warner, Austin Grill, Aventis SA, Banco Bradesco, Bank NY, Barclays, BASF, Billiton, BNP, BP Amoco, BP PLC, Bristol Myers Squibb, British Aerospace, British Sky Broadcasting, Bruker AKS, Cadbury, Canon, Citigroup, Commerce One, Comm. Bk. Australia, CRH PLC, Danske Bank, Dell Comp., Deutsche Bank (2), Diageo PLC, E ON AG, Elan (2), Embratel, Emerson Elec., Endesa, Eni, Fast Retailing, Fed. Home Mortgage, Fed. Ntl. Mtge., Fortis, Fraport, Fresenius Med., Fujitsu, GE, Gjensidige Nor Sparebank, GlaxoSmithKline (2), Group Serve, Grupo Carso, Grupo Drag., Guidant, Heineken, Henkel, Hitachi, HSBC PLC, Iberdrola, ING Gr., Intel, Intellidata, Interbrew, IBM, Invensys, ITO-Yokado, JGC, Johnson & Johnson, Kao, Koninklijke Ahold, Korea Elec., Korea Telecom, Lloyds, Lucent, Marks & Spencer, Matalan, Merck, Microsoft, Microstrat., Midway Games, Muenchener Rueckver, Nestle (2), News Corp., Nintendo, Nissan, *Bus. Int.*, $50,000+ ea.: Columbia Capital Corp., Columbia Capital LLC, MRW Enterprises, rental prop. (2); $50,000/less farm; *Real Estate*, Six prop. (5 rentals, rec./farming, all w/others).

LIEUTENANT GOVERNOR TIMOTHY KAINE

The Lieutenant Governor must be a citizen of the United States, at least thirty-five years of age, and a resident and registered voter of Virginia. He/She is the President of the Senate, but only votes to break a tie. The term is four years, and there is no limitation on the number of terms that may be served. The salary is $36,321.

POLITICAL BACKGROUND

STATEWIDE ELECTED OFFICIALS

Democratic Lt. Governor Timothy M. Kaine devoted his first year in office to building a foundation for an almost certain bid for governor in 2005. Coming off a three-year tenure as mayor of Richmond in 2001, Kaine bested two fellow Democrats in a primary for the Democratic nomination and ultimately defeated Republican Delegate Jay Katzen. Kaine won the 2001 general election with 50.35% of the vote. His margin was a wafer-thin victory over Katzen's 48.06% hold on the popular vote.

Kaine, sworn into office by his wife, Judge Anne Holton, claimed title to a largely ceremonial job that is openly acknowledged to be a proving ground in a candidate's quest for the governor's mansion. If Kaine is the Democratic nominee, he is certain to be challenged in the next gubernatorial race by Republican Attorney General Jerry W. Kilgore.

Political pundits have called Kaine "a bridgemaker," and he has publicly stated his desire to forge bipartisan cooperation in the Senate, which, going into the 2003 session, was divided with 23 Republicans and 17 Democrats.

Kaine's first General Assembly session was mostly uneventful, as the largely ceremonial job of presiding over the Senate offered few opportunities to set and direct an agenda. The Lieutenant Governor is constitutionally charged with presiding over the Senate, unable to vote except when deciding tie votes. In the 2002 session, Kaine cast the deciding vote on two bills that tied in the Senate. Senate Bill 214, sponsored by Senator Patricia S. Ticer (D-30), called for the State Board of Elections to prescribe voting materials in languages other than English if the state or a locality were to fall under federal bilingual election requirements. Kaine voted in support of the bill, although it later was killed in the House Committee on Privileges and Elections.

Republicans in 2003 were expected to make the case that Kaine's proposal, during a budget crisis, would necessitate a tax increase. Speaking to Republican activists in December, Kilgore said, "Not now, not in the future can this party be a party that supports raising taxes."

Kaine countered: "The debate this is setting up is not about taxes, but a debate about 'tell me what's a more important priority than educating the 1.1 million kids in Virginia.'"

The Lt. Governor said he had also discussed his proposal with Governor Mark Warner, a fellow Democrat, but the Governor "hasn't signed on yet," Kaine said. Going into the 2003 session, he also had not secured a sponsor for the proposed constitutional amendment or the proposed bill to increase teacher salaries. Virginia ranks 13th in the nation in per-capita income, but only 44th in state spending for schools based on that income.

As the state's financial woes intensified in fall 2002, Kaine said in September that he would trim the budget of the lieutenant governor's office to help the commonwealth save funds during the budget crisis. Kaine noted he would give up his annual discretionary allowance of $16,200 for the remainder of his term and would not ask for any state reimbursements for office-related travel or expenses.

"Our office is working with the Department of Planning and Budget to find other ways to trim costs and streamline our budget," he said. The Lt. Governor planned to offer legislation in 2003 to require the accountability of office expenses paid to elected officials, rather than the current direct payment. However, Kaine did not say he would take a pay cut. The Lieutenant Governor's annual salary is $36,321, with an office budget of $336,262 in fiscal 2002.

In 2002, Kaine also took issue with the legislature's redistricting power, saying state lawmakers should not be allowed to draw their own election districts. In an editorial published in *The Roanoke Times*, Kaine wrote that Republican lawmakers in 2001 "packed as many Democrat-leaning areas into as few legislative districts as possible." He argued that party politics should be banished from the redistricting process, instead suggesting that Virginia create a non-partisan commission, a move adopted by other states.

A citizens' advocacy group filed suit against Virginia in April 2002, challenging the congressional redistricting approved by the Republican-controlled General Assembly in 2001. As Lt. Governor, Kaine was named as a defendant in the suit, although within weeks he had filed a motion asking the court to dismiss him from the lawsuit. As Kaine noted, "the office of Lt. Governor had no part in the formulation or adoption of the Congressional District Plan voted on and passed by the Virginia General Assembly -- nor do I currently have any role in the enforcement or execution of the Congressional District Plan. More importantly, I do not wish to defend the plan because Virginia's redistricting process is indefensible."

Kaine added that his legal team, including his father-in-law, former Virginia Gov. Linwood Holton, would argue the motion at no cost to state taxpayers.

Kaine faces what promises to be a difficult battle for the governorship against the well oiled conservative machine that is building a voter base for Kilgore.

Lt. Governor Timothy M. Kaine keeping a low profile in the budget debate spoke out in early April for a compromise in the contentious state budget said that the argument should not be about the plans of the separate legislative bodies about which we raise more taxes. The debate should be about which we keep the public safe.

Kaine presiding over the Senate according to press reports said the Senate plan was best by providing about $200 million of additional funds for law enforcement agencies, courts, prisons and state police. According to newspaper accounts Kaine listed the following issues that made the budget a better guarantee of safety: Fully funds constitutionally mandated aid to local police departments, while the House version cuts the aid by $35.8.6 million; restores an additional $26.4 million in state reimbursements to local jailers that had been cut in previous budgets, while the House plan cuts an additional $16.2 million in the allocations; calls for building state prisons, while the House plan seeks one. The Senate also allocates $2.9 million for 100 more correctional officers,; backs $16.5 million more for circuit and district courts than the House plan; seeks $20 million to bump up state police starting salaries by 6.4 percent while the House plan offers no new money; proposes spending $37 million to increase the salaries of sheriffs deputies 6.4 percent, while the House plan offers no new spending.

Lt. Governor Kaine is now running for governor. His will-known political plans were on hold during the 2004 session but now he is proceeding full steam ahead to be elected Virginia's new governor in November, 2005.

Lieutenant Governor

Timothy Michael Kaine (D) Lt. Governor 2002- ; b. February 26, 1958, Minnesota; educ. Univ. Missouri (BA), Harvard Law Sch. (JD); married, Anne Holton; Catholic.

Former Mayor City of Richmond 1998-2001, Richmond City Council 1994-98.

Offices Office of the Lt. Governor, 900 E. Main St. Suite 1400, Richmond 23219; 804-786-2078; FAX 804-786-7514; ltgov@ltgov.state.va.us.

STATEWIDE ELECTED OFFICIALS

Election Results

2001 general	Timothy Kaine	(D) 925,974	50.3%	$2,695,350
	Jay Katzen	(R) 883,886	48.1%	$1,354,075
	Gary A. Reams	(L) 28,783	1.6%	$ 11,001

Campaign Contributions Realty/Constr. $513,490; Law $369,218; Individ./Colleges/Churches $237,244; Finance $165,760; Health Care $119,572; Democrats $106,918; Tech./Comm. $98,164; Pub. Empl. $74,137; Labor $72,060 (AFL-CIO $24,700, UMW $1,000); Grocery $42,255; Hotel/Tourism $39,368; Individuals $38,880; Electric $33,635 (Dominion $25,150+, Am. Electric $500); Auto Dealers/Rep. $30,825; Consultants $30,734; Computer/Office $28,250; Advertising $25,550; Beer/Wine $22,950; Tobacco $22,250 (Univ. Leaf $12,000, Philip Morris $3,000); Personnel Ag. $21,173; Retail/Comp./Furn. $20,350; Misc. Defense $16,500 (John M. Toups $11,000, Philip Odeen $5,500); Insurance/HMO $13,350; Trav. Agents $12,150; Metals $12,100; Services $11,725; Clothing $11,648; Restaurants $11,072; Trucking $10,450; Mark M. O'Connell $10,000; Coal $8,000; RR $7,875; Paper $7,500; Schools $7,375; Lumber $7,350; Recreation/Amus. Pk. $7,200; Env. Eng. $6,450; Garden $5,400; Misc. Business $5,650; Chem./Plastics $5,600; Air Transport $5,454; Funeral $4,937; Farmers/Horse/Farm Equip. $4,660; Serv. Stat./Conv. Store $3,000; Nat. Gas $2,600; Janus Corp. $2,500; Abortion Rights $1,900; Food Proc. $1,856; Gay/Lesbian $1,800; Misc. Energy $1,700.

Economic Interests 2002 *Sec.*, $50,000+ ea.: money market, 401K with bank, college savings mutual fund; $10,001-$50,000 ea.: Bristol Myers Squibb, Coca Cola, GE, Texaco; *Gifts*, $100 Rich. Metropolitan Auth. (tickets), $77 Philip Morris (gift box); *Pay. for Rep. by Assoc.*, all services performed by lawyer at prev. law firm: utilities, tel., auto dealers, cellular phone, insurance before legislature, SCC; hospital and physicians before Bd. Health, Bd. Med.; wine distrib. before ABC Bd.; *Pay. for Rep. Gen.*, all services performed by lawyer at prev. law firm: $250,001+ ea.: electric utilities, tel. util., banks, savings inst., manuf., casualty insur., other insur., other; $100,001-$250,000 ea.: gas util., oil/gas retail, life insur., retail, alcoholic bev., $50,001-$100,000 ea.: trade assn , local govt.; $10,001-$50,000 ea.: cable tv, inter/intrastate transp., prof. assn., labor org.; *Real Estate*, One prop.

ATTORNEY GENERAL JERRY KILGORE

The Attorney General must have been admitted to the bar of the Commonwealth five years before his/her election and be at least 30 years of age. The term is four years, and there is no limitation on the number of terms that may be served. The salary is $110,667.

POLITICAL BACKGROUND

While Republican Attorney General Jerry Kilgore when elected in mid-January, 2002 assumed the duties of the Attorney General to work with the governors office and state agencies Kilgore when campaigning for his office said he would help keep Virginia safe from violent predators, combat terrorism, keep drugs away from children, and protect citizens – especially seniors from fraud and abuse.

Like the position for lieutenant governor, the job of attorney general is seen as a springboard to a campaign for governor the next time around. Like Democratic Lt. Governor Timothy Kaine, Kilgore made no secret of his designs on the governor's job. Those designs would bring him into direct conflict with the governor himself.

9

Democratic legislators appealed the Republican redistricting, and a judge had overturned the plan. While Governor Gilmore was in office, the state had been planning on filing an appeal to a higher court. Once Governor Warner was elected, Democrats believed that the case would go no further. Kilgore announced he would appeal, without discussing the matter with the Governor, and further, Kilgore made it clear he intended to appeal even if Warner wanted the case dropped. Warner was eager to keep peace with Republicans and appear fair. Kilgore aggressively maneuvered his position. He put out a statement saying, "the Governor could create a conflict for this office as it continues to defend a law duly passed by the people's representatives in the General Assembly and signed by the Governor. I informed Governor Warner of the potential conflict and recommended that he consider special counsel for himself." Eventually Warner agreed to appoint special counsel for himself, and he and Kilgore released this joint agreement: "to ensure that the appeals process in *West v. Gilmore* will proceed as quickly as possible for the reasons discussed below. The Attorney General believes the *West* case was wrongly decided. The Governor believes the opinion was sensible and defensible. In our legal system, the Virginia Supreme Court is the final arbiter of state law. We believe the best interests of the Commonwealth are served by the appeals process laid out in this agreement." Kilgore won the appeal and Democratic legislators were quite unhappy that their battle against redistricting was over.

Kilgore was masterful in distancing himself from Republican scandals. When prominent Republicans were caught eavesdropping on a conference call between Democratic legislators and the Governor, Kilgore moved quickly to protect his position as the highest ranking law enforcement officer in the state. He condemned the behavior and urged an investigation. He also quickly reprimanded Speaker Vance Wilkins' behavior when it became public that the Speaker had settled out of court for sexual harassment. He released a statement, "Sexual harassment is wrong and conduct of this type, under any guise or excuse, is unacceptable and, if the allegations are true, the Speaker's moral authority to lead is seriously undermined. The payment by the Speaker of $100,000 -- has been confirmed. The reason given by the Speaker for the payment -- that it was to protect the caucus -- I interpret to be an effort to protect his position as Speaker." This quote was widely reported, and political pundits felt that as the highest elected Republican office holder that Kilgore's opinion dealt the deathblow to the Speaker's support. In both cases, Kilgore came across as ethical and statesmanlike.

During the legislative session, the Republican controlled legislature and the Democratic governor approved legislation backed by Kilgore on domestic violence, expanding the use of DNA evidence in violent crimes, and fighting terrorism. His domestic abuse bill updated Virginia's abuse laws including making it easier to convict a spouse of marital rape. It removed the requirement that married persons must be living apart or that the defendant caused bodily injury by use of force for a spouse to be convicted of rape. The bill also expanded the definition of "family abuse" to include any bodily injury. Kilgore said. "It is now time we addressed the problem of violence inside the home."

Kilgore took a bill backed by some Democrats but opposed by Republicans in the 2001 session and made it his own in the 2002 session. The Republicans championed it, and the "Stand By Your Ad" which requires full disclosure about who paid for a campaign ad and whom would benefit, and the posting of minutes on the internet of all boards, commissions, and public bodies, passed.

Kilgore was elected Virginia's 42nd Attorney General on November 6, 2001, receiving more than 60% of the vote. Prior to his election as Attorney General, Kilgore had been plucked from obscurity by then Governor George Allen to serve as Secretary of Public Safety in 1994, with some voicing concern over his rather thin resume. He went on to become a lobbyist. When Kilgore won the office of Attorney General, he was the only statewide elected official to hail from the Southwest since Wise County native Linwood Holton, Kaine's father-in-law, won the governorship in the 1970's.

The race for governor in Virginia has begun. It pits Lieutenant Governor Timothy Kaine, Democrat against Attorney General Jerry Kilgore, Republican. Odds favor the Lieutenant Governor hailing from

STATEWIDE ELECTED OFFICIALS

Richmond, the capitol in central Virginia but few would forecast the favored candidate Kaine given the combatative nature of the Attorney General. The race will be most interesting to watch and assess the various campaign strategies that both will need to use as they criss-cross Virginia.

Attorney General

Jerry Kilgore (R) Attorney General 2002- ; b. August 23, 1961, Kingsport, TN; educ. Clinch Valley College of UVA, Sch. Law William & Mary; married Martha Kilgore; Baptist.

Attorney; Secretary Public Safety 1994-97; State, Fed. Prosecutor; Assist. U.S. Attorney Western District VA; Assistant Commonwealth's Attorney Scott County; Richmond law firm Sands Anderson Marks & Miller.

Offices Office of the Attorney General, 900 E. Main St., Richmond 23219; 804-786-2071.

Election Results

2001 general	Jerry Kilgore	(R)	1,107,068	60.0%	$2,151,966
	A. Donald McEachin	(D)	736,431	39.9%	$1,638,589

Campaign Contributions Republicans $242,893 (include. National $63,332); Realty/Constr. $233,887; Law $203,248; Health Care $178,874; Tech./Comm. $154,992; Coal $146,085; Individ./Misc. co. $88,224; Electric $78,778 (Dominion $57,700, Independent Electric $6,000); Auto manuf./dealers/rep./rental $59,878 (dealers $47,978); Pub. Empl. $58,130; Finance $56,391; Insurance/HMO $54,415; Amuse. Pks., Rec. $31,950; Tobacco $29,500 (Univ. Leaf $8,000, Philip Morris $4,500); Restaurants $28,579; Chem./Plastics $26,440; Lumber $25,615; Advertising $20,530; Retail $16,610; M. G. "Pat" Robertson $15,000; Grocery $12,262; Oil $11,850; Consultants $10,250; Trucking $6,795; Conserv. Pro-Family $6,425 (Bay Shore Ent. $5,000, Natl. Conserv. Campaign $1,000), Moving $6,600; RR $6,175; Hotel/Tourism $5,800; Service Stat./Conv. St. $5,750; Paper $5,750; Schools $5,600; Nat. Gas $5,500; NRA $5,000; NN Shipping $5,000; Hwy. Co. $5,000.

Economic Interests 2002 *Sal. & Wages,* $10,000+ ea.: Sands Anderson Marks & Miller (self until 1-12-02); state VA (spouse); *Off. & Dir.,* Sands Anderson, Dir. until 1-12-02; *Sec.,* $50,000+ mutual fund; $10-001-$50,000 mutual fund; *Pay. for Talks, Mtgs. & Publ.,* $905 state (Natl. AG Conf. expenses, per diem), $400 Natl. Atty. Gen. (conf. expenses); *Gifts,* $235 Dominion Resources (Redskins tickets), $100 Charlie Condon for Gov. campaign (flight expenses), $77 Philip Morris (gift box); *Bus. Int.,* $50,000/less 1/2 interest in business building; *Pay. for Rep. by You,* lobbying legisl. & exec., each $50,001-$100,000 Brown & Root constr.; $10,001-$50,000 ea.: Com-Net Ericsson, Commissioners of Rev., VA High Growth Comm.; *Pay. for Rep. by Assoc.,* Sands Anderson Marks & Miller represents several lobbying clients, filed with the Sec. of the Commonwealth, partnership ended at this co. 1-12-02; *Pay. for Rep. Gen.,* legal or lobbying services each $50,001-$100,000 ea.: construction, communications; $10,001-$50,000 ea.: mining, pub. empl., localities; $1,001-$10,000 banks, life insur. co.; *Real Estate,* One prop. (w/spouse).

11

STATEWIDE ELECTED OFFICIALS

Notes

SENATE DISTRICT ONE, *Martin E. "Marty" Williams (R)*

POLITICAL AND LEGISLATIVE BACKGROUND

Senate District One consists of all of the City of Poquoson; the York County Precincts of Coventry, Tabb, and Bethel; the City of Hampton Precincts of Syms, Booker, Buckroe, Burbank, Fox Hill, and Phillips Precincts and part of Langley; and the City of Newport News Precincts of Denbigh, Epes, Jenkins, Oyster Point, Richneck, Windsor, Bland, Boulevard, Charles, Christopher Newport, Deep Creek, Watkins, Grissom, Hidenwood, Hilton, Palmer, Riverside, Sanford, Saunders, Warwick, Yates, Riverview, Kiln Creek, Beaconsdale, and Sedgefield.

Martin E. "Marty" Williams, a Republican, was elected in 1995, defeating the powerful and legendary Senate Majority Leader Hunter Andrews who had served since 1964. Williams, a former vice mayor of Newport News, bested Andrews with 52.5% of the vote in an expensive race, and ran unopposed in the 1999 election. Williams is a partner in Environmental Specialties Group, and the executive director of Inflammatory Skin Disease Institute.

During the 2004 session, Williams sponsored nineteen bills, of which twelve passed and two were incorporated into other bills. Bills that passed allowed toll operators to obtain vehicle owner information from the DMV; established screening requirements in York counties for automobile graveyards and junkyards; established reciprocity agreements for law-enforcement officers regarding concealed weapons; prohibited persons telephone solicitation to persons on a Do-Not-Call Registry; and authorized the governor to establish remedial programs to include small businesses along with women and minority-owned businesses under the Public Procurement Act.

Bills that failed would have exempted water supply projects that have a Virginia Water Protection Permit from needing a permit from the Virginia Marine Resource Commission and allowed the City of Newport News to construct underground utilities for a state highway project for up to ten million dollars.'

Of three resolutions one commemorative resolution was successful.

Senator SD 1

Martin E. "Marty" Williams (R) Member of Senate: 1996- ; b. March 5, 1951, Newport News; home, 9921 River Rd., Newport News 23601; educ. Ferrum College; married, LaDonna Williams; Episcopal.

Partner, Environmental Specialties Group; Executive Dir., Inflammatory Skin Disease Institute; Member: Boys & Girls Club, VA Peninsula, Bd. of Dir.; Sarah Bonwell Reg. Center, Bd. of Dir.; past Vice Mayor, City of Newport News (1990-1996).

Offices P.O. Box 1096, Newport News 23601-1096; 757-599-8683; GA Bldg. Capitol Sq., Rm. 331, Richmond 23219; 804-698-7501.

2004 Committees *Transportation, Chairman; Commerce and Labor; General Laws; Rehabilitation and Social Services; Rules.*

Senate Key Votes, 2004
Please see Introduction for more information on bills.

1) Budget Bill	FOR	5) Family Life	FOR	9)Charter Schools	FOR

FIRST CONGRESSIONAL DISTRICT

2) Feticide	FOR	6) Fire Arms	FOR	10)Legal Aid		FOR
3) Marriage	FOR	7) Open Space	AGN			
4) Child Abuse	AGN	8) Home School	FOR			

Election Results

1999	general	M. E. Williams	(R)	25,416	96.1%	$234,822

Campaign Contributions 2000-June 30, 2002 **Realty/Constr.** $35,825; **Transp.** $25,355 (Auto Dealers $16,500); **Attys.** $18,230; **Medical** $15,450; **Tech./Comm.** $11,000; **Insurance/HMOs** $5,750; **Finance** $4,750; **Tobacco** $4,041 (RJR $3,04, PM $1,000); **NNShipbldg.** $4,000; **Beer/Wine/Dist. Sp.** $3,800; **Individuals** $2,660 ($2,000 Solon Paul); **Retail** $2,500; **Electric** $2,300; **Trash** $2,000; **Natural Gas** $1,750; **Pub. Empl.** $1,810; **Coal** $1,000; **Billboards** $750; **Funeral** $750; **Serv. Stat/Conv St** $500; **Miscellaneous Energy** $500; **Consultants** $500; **Oil** $300; **Advert.** $263; **Soft Drink** $250; **Restau.** $250; **Kings Dom.** $250; **VA Automat. Merch.** $250; **Misc. Defense** $250; **Envir. Eng.** $250; **Republicans** $250.

Economic Interests, 2004 *Sal. & Wages*, $10,000+ Malcolm Pirnie Inc., Inflammatory Skin Disease Institute, wife, DIR, Riverside Hospital; Securities more than $50,000: stock , money markets; Less than $50,000: value trust, money market/stocks; Paymts for representation by you up to $10,000: Seaford Scallops, V-Dot mtg; Cumberland County, VDEQ mtg; Paymts for representation and other services generally: Water utilities, consulting; Pymts for other from $50, 000 to $100,000; counties, cities, towns, consulting; from $10,000 to $50,000; Real Estate: residential property in VA and NC; Gifts: $1005 Dominion Resources Svs, hunting trip; $179 McGuire Woods consulting, dinner; $91 Dominion Resources Svs, dinner; $ 54 Dominion Resources Svs, dinner; $67 VA Auto Dealers, dinner; $2,658 VADA Convention; $131 Altria, dinner; $93 Access Point, dinner.

SENATE DISTRICT THREE, *Thomas K. Norment, Jr. (R)*

POLITICAL AND LEGISLATIVE BACKGROUND
The Third Senatorial District includes Gloucester, James City, and New Kent Counties; the City of Williamsburg; the York County Precincts of Queens Lake, Yorktown, Waller Mill, Nelson, Magruder, Seaford, Harris Grove, Edgehill, Dare, and Harwoods Mill; and the City of Newport News Precincts of McIntosh, Reservoir, Lee Hall, and Nelson

Thomas K. Norment, Jr., an attorney and a Republican, has served since his election in 1991 when he defeated long-term incumbent William E. Fears (D), making much of Fears' opposition to tougher penalties on drunk driving. "Stormin' Norment," unopposed in 1995, defeated Democrat Lynwood W. Lewis in 1999 with 63% of the vote. As Senate Floor Leader in 2001 and a member of the Privileges and Elections Committee, Norment helped shape the redistricting process. Norment and other Senators in both parties, refused to go along with Gilmore's budget plan that severely cut agency services while putting the car tax cut at 70%, asking instead that the cut be more gradually phased in. "Cutting vital services to fund a car-tax reduction is both fiscally irresponsible and a threat to the future economy of the commonwealth," Norment was quoted in *The Richmond Times-Dispatch*. That session ended without an agreement on the budget.

During the 2004 session, Norment sponsored thirty-three bills which twenty passed and nine were carried over to the 2005 session. The bills that passed provided training standards for law-enforcement personnel in handling sexual assault and stalking cases; created a Post-Disaster Anti-Price Gouging Act; prohibited the Commonwealth from selling new sources of air emissions; amended the Charter of the City of Williamsburg; allowed localities to impose water saving ordinances during water shortages or emergencies; and allowed the James City and York counties to impose a transient occupancy tax.

15

Carried over were bills, which eliminated a requirement to use fictitious names in business entities; permitted a voter to submit an application for an absentee ballot online; and required the phase-out of business license taxes in all localities.

Eleven of thirteen resolutions passed; one of which set the schedule for conducting business during the 2004 Special Session.
Bills that failed would have created a Domestic Violence Victim Fund and provided revised civil penalties for violations regarding inoperable motor vehicles.

Norment voted against the Equal Rights Amendment which failed by one vote in the Senate Privileges and Elections Committee.

Senator SD 3

Thomas K. Norment, Jr. (R)
Member of Senate: 1992- ; b. April 12, 1946, Richmond; home, 145 Jerdone Rd., Williamsburg 23185; educ. VMI, William & Mary Law Sch.; married, Mary Carlisle Humelsine; Episcopalian.

Attorney; former mem. & Chair, James City Co. Bd. Sup.; Bd. Dir. Williamsburg & Peninsula Ch. Commerce; former prof., Christopher Newport Coll., Am. Inst. Banking; former Leg. Aide State Sen. Herb Bateman; VA, Williamsburg & Newport News Bar; James City Co. Rotary; Jamestown-Yorktown Fndn.; VA Pen. Econ. Comm.

Offices P.O. Box 1697, Williamsburg 23187-1697; 757-259-7810; GA Bldg., Rm. 427, Capitol Sq., Richmond 23219; 804-698-7503.

2004 Committees *Commerce and Labor; Courts of Justice; Finance; Privileges and Elections; Rules.*

Senate Key Votes, 2004
Please see Introduction for more information on bills.

1) Budget Bill	FOR	5) Family Life	FOR	9)Charter Schools	FOR
2) Feticide	FOR	6)Fire Arms	FOR	10) Legal Aid	FOR
3) Marriage	FOR	7) Open Space	FOR		
4) Child Abuse	FOR	8)Home School	FOR		

Election Results

1999 general	Thomas K. Norment, Jr.	(R)	24,916	62.9%	$451,992
	L. W. Lewis, Jr.	(D)	14,611	36.9%	$ 56,273

Campaign Contributions 2000-June 30, 2002 Realty/Constr. $63,665; **Attys.** $40,800; **Medical** $23,500; **Finance** $19,450; **Insur./HMOs** $17,133; **Transp.** $17,425 (Auto Deal. $13,575, Ports/Shipping $500); **Electric** $16,225 (Dom. $4,700, Indep. elec. $1,625); **Tech./Comm.** $15,985; **Pub. Empl.** $10,325; **Individuals** $9,280; **Retail** $8,545; **Beer/Wine** $5,500; **Restau./Hotel/Tour** $5,350; **Travel Ag.** $5,000; **Coal** $4,900; **NNShipbldg.** $3,800; **Tobacco** $3,750 (PM $3,500; RJR $250); **Misc. Manuf.** $2,800; **Chem./Plastics** $2,500; **Rec./Amuse. Pk.** $2,475; **Nat. Gas** $2,000; **Soft Drink** $1,800; **Pork Proc./Fishing/Farm** $1,650; **Serv. Stat./Conv. St.** $1,200; **Oil** $1,200; **Advert.** $425; **Republicans** $425; **Lumber** $300; **VA Automat. Merch.** $250.

Economic Interests, 2004 *Sal. & Wages,* $10,000+ ea.: Col. Williamsburg Fdn.; Kaufman & Canoles, P.C.; *Off. & Dir.,* Towne Bank, Dir.; *Sec.,* $50,000+ ea.: mutual funds (6), money market, stocks: Grafton Dodge, Dom. Resources, First Union, SunTrust, IBM; $10,001-$50,000 ea.: mutual fund, money market, stocks: Sara Lee, An. Busch, Oracle, law firm, Bank One, BB&T, Old Pt. Fin.,

FIRST CONGRESSIONAL DISTRICT

Gateway 2000, Nokia, CTC, First Charter, Owens Minor, Bon Air/Wmsburg Title Ins.; *Gift; $98 VCTA, dinner; $6,293 VA Sheriffs Assoc. hunting trip; $102 VA Sheriffs Assoc, hunting trip; $45 VA Sheriffs Assoc, dinner; Bus. Int.,* $50,000+ ea.:   Mill Assoc. (rentals), Hillman/Norment (realty/stocks), Kaufman & Canoles (law), JTN/Grafton Dodge (dealership); $50,000/less Thimble Shoals (realty); *Pay. for Rep. by You,* $1,001-$10,000 ea.: inmates Dept. Correct. (parole bd.), bldr. (DPOR), realtor (DPOR), developers (DPOR); *Pay. for Rep. by Assoc.,* employ. claims at Workers' Comp. and at Empl. Comm.; *Pay. for Rep. & Other Services Generally,* legal services, $250,001+ ea.: localities; manuf., insur., retail co.; $100,001-$250,000 ea.: savings inst., life insur., casualty insur., alcoholic bev.; $50,001-$100,000 ea.: loan/finance, mining, prof. assn.; $10,001-$50,000 ea.: electric, water, interstate transp., oil or gas co.; *Real Estate,* Six residential & comm. prop. w/others.

SENATE DISTRICT FOUR, *William T. "Bill" Bolling (R)*

POLITICAL AND LEGISLATIVE BACKGROUND

Senate District 4 consists of all of Caroline, Essex, Hanover, King and Queen, King William, and Middlesex Counties; and part of Spotsylvania County comprised of the Partlow, Blaydes Corner, Travelers Rest, Summit, and Battlefield Precincts.

William Bolling, a businessman and a Republican, was elected in 1995 after an expensive, heated, and vitriolic race that resulted in the close defeat of incumbent Democrat Elmo Cross, who had served in the Senate since 1976. The level of shrillness and misrepresentation brought the Bolling campaign statewide criticism, but won the seat by 574 votes. Bolling had no opposition in 1999.

During the 2004 session, Bolling sponsored eight bills of which five passed and one was carried over to the 2005 session. The bills that passed provided for orientation and training sessions for state government personnel on the provision of the Conflict of Interest Act; mandatory training regarding the legal duties of child protective service workers; that royalties would be charged for the use of state-owned bottomland.

The bills that carried over required that the permit of the Virginia Pollutant Discharge Elimination System be no fewer than five years.

Bills that failed required magistrates who issued emergency custody or temporary detention orders for seriously mentally ill individuals to name the enforcement agency and jurisdiction that would carry out the orders.

Bolling voted against the Equal Rights Amendment which failed by one vote in the Senate Privileges and Elections Committee.

17

Senator SD 4

William T. "Bill" Bolling (R) Member of Senate: 1996-; b. June 15, 1957, Sistersville, WVA; home, 7995 Strawhorn Dr., Mechanicsville 23111; educ. Univ. Charleston (B.A. Pol. Sci.); married, Jean Ann; United Methodist.

Second Vice-Pres., The Reciprocal Group; former Chairman Hanover Co. Board of Supervisors 1992-95.

Offices P.O. Box 3037, Mechanicsville 23116; 804-730-4202; FAX 804-559-2595; GA Bldg., Capitol Sq., Rm. 317, Richmond 23219; 804-698-7504.

2004 Committees *Agriculture, Conservation and Natural Resources; Education and Health; General Laws; Privileges and Elections.*

FIRST CONGRESSIONAL DISTRICT

Senate Key Votes, 2004
Please see Introduction for more information on bills.

1) Budget	AGN	5) Family Life	FOR	9)Charter Schools	FOR
2) Feticide	FOR	6) Fire Arms	FOR	10) Legal Aid	FOR
3) Marriage	FOR	7) Open Space	AGN		
4) Child Abuse	AGN	8) Home School	FOR		

Election Results

1999 general   William T. Bolling   (R)   38,136   99.7% $134,555

Campaign Contributions 2000-June 30, 2002   Republicans $34,545; **Medical** $29,316; **Realty/Constr.** $21,200; **Insur./HMOs** $13,650; **Attys.** $10,950; **Finance** $9,700; **Tech./Comm.** $7,700; **Transp.** $7,400 (RR $1,750; Auto Dealers $1,300); **Farmers/Fishing/Horse** $6,900; **Individ.** $5,950; **Retail/Busin.** $4,550 (Jacob Assoc. $1,000); **Serv. Stat./Conv. St.** $3,700; **Beer/Wine** $3,400; **Electric** $3,250; **Pub. Empl.** $2,400; **Tobacco--PM** $1,800; **Quarries** $1,500; **Coal** $1,250; **Paper** $1,250; **Rec./Amuse. Pk.** $1,000; **Funeral** $750; **NRA** $500; **Soft Drink** $500; **Ashland Milling** $500; **Nat. Gas** $500; **Oil** $500; **VA Nat. Res.** $500; **NNShipbldg.** $500; **Trash** $250.

Economic Interests, 2004   *Sal. & Wages*, $10,000+ The Reciprocal Group; *Off. & Dir.*, Reciprocal Gr., 2nd VP; *Sec.*, $50,000+ ea.: mutual funds (3); $10,001-$50,000 ea.: mutual funds (7), stocks: Capital One, Prudential, Sun Microsystems; *Pay. for Talks, Mtgs., & Publ.* $10,000 to $50,000: Inter/Intra state Insurance companies; $250,000 and over: Life Insurance, Casualty Insurance Companies; Gifts: $85 Altria, dinner; $132 VA Cable, dinner.

SENATE DISTRICT SEVENTEEN, *R. Edward Houck (D)*

POLITICAL AND LEGISLATIVE BACKGROUND
Senate District 17 consists of all of Culpeper, Louisa, Madison, and Orange Counties; the Spotsylvania County Precincts of Grange Hall, Maury, Plank Road, Frazers Gate, Belmont, Brokenburg, Todd's Tavern, Holbert, Salem, and Dient's Mill, and the City of Fredericksburg's District 1, District 3, and District 4 Precincts and part of the District 2 Precinct.

Edward "Edd" Houck, a school administrator and a Democrat, has served since 1983. The seat opened on the retirement of conservative Republican, Eva Scott, the first woman elected to the Virginia Senate. Houck defeated Republican Patrick McSweeney by 54.5% of the vote, and has won over Republican opposition ever since. Houck had served as Senate Democratic Caucus Chairman, but resigned saying they spent too much time arguing over roads and not enough on education.

During the 2004 session, Houck sponsored ten bills, eight passed and two were carried over to the 2005 session. The bills that passed granted access to committee and subcommittee; meetings of boards of directors of property owner's associations; permitted reorganization of record exemptions of the Freedom of Information Act; and granted photo identification cards to retired law enforcement officers.

Carried over to the 2005 session were bills to license inpatient hospice facilities and to allow localities in their subdivision ordinances to determine adequate water supply sources.

Six resolutions were passed including one to designate the second week of February National Courtesy Week.

19

Senator SD 17

R. **Edward "Edd" Houck (D)** Member of Senate: 1984-; b. Sept. 11, 1950, Smyth Co.; home, 306 Woodfield Dr., Spotsylvania 22553; educ. Wytheville Comm. Coll. (A.S.), Concord Coll. (B.S. Ed.), Univ VA (M. Ed.); married Dana Kee Blankenship; Episcopalian.

Dir. Student Services, Fredericksburg City Sch.; former chair Dem. Caucus; Chm. Rappahannock River Basin Study Comm.; Comm. on Youth, (past Chm.); Spotsylvania 4-H Adv. Com.; Ruritan; UVA Sch. Educ. Fnd., Bd. Dir.; Pi Kappa Alpha, past pres.; Fredericksburg Area Ch. Commerce; VA High School League. Awards: 1997 VA Fed. Council Exceptional Children; 1997 Child Advocate of Yr. VA Chap. Am. Ped. Assn.; 1997 Leg. Yr. VA Sheriff's Offices P.O. Box 7, Spotsylvania 22553-0007; 540-786-2782; FAX 540-891-8805; GA Bldg., Capitol Sq., Rm. 326, Richmond 23219; 804-698-7517.

2004 Committees *Education and Health; Finance; General Laws; Rules; Transportation.*
Senate Key Votes, 2004
Please see Introduction for more information on bills.

1) Budget Bill	FOR	5) Family Life	FOR	9)Charter Schools	FOR
2) Feticide	FOR	6) Fire Arms	FOR	10) Legal Aid	FOR
3) Marriage	FOR	7) Open Space	FOR		
4) Child Abuse	**???**	8) Home School	**???**		

Election Results

1999 general	R. "Edd" Houck	(D)	27,605	60.1%	$270,951
	A. M. Sheridan, Jr.	(R)	18,334	39.9%	$301,605

Campaign Contributions 2000-June 30, 2002 **Medical** $9,300; **Tobacco--PM** $2,250; **Attys.** $2,250; **Pub. Empl.** $2,000; **Realty/Constr.** $1,950; **Transp.** $1,700 (Auto Dealers/Manuf. $1,450); **Tech./Comm.** $1,500; **Democrats** $1,000; **Electric** $750; **Finance** $750; **Beer/Wine** $750; **Individ.** $500; **Nat. Gas** $350; **Horse Farm** $250; **Pest Contr.** $250; **Advert.** $250; **Restau.** $150.

Economic Interests, 2004 *Sal. & Wages*, $10,000+ ea.: Spotsylvania Co. Pub. Sch., Fredericksburg City Sch.; *Gifts*, $115VA Auto Dealers, legislative dinner; $102 Old Dominion Hwy Contractors Assoc, legislative dinner; $158 Altria, legislative dinner; $346 Altria, NASCAR Nextel race; $336 Altria, NASCAR Nextel race; $52 Cambridge Healthcare Holdings, legislative dinner.

SENATE DISTRICT TWENTY-EIGHT, *John H. Chichester (R)*

POLITICAL AND LEGISLATIVE BACKGROUND
Senate District 28 consists of all of King George, Lancaster, Northumberland, Richmond, Stafford, and Westmoreland Counties; the Fauquier County Precincts of Catlett, Lois, and Morrisville; a part of Prince William County's Quantico Precinct; and part of the City of Fredericksburg's District 2 Precinct.

John H. Chichester, an insurance business owner and a Republican, ran as a Democrat in 1969 against George Rawlings in a House primary. Chichester lost and left the Democrats, claiming they were too liberal. In 1978, Chichester, vastly outspent by his opposition, won a special Senate election, filling a vacancy created by the death of veteran legislator Paul Manns. He has defeated Democratic opposition since, and was unopposed in 1995 and 1999. In 1980, on the Equal Rights Amendment, he abstained, invoking Rule 36, refraining upon an "immediate, private or personal interest." This stopped approval of

the ERA in the Virginia Senate. In 1985, Chichester ran unsuccessfully for Lt. Governor against Senator L. Douglas Wilder.

With the shift in political power in the Senate, Chichester became Co-Chair of the powerful Senate Finance Committee, and in 2000, with Republicans in the majority, he became the chairman. The 2001 session began and ended with Chichester and Governor James Gilmore, both Republicans, at odds over the budget, which is covered in fuller detail in the "Introduction" to *The 2002 Almanac of Virginia Politics*. Gilmore wanted to intensify the phasing out of the car tax above all else, as part of his "legacy." Chichester maintained the original "deal" of the "car tax cut" language allowed a slowing of the phase out as warranted by economics. Chichester and the majority of the Senate held firm that it was not worth the loss of necessary services to the public to eliminate the car tax at the 70% rate which Gilmore stuck to, but that a 55% phase out for the current year would be feasible. In the early part of the 2002 session, *The Washington Post* noted other legislators acknowledged Chichester and the finance committee were correct that Gilmore "was overstating revenue" to pay for the car tax cut. As a result, Chichester said, "A $3.6 billion problem can't be fixed with a nip here and a tuck there. It can only be fixed with real, lasting budget reductions that involve a lot of pain."

During the 2004 session, Chichester sponsored ten bills, three passed. These bills authorized the Higher Education Bond Bill Act of 2004; the Parking Facilities Bond Bill of 2004; and changed the name of Mary Washington College to the University of Mary Washington.

A resolution established a subcommittee to study the administrative and financial relationships between the State and its higher educational institutions.

Failed bills would have amended the Appropriations Act of 2003, authorized bonds for the Virginia Public Building Authority and Virginia College Building Authority; and increased the per pack excise tax on cigarettes.

Senator SD 28

John H. Chichester (R) Member of Senate: 1978-; b. Aug. 26, 1937, Fredericksburg; home, 135 Lake Shore Dr., Fredericksburg 22495; educ. Augusta Mil. Acad., attending VPI, Bus. Admin.; married Karen L. Williams; Presbyterian.

Manager and Owner Chichester Ins. Co.; US Army Reserves 1956-62 incl. active duty; Mason 32 degree; Rotary past pres.; Jaycees; Acca Shrine; Fredericksburg Lodge No. 4 AF & AM.

Offices P.O. Box 904, Fredericksburg 22404-0904; 540-373-5600; GA Bldg., Capitol Sq., Rm. 626, Richmond 23219; 804-698-7528.

2004 Committees *Finance, Chair; Agriculture, Conservation and Natural Resources; Commerce and Labor; Rules.*

21

FIRST CONGRESSIONAL DISTRICT

Senate Key Votes, 2004

Please see Introduction for more information on bills.

1) Budget Bill	FOR	5) Family Life	FOR	9) Charter Schools	FOR
2) Feticide	FOR	6) Fire Arms	FOR	10) Legal Aid	FOR
3) Marriage	FOR	7) Open Space	FOR		
4) Child Abuse	AGN	8) Home School	FOR		

Election Results

1999 general	John H. Chichester	(R)	29.548	98.9%	$67,337

Campaign Contributions 2000-June 30, 2002 **Medical** $13,200; **Tech../Comm.** $9,500; **Pub. Empl.** $7,500; **Insur./HMOs** $6,500; **Attys.** $6,250; **Transp.** $3,900 (Auto Dealers $1,250); **Realty/Constr.** $3,750; **Finance** $3,250; **Tobacco** $2,957 (PM $2,500, B&W $457); **Electric** $2,493; **Chem./Plastics** $1,250 (Dupont $1,000); **Individ./Private College** $1,200; **Serv. Stat./Conv. St.** $1,000; **Nat. Gas** $1,000; **Coal** $1,000; **Soft Drink** $1,000; **Consult.** (Alan Voorhees) $1,000; **Fishing** $900; **Quarries** $750; **Beer** $750; **VA Manuf. Assn.** $500; **Committee for Fiscal Integrity** $500; **Oil** $300; **Trash** $250; **VA Automat. Merch.** $250.

Economic Interests, 2004 : Offices and Directorships: National Bank of Fredericksburg, Director; Northern Neck Insurance Company, Director;; Business Interests $50,000 or less: Chichester, Inc.; Paymt for talks, meetings, and publications: $190 state, SLC meeting; $1,031 state, SLC meeting; $400 state, SLC mtg; $250 state, registration fee, $802 state, travel lodging; $300 state, per diem; $200 state, registration fee, $1,246 state, SLC; $400 state, SLC, per diem; $370 Southern Regional Education Bd, SREB travel; $313 Southern Regional Education Bd. Lodging; sec. more than $50,000: municipal bonds, stocks, mutual funds, less than $50,000: mutual bonds, stocks; Gifts: $54 GlaxoSmithKline, dinner; $103 VA State Police Assoc, leather jacket; $114 VA State Police Assoc, plaque; $66 Dominion Resources, dinner; $65 Carillon Health System, dinner; $150 Carillon Health System, dinner, lodging at Regional Business Leaders Mtg; $150 Treasurers Assoc .of VA, Red Sox Baseball tkts; $428 Norfolk Southern, flight to Roanoke; Real Estate: vacant land and vacant house.

HOUSE DISTRICT TWENTY-EIGHT, *William James Howell (R)*

POLITICAL AND LEGISLATIVE BACKGROUND

House District 28 consists of all of the City of Fredericksburg; and part of Stafford County comprised of the Garrisonville, Widewater, Aquia, Courthouse, Brooke, Grafton, Falmouth, Gayle, Ferry Farm, Chatham, and White Oak Precincts, and part of the Simpson Precinct.

William J. Howell, an attorney and a Republican, has represented the district since 1987. In that year, he won a three-way race after the retirement of the incumbent, Thomas Moncure. Howell faced no opposition in 1989 and 1997. He has easily overcome opposition in all other elections, including the 2001 election, when Howell won with 63.8% of the vote over Democratic challenger Noreen C. Crowley. With the shift in political party power, Howell became the co-chairman of the Courts of Justice Committee, and in 2002, the chairman.

FIRST CONGRESSIONAL DISTRICT

During the 2004 session, Howell sponsored two successful resolutions,. One resolution designated the Virginia Historical Society as the official state society in Virginia. The second resolution confirmed appointments to the retirement system board of trustees.

As Speaker of the House, Howell would generally sponsor few bills.

Delegate HD 28

William J. Howell (R) Member of House: 1988-; Speaker of the House: 2003- ; b. May 8, 1943, Washington, D.C.; home, 6 Hunters Ct., Falmouth 22405; educ. Univ. Richmond (B.S., Bus. Admin.), Univ. VA Sch. Law (LL.B.); married Cecelia Stump; Baptist.

Attorney; Rappahannock United Way (past pres. & camp. chair.); Vice Chm. Bd. Dir. Mary Washington Hospital; VA State Cham. Comm. (past dir.); Bd. Dir. Rappahannock YMCA; Bd. Dir. Rappahannock Hospice; Spotslyvania Cham. Commerce (past pres.).

Offices P.O. Box 8296, Fredericksburg 22404-8296; 540-371-1612; GA Bldg., Capitol Sq., Rm. 635, Richmond 23219; 804-698-1028.

2004 Committees *Speaker of the House; Rules, Chair.*

House Key Votes, 2004
Please see Introduction for more information on bills.

1) Budget Bill	AGN	5) Family Life	FOR	9) Morning After	AGN
2)Feticide	FOR	6) Fire Arms	FOR	10) Legal Aid	FOR
3) Marriage	FOR	7)Open Space	FOR		
4) Abortion	FOR	8) Home School	AGN		

Election Results

2004 general	William J. Howell	(R) 10,964	98.0%		$234,909

Campaign Contributions 2004 Business/Retail Svs $46,975; Health Care $11,050; Tech/Comm. $10,750; Finance/Ins $8,500; Energy $6,100; Transportation $4,750; Agriculture $3,200; Mfg $1,750; Law $1,500; Realty/Construction $1,000; Public Employees$500.

Economic Interests, 2004 *Off. & Dir.*, Virginia Heartland Bank, Dir.; *Sec.*, $50,000+ ea.: Mutual funds (2); $10,001-$50,000 ea.: stocks in Bank of Am., BB&T, VA Comm. Financial Corp.; *Pay. for Talks, Mtgs., & Publ.*, $1,100 Am. Legislative Exchange Council, expenses at annual mtg; $150 VA Petroleum Assoc, hotel room at annual mtg; $142 VA Chamber of Commerce, lodging, Bd of Directors mtg.; $1,057 Republican legislative campaign, NCSI Mtg; $2999 Altria, transportation to Michigan and dinner; $450 Republican legislative campaign, lodging; $68 MCI, dinner; $159 Altria PMUSA open house, dinner; $152 Altria, Kraft Days reception; *Gifts*, $118 Washington Gas, dinner:$45 VA Agribusiness council, dinner; *Real Estate*, Two prop. (business, recreational).

FIRST CONGRESSIONAL DISTRICT
HOUSE DISTRICT FIFTY-FOUR, *Robert D. "Bobby" Orrock, Sr. (R)*

POLITICAL AND LEGISLATIVE BACKGROUND
House District 54 consists of a part of Caroline County comprised of the Woodford Precinct; and part of Spotsylvania County comprised of the Travelers Rest, Maury, Summit, Frazers Gate, Belmont, Brokenburg, Todd's Tavern, Holbert, Salem, Battlefield, and Brent's Mill Precincts.

Robert D. "Bobby" Orrock, Sr., a high school agriculture teacher in Hanover County, and a Republican, first won election in 1989. Orrock unseated four-term incumbent Robert W. Ackerman (D), a former county attorney in Spotsylvania and Stafford Counties. Orrock has easily defeated challenges since then, facing no opposition in the 1997-2001 elections. With the 2001 redistricting, Orrock found his district revised close to its original composition a decade ago, when he moved his home after being placed in the same district with another Republican. "It's basically what I asked Democrats for 10 years ago, and they rejected it summarily."

During the 2004 session, Orrock sponsored eighteen bills, twelve passed and three were carried over. The bills that passed provide for education specialists in the Department of Agriculture and Consumer Services and transferred were regulations for animal control officers from the Department of Criminal Justice Service to the State Veterinarian; localities are now permitted to issue free vehicle licenses to active auxiliary members of volunteer fire departments.

Carried over bills allow localities to devise a procedure to forgive back taxes on real property transferred to a 501K (3) organization that constructs affordable single-family dwelling units; increase the number of the Pest Control Board; and abolish the Electric Utility Restructuring Act and the Commission on Electric –Utility Reconstructing.

Failed bills would have provided for an award by the court to the prevailing party associated with either trial or with the recovery of judgment; revised the formula for distribution of the fee charged and collected for motor vehicles, imposed would be a two percent sales tax on motor fuels in cities and counties also in the City of Fredericksburg, Caroline and Spotsylvania.

Delegate HD 54

Robert Dickson "Bobby" Orrock, Sr. (R) Member of House: 1990-; b. Nov. 13, 1955, Fredericksburg; educ. Germanna Comm. Coll., VPI & SU (BS, Ag. Ed.), VA State Univ. (M.S. Agr. Ed.); married Betsy Malinda Massey; Baptist.

School Teacher; Ladysmith/Spotsyl. Vol. Res. Squad; Teacher of the Yr.; Tri-Cty. Soil/Water Cons. Dist.; Outstanding Voc. Ag. Inst., VA State Dairyman's Assn. & Farm/Home Elec. Coun.; Bd., Rappahannock Emer. Med.; VA Game Comm. Hunter Safety Instr.; VA Coop. Ext. Leadership; VA & Fredericksburg Jaycees Awards. Offices P.O. Box 458, Thornburg 22565; 540-891-1322; GA Bldg., Capitol Sq., Rm. 411, Richmond 23219; 804-698-1054.

2004 Committees *Agriculture, Chesapeake and Natural Resources; Counties, Cities and Towns; Finance; Health, Welfare and Institutions.*

House Key Votes, 2004
Please see Introduction for more information on bills.

1) Budget Bill	FOR	5) Family Life	FOR	9) Morning After	FOR

2) Feticide	FOR	6) Fire Arms	FOR	10) Legal Aid	FOR
3) Marriage	FOR	7) Open Space	FOR		
4) Abortion	AGN	8) Home School	FOR		

Election Results

2004 general   Robert D. "Bobby" Orrock (R)   13,930   98.3% $21,852

Campaign Contributions 2004 : Health Care $3,650; Realty/Construction $2,750; Business/Retail Svs $2,000; Energy/ Natural Resources $1,700; Agriculture $1,450; Transportation $1,350; Law $1,300; Finance, Ins. $1,150; Technology/Communication $750; Misc. $500; Public Employees $500; Defense $500; Undetermined $200

Economic Interests 2004: Salary or wages of more than $10,000: Spotsylvania County Public Schools (self), Mary Baldwin College (wife); Paymts for talks, meetings, and publications: $$1,362 & $410 for

HOUSE DISTRICT FIFTY-FIVE, *Frank Hargrove, Sr. (R)*

POLITICAL AND LEGISLATIVE BACKGROUND

House District 55 consists of part of Hanover County comprised of the Ashland, South Ashland, Ashcake, Beaverdam, Blunts, Wilmington Parish, Goddin's Hill, Clay, Chickahominy, Shady Grove, Atlee, Cool Spring, Courthouse, Rural Point 502/ Newman 503, Village, Mechanicsville, Farrington, Montpelier, Rockville, and Elmont Precincts.

Frank D. Hargrove, Sr., a retired insurance agent and a Republican, was first elected in 1981. The district was then a four-member district made up of Hanover and Henrico Counties. D. Wayne O'Bryan, the incumbent Democrat from Hanover, was Hargrove's principal opponent. Hargrove campaigned for higher teacher salaries and tougher criminal laws and against the Equal Rights Amendment. He was actively supported by former Governor Mills Godwin. Hargrove was unopposed from 1982 to the 1993 election when he defeated two challengers by 79.6%. He was unopposed in 1995 and 1997. In the 1999 election, Hargrove won by 80% over two Independent challengers. He was unopposed in 2001 Hargrove was appointed by the Speaker of the House to serve on the Joint Legislative Audit and Review Commission.

During the 2004 session, Hargrove sponsored thirteen bills, eight passed and two carried over to the 2005 session. The bills passed amended the Public Private Education Facilities and Infrastructure Act of 2002 to require local public entities to have independent design professionals prior to proceeding under the Act.

Carried over were bills that clarified the health care services do not include dental services which are not managed health care insurance plans. Also required are performance bonds in private construction projects when contracts exceeded $250,000.

Eight resolutions passed, seven were commending.

Bills that failed would have abolished the death penalty for Class 1 felonies; and allowed those who issued motor vehicle liability insurance to exclude coverage for punitive damages.

Hargrove voted against ratifying the Equal Rights Amendment which failed by six votes in the House Privileges and Elections Committee.

Delegate HD 55

FIRST CONGRESSIONAL DISTRICT

Frank DuVal Hargrove, Sr. (R) Member of House: 1982-; b. Jan. 26, 1927, Elmont; home, 13033 Old Ridge Rd., Beaverdam 23015; educ. VPI (B.S., Bus.); married Oriana Dale Robertson; Methodist.

Retired chairman bd. A.W. Hargrove Ins. Agency; past pres. Hanover Assn. of Bus.; Bd. Dir. Hanover Mental Health Assn.; Mechanicsville Bus. Assn.; Bd. Trust. Ferrum Col.; Bd. Dir. VA Assn. Ins. Agents; US AAF 1943-45; Mason; Randolph Macon Col. Bd. Trust; Ashland Kiwanis; Am. Legion; Hanover Humane Soc.; Ashland-Hanover Leadership Council.

Offices 10321 Washington Hwy., Glen Allen 23059; 804-550-4000; GA Bldg., Capitol Sq., Rm. 821, Richmond 23219; 804-698-1055.

2004 Committees *Commerce and Labor; Privileges and Elections; Rules; Transportation.*

House Key Votes, 2004
Please see Introduction for more information on bills.

1) Budget Bill	FOR	5)Family Life	AGN	9) Morning After	FOR
2) Feticide	FOR	6)Fire Arms	FOR	10) Legal Aid	FOR
3) Marriage	FOR	7) Open Spaces	FOR		
4)		8)			

FIRST CONGRESSIONAL DISTRICT
21

Election Results

2004 general	Frank D. Hargrove, Sr.	(R)	19,107	99.8%	$19,502

Campaign Contributions 2004 : Health Care $4,750; Finance/Insurance $2,750; Realty/Construction $2,750; Tech/Communication $1,845; Law $1,750; Energy/ Natural Resources $1,750; Single issue groups $1,000; Business/ Retail $1,000; Agriculture $500

Economic Interests, 2004 Sec., $50,000+ ea.: bonds (18), stocks in: Philip Morris, Harley-Davidson; $10,001-$50,000 ea.: bonds (2), stocks in Kraft Foods, United Parcel Service, mutual funds; *Gifts*, $90 Bon Secours, Legislative reception and dinner; $63 Bon Secours, reception; Business Interests: Lynchburg Harley-Davidson, dealership; 2 rental properties; Real Estate: office bldg, open land.

HOUSE DISTRICT NINETY-ONE, *Thomas Donald "Tom" Gear (R)*

POLITICAL AND LEGISLATIVE BACKGROUND
House District 91 consists of all of the City of Poquoson; part of the City of Hampton comprised of the Syms, Booker, Burbank, Langley, and Phillips Precincts and parts of the Buckroe, Fox Hill, and Magruder Precincts; and part of York County comprised of the Seaford, Harris Grove, and Dare Precincts.

Thomas D. "Tom" Gear is the delegate for the 91st House District. Retired from printing, and a former member of the Hampton City Council, Gear is a Republican. Although Gear was unopposed in the 2001 general election, he won an intensely close race in the August 2001 Republican Primary, defeating one term incumbent Phil Larrabee, Jr., an optometrist, by a narrow margin of 40 votes in an election decided by only 12.6% of the registered voters, the highest voter turnout in the nine Republican Primaries held that year.

During the 2004 session, Gear sponsored nine bills, five passed and two carried over to the 2005 session. The bills that passed changed the name of the York County-Proquoson Circuit Court to the York County Circuit Court; required new or renewal fire insurance policies that exclude flood damage coverage to permit the addition of a flood policy for an additional premium.

Carried over bills authorized hurricane deductibles for homeowners insurance and established a public defender's office in the City of Hampton.

A resolution failed that required the Department of Transportation to study the expansion of the Hampton Roads Bridge Tunnel.

A bill that failed would have allowed owners of antique motor vehicles to transfer their license plates to other vehicles.

Delegate HD 91

Thomas D. "Tom" Gear (R) Member of House: 2002- ; b. May 2, 1949, Hampton; home, 43 Mohawk Road, Hampton; married, Janice Graham Sigler; Catholic. Printing; Hampton City Council 1998-2001; National Guard 1968 - 1974; Member: St. Joseph's Church; Am. Legion Post 48; Northampton Lions Club; Relay for Life; Phoebus Civic Assn.; Hampton Historical Soc.; Knights of Columbus.

Offices; P.O. Box 7496, Hampton 23666; 757-825-1943; GA Bldg, Rm. 708, Capitol Sq., Richmond 23219; 804-698-1091.

2004 Committees *General Laws; Science and Technology; Transportation.*
House Key Votes, 2004 *Please see Introduction for more information on bills.*

1)Budget Bill	FOR	5)Family Life	AGN	9) Morning After	FOR
2)Feticide	FOR	6)Fire Arms	FOR	10)Legal Aid	AGN
3) Marriage	FOR	7)Open Spaces	FOR		
4) Abortion	FOR	8)Home School	FOR		

Election Results

2004 general	Thomas D. Gear	(R)	15,126	94.9%	$90,051

Campaign Contributions 2004 Realty/Constr. $5,200; Business/Retail Svs $4,500; Misc $2,700; Transportation $2,650; Finance/Ins $1,785; Public Employees $1,550; Law $1,550; Energy $1,550; Agriculture $1,425; Political $1,250; Health Care $950; Tech/ Communications $750; Undetermined $250; Single issue groups $100

Economic Interests, 2004 *Sal. & Wages,* $10,000+ ea.: TNT Entertainment, Inc., Riverside Hospital, Gear Enterprises, Inc.; *Off. & Dir.,* Pres. of: Gear Adv., TNT Entertainment, Gear Ent. President; *Pers. Liabil.,* $50,000+ ea.: Banks (self), (family); other loan/finance (self), (family); banking/leasing co. (self), (family); *Sec.,* $50,000+ ea.: stock in: Gear Adv., TNT Ent. (rental); $10,001-$50,000 Printing Prop. (rental); *Gifts,* $300 City Hampton (jazz festival); *Bus. Int.,* $50,000+ ea.: Gear Adv. (printing), TNT Ent. (rental),. Printing Properties (rental); $50,000/less Gear Ent. (dances); *Pay. for Rep. Generally,* $100,001-$250,000 ea.: printing services for banks savings institutions, other insurance, professional associations, cities counties and towns; *Real Estate,* four commercial properties/ Gifts: $152 Altria, Kraft Days, reception, $131 Altria, dinner.

HOUSE DISTRICT NINETY-THREE, *Phillip Andrew Hamilton (R)*

POLITICAL AND LEGISLATIVE BACKGROUND
House District 93 covers part of James City County comprised of the Roberts B and Roberts A Part 2 Precincts and part of the Roberts A Part 1 Precinct; and part of the City of Newport News comprised of the Epes, McIntosh, Reservoir, Richneck, Windsor, Watkins, Palmer, Kiln Creek, and Beaconsdale Precincts, and parts of the Lee Hall and South Morrison Precincts.

Philip A. Hamilton, a school administrator and a Republican, has served since 1988, following the death of Republican Everett Hogge, who had been elected in 1987, after more than 80 years of Democratic control in the district, and the retirement that year of incumbent Ted Morrison. Hogge, seriously ill during much of the 1988 session, died in April. Hamilton, Hogge's campaign manager, won the seat in a November 1988 special election. Hamilton ran unopposed in 1989, easily defeated Democratic opposition thereafter, and has been unopposed since the 1997 election.

During the 2004 session, Hamilton sponsored twenty-one bills, eight passed and three carried over to the 2005 session. The bills that passed required juvenile and domestic violence courts to hold hearings for the involuntary commitment of minors, also license were regulated for teachers who provided special education instructions; and permitted the Board of Education to waive requirement to add additional instructional days to compensate for school closings due to a state of emergency.

Three bills were carried over to the 2005 session which set procedures for the magistrate to issue temporary detention orders for the mentally ill; established the public defender's office in Newport News City; and granted state income tax credit for the purchase of long term insurance.

Six of eight resolutions were passed. These established a Crime Commission to study campus safety at public and private institutions of higher education; continued the Commission to Review, Study and Reform Educational Leadership; and authorized the Board of Education to develop a statewide articulation agreement on career and technical education.

Bills that failed would have licensed midwifery; changed the indexed income tax brackets; and established a public defender's office in any judicial circuit that does not have one.

Delegate HD 93

Philip   Andrew   Hamilton   (R)
Member of House: 1989-; b. April 9, 1952, Richmond; home, 915 Willow Point, Newport News 23602; educ. Univ. Richmond (B.A.), Col. Wm. & Mary (M. Ed.; C.A.G.S.); married Brenda Kay Land Stallard, separated; Roman Catholic.

School Admin.; Natl. & VA Assn. Sec. Sch. Prin., Newport News Assn. Mid. Sch. Princ.; VA PTA Life Member; Who's Who Am. Edu. 1987-88; Outstanding Young Men of America.

Offices   P.O. Box 1585, Newport News 23601; 757-249-2580; GA Bldg., Capitol Sq., Rm. 501, Richmond 23219; 804-698-1093.
2003 Committees *Health, Welfare and Institutions, Chair; Appropriations; Education.*

House Key Votes, 2004
Please see Introduction for more information on bills.

1)Budget Bill	FOR	5)Family Life	FOR	9) Morning After	FOR
2) Feticide	FOR	6)Fire Arms	FOR	10) Legal Aid	FOR
3) Marriage	FOR	7)Open Space	FOR		
4) Abortion	FOR	8)Home School	FOR		

Election Results
2004   general   Phillip A. Hamilton   (R)   10,260   96.0% $138,434

Campaign Contributions 2004 : Health Care $38,363; Realty/ Construction $10,500; Law $6,250; Business/Retail Svs $4,200; Transportation $3,250; Energy $3,200; Public Employees $3,050; Finance/Ins $3,050; Agriculture $1,400; Technology/Communication $800; Misc. $250; Mfg $250.

Economic Interests, 2004 *Sal. & Wages*, $10,000+ ea.: Newport News Pub. Sch.; *Pers. Liabil.*, $10,001-$50,000 ea.: VA Educators' Credit Union, 2 credit cards; *Sec.*, $10,001-$50,000 ea.: mutual fund; *Pay. for Talks, Mtgs., & Publ.*, $2,124 state (ALEC Convention, travel expenses); sec more than $50,00: mutual fund, stock.

HOUSE DISTRICT NINETY-FOUR, *George Glenn Oder (R)*

POLITICAL AND LEGISLATIVE BACKGROUND
House District 94 consists of part of the City of Newport News comprised of the Denbigh, Jenkins, Oyster Point, Bland, Boulevard, Charles, Christopher Newport, Deep Creek, Grissom, Hidenwood, Hilton, Nelson, Riverside, Sanford, Warwick, Yates, Riverview, River, and Sedgefield Precincts and part of the Lee Hall Precinct.

G. Glenn Oder, a landscape architect and a Republican won this open seat in 2001 with 53.7% of the vote over Democrat John C. Miller in an election costing in excess of $248,000. The seat was opened with the retirement of Democrat Alan A. Diamonstein who had served since 1968. Diamonstein was a strong advocate for colleges and universities as well as education in general. Diamonstein ran in the Democratic Primary in 2001 against three other candidates for the office of Lt. Governor, but lost.

During the 2004 session, Oder sponsored sixteen bills, nine passed and two were carried over to the 2005 session. The bills that passed set procedures for the re-enrollment of students in higher educational institutions that were called to active duty; and established a combined license for fresh and salt water fishing.

Bills that carried over would have authorized an independent audit for the Department of Transportation at least every two years.

Bills that failed would have authorized the Marine Resources Commission to convey a permanent easement to the City of Newport News to construct a reservoir project; exempted motor vehicles from the current or immediately proceeding year from safety inspections if the vehicle had been driven fewer than 50,000 miles; and allowed free clinics to buy procurements from the Division of Purchase and Supply.

Delegate HD 94

George Glenn Oder (R) Member House: 2002-; b. April 24, 1957, Newport News, home, 213 Robin Drive, Newport News 23606; educ. VA Tech; married, Mary Catherine Bowen; Baptist.

Landscape Architect; Member: First Baptist Church, Deacon; Newport News Republican City Committee, Treas.; Friends of Lee Hall Depot; Harrison S. Lear, Inc., Dir.; Peninsula Housing & Building Assn., past pres.; Newport News Planning Admin., past member; VA Tech Landscape Arch. Review Bd.; Am. Soc. of Landscape Arch., member. Offices P.O. Box 6161, Newport News 23606, 757-930-8683; GA Bldg., Rm. 505, Capitol Sq., Richmond 23219; 804-698-1094.

2004 Committees *Counties, Cities and Towns; General Laws; Transportation.*

House Key Votes, 2004
Please see Introduction for more information on bills.

1)Budget Bill	FOR	5) Family Life	FOR	9) Morning After	FOR
2) Feticide	FOR	6) Fire Arms	FOR	10)Legal Aid	FOR
3) Marriage	FOR	7) Open Space	FOR		
4) Abortion	FOR	8) Home School	FOR		

Election Results
2004 general	G. Glenn Oder	(R)	9,691	92.9%	$48,267

FIRST CONGRESSIONAL DISTRICT

Campaign Contributions 2004: Real Estate $23,000; Law $10,850; Finance/Ins $8,400; Health Care $8,050; Political $4,700; Transportation $4,500; Undetermined $3,050; Energy $2,500; Business/Retail $1,750; Tech/ Communication $1,750; Defense $1,000; Mfg $750; Agriculture $750; Public Employees $500; Misc $200.

Economic Interests, 2004 Sal. & Wages, $10,000+ ea.: Kaufman Canoles Consulting, Witt, Mares & Co., PLC; Off. & Dir., Virginia Company Bank, Dir., Harrison & Lear, Dir.; Sec., $10,001-$50,000 ea.: partnership interests in: Running Man Develop. Co.; Pay. for Rep. by Associates: Real Estate developers and property owners; DEQ, VDOT, DGS, Governors office; Paymts for representation and other from $10,000 to $250,000: Legal consultation and representation for electric company, gas utilities, telephone companies, cable, water, oil and gas companies, savings and loan, mfg companies, mining companies, Insurance companies; other: real estate, architect consulting, development; Real Estate: recreational; Gifts: $109 Access Point Public Affairs, event; $79 Hampton Roads Maritime Assoc, event; $109 Altria, event; $104 Old Dominion Hwy Contractors, event; $300 VA Agribusiness, gift; $57 VA Cable , dinner; $59 Dominion Resources, event.

HOUSE DISTRICT NINETY-SIX, *Melanie Lynn Rapp (R)*

POLITICAL AND LEGISLATIVE BACKGROUND
House District 96 contains part of James City County comprised of the Stonehouse A and Stonehouse B Precincts and parts of the Berkeley A, Berkeley B, Powhatan A, and Powhatan B Precincts; part of the City of Newport News comprised of the Saunders Precinct; and part of York County comprised of the Queens Lake, Yorktown, Waller Mill, Nelson, Magruder, Coventry, Edgehill, Harwoods Mill, Tabb, and Bethel Precincts.

Melannie L. Rapp, an accounting manager and a Republican, has served as delegate for this district since she won a special election, December 19, 2000. The seat had opened when Jo Ann Davis was elected to Congress, following the retirement of Herbert Bateman. Davis, who had served since her election in 1997, successfully ran for the Republican nomination for the First Congressional District seat, despite Gov. Gilmore's endorsement of her main opposition. Davis went on to win the general election.

Rapp won a narrow 230 vote victory against Democrat Patrick R. Pettitt, winning with 51% of the vote. Both candidates opposed the controversial King William Reservoir to supply water to the developing Newport News. Rapp, a strong anti-choice candidate, supported Gov. Gilmore's no car tax agenda. In the 2001 general election, Rapp held her own, and defeated three candidates, winning with 46.2% of the vote, including another rematch with Pettitt, Independent H. R. "Dick" Ashe, and Libertarian candidate Robert L. Stermer III. Rapp increased her win over Pettitt to a 1,713 vote margin in this election which cost more than $265,000.

During the 2004 session, Rapp sponsored eleven bills that passed; one was carried over to the 2005 session. Bills that passed authorized governing bodies in counties to restrict parking on secondary system highways, authorized the disclosure of finance information required of candidates, campaign committees, and other persons; created the Post-Disaster Anti-Price Gouging Act; localities were allowed to refer to an industrial development authority as an economic development authority; conditions were set for issuing amended certificates of public need in nursing home projects.

Carried over to the 2005 session was a bill, which provided for the removal of elected officials for certain criminal convictions.

The only bill to fail would have provided instructions for compliance with disclosure requirements for campaign advertisements.

FIRST CONGRESSIONAL DISTRICT

Delegate HD 96

Melanie Lynn Rapp (R) Member House: 2001- ; b. Sept. 5, 1964, Lake Worth, Fl.; home, P.O. Box 8123, Yorktown 23693; educ. Christopher Newport Univ. (B.A.); Baptist.

Accounting manager; member Liberty Baptist Church, Natl. Right to Life, VA Soc. for Human Life, Family Foundation, Concerned Women for America, Rep. Party of VA (Eastern vice ch.), York Republican Women's Club.
Offices P.O. Box 1529, Yorktown 23692; 757-886-1000; GA Bldg., Capitol Sq., Rm. 520, Richmond 23219; 804-698-1096.

2004 Committees *Education; General Laws; Privileges and Elections.*

House Key Votes, 2004
Please see Introduction for more information on bills.

1) Budget Bill	FOR	5) Family Life	AGN	9) Morning After	FOR
2) Feticide	FOR	6) Fire Arms	FOR	10)Legal Aid	FOR
3) Marriage	FOR	7) Open Spaces	AGN		
4) Abortion	FOR	8) Home School	FOR		

Election Results

2004 general	Melannie L. Rapp	(R)	9,888	54.1%	$148,231
	Philip Forgit	(D)	8,175	45.7%	$177,141

Campaign Contributions 2004: Real Estate $4,050; Business $1,750; Finance/ Ins $1,500; Law $1,450; Transportation $1,350; Energy $1,250; Health Care $700; Public Employees $500; Technology/Communication $500; Agriculture $500; Undetermined $222; Misc $85.

Economic Interest 2004 Salary & Wages: Denbridge Baptist Christian School. No listings under Officers and Directorships, Personal Liabilities, Securities, Payments for Talks, Meetings, and Publications, or Gifts.

HOUSE DISTRICT NINETY-SEVEN, *Ryan T. McDougle (R)*

POLITICAL AND LEGISLATIVE BACKGROUND
House District 97 consists of all of New Kent County; part of Caroline County comprised of the Madison, Reedy Church, and Mattaponi Precincts; part of Hanover County comprised of the Battlefield, Old Church, Cold Harbor, Black Creek, Studley, and Stonewall Jackson Precincts; part of Henrico County comprised of the Chickahominy, Nine Mile, and Antioch Precincts; part of King and Queen County comprised of the Owenton and Clark's Precincts; part of King William County comprised of the Second-B, Third, Fourth and Fifth Precincts and part of the Second-A Precinct; and part of Spotsylvania County comprised of the Partlow and Blaydes Corner Precincts.

The Mattaponi and Pamunkey Indian Reservations are located in King William. In early 1998, the Rappahannock Tribe swore in the first woman chief of a recognized tribe in Virginia since Cockacoeske, ruler of the Pamunkey tribe in the 1600's. G. Anne Richardson, or Queen Anne of the Rappahannock, comes from a long line of Rappahannock chiefs.

During the 2004 session, McDougle sponsored eighteen bills, eight passed. Bills that passed set a mandatory punishment on the third or subsequent offense of driving on a suspended or revoked license; set forth procedures for taking blood samples while driving under the influence of alcohol or drugs. Established procedures when traffic signals were not in operation; and granted access of DMV records to insurance companies.

Bills carried over exempted certain energy efficient products from retail taxes and provided that a circuit or district court could allow a person from another jurisdiction to work on state, county, city or town property.

Bills which failed would have designated private roads as highways for law enforcement purposes; and would have struck the separate provision for ending spousal support when the paying spouse is cohabitating with another.

Delegate HD 97

Ryan Todd McDougle (R) Member House: 2002 ; b. November 9, 1971, Richmond; home, 6323 Draperfield Road, Mechanicsville 23111; edu. James Madison Univ., College of Williams & Mary; single; Baptist. Attorney; Member: Shalom Baptist Church; Hanover Ruritan, A.F. & A.M. Lodge #344.

Offices P.O. Box 187, Mechanicsville 23111; 804-730-1026; GA Bldg., Rm. 715, Capitol Sq., Richmond 23219; 804 698 1097.

2004 Committees *Courts of Justice; General Laws; Transportation.*

House Key Votes, 2004
Please see Introduction for more information on bills.

1) Budget Bill	FOR	5) Family Life	AGN	9) Morning After	FOR
2) Feticide	FOR	6) Fire Arms	FOR	10) Legal Aid	FOR
3) Marriage	FOR	7) Open Space	NV		
4) Abortion	FOR	8) Home School	FOR		

Election Results

2004 general	Ryan T. McDougle	(R)	11,726	99.4%	$59,782

Campaign Contributions 2004 : Law $10,083; Transportation $6,000; Realty/Construction$5,750; Business/Retail Svs $5,375; Agriculture $2,800; Health Care $2,400; Energy $2,250; Tech/Communication $2,250; Finance/Ins $2,000; Candidate Self-Financing $1,450; Misc. $500; Public Employees $450; Undetermined $250; Mfg $250; Political $250.

Economic Interests, 2004 *Sec to* $50,000: Trigon, stock; Offices and Directorships: McDougle Law Firm, principal; Capital Results (spouse), principal; Custom Mktg, principal; Business Interests: 3M Farms, investment; Winfrey Family LLC, investment; Paymts for talks, meetings, publications: NCSL, technical conference, Savannah; travel/lodging; NCSL, JNET Conference, Harrisburg; travel/lodging; Paymts for other to $50,000: legal services to client; Gifts: $194 Old Dominion Hwy Contractors, dinner; $60 CSK, dinner; $84 VA Agribusiness Council, golf outing; $208 Home Depot, day at the races; $152 Altria, Kraft Recreation; $109 Altria, dinner; $100 Altria, golf outing; $120 VA Tech. football tkts; Real Estate: three open land and a house.

HOUSE DISTRICT NINETY-EIGHT, *Harvey B. Morgan (R)*

POLITICAL AND LEGISLATIVE BACKGROUND
House District 98 consists of all of Essex, Gloucester, Mathews, and Middlesex Counties; part of King and Queen County comprised of the Shackleford's, Courthouse, and Old Mill Precincts; and part of King William County comprised of the First Precinct and part of the Second-A Precinct.

Harvey Morgan, a retired pharmacist and a Republican, was first elected to the House in 1979 on a right-to-work platform that included opposition to the ERA. He succeeded retiring Democrat John Warren Cooke, a former Speaker of the House, who had served in the General Assembly since 1942. Morgan defeated Democratic opposition in 1989 and 1991, trounced an Independent challenger in 1993, and had been unopposed since then until 2001, when Morgan easily defeated Democrat K. J. Havens with 74.6% of the vote. Morgan has received consistently strong backing from constituents in the 98th, despite two redistricting changes. Morgan's legislative interests have supported health and the environment, including public smoking restrictions, mental health, and assisting troubled youth.

During the 2004 session, Morgan sponsored thirty bills, thirteen passed; nine were carried over to the 2005 session. Bills which passed authorized the killing of beavers due to the destruction of property; required certification for vocational rehabilitation counselors; authorized the suspension of licenses of drivers who were believed to be incompetent; prohibited telephone solicitation to persons on a No-Act-Call registry drug dispensing systems by pharmacy technicians.

Bills carried over to the 2005 session set eligibility for transitional severance benefits; allowed the use of internet database for payday loan borrowers and set restrictions on loans made to spouses of military personnel.

Seven of nine resolutions passed which established a Redistricting Commission to redraw the boundaries of congressional and legislative districts and established a Joint Committee on Health Care to study the access and availability of geriatricians.

Bills that failed would have prohibited smoking in restaurants in Gloucester County; provided hearing protection devices to patrons in hotels and restaurants that provide musical entertainment; created a Natural and Historic Resource Fund and Commission; and make changes in the provisions for electric utility restructuring.

Delegate HD 98

Harvey B. Morgan (R) Member House: 1980-; b. Aug. 18, 1930, Gloucester; home, PO Box 949, Gloucester 23061; educ. Hampden-Sydney Coll. (B.A.) and Med. Coll. VA (B.S.), Pharmacy; U.S. Navy 1955-57; married Mary Helen Osborn; Presbyterian.

Retired pharmacist and Assistant Clinical Professor of Pharmacy MCV; Dir. Alumni Ret. Sch. Pharmacy MCV; Member: Friends of Dragon Run; Council of Indians; Joint Comm. Health Care; Atlantic States Marine Fisheries Comm.; Kiwannis (past Dir.); Chesapeake Bay Fndn.; VA Small Bus. Council; VA Pharmacist of Yr. 1978.

Offices P.O. Box 949, Gloucester 23061; 804-693-4750; GA Bldg., Capitol Sq., Rm. 521, Richmond 23219; 804-698-1098.

2004 Committees *Commerce and Labor, Chair; Appropriations; Rules.*

House Key Votes, 2004
Please see Introduction for more information on bills.

1) Budget Bill	FOR	5) Family Life	FOR	9) Morning After	AGN
2) Feticide	FOR	6) Fire Arms	FOR	10)Legal Aid	FOR
3) Marriage	FOR	7) Open Space	FOR		
4) Abortion	AGN	8) Home School	AGN		

Election Results

2004 general	Harvey B. Morgan	(R)	15,089	78.8%	$91,350
	Michael Rowe	(I)	5,141	21.1%	$5,359

Campaign Contributions 2004 :   Health Care $17,800; Finance/Ins; $10,220; Energy $6,050; Realty/Construction $5,902; Technology/ Communication $4,000; Law $3,735; Agriculture $2,854; Misc $2,760; Transportation $2,235; Business/Retail Svs $2,125; Public Employees $1,045; Defense $1,000; Mfg $700; Single-Issue Groups $525; Undetermined $170; Political $50.

Economic Interests, 2004 *Off. & Dir.*, Morgan Prop., President.; DuVal Avenue, LLC, Manager, *Pers. Liabil.*, $50,000+ individual; *Sec.*, $50,000+ ea.: stocks in: Morgan Prop., C&F Financial Shares, Bristol-Meyers; $10,001-$50,000 ea.:   stocks in: DuVal Ave. (realty), Merck, Chesapeake Fin., Firs VA Bank shares, Susquehanna Bank shares; *Pay. for Talks, Mtgs., & Pub.*, $976NCSL Spring Forum, travel, lodging, meals; $1,371 NCOIL , travel, meals, lodging; $1,891 NCSL, lodging; $1,430 NCOIL, travel, lodging, meals; Personal Liabilities to $50,000: Banks; Business Interests $50,000 or less: two rental properties, Real Estate: 2 lots of open land and an apartment; Gifts: $139 VA Chamber of Commerce, food/beverages; $103 Access Point Public /ALERT, food/beverages; $96 EPIC Pharmacies, food; $78 State Farm Ins., food; $68 MCI, food; $80 VA Tech, 2 football tkts; $765 Wolf Trap, 2 tkts & Lodging; $204 Epic Pharmacies, 2 tkts Wolf Trap, lodging; $65 Covanta Energy, food; $314 VA Health Quality Ctr, food/lodging; $166 Constellation Energy Group, Direct Energy Mktg., Strategic Energy, Washington Gas Energy Service, food; $333 VACO, lodging, food.

HOUSE DISTRICT NINETY-NINE, *Albert C. Pollard, Jr. (D)*

POLITICAL AND LEGISLATIVE BACKGROUND

House District 99 consists of all of King George, Lancaster, Northumberland, Richmond, and Westmoreland Counties; and part of Caroline County comprised of the Bowling Green and Port Royal Precincts.

Albert C. Pollard, Jr., a timber investment owner and property manager, and a Democrat, has been the delegate for this district since 1999. He won a hard fought election over Republican Henry Hull, to fill the seat opened by the retirement of Tayloe Murphy, Jr., also a Democrat, who had served since 1981. Pollard had been Murphy's legislative assistant for four sessions. *The Daily Press* called Murphy "the father of most major pieces of environmental legislation in Virginia." *The Virginian-Pilot* enumerated several: The Chesapeake Bay Preservation Act, The Water Quality Improvement Act, a state ban on phosphate detergents, restrictions on TBT - a toxic pesticide in boat paint, and regulating poultry wastes. Murphy stumped for Pollard, a former director of the Virginia chapter of the Sierra Club. In the 2001 election and following redistricting, Pollard easily won with 61.5% of the vote over Republican R. Allen Webb. Webb had just won an August Republican Primary, defeating R. R. Fountain.

Pollard, in a *Richmond Times-Dispatch* op-ed in 2000, decried "the influence of special interests and the heavy-handedness of party politics," urging significant campaign finance reform, seating in the Assembly by region rather than by party, and better education of the electorate.

During the 2004 session, Pollard sponsored twenty-one bills, four passed, seven were carried over to the 2005 session. Bills passed allowed circuit court judges to participate in the selection of grand jurors; exempted trailer dealers from licensing utility/cargo trailers that weigh more than 3,000 pounds; and provided that law enforcement benefits without five years or more years of service can receive minimum retirement benefits without service under a specific retirement system.

Seven bills were carried over which would prohibit campaign areas in polling places; withdrew the Commonwealth from participating in the No Child Left Behind Act; and imposed a water quality improvement fee.

Two resolutions were carried over which would authorize a JLARC study of the fiscal implications of state compliance with the No Child Left Behind Act and proposed a constitutional amendment regarding
unfounded state mandates.

Delegate HD 99

Albert C. Pollard, Jr. (D) Member House: 2000-; b. Sept. 18, 1967, Washington, D.C.; home, 5202 Irvington Road, Irvington 22480; educ. VCU (B.S. Urban Studies); married, Mariah Nottingham Mears; Episcopalian.

Property management; member Lancaster Co. Chamber Comm., Reedsville Fisherman; awards Magna cum laude graduate VCU 1991.

Offices P.O. Box 1256, White Stone 22578; 804-436-9117; GA Bldg., Rm. 816, Capitol Sq., Richmond 23219; 804-698-1099.

2004 Committees *Militia, Police and Public Safety; Transportation.*

House Key Votes, 2004
Please see Introduction for more information on bills.

1) Budget Bill	AGN	5) Family Life	FOR	9) Morning After	AGN
2) Feticide	FOR	6) Fire Arms	FOR	10) Legal Aid	FOR
3) Marriage	AGN	7) Open Space	FOR		
4) Abortion	AGN	8) Home School	AGN		

Election Results

2004 general	Albert Pollard, Jr.	(D)	12,738	64.8%	$157,433
	Shawn Donahue	(R)	7,969	35.1%	$ 94,468

Campaign Contributions 2004 Transportation $3,000; Agriculture $2,250; Law $1,500; Health Care $1,000; Finance/Ins $750; Realty/Construction $750; Business/Retail Svs $750; Public

FIRST CONGRESSIONAL DISTRICT
Employees $500; Mfg $500; Energy $500; Defense $250; Tech/Communication $250; Undetermined $148; Political $129.

Economic Interests 2004: Salary & Wages in excess of $10,000: AM-PM, LLC, President, Bay Etching and Imprinting, Chairman of the Board; sec to $50,000: I-shares, mutual funds, stocks in own companies; Real Estate: AM-PM, LLC, business, 2 residential, 1 industrial, 1/6th ownership.

HOUSE DISTRICT ONE HUNDRED, *Lynwood W. Lewis, Jr. (D)*

POLITICAL AND LEGISLATIVE BACKGROUND
House District 100 consists of all of Accomack and Northampton Counties; part of the City of Hampton comprised of part of the Buckroe Precinct; and part of the City of Norfolk comprised of parts of the Bayview School, Ocean View Center Part 1, Ocean View School, Titustown Center, and Zion Grace Precincts.

Robert S. Bloxom was replaced by Lynwood W. Lewis in 2004.

During the 2004 session, Lewis sponsored five bills, two passed and one was carried over to the 2005 session. The bills that passed established a penalty for the possession or transportation of explosives by convicted felons and authorized the Governor to conduct an annual statewide drill in response to emergencies and disasters.

Bills carried over would require localities to exempt farm property and products from the personal property tax and provided for an additional distribution of the state recordation tax to localities.

Delegate HD 100

Lynwood W. Lewis (D) Member House 2004 – ; b. Nov. 26, 1961, Nassawasox, VA, educ. Hampden-Sydney College (B.A., 1984), T. C. Williams School of Law, University of Richmond (J.D., 1988), Methodist.

Attorney; Eastern Shore Community College Board, Eastern Shore United Way Board, Eastern Shore Literacy Council Board, Eastern Shore Historical Society Board, Eastern Shore Hampden-Sydney Alumni (President), Onancock Rotary.

P.O. Box 760, Accomac, VA 23301, (757) 787-1094; FAX: (757) 787-2356; P.O. Box 406, Richmond, VA 23218, Rm 422, (804) 698-1000, FAX: (804) 786-6310.

2004 Committees *Finance; Militia, Police and Public Safety.*

House Key Votes, 2004
Please see Introduction for more information on bills

1) Budget Bill	AGN	5) Family Life	FOR	9) Morning After	FOR
2) Feticide	FOR	6) Fire Arms	FOR	10) Legal Aid	FOR
3) Marriage	FOR	7) Open Space	FOR		
4) Abortion	AGN	8) Home School	AGN		

Election Results

2004 general	Lynwood W. Lewis	8,528	59.3%	$265,666

FIRST CONGRESSIONAL DISTRICT
Thomas Dix (R)   40.7% $148,281

Campaign Contributions 2004   Law $8350; Health Care $4,900; Finance/Ins $4,270; Realty/Construction $3,300; Business/Retail Svs $2,600; Energy $2,450; Public Employees $2,050; Transportation $2,000; Tech/Communication $1,750; Agriculture $1,250; Mfg $1,150; Misc $750; Undetermined $500; Organized Labor $250; Defense $150.

Economic Interests, 2004   *Sal. & Wages*, $10,000+ Vincent Northam & Lewis, law firm; Personal Liabilities to $50,000: banks; Business Interests: Vincent Northam & Lewis; Paymts for representation, other services generally to $10,000: Banks, real estate, VA Dept of Transportation, condemnation work by law partners; value to $$50,000: State Farm Ins, defense by law partner, general legal services, collections; Gifts: $80 Allstate Insurance, dinner; $80 Verizon, dinner.

Notes

SECOND CONGRESSIONAL DISTRICT

SENATE DISTRICT SIX, *Dimitrios Nick Rerras (R)*

POLITICAL AND LEGISLATIVE BACKGROUND

The Sixth Senatorial District consists of Accomack, Mathews, Northampton Counties; the City of Norfolk Precincts of Granby, Northside, Titustown Center, Tucker House, Zion Grace, Crossroads, Suburban Park, Therapeutic Center, Wesley, Willard, Azalea Gardens, Barron Black, Houston, Bayview School, Bayview United, East Ocean View, Larrymore, Little Creek, Ocean View School, Oceanair, Tarralton, 3rd Presbyterian, Ocean View Center Part 1, and Ocean View Center Part 2; and parts of the City of Virginia Beach's Lake Smith, Bayside, and Chesapeake Beach Precincts.

D. Nick Rerras, a businessman and a Republican, was elected in 1999, defeating veteran and long-time incumbent Democrat Stanley Walker in their second election encounter. Rerras is the son of Greek immigrants, born and raised in Norfolk, and a veteran serving in the U.S. Army. He campaigned on a program to keep violent criminals off the street, investing in children with high standards in schools, supporting the return of lottery profits to the localities, and lowering tuition costs at Virginia colleges.

Walker had represented this area for more than three decades, serving first in the House from 1964-1971, and then in the Senate, developing strong legislation for women, children, and education. Walker had been the President Pro Tempore of the Senate since 1988. Walker died in 2001.

During the 2004 session, Rerras sponsored eleven bills, six passed and two were carried over to the 2005 session. Bills passed provided that bail would be denied to anyone arrested for DUI who had three previous convictions within the past five years for DUI manslaughter or maiming; North Hampton County was authorized to appropriate funds from the Glebe Fund for courthouse improvements to comply with the Americans for Disabilities Act; and provided that volunteer firefighters and squad members who were assaulted were in a protected class which made the perpetrator guilty of a Class 6 felony.

Bills carried over would have authorized the governor to operate the vessel Virginia under an agreement with the Maritime Heritage Foundation and provided that during a state of emergency declared by the governor local authorities could enforce a curfew.

Eleven resolutions were successfully passed.

Senator SD 6

Dimitrios Nick Rerras (R) Member Senate: 2000- ; b. Feb. 9, 1957, Norfolk; home, 1821 Hartford Dr., Norfolk 23518; educ. Associates degree Electronics Technology; married, Gayle; Greek Orthodox.

Businessman; U.S. Army; Member: Hampton Rds. Chamber Commerce Plan 2007 Technology Comm.; Armed Forces Communications and Electronics Assn.; Bromley Civic League; Gov. Education Reform Comm. (Allen).

Offices 1518 Springmeadow Blvd., Norfolk 23518-4814; 757-855-7044; GA Bldg., Capitol Sq., Rm. 305, Richmond 23219; 804-698-7506.

2004 Committees *Agriculture, Conservation and Natural Resources; Courts of Justice; Rehabilitation and Social Service; Transportation.*

SECOND CONGRESSIONAL DISTRICT

Senate Key Votes, 2004
Please see Introduction for more information on bills.

1) Budget Bill	FOR	5) Family Life	FOR	9) Charter School	FOR
2) Feticide	FOR	6) Fire Arms	FOR	10) Legal Aid	FOR
3) Marriage	FOR	7) Open Space	FOR		
4)Child Abuse	AGN	8) Home School	FOR		

Election Results

1999 general	D. N. Rerras	(R)	11,621	59.2%	$288,893
	Stanley C. Walker	(D)	7,966	40.6%	$489,586

Campaign Contributions 2000-June 30, 2002 Realty/Constr. $25,409; **Transp.** $21,390 (Auto Dealers $6,540, Ports/Shipping $4,400); **Attys.** $9,500; **Medical** $9,450; **Tech./Comm.** $7,915; **Individ.** $7,005; **Finance** $5,900; **Beer/Wine/Dist. Sp.** $5,500; **Restau./Hotel/Tour** $4,586; **Insur./HMOs** $3,515; **Electric** $3,000; **Pub. Empl.** $2,895; **Retail** $2,500; **Shipbldg.** $2,300 (NNShipbldg. $1,250); **Farm/Poultry/Fish** $2,000; **Nat. Gas** $1,750; **Coal** $1,500; **Tobacco--PM** $1,300; **Oil** $850; **Misc. Manuf.** $750; **Republicans** $550; **Kings Dom.** $500; **Retail Merch. Norfolk** $500; **Soft Drink** $450; **Serv. Stat./Conv. St.** $350; **Gun Rts.** $300; **Billboards** $250; **Trash** $250; **Misc. Defense** $250; **Pawn Shops** $200; **Lumber** $150; **Advert.** $50.

Economic Interests, 2004 *Sal. & Wages,* $10,000+ Allied Technology Group; *Pay. for Talks, Mtgs., & Pub.*, $4,547 Conference on issues concerning Greece and Greek people in Athens, Greece, travel, expenses; Gifts: $63 Bon Secours, legislative dinner; $79 Hampton Rds Maritime Assoc, legislative dinner; $147 Altria, dinner; $62 Dominion Resources, dinner; Real Estate: Second home in Cape Charles.

SENATE DISTRICT SEVEN, *Frank W. Wagner (R)*

POLITICAL AND LEGISLATIVE BACKGROUND

Senate District 7 includes the City of Virginia Beach Precincts: Kingston, Mt. Trashmore, Malibu, Old Donation, Aragona, Ocean Park, Thoroughgood, Davis Corner, Point O' View, Arrowhead, Larkspur, Providence, Thalia, Witchduck, Pembroke, Bonney, Brandon, Bellamy, Centerville, Stratford Chase, Homestead, Shannon, Meadows, Forest, Colonial, Shell, Round Hill, and Woodstock (25)/Fairfield (26); parts of Lake Smith, Bayside, Chesapeake Beach, Little Neck, and Rosemont Forest.

Frank W. Wagner, a Republican, won the 2000 special election to replace Senator Edward Schrock who won a seat in the U.S. Congress, after Democrat Owen Picket did not seek re-election. Wagner is a shipyard owner who served in the Navy for nine years. He had been a delegate for House District 21 since 1991. Schrock, also a Republican, and a retired Navy captain, had defeated incumbent Democrat Clancy Holland in 1995.

While Wagner was in the House, he served on the Privileges and Elections Committee, and introduced a bill to reform campaign financing, but delayed the provision that required disclosure. *The Virginian-Pilot* reported that Wagner was later criticized when it was revealed that his shipyard "had fraudulently billed the U.S. Navy in 1997 and 1998." Wagner agreed to pay $400,000. Wagner petitioned the judge to have the case sealed, and he was criticized for keeping voters in the dark.

During the 2004 session, Wagner sponsored twenty bills, ten passed. These made failure to comply with traffic signals a traffic violation, which is punishable by a fine; allowed local jurisdictions to combine storm water fees with bills for water, sewer, real property or other billings; and provided that multidisciplinary teams could provide consultation in cases of child abuse or neglect.

Two bills carried over would have directed the Board of Education to establish guidelines for local school boards for granting diplomas upon satisfactory completion of coursework and twenty-two credits; modified the guidelines for variable and fixed costs calculations for child support in shared custody cases.

Bills that failed would have established procedures for disposing unattended, immobile, and recovered stolen vehicles; provided that carnal knowledge of a child who is thirteen years of age or older by an adult in a custodial or supervisionary relationship is a Class 3 felony; required four year higher educational institutions to maintain a ration of in-state and out-of-state student population that is no less than seventy-five percent in-state students in the freshman class; and expanded the boundaries by the Chesapeake Bay Preservation Act to include the watershed of the Chesapeake Bay.

Senator SD 7

Frank Warren Wagner (R) Member Senate: 2001- ; Member House: 1992-2000; b. July 18, 1955, Ruislip, England; home, 4304 Alfriends Trail, Virginia Beach 23455; educ. U.S. Naval Academy (B.S. Ocean Engineering); married, Susan O'Rourke; Methodist.

Shipyard Owner; Optimists Club; PTA, Pembroke Meadow Elementary School; US Navy 1973-82; Naval Academy Alumni Assn.

Offices P.O Box 68008, Virginia Beach 23471; 757-671-2250; FAX 757-244-7866; GA Bldg., Rm. 312, Capitol Sq., Richmond 23219; 804-698-7507.

2004 Committees *General Laws;Commerce and Labor; Rehabilitation and Social Services; Transportation.*

Senate Key Votes, 2004
Please see Introduction for more information on bills.

1) Budget Bill	AGN	5) Family Life	FOR	9) Charter School	FOR
2) Feticide	FOR	6) Fire Arms	FOR	10) Legal Aid	FOR
3) Marriage	FOR	7) Open Space	FOR		
4) Child Abuse	AGN	8) Home School	FOR		

Election Results

2001 special	Frank W. Wagner	(R)	11,041	68.8%	$133,463
	Louisa M. Strayhorn	(D)	4,998	31.1%	$ 83,226

Campaign Contributions 2000-June 30, 2002 Realty/Constr. $11,625; **Transp.** $9,521 (Auto Dealers $4,671, Shipping/Boats $4,100); **Finance** $8,400; **Attys.** $4,535; **Republicans** $3,408; **Insur./HMOs** $3,125; **Medical** $3,085; **Exec. Recruit./Temp.** $2,563; **Beer/Wine** $2,200; **Tech./Comm.** $1,560; **Electric** $1,320; **Individual** $1,130; **Pub. Empl.** $1,100; **NNShipbldg.** $1,000; **Chem./Plastics** $1,250; **Tobacco--PM** $750; **Coal** $750; **Fishing** $600; **Trash** $500; **Retail Merch. Norfolk** $500; **Nat. Gas** $500; **Sales Systems** $500; **Misc. Manuf.** $400; **VA Automat. Merch.** $250; **Serv. Sta./Conv. St.** $200.

Economic Interests, 2004 *Sal. & Wages*, $10,000+ Davis Boat Works; *Off. & Dir.*, Venture Dynamics, Pres.; Davis Boat Works, Pres/VP.; O'Rourke Ltd., Treas.; *Pers. Liabil.*, $50,000+ ea.: stock/or other brokerage co., ship repair; *Sec.*, $50,000+ ea.: mutual funds (3), bonds, stock in: PC Connection, Gateway Holdings, United Def. Ind., Invest Ventura; $10,001-$50,000ea.: mutual fds. (5), bonds (2), stocks in: Blackrock Municipal, Cendant, Markel, Town Bank Portsmouth, Volkswagen, Walmart Mexico, GE; *Gifts*, $70 Geico, dinner; $3,814 VA Auto Assoc. , VADA convention' $67 VA Auto Assoc., dinner; $79 Hampton Rds Maritime Assoc., dinner; $102 Old Dominion Hwy Assoc. , dinner; $88 Reynolds Co., briefcase; $72 ALERT, dinner; $179 General Motors, dinner; *Bus. Int.*, $50,000+ ea.: Davis Boat Works, Venture Dynamics (marine repair); $50,000/less ea.: O'Rourke (retail), rental prop. (w/spouse); *Pay. for Rep. & Other Services Generally*, marine repairs: $250,001 + ea.: interstate transp., intrastate (tugs & barges), fishing vessel repair; $10,001-$50,000 concrete industry marine repairs; *Real Estate*, Two prop. and open land(one w/spouse).

SENATE DISTRICT EIGHT, Kenneth W. "Ken" Stolle (R)

POLITICAL AND LEGISLATIVE BACKGROUND
Senate District 8 consists of the City of Virginia Beach Precincts of North Beach, South Beach, Linkhorn, Alanton, London Bridge, Cape Henry, Plaza, Holland, Capps Shop, Windsor Oaks, Kings Grant, Wolfsnare, Lynnhaven, Oceana, Magic Hollow, Landstown, Hunt, Eastern Shore, Hilltop, Strawbridge, Ocean Lakes (3)/Red Wing (30)/Sigma (31)/Culver (63), Seatack (5)/Rudee (72), and Trantwood (9)/Great Neck (10), and parts of the Courthouse and Little Neck Precincts.

Kenneth W. Stolle is a former policeman who read for the law to become a lawyer. A Republican, Stolle defeated incumbent Democrat Sonny Stallings with 54% of the vote in 1991. Stallings had served since 1988. Charges of special interests became a part of the campaign with Stolle endorsed by the National Rifle Association, heavy tobacco industry contributions, and money from the anti-choice Family Life cable TV channel owned by Pat Robertson which donated $5,000 to Stolle's campaign. Robertson's son, Gordon, had chaired the Second District GOP Committee. Stolle ran unopposed in both the 1995 and 1999 elections. Stolle chairs the Courts of Justice Committee and serves on the State Crime Commission. As the majority whip, he holds a commanding position in the Senate.

During the 2004 session, Stolle sponsored thirty-nine bills, twenty-seven passed and eight were carried over to the 2005 session. Those bills passed eliminated the Wireless E-911 Board making the quarterly payments to eligible providers, set a ceiling on appeal bonds; adjusted the maximum credit a former judge can transfer to the Judicial Retirement System, created Racketeer Influenced and Corrupt Organization Act (RICO); established the Chief Justice as a member and chairman of the Committee on the District Courts, established a penalty for driving after forfeiture for a DUI conviction; regulated and licensed bail enforcement agents; authorized that a writ of actual innocence would be issued based on non-biological evidence in a felony conviction; and required that the privacy of health records and their access comply with federal regulations.

Bills carried over allowed hunting during certain hours on Sunday; increased the retirement allowance of state police officers for services rendered in hazardous positions.

Of the thirteen resolutions, one authorized the Department of Game and Inland Fisheries to study firearms hunting ordinances.

Bills that failed would have increased the number of judges in the 15th and 27th juvenile and domestic relations district court, set a penalty in the commission of a larceny; and allow the Chief Justice to designate senior retired, or active judges of the Court of Appeals to serve on panels of the Supreme Court.

Senator SD 8

Kenneth W. "Ken" Stolle (R) Member Senate: 1992-; b. July 7, 1954, Washington, DC; home, 780 Lynnhaven Pkwy, Virginia Beach 23452; educ. Berry College (BS), Virginia Reading Law Program, passed VA Bar 1983; married, Deborah Laux; Roman Catholic.

Attorney; Virginia Beach Police Dept., Silver Star Bravery & Merit; Intelligence Officer, Lt., US Naval Res.; Special Pros., Comm. Atty. Virginia Beach; member, VA Trial Lawyers Assn., 1992, 1996 Senator of the Yr. Frat. Order of Police, Knights of Columbus, Chm. Rep. Party VA Beach 1990.

Offices 700 Pavillon Center, Virginia Beach 23451; 757-486-5700; FAX 757-486-8020; GA Bldg., Capitol Sq., Rm. 426, Richmond 23219; 804-698-7508.

2004 Committees *Courts of Justice, Chair; Commerce and Labor; Finance; Privileges and Elections; Rules.*

Senate Key Votes, 2004
Please see Introduction for more information on bills.

1) Budget Bill	FOR	5) Family Life	FOR	9) Charter Schools	FOR
2) Feticide	FOR	6) Fire Arms	FOR	10) Legal Aid	FOR
3) Marriage	FOR	7) Open Space	FOR		
4) Child Abuse	FOR	8) Home School	FOR		

Election Results

1999 general	K. W. Stolle	(R)	25,459	97.6%	$209,781

Campaign Contributions 2000-June 30, 2002 Attys. $21,125; **Realty/Constr.** $18,170; **Medical** $18,027; **Finance** $16,640; **Pub. Empl.** $13,170; **Insur./HMOs** $11,500; **Tech./Comm.** $10,594; **Transp.** $9,065 (Auto Dealers $3,915, Ports/Shipping/Boats $3,250); **Electric** $9,064; **Beer/Wine** $5,089; **Republicans** $2,270; **Restau./Hotel.Tour.** $1,950; **Tobacco** $1,750 (PM $1,500, RJR $250); **NNShipbldg.** $1,500; **Horse/Trainers** $1,250; **Retail** $1,200; **Rec./Amuse. Pk.** $1,000; **Nat. Gas** $1,000; **Oil** $500; **Coal** $500; **Retail Merch. Norfolk** $500; **Honeywell** $500; **Soft Drink** $350.

Economic Interests 2004: Salary & Wages in excess of $10,000: Kaufman & Canoles, PC; Paymt for representation by you to $10,000: VA Oncology Assoc, legal, Sentara, Quemasters Billards, legal; to $50,000: VA Bch Eye Center, legal; Paymts for talks, meetings, publications: $1,049 VA Sheriffs Assoc, meeting; Paymts for presentation by associates: Various Associates and Partners of Kaufman & Canoles law firm, Va workman's comp. employment commission, state corp., DOCPN; Gifts: $92 GEO Group, dinner; $192 VA Sheriffs Assoc, dinner; $2,102 VA Sheriffs Assoc., hunting trip; $6,351 VA Sheriffs Assoc., hunting trip; $79 Hampton Rds Maritime Assoc., reception.

HOUSE DISTRICT TWENTY-ONE, *John J. Welch III (R)*

POLITICAL AND LEGISLATIVE BACKGROUND
House District 21 consists of part of the City of Virginia Beach comprised of the Mt. Trashmore, Malibu, Thalia, Windsor Oaks, Timberlake, Glenwood, Forest, Rosemont Forest, Round Hill, and Dahlia Precincts and parts of the Bellamy, Colonial, Little Neck, and Salem Precincts.

John J. Welch III, a chiropractor and a Republican, was first elected in a special January 2001 election. The seat was opened when Republican Frank W. Wagner, who had served in this seat since 1992, won the special election for Senate District 7. Welch defeated Democrat Alan P. Holmes with 61.4% of the vote in an election decided by only 4,123 voters. Although Welch was unopposed in the November 2001 election, he was challenged earlier in an August Republican Primary. Welch defeated M. A. "Peggy" Totin, winning with 63.8% of the vote in a primary decided by 3.9% of the registered voters.

Welch sponsored seven bills in the 2004 session, four passed. Bills passed increased the area of the foot where a podiatrist could perform foot amputations; established post election security procedures for election materials; and required the use of reflective materials when using steel plates for highway repairs;

No bills were carried over.

Bills that failed would have provided that animals could not be used as prizes in carnivals, or fairs; all roadwork must comply with the Virginia Department of Transportation; and meal and lodging tax cannot be increased without a voter referendum.

One of the two resolutions was successful.

Delegate HD 21

John J. **Welch III (R)** Member House: 2001-; b. June 20, 1961, Falls River, Massachusetts; educ. Hawaii Pacific Col., Edison Comm. Col., Parker Col. of Chiropractic (Ph.D.); married Carol C. Gaudreau; Catholic.

Chiropractor, entrepreneur; US Army 1982-90; awards: Who's Who of Am. Junior Colleges; Who's Who in Professional Cols.; NCO/Soldier of the Year, 82nd Airborne Div.

Offices 334 Lynn Shores Dr., Virginia Beach 23452; 757-340-2800; GA Bldg., Rm. 519, Capitol Sq., Richmond 23219; 804-698-1021.

2004 Committees *Finance; Health, Welfare & Institutions; Transportation.*

House Key Votes, 2004
Please see Introduction for more information on bills.

1) Budget Bill	FOR	5) Family Life	FOR	9) Morning After	FOR
2) Feticide	FOR	6) Fire Arms	FOR	10) Legal Aid	FOR
3) Marriage	FOR	7) Open Space	AGN		
4) Abortion	FOR	8) Home School	FOR		

Election Results

2004 general	J. J. Welch III	(R)	10,563	61.9%	$82,644
	Tim Jackson	(D)		38.0%	$ 9,699

Campaign Contributions 2004 Health Care $12,925; Realty $4,755; Business/Retail Svs $4,663; Finance/Ins $4,290; Law $3,900; Transportation $3,500; Misc $2,620; Agriculture $2,610; Energy $2,350; Political $1,750; Tech/communication $1,500; Public Employees $880; Defense $500; Mfg $250; Candidate Self-Financed $250; Undetermined $150.

Economic Interests, 2004 *Sal. & Wages*, $10,000+ Sentana Medical Group; Officers and Directorships: VA Motion Xray, Vice President, North Florida Motion Xray, President, Strike Screening Center, Vice President; sec more than $50,000: Fidelity, stocks, bonds; Personal Liabilities to $50,000: banks loan finance companies; more than $50,000: banks; Gifts: $109 Altria, dinner; $102 Old Dominion Hwy Assoc., dinner; $203 VCTA, dinner; $62 Dominion Power, dinner; $335 City of Va Bch, reception/cruise.

HOUSE DISTRICT EIGHTY-ONE, *Terrie L. Suit (R)*

POLITICAL AND LEGISLATIVE BACKGROUND
House District 81 consists of part of the City of Chesapeake comprised of the Bethel, Bells Mill, Indian Creek, Green Sea, Grassfield Part 1, and Grassfield Part 2 Precincts; and part of the City of Virginia Beach comprised of the Creeds, Capps Shop, Blackwater, and Ocean Lakes (3)/ Red Wing (30)/ Sigma (31)/ Culver (63) Precincts and parts of the Magic Hollow, Oceana, Seatack (5)/Rudee (72), and Strawbridge Precincts.

Terrie L. Suit, a businesswoman and a Republican, was elected in 1999, defeating the incumbent Democrat, Glenn R. Croshaw by 373 votes. Croshaw had represented the area for 13 years. Suit came to Virginia from San Diego, was reared in a military family, and has lived in Virginia Beach for a decade.

She was appointed to the state Real Estate Board by Governor George Allen in 1997 and reappointed by Gilmore. Suit was unopposed in the 2001 election.

During the 2004 session, Suit sponsored twenty-four bills, fourteen passed and two were carried over to the 2005 session. Bills which passed provided for winner-take-all, "Lucky Seven" games under charitable gambling; allowed the court to decide the best interest of a child in custody and investigation cases; a penalty for theft of oysters and clams; and a procedure for awarding contracts for examination service of regulatory boards.

Bills which were continued provided for overtime compensation for law enforcement employees and authorized resale disclosures under the Condominium and Property Owner's Association Act.

Failed bills would have granted coverage for windstorms and hail under homeowner's insurance; established management plan for the Menhaden fishery; and established a procedure for awarding contracts for examination services by regulatory boards under the Department of Professional and Occupational Regulations.

Delegate HD 81

Terrie Lynne Suit (R)   Member House 2000- ; b. Oct. 3, 1964, Orleans, France; home, 3304 Ives Rd., Virginia Beach 23457; educ. Southwestern Comm. College; Tidewater Comm. College; married, Thomas F. Suit; Presbyterian.

Home lender; Member: Hampton Roads Chamber Comm.; Military Diplomats; Hampton Roads Republican Professional's Network; Virginia Beach Republican Women's Club.

Offices P.O. Box 7031, Virginia Beach 23457; 757-421-3309; GA Bldg., Capitol Sq., Rm. 721, Richmond 23219; 804-698-1081.

2004 Committees *Agriculture, Chesapeake and Natural Resources; Counties, Cities and Towns; General Laws.*

House Key Votes, 2004
Please see Introduction for more information on bills.

1) Budget Bill	FOR	5) Family Life	FOR	9) Morning After	AGN
2) Feticide	FOR	6) Fire Arms	FOR	10) Legal Aid	FOR
3) Marriage	FOR	7) Open Space	AGN		
4) Abortion	AGN	8) Home School	FOR		

Election Results

2004 general	Terrie Suit	(R)	11,445	69.6%	$194,927
	Sharon Bivens	(I)		5.4%	$427
	Lois Williams	(D)		2.5%	$131,180

Campaign Contributions 2004 Realty/Constr. $17,955; Energy $5,100; Law $4,900; Finance/Ins $4,625; Business/Retail Svs $4,550; Political $3,450; Health Care $3,350; Tech/Communications $2,750; Transportation $2,250; Agriculture $1,400; Mtg $1,000; Defense $775; Single-issue Groups $610; Public Employees $600; Misc $395; Undetermined $350.

Economic Interests, 2004 *Sal. & Wages*, $10,000+ ea.: U.S. Navy, Country wide Home Loans; Officers and Directorships: OMG, Director: Paymts for talks, meetings, and publications: $2,272 House, conference on environment; committee of NCSL, travel, lodging; $1,300 NCSL, spoke as representative for VA at conference; travel, lodging; Gifts: $56 McGuire Woods, dinner mtg; $101 VCTA, dinner mtg; Real Estate: three condos in VA, one in Wisconsin.

HOUSE DISTRICT EIGHTY-TWO, *Harry R. "Bob" Purkey (R)*

POLITICAL AND LEGISLATIVE BACKGROUND
House District 82 consists of part of the City of Virginia Beach comprised of the North Beach, South Beach, Linkhorn, Alanton, Kingston, Cape Henry, Kings Grant, Wolfsnare, Lynnhaven, Eastern

SECOND CONGRESSIONAL DISTRICT

Shore, Hilltop, and Trantwood (9)/ Great Neck (10) Precincts and parts of the Little Neck, Oceana, and Seatack (5)/ Rudee (72) Precincts.

Harry R. "Bob" Purkey, a stockbroker and a Republican, has represented the area since 1985, often running unopposed and easily defeating the rare opposition. In 1999, Purkey defeated Independent C. S. "Steve" Vinson. Following the 2000 session, Purkey suffered a mild stroke, but recovered. Purkey was unopposed in the 2001 election.

During the 2004 session, Purkey sponsored twenty-six bills, six passed; seven were carried over to the 2005 session. Bills that passed allow interest to be paid to owners of unclaimed property, permit electronic filing of reports of unclaimed property; establish certification requirements for occupational therapy and limit a certain percentage of revenues, which a nonprofit organization could use for administrative costs in order to maintain exempt status.

Bills carried over would have created the Virginia Entrepreneurial Encouragement Program as a tax incentive to start up businesses, required the Governor to automatically reduce general fund appropriations if general fund revenue collections exceeded the revenue growth estimate; and made it unlawful for anyone other than a family member to solicit an absentee ballot application or ballot in a hospital, nursing home, or assisted living facility.

Failed bills would have set a penalty for possessing an open container of alcohol in an automobile; allowed the Virginia Insurance Plan for Seniors to assist in the purchase of prescription drugs by those who are eligible for Medicaid and Medicare, but who do not qualify for prescription coverage under Medicaid; required members of the General Assembly who received an annual allowance for expenses and supplies by the general appropriations act to file an annual disclosure statement; and provided that anyone who attended an alcohol safety action program while under the influence of alcohol was guilty of a misdemeanor, which was punishable by a fine, and permanent revocation of his driver's license.

Delegate HD 82

Harry R. "Bob" Purkey (R) Member House: 1986-; b. July 13, 1934, Parsons, West VA; home, 2352 Leeward Shore Dr., Virginia Beach 23451; educ. Old Dom. Univ. (B.S.) Bus. Adm./Economics; USAR 1957-62; married Sonja Helene Firing; Methodist.

Vice Pres., Merrill, Lynch, Pierce, Fenner & Smith; past Dir. Ind. Devel. Auth.; Dir., Sanctuary of Tidewater; Dir. Old Dominion U. Intercoll. Fndn., Educ. Fndn. (Dir.); VA Beach Rep. Party (past chm.); Chamber of Com.; Phi Kappa Phi Honor Soc.; Gov. Comm. Govt. Reform Strike Force; Tidewater Auto Assn.; Sel. Comm. Transp.

Offices 2352 Leeward Shore Dr., Virginia Beach 23451; 757-481-1493; GA Bldg., Cap. Sq., Rm. 415, Richmond 23219; 804-698-1082.

2004 Committees *Commerce and Labor; Finance; Health, Welfare and Institutions; Science and Technology.*

House Key Votes, 2004

Please see Introduction for more information on bills.

1) Budget Bill	FOR	5) Family Life	FOR	9) Morning After	FOR
2) Feticide	FOR	6) Fire Arms	FOR	10) Legal Aid	FOR
3) Marriage	FOR	7) Open Space	FOR		
4) Abortion	FOR	8) Home School	FOR		

50

SECOND CONGRESSIONAL DISTRICT

Election Results

2004 general   Harry R. Purkey   (R)   17,663   97.3% $28,647

Campaign Contributions 2004 Health Care $6,500; Finance/Ins $4,450; Energy $4,250; Business/ Retail Svs $1,100; Transportation $950; Law $850; Agriculture $500; Political $250; Tech/ Communication $250; Mfg $150.

Economic Interests, 2004 *Sal. & Wages*, $10,000+ Merrill Lynch; *Off. & Dir.*, Bobson Properties LLC, Partner, owner; *Sec.*, $50,000+ ea.: mutual funds (4), money markets (3), retirement fund, stocks in: Merrill Lynch plans & IRA (6), Norfolk Southern; $10,001-$50,000 ea.: money market, stocks in: Exxon, Phillips Pete, Shell Oil, Rap. Dutch Pete, GE, Johnson & Johnson, Tenet Health, Pfizer, Microsoft, JP Morgan, Alcoa, Verizon, AT&T, Pepsi Cola, Coca Cola, Texas Instr., Lucent; *Gifts:* $140 McCaull, dinner/ reception; $136 Johnson & Johnson, dinner; *Bus. Int.*, $50,000+ Bobson Properties (rental); *Pay. for Rep. & Other Services Generally*, financial services $10,001-$50,000 ea.: medical retirement, fertilizer co., money managers, food proc., auto assn., law firms, health care services, farming, realty; $1,001-$10,000 ea.: heating oil, ice co., chemical, restaurants, non-profit, homeowners assns., retail, landscaping; *Real Estate*, One prop. (Bobson Prop.).

HOUSE DISTRICT EIGHTY-THREE, *Leo C. Wardrup, Jr. (R)*

POLITICAL AND LEGISLATIVE BACKGROUND

House District 83 consists of part of the City of Virginia Beach comprised of the Old Donation, Aragona, Ocean Park, Thoroughgood, Lake Smith, Bayside, Davis Corner, Chesapeake Beach, Witchduck, Pembroke, Bonney, Meadows, and Shell Precincts, and part of the Shannon Precinct.

Leo C. Wardrup, Jr., a financial consultant, retired Naval captain, and a Republican, has represented the area since 1991, when he won an open seat with 56.6% of the vote over two challengers. That year veteran legislator J. W. O'Brien retired after serving since 1974, and after he had worked 15 years getting the Virginia lottery bill through the legislature. In 1993 and 1995, Wardrup defeated opposition easily, and was unopposed in 1997. In 1999, Wardrup defeated Democrat S. W. "Sam" Meekins, Jr. In 2001, Wardrup won with 58.5% of the vote over Democrat Afshin Farashahi.

During the 2004 session, Wardrup sponsored thirteen bills, six passed and two were carried over to the 2005 session. Two resolutions were sponsored.

Bills that passed required notices to homeowners of changes in deductibles by their insurance companies; authorize limited use of the over-the-road operation of golf carts; increase the uniformity issuance and qualifications for special license plates; clarify that tax returns may be filed with the Department of Taxation or the local commission of revenues; and allow the Commonwealth Transportation Commission to make agreements with towns and cities regarding the design of right-of-way highways.

Bills continued would impose a tax on newspaper publishers to generate revenue for environmental activities in the commonwealth and repealed the tolls on I-81, which applied to all vehicles subject to the toll.

Bills that failed would have provided an annual appropriations for scholarships for shipyard workers enrolled in a program at Tidewater Community College; required that Virginia Department of Transportation to have a highway logo sign program and repealed the newspaper, magazine, and newsletter exemption of the business, professional, and occupational license (BPOL) tax.

Delegate   HD 83

Leo C. Wardrup (R)   Member House: 1992-; b. Sept. 5, 1936, Middlesboro, KY; home, 2208 Sunvista Dr., Virginia Beach 23455; educ. Univ. of NC (BA), George Washington Univ. (MBA), Naval War College (MS); married, Gloria Anne Wirth; Episcopalian.

Financial Analyst and Consultant; Active duty, U.S. Navy, 1958-1986; retired Captain, Supply Corps, USN; Navy League; Disabled American Veterans; Phi Beta Kappa; American Legion; Fleet Reserve Assn.; VA Beach Dev. Auth. (V. Chmn.).

Offices   Box 5266, Virginia Beach 23471; 757-490-8383; GA Bldg., Rm. 722, Capitol Sq., Richmond 23219; 804-698-1083.

2004 Committees   *Appropriations; Rules; Science and Technology; Transportation.*

House Key Votes, 2004
Please see Introduction for more information on bills.

1) Budget Bill	FOR	5) Family Life	FOR	9) Morning After	FOR
2) Feticide	FOR	6) Fire Arms	FOR	10) Legal Aid	AGN
3) Marriage	FOR	7) Open Space	FOR		
4). Abortion	FOR	8) Home School	FOR		

Election Results

2004 general	Leo C. Wardrup, Jr.	(R)	9,241	97.5%	$105,287

Campaign Contributions 2004   Transportation $7,250; Realty $5,125; Law $3,750; Health Care $3,750; Finance/Ins $3,500; Business/Retail Svs $3,100; Energy $3,100; Political $2,700; Tech/Communication $1,356; Public Employees $1,000; Mfg $1,000; Agriculture $1,000.

Economic Interests, 2004   *Sal. & Wages,* $10,000+ Triton Industries (spouse); *Sec.,* $50,000+ ea.: mutual fund, Merrill Lynch money fund, IRA (2), mortgage loan service demand notes; $10,001-$50,000 ea.: mutual funds (3), stock in SouthTrust Bank; *Pay. for Talks, Mtgs., & Pub.,* $1,769 state (ALEC expenses, per diem);, $1,653 ALEC conference, travel, per diem; ALEC registration fee; $1,367 Commonwealth of VA, conference, travel, per diem; $500 VA Transportation summit, lodging/meals; *Real Estate,* House, rental apts, open land; Gifts: $125 UPS, hot air balloon ride; $100 VA Auto Dealers, dinner.

HOUSE DISTRICT EIGHTY-FOUR, *Robert F. McDonnell (R)*

POLITICAL AND LEGISLATIVE BACKGROUND
House District 84 consists of part of the City of Virginia Beach comprised of the London Bridge, Plaza, Holland, Courthouse, Green Run, Landstown, and Hunt Precincts and parts of the Magic Hollow, Salem, and Strawbridge Precincts.

Robert F. McDonnell is a prosecutor, and a Republican, who has served since 1992. In his first run for political office, McDonnell upset veteran Democrat Glenn B. McClanan, who had served since 1972, winning with 52.8% of the vote. McDonnell easily defeated Democratic opposition in 1993,

SECOND CONGRESSIONAL DISTRICT

and ran unopposed in 1995 and 1997. But in 1999, Democrats, in their all out effort to keep control of the legislature that had been gradually slipping, backed Democrat Frank Drew, a popular sheriff in Virginia Beach. McDonnell won with 55.3% of the vote in an expensive race. In 2001, McDonnell was again unopposed.

During the 2004 session, McDonnell sponsored thirty-nine bills, twenty–seven passed, five were carried over. Bills that passed, created the Racketeer Influenced and Corrupt Organization Act (RICO); clarified that eighteen year olds are covered by the criminal statue governing the use of computers to solicit sexual activity with children; prohibited the recording of a motion picture, which is running in a movie theater and made it a misdemeanor; denied bail to a person arrested for DUI if there were three previous DUI convictions; provided that chief circuit court judge's authority to appoint magistrates is done in consultation with the chief general district and juvenile court judge and that all appointments are for four years, even to fill a vacancy; and expanded the list of criminal activity by gangs to include the distribution, transportation, and recruitment of juveniles into street gangs.

Eight resolutions passed including proposing a JLARC study financing trauma centers in hospitals and one urging Congress to enact a constitutional amendment to protect the institution of marriage.

Bills that failed would have increased the number of judges in the circuit courts, increased the numbers of judges in juvenile and domestic relation district courts, and amended the definition of explosive to exclude small arms ammunition that is in the original packing.

Delegate HD 84

Robert F. McDonnell (R) Member House: 1992- ; b. June 15, 1954, Philadelphia, PA; home, 2501 Woods Hole Ct., Virginia Beach 23456; educ. Univ. of Notre Dame (BBA), Boston Univ. (MSBA), Regent Univ. (JD, MA); married Maureen Gardner; Catholic.

Attorney; member, American and VA Bar Assn., Notre Dame Alumni Assn., Regent Univ. Law School (Bd. of Visitors); Bd of Dir.: Teen Challenge, CADRE, Ships at Sea; U.S. Army Reserve Officer.

Offices P.O. Box 62244, Virginia Beach 23466-2244; 757-671-8484; GA Bldg., Rm. 529, Capitol Sq., Richmond 23219; 804-698-1084.

2004 Committees *Courts of Justice, Chair; Commerce and Labor; Health, Welfare and Institutions; Rules.*

House Key Votes, 2004

Please see Introduction for more information on bills.

1) Budget Bill	FOR	5) Family Life	FOR	9) Morning After	FOR
2) Feticide	FOR	6) Fire Arms	FOR	10) Legal Aid	FOR
3) Marriage	FOR	7) Open Space	FOR		
4) Abortion	FOR	8) Home School	FOR		

Election Results

SECOND CONGRESSIONAL DISTRICT

2001 general   Robert F. McDonnell   (R)   10,727   98.1% $107,695

(2004 Campaign contributions are missing)

2002 Campaign Contributions   **Attys.** $4,743; **Medical** $4,700; **Realty/Constr.** $4,350; **Transp.** $3,100 (Auto Dealers $2,250); **Finance** $2,925; **Pub. Empl.** $2,350; **Electric** $1,750; **Tobacco** $1,500 (PM $1,000, UST $500); **Tech./Comm.** $1,425; **Beer/Wine** $1,350; **HMOs** $1,000; **Kings Dom.** $500; **Restaur.** $300; **Sheetz PAC** $250; **Coal** $250; **VA Retail Merch. Assn.** $250; **Republicans** $250; **Both Management Serv.** $200; **Hampton Roads Ptnship** $125.

Economic Interests, 2004   *Sal. & Wages,* $10,000+ Huff, Poole & Mahoney, P.C.; *Off. & Dir.,* NU International, Pres. (spouse); *Pers. Liabil.,* $10,001-$50,000 ea.: banks (self); *Sec.,* $50,000+ stock own law firm; *Gifts,* $78 State Farm Ins., dinner; $90 Geo Group, Inc., dinner; $63 Bon Secours, dinner; $74 Bon Secours, dinner; *Bus. Int.,* $50,000+ law firm; $50,000/less: Race Horse Properties, rentals; *Pay. for Rep. by You,* $1,001-$10,000 ea.: Tycorp, restaurant, legal services; Dept of Taxation; *Pay. for Rep. by Assoc.: retail/ Mfg/Ins.,* workers comp. commission; *laboratories/contractors, Dept of professional Occupational Regulations, Health Care, Dept of Health Professionals; Other:* retail, manuf., services before Wkers. Comp.; commun., insur. before SCC; *Pay. for Rep. & Other Serv. Gen.,* $250,001+ ea.: chemicals, aircraft, consumer prod., food, constr., casualty insur., retail co.; $100,001-$250,000 ea.: other insur. co., prof. assn.; $50,001-$100,000 ea.: banks, life insur.; $10,001-$50,000 ea.: electric, telephone, oil/gas, localities; $1,001-$10,000 ea.: gas, cable tv, interstate transp.; Real Estate: timeshare, open land.

HOUSE DISTRICT EIGHTY-FIVE, *Robert "Bob" Tata (R)*

POLITICAL AND LEGISLATIVE BACKGROUND

House District 85 consists of part of the City of Virginia Beach comprised of the Point O' View, Arrowhead, Larkspur, Providence, College Park, Brandon, Centerville, Stratford Chase, Homestead, Sherry Park, and Woodstock (25)/Fairfield (26) Precincts and parts of the Bellamy, Colonial, and Shannon Precincts.

Robert "Bob" Tata, a realtor, retired high school counselor, and a Republican, has served since 1984 when he defeated one year incumbent, Julie Smith, in 1983 and again in 1985. In 1991 he defeated another woman, Sandra W. Brandt, who was pro-choice. She was critical of Tata for voting against the 3-day waiting period for gun purchases. In 1993, Tata won over Independent Harry W. Rogers by 86.4%. He was unopposed in 1987 and 1989. He has been unopposed since 1995.

During the 2004 session, Tata sponsored fourteen bills, seven passed; two were carried over to the 2005 session. Bills that passed provide group life and accident insurance for state employees and retirees with twenty years of service; permitted the Virginia Retirement system (VRS) to recover overpayments of benefits paid for VRS administration programs; that Virginia Retirement benefits be paid to the successor of a deceased worker with an affidavit that certified that the value of the estate did not exceed the maximum value allowed under the Virginia Small Estate Act; and provided that a good cause for leaving employment was to accompany a spouse to a new military assignment from which the current place of employment was not reasonably accessible. The bill was incorporated into HB 177.

One resolution passed which urged schools to provide diversified health, nutrition, and physical education activities for students.

A bill that failed would have increased the monthly health insurance credits for retired teachers.

SECOND CONGRESSIONAL DISTRICT

Delegate HD 85

Robert "Bob" Tata (R) Member House: 1984-; b. Jan. 27, 1930, Detroit, MI; home, 4536 Gleneagle Dr., Virginia Beach 23462; educ. U VA (B.S., M.S.); Old Dom. Univ.; VPI (adv. endorsement); married Martha Jeraldine Morris; Catholic.

Retired High School Counselor & Coach; Former Realtor; US Army (1954-56).

Offices 4536 Gleneagle Dr., Virginia Beach 23462; 757-499-2490; GA Bldg., Capitol Sq., Rm. 801, Richmond 23219; 804-698-1085.

2004 Committees *Appropriations; Commerce and Labor; Education.*

House Key Votes, 2004
Please see Introduction for more information on bills.

1) Budget Bill	FOR	5) Family Life	FOR	9) Morning After	AGN
2) Feticide	FOR	6) Fire Arms	FOR	10) Legal Aid	FOR
3) Marriage	NV	7) Open space	FOR		
4) Abortion	FOR	8) Home School	FOR		

Election Results

2004 general	Robert Tata	(R)	16,837	73.5%	$90,570
	Eric Potter	(I)		26.4%	$25,395

Campaign Contributions 2004 Health Care $6,350; Finance $$5,000; Energy $4,000; Realty $3,850; Law $3,356; Business/Retail Svs $2,450; Transportation $1,850; Public Employees $1,500; Tech/ Communication $1,250; Political $1,000; Agriculture $1,000; Defense $500; Mfg $400.

Economic Interests, 2004 *Sal. or Wages,* $10,000+ ea.. retirement Norfolk City (self) and VA Beach Public Schools (spouse); *Sec.,* $50,000+ ea.: mutual fund, stock in Bank America; $10,001-$50,000 ea.: mutual fund, IRA (2); *Pay. for Talks, Mtgs., & Publ.,* $1,531 ALEC, reimbursement; $500 ALEC, scholarship   ; *Gifts,* $79 Kemper consulting, legislative dinner; $136 Mac Cauley & Burtch, legislative dinner; $125 Reynolds, golf outing; $147 Altria, legislative dinner; $63 Bon Secours, dinner; *Bus. Int.,* $50,000+ ea.: Farm, rental condominium (spouse); *Real Estate,* Farm and condo.

HOUSE DISTRICT EIGHTY-SIX, *Thomas D. Rust (R)*

POLITICAL AND LEGISLATIVE BACKGROUND

House District 86 consists of part of Fairfax County comprised of the Floris 203/Frying Pan 235, Herndon #1, Herndon #2, Herndon #3, Hutchison, Stuart, and Franklin Precincts; and part of Loudoun County comprised of the Guilford, Sully, Park View, and Rolling Ridge Precincts, and parts of the Cascades and Forest Ridge Precincts.

SECOND CONGRESSIONAL DISTRICT

Thomas D. Rust, a civil engineer and a Republican, is the delegate for this reconfigured district. Rust won an August 2001 Republican Primary, defeating Steve D. Whitener with 64.0% of the vote in an election decided by 8.2% of the registered voters. In the November 2001 general election, Rust defeated Democrat James G. Kelly with 62.9% of the vote. The seat was opened with the retirement of Donald L. "Don" Williams, a Democrat, who resigned following the redistricting process, which restructured the boundaries, and pitted Williams against Thelma Drake. Williams had served in the Hampton Roads area since his election in 1997, following the retirement of George Heilig who had served for 26 years.

During the 2004 session, Rust sponsored sixteen bills, four passed; five were carried over to the 2005 session. Bills that passed authorized the towns of Herndon and Vienna to impose a local tax on telecommunications services; authorized the issuance of a homeowner's policy, with the written consent of the insured to exclude from coverage any liability from injury caused by a dangerous animal owned or in the care of the insured (incorporated HB 1332); provided for a civic penalty for failure to pay a toll.

Bills carried over provided that taxpayers who are to receive a refund can voluntarily check off a contribution to the Virginia Responders Fund on the income tax; permitted public higher educational institutions to contract for construction projects without the approval of the Bureau of Capital Centtay Management, as long as they complied with the Virginia Public Procurement Act policies; and provide that contracts for professional services by a public body would only be with U.S. citizens, legal resident aliens or individuals with valid visas.

Three resolutions passed, one provided for a joint subcommittee to study the feasibility and appropriations of implementing JLARC recommendations on elementary and secondary school funding.

Bills that failed would have allocated funds for urban and secondary highways constructions; granted Loundon County the authority to regulate the use and occupancy of buildings; and reserved Virginia's transportation construction and maintenance allocation systems.

Delegate HD 86

Thomas Davis Rust (R) Member House: 2002- ; b. July 21, 1941, Front Royal, VA; home, 1020 Monroe Street, Herndon 20170-3213; educ. VA Tech (B.S.), George Wash. Univ. (M. Pub. Wks.), Univ. VA (Masters Urban/Env. Planning); married, Ann Edwards; Episcopal.

Civil Engineer; Herndon Town Council 1971-76, Mayor 1976-84, 1990-2001; Member: VA Tech Bd. Visitors; Northern VA Reg. Comm.; Northern VA Transp. Coord. Council, Exec. Comm.; Fairfax Commi. 100; Am. Planning Assn.; Am. Inst. Certified Planners; Fairfax/Falls Church United Way (former chair); Dulles Area Transp. Assn.; Northern VA Comm. Fndn.; Am. Red Cross, Hon. Dir.; Awards: Patrick Henry 2001; Acad. Distinguished Alumni Dept. Civil & Envir. Eng., VA Tech, 2001; Best of Herndon-Dulles; Who's Who US 1998; Vecinos Unidos, assistance to Hispanic Youth 1997; Man of Yr., Herndon Jaycees 1979.

Offices 730 Elden St., Herndon 20170; 703-437-9400; GA Bldg., Rm. 516, Capitol Sq., Richmond 23219; 804-698-1086.

2004 Committees *Education; Science and Technology; Transportation.*

House Key Votes, 2004
Please see Introduction for more information on bills.

1) Budget Bill	FOR	5) Family Life	FOR	9) Morning After	FOR
2) Feticide	FOR	6) Fire Arms	FOR	10) Legal Aid	FOR
3) Marriage	FOR	7) Open Space	AGN		
4) Abortion	FOR	8) Home School	FOR		

Election Results

2001 general	Thomas D. Rust	(R)	9,175	62.9%	$195,830
	James G. Kelly	(D)	5,388	36.9%	$ 17,223

Campaign Contributions 2004   Realty/Constr. $48,850; Political $5,750; Law $5,600; Business $5,543; Energy $4,500; Finance $4,100; Tech/Communication $3,600; Defense $3,500; Health Care $3,250; Public Employees $2,652; Transportation $2,500; Agriculture $2,000; Misc $1,000; Undetermined $350; Mfg $250; Candidate Self-financing $250.

Economic Interests, 2004   *Sal. or Wages*, $10,000+ ea.:   Patton Harris Rust & Assoc., US House Rep.; *Off. & Dir.*, Patton Harris Rust & Assoc., Chairman & Sr. VP; *Sec.*, $50,000+ ea.:   mutual fund, realty partnership, stocks in: own firm, F&M Natl.; $10,001-$50,000 ea.:   realty partnership, mutual funds (4); *Gifts*, $101 Northern VA Tech Council, dinner; $190 Greater Washington Bd of Trade, dinner; $225 VA Tech, football tkts; $50 Washington Gas, breakfast; $62 Washington Gas, dinner; $74 Dominion Power, dinner; *Bus. Int.*, $50,000+ Patton Harris Rust & Assoc. (engineering); $50,000/less ea.:   F&M Bank-NOVA, rental properties (4); *Pay. for Rep. & Other Services Generally*, engineering $250,001+ ea.:   gas util., tcl., retail co., other; $100,001-$250,000 water util., localities; $50,001-$100,000 prof. assn., other insur. co.; $10,001-$50,000 ea.:   cable TV, inter/intrastate transp., oil/gas, banks, savings, loan/finance, manuf.; $1,001-$10,000 ea.:   electric, mining, life insur., casualty insur., alcoholic bev., trade assn.; *Real Estate*, Five groups of properties (commercial, recreational) w/others.

HOUSE DISTRICT EIGHTY-SEVEN, *Paula Miller (R)*

POLITICAL AND LEGISLATIVE BACKGROUND
House District 87 consists of part of the City of Norfolk comprised of the Northside, Crossroads, Therapeutic Center, Wesley, Bayview United, East Ocean View, Larrymore, Little Creek, Oceanair, Tarrallton, Third Presbyterian, and Ocean View Center Part 2 Precincts and parts of the Azalea Gardens, Barron Black, Bayview School, Granby, Ocean View Center Part 1, Ocean View School, Titustown Center, Tucker House, and Zion Grace Precincts.

Paula Miller replaced Thelma Drake in the 2004 election. There is no legislative record.

Delegate HD 87

Paula Miller (D) House Member 2005 - ; b Aug. 1, 1959, Batavia, NY, educ. Genessee Community College, NY (AS mass communications, 1979, State University of NY at Genesso (BA, cum laude, speech communication, 1981), married George Edward, III, children George Edward IV, and Molly; Roman Catholic.

Information Officer, VA Sheriffs Office, Pinewell Civic League, VA Beach Crime Solvers Bd., Holy Trinity School PTO, Pungo Strawberry Festival (board), Mayors Task Force on Ocean View (former member), Legends in Music Committee.

937 Wells Parkway, Norfolk, VA 23503, (757) 587-8758, FAX (757) 480-8757; P.O. Box 406, Richmond, VA 23218, (804) 698-1087, FAX (804) 789-6310.

2004 Committees Militia Police and Public Safety, Science and Technology.

House Key Votes, 2004 Not in office during voting.
Please see Introduction for more information on bills.

Election Results

2004 general	Paula Miller	(R)	8,267	50.5%	$192,316
	Michael Ball	(D)		49.3%	$91,324

Campaign Contributions 2004 not available

Economic Interests, 2004 *Sal. or Wages*, $10,000+ ea.: VA Beach Sheriffs Office, Norfolk Circuit Court (husband); Personal Liabilities: other loan or finance companies, car loan.

HOUSE DISTRICT EIGHTY-EIGHT, *Mark Lanze Cole (R)*

POLITICAL AND LEGISLATIVE BACKGROUND
House District 88 consists of part of Fauquier County comprised of the Lois, Morrisville, Remington, and Opal Precincts; part of Spotsylvania County comprised of the Grange Hall and Plank Road Precincts; and part of Stafford County comprised of the Hartwood, Hampton, Rock Hill, Roseville, Ruby, Stefaniga, Griffis, and Potomac Hills Precincts, and part of the Simpson Precinct.

Mark I. Cole, a systems analyst and a Republican is the delegate for this district. In an August 2001 Republican Primary, Cole defeated four other contenders, winning with 35.5% of the vote in an election
decided by 8.4% of the registered voters. In the November 2001 general election, Cole defeated Democrat W. L. "Bill" Jones with 65.8% of the vote in an election costing over $227,000.

The seat was opened with the retirement of veteran legislator Thomas W. Moss, Jr., a Democrat and an attorney. Moss had held office since 1966, becoming the Speaker of the House in 1991. In 1999, with the shift of House control to the Republicans, Moss lost his role as Speaker of the House which he had held for eight years. With the redistricting process completed, Moss opted to retire from the House, and to seek the position of city treasurer which he easily won.

SECOND CONGRESSIONAL DISTRICT

During the 2004 session, Cole sponsored twenty bills, six passed; four were carried over to the 2005 session. Bills passed change the financial criteria that the localities use for determining eligibility for real estate exemption for the elderly or disabled by increasing their asset thresholds prior to the imposition of reduced real estate taxes; repeal provisions that authorize counties to require a permit for the sale and purchase of revolvers; and approved that no more than one-third of the annual secondary highway funds granted to a county be used to reimburse the county for debt service for bonds.

Bills carried over would have repealed the July 1, 2006 sunset provision on vehicles displaying clean fuel vehicle license plates on using HOV lanes.

Five of six resolutions were successful.

Bills which failed provided that a water and waste authority could suspend connections to its water and sewer systems when mandatory water conservation measures were imposed; and required that lobbyists who spend more than $50,000 during the General Assembly session register, file biweekly reports of expenditures and file an annual disclosure statement.

Delegate HD 88

Mark Lanze Cole (R) Member House: 2002- ; born June 6, 1958, Louisville KY; home, 3800 Wilburn Dr., Fredericksburg 22407; educ. Mary Washington College (B.L.S.), Germann Comm. College (A.A.S.), Western Ky Univ. (B.S.); married, Eugenia Ann Fairchild; Baptist.

Systems Analyst, Project Manager; Spotsylvania Co. Bd. Supervisors 2000-2002; U.S. Navy 1980-1985; U.S. Navy Reserve 1985-2001; Member: Colonial Baptist Church; Fredericksburg Metrop. Planning Org.; High Growth Coalition; Quantico Civilian-Military Council; Awards: Navy Commendation Medal (twice); Navy Achievement Medal (twice); AEGIS Excellence Award.

Offices P.O. Box 6046, Fredericksburg 22403; 540-752-8200; GA Bldg., Rm. 808, Capitol Sq., Richmond 23219; 804-698-1088.

2004 Committees *Finance; Privileges and Elections; Science and Technology.*

House Key Votes, 2004
Please see Introduction for more information on bills.

1) Budget Bill	AGN	5) Family Life	AGN	9) Morning After	FOR
2) Feticide	FOR	6) Fire Arms	FOR	10) Legal Aid	AGN
3) Marriage	FOR	7) Open Space	FOR		
4) Abortion	FOR	8) Home School	FOR		

Election Results

2004 general	Mark L. Cole	(R)	9,926	71.2%	$82,314
	Charles Feldbush	(D)		28.7%	$5,159

Campaign Contributions 2004 Realty $4,500; Energy $3,325; Law $2,305; Tech/ Communication $2,000; Transportation $1,750; Finance $1,625; Defense $1,500; Business/Retail Svs $1,250; Agriculture $1,250; Misc. $1,000; Political $1,000; Single-Issue Groups $500; Public Employees $250; Health Care $250; Mfg $200.

Economic Interests, 2004 *Sal. or Wages*, $10,000+ ea.: Northrop Grumman (Logicon), Christ Academy, U.S. Navy Reserve, Rugged Warehouse, Hilldrup Moving & Storage; *Off. & Dir.*, Northrop Grumman (Logicon), Proj. Manager; U.S. Navy Reserve, Commander; Spotsylvania Co., Supervisor;

Christ Academy, Teacher; *Sec.*, $50,000+ Northrup Grumman retirement (stocks, bonds, mut. funds); *Pay. for Rep. & Other Services Gen.*, $50,001-$100,000 Project management Northrop Grumman; $10,001-$50,000 Spotsylvania Co.; Gifts: $100 VA Auto Dealers Assoc., dinner; $130 Altria, legislative dinner; $159 Altria, open house; $50 VA Agribusiness Council, banquet.

HOUSE DISTRICT NINETY, *AlgieT. Howell,Jr. (D)*

POLITICAL AND LEGISLATIVE BACKGROUND
House District 90 consists of part of the City of Chesapeake comprised of the Indian River, Norfolk Highlands, Oaklette, and Tanglewood Precincts; part of the City of Norfolk comprised of the Bowling Park, Union Chapel, Brambleton, Campostella, Chesterfield, Coleman Place Presbyterian, Easton, Fairlawn, Houston, Ingleside, Poplar Halls, and Sherwood Rec Center Part 1 Precincts and parts of the Azalea Gardens, Barron Black, and Sherwood Rec Center Part 2 Precincts; and part of the City of Virginia Beach comprised of the Baker Precinct.

Winsome Earle Sears was replaced by Algie T. Howell in the 2004 election. There is no legislative record.

Delegate HD 90

Algie T. Howell (R) Member House 2004 - ; Jan. 8, 1938, Holland, VA, educ. Norfolk Division, VA State College (BS, 1967), Hampton Institute (MA 1973), married Lesser B. , children: Algie T. III, Alesia, Howell, Allen; Protestant.

USAF (1956-60), Business Owner; Hampton Roads Light Rail Representative, NEA, life member, Norfolk Public School Bd. member, Norfolk Parks and Rec. Commission, former Norfolk Chapter of SCL (President), USAF Squadron Airman Award (1956,57), Natl. Defense Education Fellowship Award (1960), Distinguished Service Award (1992) Life Saver Commendation Award (2002), and others.

P.O. Box 12865, Norfolk, VA 23541, (757) 466-7525; FAX (757) 466-7526; P.O. Box 406, Richmond, VA 23218, Rm. 717, (804) 698- 1090, FAX (804) 786- 6310.

2004 Committees General Law, Health, Welfare and Institutions, Science and Technology.

House Key Votes, 2004 Not in office
Please see Introduction for more information on bills.

1) Budget Bill	5) Family Life	9) Morning After
2) Feticide	6) Fire Arms	10) Legal Aid
3) Marriage	7) Open Space	
4) Abortion	8) Home School	

Election Results
2004 general	Algie T. Howell	(R)	6,696	99.4%	$ 25,100

SECOND CONGRESSIONAL DISTRICT

Campaign Contributions 2004 Health Care $3,750; Business $2,250; Public Employees $2,000; Realty $1,600; Transportation $1,500; Finance $1,500; Law $1,428; Political $1,050; Energy $1,000; Misc $775; Tech/Communications $750; Agriculture $750; Undetermined $200.

Economic Interests, 2004 *Pers. Liabil.*, $10,001-$50,000 ea.: Owner Algie's Barber & Beauty Shop; Officers & Directorships: Algie's Enterprises, Inc., President, Freeman House, Inc., Treasurer; Paymts for talks, meetings, publications: $300 Camptown School Reunion committee; Gifts: $96 Dominion VA Power, dinner; $79 Kemper Consulting ,dinner; Business Interests $50,000 or less: Algie's Enterprises, Inc., Freeman House, Inc, four rental properties; Real Estate: five houses, business, rental properties.

THIRD CONGRESSIONAL DISTRICT

SENATE DISTRICT TWO, *Mamie E. Locke (D)*

POLITICAL AND LEGISLATIVE BACKGROUND

Senate District 2 consists of the City of Hampton Precincts of Aberdeen, Bassette, City Hall, Cooper, East Hampton, LaSalle, Lee, Pembroke, Phenix, Phoebus, River, Smith, Tarrant, Wythe, Forrest, Jones, Kecoughtan, Kraft, Magruder, Mallory, Northampton, Tucker Capps, and Tyler, and part of Langley; the City of Newport News Precincts of Briarfield, Carver, Chestnut, Downtown, Dunbar, Huntington, Jefferson, Magruder, Marshall, New Market, Newsome Park, Reed, River, South Morrison, Washington, and Wilson; the City of Portsmouth Precincts of 37 / 38; and the City of Suffolk's Harbour View Precinct.

Mamie E. Locke replaced Walter Maxwell in the 2004 election.

During the 2004 session, Locke sponsored six bills, three passed and one was carried over. Bills which passed extended the sunset provision for the Neighborhood Assistance Act from 2004 to 2009; amended the provisions for prohibiting persons from keeping inoperable vehicles on certain property except within a fully enclosed structure; and instructed school boards to notify parents of the educational rights of students who failed to graduate.

A bill carried over which would have increased the size of the State Board of Corrections which was to have three community leaders, three elected officials, three members of the medical profession, and three citizens who have incarcerated family members.

Four resolutions were successful.

Bills that failed would have provided for a percentage of the state general sales tax and all water craft sales taxes to the City of Hampton and created the Virginia Targeted Jobs Grants Program.

Senator SD 2

Mamie E. Locke (D) Member Senate: 2004 - ; b. Mar. 19, 1954, Brandon, MS., educ. Tougaloo College (BA), Atlanta University (MA, PhD); Roman Catholic.

Dean, School of Liberal Arts & Education, Hampton University.

P.O. Box 3006, Hampton, VA 23663, (757 825-5880, FAX (757) 825-7372; P.O. Box 396, Richmond, VA 23128, (804) 698-7502, FAX (804) 698-7651.

2004 Committees Agriculture, General laws, Conservation and Natural Resources, Rehabilitation and Social Services.

Senate Key Votes, 2004
Please see Introduction for more information on bills.

1) Budget Bill	FOR	5) Familty Life	FOR	9)Charter School	FOR
2) Feticide	AGN	6) Fire Arms	AGN	10) Legal Aid	FOR
3) Marriage	AGN	7) Open Space	FOR		
4) Child Abuse	FOR	8) Home School	AGN		

Election Results -----NO RECORD OF ELECTION

Economic Interests, 2004 *Sal. & Wages*, $10,000+Hampton University;Officers & Directorships: Towne Bank, Director; Personal Liabilities to $50,000: Banks, loan or finance companies; More than $50,000: mortgage company; Business Interests $50,000 or less: rental property; *Gifts:*$76 Geico/State Farm, dinner; $176 King's Dominion, 4 tkts; $71 VA Cable, dinner; $56 Dominion Power, dinner; $120 Feld Entertainment, circus tkts; $50 gift certificate to Mortons Steak House; $72 VA Pharmacists Assoc., health screening; $140 Science Museum of VA, two memberships; $280 Colonial Athletic League, game tks; $150 Norfolk State University, MEAC game tks; $75 Kemper Consulting, dinner; $96 Dominion Power, dinner; $500 VA Horse council, trail ride; *Real Estate,* townhouse.

SENATE DISTRICT FIVE, *Yvonne B. Miller (D)*

POLITICAL AND LEGISLATIVE BACKGROUND
Senate District 5 consists of the City of Chesapeake Precincts: Crestwood, Georgetown, Oaklette, South Norfolk Fire Station, Carver School, and Providence Church of Christ; the City of Norfolk Precincts of Canterbury, Ghent Square, Immanuel, Lafayette Library, Lafayette Presbyterian, Lambert's Point, Larchmont Library, Larchmont Recreation Center, Maury, Ohef Sholom, Park Place, St. Andrews, Stuart, Ballentine, Tanner's Creek, Bowling Park, Coleman Place School, Lafayette-Winona, Lindenwood, Monroe, Norview Methodist, Norview Recreation Center, Rosemont, Sherwood School, Union Chapel, Berkley, Brambleton, Campostella, Chesterfield, Coleman Place Presbyterian, Easton, Fairlawn, Hunton Y, Ingleside, Poplar Halls, Young Park, Sherwood Rec Center Part 1, and Sherwood Rec Center Part 2; and the City of Virginia Beach Precincts: College Park, Sherry Park, and Baker.

Dr. Yvonne Miller was the first African-American woman elected to the Virginia House and the Senate. Serving for her 19th session as a member of the General Assembly, Miller ranks seventh in terms of seniority in the Senate. A Democrat and an educator, she won the House seat on a platform of education, women's rights, and sex equality. She met her first opposition in the Senate race for the seat vacated by the late Senator Peter K. Bablas, who had served from 1968-1987. In a hard fought contest, she defeated two opponents. In 1991, Miller easily defeated two challengers, beat back Republican opposition in 1995, and ran unopposed in 1999 Miller chaired the Senate Rehabilitation and Social Services Committee from 1996 to 1999, until the shift in political power put Republicans at the helm of all committees.

During the 2004 session, Miller sponsored twelve bills; four passed and two were carried over to the 2005 session. Bills that passed directed the Department of Social Services to provide a subsidized custody program for children who are living with relatives and for whom reunification with their natural parents and adoption relatives is not an option; defined kinship care as the full-time care, nurturing, and protection of children by relatives, and amended the Virginia-Asian Advisory Board to include advising the Governor on issues affecting Asian-American communities.

Two bills carried over require the Board of Dentistry to establish regulations for the safe use of dental amalgams that contain mercury and provided that in health maintenance organizations "net worth" and "capital and surplus" have the same meaning.

There were twelve resolutions of which ten were successful.

Bills that failed would have provided for a referendum that considered a constitutional amendment to restore the civil rights of persons convicted of non-violent felonies; have raised the minimum wage to

$6.50 per hour, a sum greater than the federal wage; and under workman's compensation, eliminated the requirement that an employer offer a choice of three physicians to the employee.

Senator SD 5

Yvonne B. Miller (D) Member Senate: 1988-; Member House 1984-88; b. July 4, 1934, Edenton, NC; home, 2816 Gate House Rd., Norfolk 23504; educ. VA State Coll. (B.S.), Columbia Univ. (M.A.), Univ. Pittsburgh (Ph.D.); C.H. Mason Mem. Church of God in Christ.

Retired Prof., Dept. Early Childhood/Elementary Educa. Norfolk State Univ.; member: Am. Assn. Univ. Prof., AAUW, Natl. Alliance Black Sch. Educators (life mem.), VA Assn. Early Childhood Educa., NEA (life mem.), Zeta Phi Beta Sorority, Inc.; LINKS; 1st Vice Chmn. Dem. Party VA; Dem. Natl. Comm.; Assn. State Dem. Chairs; Sec., Senate Democratic Caucus.

Offices 2816 Gate House Rd., Norfolk 23504-4021; 757-627-4212; FAX 627-7203; GA Bldg. Capitol Sq., Rm. 315, Richmond 23219; 804-698-7505.

2004 Committees *Rehabilitation and Social Services; Commerce and Labor; General Laws; Transportation.*

Senate Key Votes, 2004
Please see Introduction for more information on bills.

1) Budget Bill	FOR	5) Family Life	FOR	9)Charter Schools	FOR
2) Feticide	FOR	6) Fire Arms	AGN	10) Legal Aid	FOR
3) Marriage	AGN	7) Open Space	FOR		
4).Child Abuse	FOR	8) Home School	AGN		

Election Results

1999 general	Yvonne B. Miller	(D)	17,464	97.6%	$96,946

Campaign Contributions 2000-June 30, 2002 Org. Labor $7,250; (AFL CIO $2,800, Intl. Longsh. $2,000); **Democrats** $5,100; **Finance** $3,500; **Attys.** $2,900; **Churches/Pastors** $2,600; **Tech./Comm.** $2,450; **Realty/Constr.** $2,250; **Beer/Wine** $2,000; **Transp.** $1,750 (Auto Dealers/Manuf. $1,350); **Medical** $1,350; **Restau.** $1,000; **Pub. Empl.** $850; **NNShipbldg.** $800; **Electric** $500; **Insurance** $350; **Retail Merch. Norfolk** $250; **Retail** $200; **Misc. Defense** $200; **Individ.** $200; **Serv. Sta./Conv. St.** $150.

Economic Interests, 2004 *Sal. & Wages,* $10,000+ ea.: VA Retirement from Norfolk State University, Social Security; *Sec.,* $10,001-$50,000 stock in American Funds; Sec to $50,000: American Funds, stocks; *Pay. for Rep. by You,* $,976 NCSL, travel expenses; $2,610 CSG annual mtg, expenses; $1,200 Women in Gov't, expenses; $1,400 Annual mtg in Tucson, expenses; $1,050 Southern Women in Public Service, annual mtg, expenses;$1,100 Southern Regional conference, expenses; $1,160 Natl Democratic Party Convention, expenses; $730 Kinship care/NBCL/AARP, travel expenses; $1,500 BNCL Annual mtg, expenses; Gifts: $100 Mr A. Albert, banqet; $50 Sherrif Newhart, festival; $68 MCI & Frazier BlaylockCovanta Energy Group, dinner; $150 Mr Lindsay, first Citizens dinner; $89 Altria, reception; $79 Hampton Rds Maritime, Commonwealth club; $75 Hampton Rds maritime, banquet; $150 Dominion Resources, NSU Gree & Gold Ball; $50 Commonwealth Financial Service Assoc., dinner; $50 Natl Democratic Pary, luncheon; $50 NCSL presidential reception; $50 NCSL, Presidents reception; $100 VA Arts Festival, Boys Choir of Harlem; $80 Iota Omega Chapter Sorority, Ebony Fashion Flair; $50 NSU/SNEA, $150 Honorable Pickett, banquet; $2,232 Jimmy Rogers, JJ dinner and MEAC tkts; $220 Ms Forbes, CIAA tkts; $110 VA State University, CIAA tkts; $50 Norfolk Southern, luncheon; $200 Norfolk University, football games; $60 Hathaway & Assoc., dinner; $90 Mr Herger & Mr Bylor, dinner; $96 Mr Gilligan, dinner.

SENATE DISTRICT NINE, *Benjamin L. Lambert III (D)*

POLITICAL AND LEGISLATIVE BACKGROUND
Senate District 9 includes all of Charles City County; Henrico County Precincts: Brookland, Adams, Azalea, Brook Hill, Central Gardens, Chamberlayne, East Highland Park, Fairfield, Glen Lea, Greenwood, Highland Gardens, Hungary, Longdale, Ratcliffe, Upham, Wilkinson, Yellow Tavern, Maplewood, Landmark, Cedar Fork, Chickahominy, Donahoe, Eanes, Elko, Fairmount, Glen Echo, Highland Springs, Laburnum, Masonic, Town Hall, Montrose, Pleasants, Sandston, Seven Pines, Sullivans, Mehfoud, Whitlocks, Nine Mile, Dorey, and Antioch; and the City of Richmond Precincts: 206, 208, 211-213, 301-308, 402-404, 412, 501-505, 508, 602-604, 606-608, 701, and 909.

Benjamin L. Lambert III, an optometrist, has served in the Assembly since 1977. He was first elected to the House of Delegates as part of what was then Richmond's all Democratic, five-member, at-large delegation in the House. In 1985, he defeated opposition and won a special election to the state Senate for the seat vacated by then Lt. Gov. L. Douglas Wilder. Lambert has been unopposed ever since.

During the 2004 session, Lambert sponsored fourteen bills, ten passed and three were carried over to the 2005 session. Bills that passed created the Brown v. Board of Education Scholarship Fund to assist students who were enrolled in Virginia public schools between 1954 – 1964 in jurisdictions where schools were closed rather than follow the Supreme Court order to integrate schools; extended the sunset date for mayor business facility job tax credit to January 2010; and required housing authorities to adopt a "no-trespass" policy to protect residents.

Bills carried over would have created the Economic Development Incentive Act and provided a tax credit against individual income taxes for some long-term care insurance premiums.

A bill that failed would have stipulated that sheriff's office could use unmarked vehicles.

Senator SD 9

THIRD CONGRESSIONAL DISTRICT
Benjamin Joseph Lambert III (D) Member Senate: 1986-; Member House 1978-86; b. Jan. 29, 1937, Richmond; home, 3109 Noble Ave., Richmond 23222; educ. VA Union Univ. (B.S.); Mass. Coll. of optometry (O.D.); married Carolyn Morris; Baptist.

Optometrist; Richmond Med. Soc.; VA Optometric Assn.; Richmond Optometrist Assn. (past pres.); NAACP; Crusade for Voters; Black History Museum; VA Union Univ. Bd. Trustees; Richmond Renaissance; Southern Reg. Educa. Bd.; Bd. Dir.: VA Power, Dom. Reso., Consol. Bank & Trust, Student Loan Marketing Assn., VCU Hospital Authority; Optometrist of Yr. (1979, Natl.; 1980 VA).

Offices 904 N. First St., Richmond 23219; 804-643-3534; FAX 804-643-3535 GA Bldg., Capitol Sq., Rm. 311, Richmond 23219; 804-698-7509.

2004 Committees *Education and Health; Finance; General Laws; Privileges and Elections.*

Senate Key Votes, 2004
Please see Introduction for more information on bills.

1) Budget Bill	FOR	5) Family Life	FOR	9)Charter Schools	FOR
2) Feticide	FOR	6) Fire Arms	FOR	10) Legal Aid	FOR
3) Marriage	AGN	7) Open Space	FOR		
4) Child Abuse	NV	8) Home School	AGN		

Election Results
1999   general   Benjamin J. Lambert III   (D)   9,571   99.3% $44,752

Campaign Contributions 2000-June 30, 2002   **Medical** $7,900; **Tobacco--PM** $1,250; **Tech./Comm.** $1,200; **Attys.** $750; **Nat. Gas** $350; **Transp.** $250; **Insur.** $200; **Realty/Constr.** $200.

Economic Interests, 2004 *Sal. & Wages*, $10,000+ ea.: Dominion Resources, U.S.A. Education, Inc. (Sallie Mae); *Off. & Dir.*, Dir.: Dominion Resources, U.S.A. Education, Inc. (Sallie Mae), Consol. Bank & Trust; *Sec.*, $50,000+ ea. Stocks in: Dom. Res., Sallie Mae; $10,001-$50,000 stock in Consol. Bank & Trust; *Pay. for Talks, Mtgs., & Publ.*, $1,305 Natl. Chain Drug Stores (conf., expenses); *Gifts*, $148 Altra, dinner; $159 Altria, open house; $97 Dominion Resources, dinner; $54 Bon Secours, dinner; *Bus. Int.*, $50,000+ restaurant and Cafe; *Real Estate*, Commercial property/land.

SENATE DISTRICT SIXTEEN, *Henry L. Marsh III (D)*

POLITICAL AND LEGISLATIVE BACKGROUND
Senate District 16 consists of Dinwiddie County; the City of Petersburg; the Chesterfield County Precincts of Bellwood, Enon, Drewry's Bluff, Point of Rocks, and Dutch Gap; the Prince George County Precincts of Richard Bland College, Union Branch, Rives, and Jefferson Park; the City of Hopewell's Ward 6 and Ward 7 Precincts; and the City of Richmond's Precincts 509, 510, 609, 610, 702-707, 802, 806, 807, 810- 813, 902, 903, 906, 908, 910, and 911.

THIRD CONGRESSIONAL DISTRICT

Henry L. Marsh III, an attorney and a Democrat, has represented the area since 1991. Before redistricting, Elmon Gray (D) had been the senator from this district for 20 years. Marsh won the Democratic primary over four other candidates. Marsh, who had been on the Richmond City Council for 25 years, and mayor for five, refused to give up his city seat at first, stirring controversy. Senator Louise Lucas (D-18), also elected that year, and likewise reluctant to leave her local government position, announced in late 1991 she would resign her local seat. Marsh resigned his second position soon after that. Marsh ran unopposed in 1995 and 1999.

During the 2004 session, Marsh sponsored twenty bills, eight passed and six were carried over to the 2005 session. Bills that passed require judges to appoint an interpreter for non-speaking persons if they were a subject or a witness in a mental commitment proceeding; allowed local jurisdictions to decide if the locality or the individual paid the cost of finger printing for criminal record checks; required that reports of divorces, annulments, and adoption records delete racial designations.

Bills carried over would have provided for good conduct allowances for prisoners depending on their performance and conduct; excluded claims of physical or sexual assault from the Prisoner Litigation Reform Acts; and required that state police collect information on the race, ethnicity, color, age, or gender of the alleged offender and the reason for the traffic stop.

Thirteen out of fourteen resolutions passed including establishing a Joint Commission on Health Care to study mental health needs and treatment as well as a joint subcommittee to study access and costs of oral health care.

Bills which failed would have prohibited the Commonwealth from executing prisoners who were sentenced to death; required a criminal history check when firearms were sold at a gun show; required the boards of visitors of public universities to establish admission policies that prohibit preferential admissions for applicants who were related to an alumnus; and required the Secretary of Education to create and implement an equal education opportunity plan for all students in the Commonwealth.

Senator SD 16

Henry L. Marsh III (D) Member of Senate: 1992- ; b. Dec. 10, 1933, Richmond; home, 3211 Que St., Richmond 23221; educ. VA Union Univ. (BA), Howard Univ. (JD); married, Diane Harris Marsh; Methodist.

Attorney; former Mayor, City of Richmond, 1977-82; City Council 10 terms; Natl. Caucus of Local Elected Officials (past pres.); Richmond Renaissance; Alpha Phi Alpha; Alpha Beta Boule.

Offices 600 East Broad St., Suite 402, Richmond 23219-1800; 804-648-9073; GA Bldg., Capitol Sq., Rm 329, Richmond 23219; 804-698-7516.

2004 Committees *Courts of Justice; Local Government; Rehabilitation and Social Services; Transportation.*

THIRD CONGRESSIONAL DISTRICT

Senate Key Votes, 2004
Please see Introduction for more information on bills.

1) Budget Bill	FOR	5) Family Life	FOR	9) Charter Schools	AGN
2) Feticide	FOR	6) Fire Arms	AGN	10) Legal Aid	FOR
3) Marriage	AGN	7) Open Space	FOR		
4) Child Abuse	FOR	8) Home School	AGN		

Election Results

1999 general	Henry L. Marsh III	(D)	12,806	99.3%	$78,649

Campaign Contributions 2000-June 30, 2002 Attys. $8,000; **Finance** $7,250; **Transp.** $6,175; **Attys.** $5,500; **Medical** $4,265; **Tech./Comm.** $3,780; **Electric** $3,750; **Tobacco** $2,698 (PM $2,448, RJR $250); **Retail** $2,475 (Groc. $1,350); **Realty/Constr.** $2,050; **Hotel/Tourism** $1,986; **Beer/Wine/Dist. Spirits** $1,875; **Intnl. Br. Electrical Wkers.** $1,750; **NNShipbldg.** $1,500; **Secur./Detect.** $1,250; **Individ.** $1,140; **Rec./Amuse. Pk.** $1,100; **Dupont** $1,000; **Democrats** $1,000; **Pub. Empl.** $750; **Honeywell** $500; **Insur.** $500; **Northrup Grumman** $500; **Serv. Stat./Conv. St.** $250; **Billboards** $200.

Economic Interests, 2004 *Sal. & Wages*, $10,000+ Hill, Tucker & Marsh Law; *Per. Liabil.*, $50,000+ ea.: Banks (self), banks (family); *Sec.*, $10,001-$50,000 stock in own firm; *Pay. for Talks, Mtgs., & Publ.*, $1,719 state HCSL mtg, expenses; *Gifts*, $1,395 VA Trial Lawyers, Assoc., convention; $152 Altria, Kraft days Reception; $189 Altria , reception; $159 Altria, open house; $71 VCTA Telecommunications, dinner; $96 Dominion, dinner; *Bus. Int.*, $50,000+ Hill, Tucker & Marsh Law; $50,000/less rental prop. (spouse); *Pay. for Rep. by You*, legal $1,001-$10,000 ea.: restaurant; *Pay. for Rep. & Other Services Gen.*, legal representation $1,001-$10,000 ea.: legal services to higher education institutions, churches, Dept of Professional & Occupational Regulations; *Real Estate*, One commercial prop. (spouse).

HOUSE DISTRICT SEVENTY, *Dwight Clinton Jones (D)*

POLITICAL AND LEGISLATIVE BACKGROUND
House District 70 consists of part of Chesterfield County comprised of the Drewry's Bluff Precinct and part of the Bellwood Precinct; part of Henrico County comprised of the Central Gardens, Eanes, Glen Echo, Laburnum, Masonic, Montrose, Sullivans, and Mehfoud Precincts; and part of the City of Richmond comprised of the 403, 508, 701, 702, 703, 704, 705, 806, 811, 812, 813, 903, and 906 Precincts, and parts of the 402 and 609 Precincts.

Democrat Dwight C. Jones has served since 1993. Jones is a minister for the First Baptist Church in South Richmond. The district was formerly served by Democrat Roland "Duke" Ealey until his death in 1992, and then by another Democrat, Lawrence D. "Larry" Wilder, Jr., who chose not to run in 1993. Jones won a fiercely fought Democratic primary, and tough Republican opposition. In 1995, Jones fended off Republican opposition, and was unopposed in 1997, 1999, and 2001. After the 2000 session, Jones was appointed by the Republican leadership as the first black member of the Joint Legislative Audit Review Commission.

During the 2004 session, Jones sponsored sixteen bills, three passed; four were incorporated into other bills. Bills passed require vision test for persons eighty years old or older who wanted to apply for or renew a driver's license; authorized the Board of Health to set criteria for developing and maintaining an emergency plan for the public water supply to obtain pure water during an extended power outage; and facilitated the efforts of localities to abate nuisances and dispose of delinquent properties.

No bills carried over to the 2005 session.

68

Out of eight resolutions, two provided for a JLARC Commission to study the use and financing of trauma centers and direct the Secretary of Public Safety to stop utilizing beds in the Department of corrections to house out-of-state prisoners.

Bills that failed would have prohibited the use of hand-held cell phones while driving; subjected both custodial and non-custodial parents to penalties for failure to comply with court orders pertaining to divorce, custody, visitation, and support; made the Director of Development of Minority Business Enterprise the Governor's key advisor on minority business issues.

Delegate HD 70

Dwight Clinton Jones (D) Member House: 1994- ; b. Feb. 3, 1948, Philadelphia, PA; home, Richmond; educ. Virginia Union Univ. (B.A., Sociology), VU Sch. of Theology (M.Div.); Baptist.

Minister, First Baptist Church, South Richmond; former Chm., Richmond City Pub. School Bd.; Richmond Renaissance, Bd. Dir.; Natl. Council of Churches; S. Richmond Sr. Cntr. (co-founder, pres.); Natl. Baptist Conv. (bd. & sec. comm. on housing).

Offices P.O. Box 2347, Richmond 23218-2347; 804-233-7679; FAX 233-7683; GA Bldg., Rm. 508, Capitol Sq., Richmond 23219; 804-698-1070.

2004 Committees *Commerce and Labor; Counties, Cities and Towns; Transportation.*

House Key Votes, 2004
Please see Introduction for more information on bills.

1) Budget Bill	FOR	5) Family Life	FOR	9) Morning After	FOR
2) Feticide	FOR	6) Fire Arms	AGN	10) Legal Aid	FOR
3) Marriage	FOR	7) Open Space	FOR		
4) Abortion	AGN	8) Home School	AGN		

Election Results

2004 general	Dwight Clinton Jones	(D)	10,978	99.1%	$19,250

Campaign Contributions 2004 Health Care $4,350; Finance $2,750; Energy $2,000; Realty $1,500; Law $1,250; Transportation $1,000; Public Employees $1,000; Tech/Communication $750; Organized Labor $500; Agriculture $500; Political $450; Mfg $250; Business/Retail Svs $225.

Economic Interests, 2004 *Sal. & Wages,* $10,000+ ea.: First Baptist Church of South Richmond; *Sec.,* $10,001-$50,000 mutual fund; *Gifts,* $334 Dominion Resources, football tks, dinner; $84 Dominion, dinner; $89 Altria, reception; *Real Estate,* One prop.

HOUSE DISTRICT SEVENTY-ONE, *Viola Osborne Baskerville (D*

THIRD CONGRESSIONAL DISTRICT

POLITICAL AND LEGISLATIVE BACKGROUND

House District 71 consists of part of Henrico County comprised of the Hilliard, Stratford Hall, and Summit Court Precincts; and part of the City of Richmond comprised of the 203, 206, 207, 208, 211, 212, 213, 301, 302, 303, 304, 305, 306, 307, 308, 309, 505, 602, 603, 606, 607, 608, 706, and 707 Precincts.

Viola Baskerville was elected to District 71 in 1997. A Democrat and an attorney, Baskerville is a former member of Richmond City Council. Baskerville defeated Leonidas Young II, a former Richmond mayor, in the Democratic Primary with 68.2% and won the general election with an 85.5% of the vote over Virginia Reform Party candidate Bernard J. Artabzon. The seat was opened when fellow Democrat Jean Cunningham retired. Cunningham had served the area since 1986, supporting women's rights, children's rights, and gun control. Baskerville ran unopposed in 1999. In 2000, she co-chaired with Senator John Watkins the Central Virginia Caucus, a local legislative coalition. Baskerville trounced Republican opposition in the 2001 election, winning with 75.9% of the vote. T. C. Elliott carried the Henrico precincts, while Baskerville captured the Richmond vote.

During the 2004 session, Baskerville sponsored sixteen bills; three passed, four were carried over, two were incorporated into other bills. Bills that passed amended the Charter of the City of Richmond; allowed city council members to be paid on the same payroll cycle as city employees; and insured the admission of students whose parents are deployed outside the limited States in public schools in the commonwealth without tuition.

Bills carried over would have prohibited court clerks from posting on court websites to agencies any documents containing personal information; allowed individuals to contribute an income tax refund to the Pre-Release and Post-Incarceration Services Fund; and established the Virginia clean Elections Act and Fund to provide an alternative way to publicly finance candidates for governor, lieutenant governor, and attorney general.

Four out of twelve resolutions passed.

Bills that failed would have removed the state tax from estates valued at $10 million or less or if assets were held in a closely held business or working farm; required school boards to provide alternative education programs for disruptive, suspended, or expelled students; and increased the grants to caregiver's of mentally or physically impaired relatives from $500,000 to $3,000,000.

Delegate HD 71

Viola Osborne Baskerville (D), Member House 1998- ; b. Oct. 29, 1951, Richmond; home 3223 Hawthorne Ave., Richmond 23222; educ. College William and Mary (B.A.), Univ. Iowa, College of Law (J.D.); married Archer Lewis Baskerville; Episcopalian.

Attorney; Member: Make Women Count (Adv. Bd.), Richmond Chapter 100 Black Women, Ginter Park Residents' Association, Richmond Renaissance, University of Richmond Service Associates.

Offices   P.O. Box 406, Richmond 23218; GA Bldg., Capitol Sq., Rm. 525, Richmond 23219; 804-698-1071.

THIRD CONGRESSIONAL DISTRICT
2004 Committees *Health, Welfare and Institutions; Science and Technology.*

House Key Votes, 2004
Please see Introduction for more information on bills.

1) Budget Bill	AGN	5)Family Life	AGN	9) Morning After	AGN
2) Feticide	AGN	6) Fire Arms	AGN	10) Legal Aid	AGN
3) Marriage	AGN	7) Open Space	AGN		
4) Abortion	AGN	8) Home School	AGN		

Election Results
2001 general	Viola Osborne Baskerville (D)	10,515	99.7%	$62,413

Campaign Contributions 2004   Health Care$9,360; Realty $5,500; Misc $3,175; Law$3,100; Finance $2,250; Tech?Communication $2,000; Energy $1,500; Agriculture $1,250; Public Employees $1,100; Transportation $1,000;Business/Retail Svs $1,000; Mfg $250; Organized Labor $250; Political $200; Undetermined $110.

Economic Interests, 2004   *Sal. & Wages*, Richmond Cardiology Assoc., RCA Profit Sharing Plan; *Off. & Dir.*, Richmond Cardiology Assoc., Pres. (spouse); *Pers. Liabil.*, $50,000+ ea. banks (self, 3 banks); banks (family); Richmond Cardiology (spouse), Rich. Card. Assoc. Profit Sharing (spouse); *Pay. for Talks, Mtgs., & Pub.*, $4,000 Center for Women Policy Studies (expenses), $200 Open Society (conf., expenses); *Gifts*, $152 Altria, Kraft Days reception; $159 Altria, PMUSA; $61 McGuire Woods Consulting, Inc., dinner; $71 VA Cable, dinner; $514 Apollo Theater Foundation, air travel; $225 Apollo Theater Foundation, hotel; $75 Apollo Theater Foundation, limo service; $119 VA Foundation Humanities, hotel; $133 Regent University, hotel, breakfast; $347 Natl Caucus of Black Legislators, air travel; $334 Natl Caucus of Black Legislators; $333 Geico, dinner.

HOUSE DISTRICT SEVENTY-FOUR, *Floyd Hugo Miles, Sr. (D)*

POLITICAL AND LEGISLATIVE BACKGROUND
House District 74 consists of all of Charles City County; part of Henrico County comprised of the Adams, Azalea, Bloomingdale, Brook Hill, Canterbury, Chamberlayne, East Highland Park, Fairfield, Glen Lea, Greenwood, Highland Gardens, Hungary, Longdale, Randolph, Ratcliffe, Upham, Wilkinson, Yellow Tavern, Maplewood, Chipplegate, Landmark, Cedar Fork, Donahoe, Elko, Fairmount, Highland Springs, and Pleasants Precincts; part of the City of Hopewell comprised of the Ward 2 and Ward 6 Precincts; part of the City of Richmond comprised of the 604 Precinct; and part of Prince George County comprised of part of the Courts Building Precinct.

Floyd H. Miles, Sr., a Democrat and a former member of the Charles City County Board of Supervisors, was elected in 2001. Miles won with 61.1% of the vote over two Independent candidates, Terone B. Green and Victor A. Motley, Sr. The seat was opened when incumbent Donald McEachin (D) ran for Attorney General, winning the Democratic Primary against three other candidates, but losing the state election. McEachin, an attorney, had served since his election in 1995 when he defeated veteran legislator Bob Ball in a hard fought and expensive Democratic primary.

Miles, a 14-year veteran of the Charles City County Board of Supervisors, served as Chairman of that board when Charles City topped the news by accepting out-of-state trash. During the controversy, Miles told the *Associated Press*, "We were willing to trade off the handling of other people's trash in return for having such a safe facility."

During the 2004 session, Miles sponsored six bills, three passed; two were carried over to the 2005 session. Bills that passed allow the State Police to sell or use unclaimed property that it has been possessed for more than sixty days, required all heads of departments in the executive branch to report the Chief Information Officer all incidents that threaten the security of the Commonwealth's databases; and repealed the optimal supplemental health insurance credit for retired state employees.

Two bills carried over would have allowed Charles City County to impose an admissions tax and would have provided services by the state Police to the governor and his immediate family for limited periods of time.

There were eight resolutions of which five passed.

Delegate HD 74

Floyd Hugo Miles, Sr. (D) Member House: 2002-; b. June 29, 1949, Charles City; home, 7420 Ruthville Rd., Providence Forge 23140; educ., VA Union Univ. ; married Clem Elizabeth Wallace; Baptist.

Retired; Charles City County Board of Supervisors, 14 years; Member Little Elem Baptist Church.

Offices P.O. Box 406, Richmond 23218; GA Bldg., Capitol Sq., Rm. 420, Richmond 23219; 804-698-1074.

2004 Committees *Agriculture, Chesapeake and Natural Resources; General Laws.*

House Key Votes, 2004
Please see Introduction for more information on bills.

1) Budget Bill	FOR	5) Family Life	FOR	9) Morning After	AGN
2) Feticide	AGN	6) Fire Arms	AGN	10) Legal Aid	FOR
3) Marriage	AGN	7) Open Space	FOR		
4) Abortion	AGN	8) Home School	AGN		

Election Results

2004 general	Floyd H. Miles, Sr.	(D) 10,451	99.3%	$16,612

Campaign Contributions 2004 Agriculture $2,499; Energy $2,000; Health Care $1,300; Law $1,250; Tech/Communications $1,250; Public Employees $1,000; Transportation $750; Political $600; Finance $500; Mfg $250; Organized Labor $250; Business/Retail Svs $250; Realty $250.

Economic Interests, 2004 *Sal. & Wages*, $10,000+ Philip Morris USA, Charles City Co. Schools; *Pers. Liabil.*, $10,001-$50,000 banks (self), loan or finance co. (family), Chrysler Credit (family); *Sec.*, $50,000+ stocks in Philip Morris, Bus. Interest $50,000 or less: Clear Miles Beauty Consultant; Gifts: $346 Altria, NASCAR race; $90 Dominion Power, dinner; $50 VA Agribusiness Council, banquet; $152 Altria, Kraft Days reception; $131 Altria, dinner; $159 Altria, PMUSA Open House.

HOUSE DISTRICT EIGHTY, *Kenneth R. "Ken" Melvin (D)*

POLITICAL AND LEGISLATIVE BACKGROUND
House District 80 consists of part of the City of Chesapeake comprised of the Johnson Park Precinct; part of the City of Norfolk comprised of the Ohef Sholom, St. Andrew's, and Berkley Precincts and parts of the Canterbury and Hunton Y Precincts; and part of the City of Portsmouth comprised of the 1, 5, 7, 9, 13, 14, 16, 17, 19, 20, 21, 26, 27, 28, 29, 31, and 32 Precincts.

Kenneth R. Melvin, a Democrat and an attorney, has served his area since 1985. He defeated incumbent Clives Manning in the 1985 primary that year. Manning had served in the House since 1968. Manning stressed his seniority and Melvin used the theme, "in touch with our community." Melvin was unopposed until 1993 when he soundly defeated Independent challenger James W. Holley III with 79.2% of the vote. Melvin won the 1995 election by garnering 76.9% of the vote over Republican F. E. "Dutch" Andrews, Jr. Melvin has been unopposed since the 1997 election.

During the 2004 session, Melvin sponsored seven bills, five passed; one was carried over to the 2005 session. Bills passed allow attorneys who provide pro bono custody and visitation services to indigent clients be covered by the Commonwealth's risk management program; clarified that a former justice of the Supreme Court or a judge of the Court of Appeals may retire and subsequently be appointed as a senior justice or judge; and provided that a property bail bondsman needed a certificate from only one circuit court judge to be able to operate state-wide.

One bill carried over which directed school boards to require applications from school employees regarding prior convictions.

Delegate HD 80

Kenneth Ronald Melvin (D) Member House: 1986-; b. Sept. 18, 1952, Fayetteville, NC; home, 14 Eleanor Ct., Portsmouth 23701; educ. Colby College (BA), Georgetown Univ. Law Center (J.D.); married Sylvia LaVerne Hodges; Baptist.

Attorney; Partner Melvin & Gourdine; former Commissioner Portsmouth Redev. & Housing Auth.; Bd. mem. Tidewater Leg. Aid Soc.; former Trial Atty. US Dept. Just.; Portsmouth Br. NAACP, leg. counsel; AM., Old Dom., & Norfolk Portsmouth Bar Assns.; VA State Bar Bd. of Gov.

Offices 801 Water St., Suite 300, Portsmouth 23704; 757-397-2800; GA Bldg., Capitol Sq., Rm. 502, Richmond 23219; 804-698-1080.

2004 Committees *Courts of Justice; Finance; Health, Welfare and Institutions.*

House Key Votes, 2004
Please see Introduction for more information on bills.

1) Budget Bill	AGN	5) Family Life	FOR	9) Morning After	AGN
2) Feticide	AGN	6) Fire Arms	FOR	10) Legal Aid	AGN
3) Marriage	AGN	7) Open Space	AGN		
4) Abortion	AGN	8) Home School	AGN		

Election Results

2004 general   Kenneth R. Melvin   (D)   14,290   97.9% $41,798

Campaign Contributions 2004   Health Care $2,000; Finance $1,000; Energy $1,000; Business/Retail Svs $750; Organized Labor $500; Tech/Communications $250; Realty $250; Public Employees $100.

Economic Interests, 2004   *Sal. & Wages*, $10,000+ ea: Portsmouth Public Schools; *Off. & Dir.*, Marcus, Santoro, Kozak & Melvin, Vice Pres.;   *Sec.*, $50,000+ ea.: Money market, mut. fund; $10,001-$50,000 ea.: mutual funds (7); *Gifts*, $56 Dominion Power, dinner; $95 Dominion Power, dinner; $71 VA Cable , dinner; $360 King's Dominion, tks; $364 King's Dominion, tks; *Bus. Int.*, $50,000/less: rental prop. w/spouse.

HOUSE DISTRICT EIGHTY-NINE, *Kenneth C. Alexander (D)*

POLITICAL AND LEGISLATIVE BACKGROUND
House District 89 consists of part of the City of Norfolk comprised of the Ghent Square, Immanuel, Lafayette Library, Lafayette Presbyterian, Lambert's Point, Maury, Park Place, Stuart, Suburban Park, Willard, Ballentine, Tanner's Creek, Coleman Place School, Lafayette-Winona, Lindenwood, Monroe, Norview Methodist, Norview Recreation Center, Rosemont, Sherwood School, and Young Park Precincts and parts of the Granby, Hunton Y, Sherwood Rec Center Part 2, Titustown Center, and Tucker House Precincts.

Delegate HD 89

Democrat Kenneth C. Alexander, a funeral director, is the new delegate for this district. Alexander captured 73% of the vote against Republican Linda Horsey and Independent Sherry White-Battle in a special election in August of 2002 in an election settled by 15.17% of the voters. The election was necessary with the resignation of Jerrauld C. Jones, following his appointment by Governor Mark Warner to head the state Juvenile Justice Department. Jones, a Democrat and an attorney, served in the House for 14 years without opposition except for 1991 when he won with 80.3% of the vote. For eight of those years, he chaired the Legislative Black Caucus. Jones unsuccessfully ran in the 2001 three-way democratic primary, which was ultimately won by Tim Kaine.

Alexander served as vice chairman of the City of Norfolk's Planning Commission and in several civic roles. In a *Virginian-Pilot* editorial urging readers to vote for Alexander, the paper was impressed with his willingness to voice the need for the state to raise revenue to pay for service and his "training at the Sorensen Institute for Political Leadership at the University of Virginia, which grooms candidates for political office."

During the 2004 session, Alexander sponsored two bills, one passed, nine resolutions were successful.
The bill that passed clarified that persons who become 18 by the November presidential election date could vote in the presidential primary earlier in the year.

THIRD CONGRESSIONAL DISTRICT

Kenneth Cooper "Ken" Alexander (D) Member House: 2003- ; b. Oct. 17, 1966, Norfolk; home, Norfolk; educ. John Tyler Comm. Coll., Old Dom. Univ. (B.S.); married Donna Burnley; Baptist.

Funeral Director/Mortician; Member: Norfolk Fun. Dir. & Embalmers Assn. (former pres.), Natl. Fun. Dir. (former district gov.), VA Morticians Assn. (former pres.), Tidewater Fun. Dir. Assn., Norfolk Planning Comm. (vice-chair), Greater norfolk Corp. (exec. comm.), Tidewater Business Fin. (bd. mem.), Empowerment 2010 (bd. mem.), Norfolk Econ. Develop. Auth. (former member), Beacon Light Comm. Housing Develop. (former pres.); Awards: Alpha Kappa Alpha Sorority Mid-Atlantic Region's Citizen of the Year 2002. Southside Sr. Cntr. Vol. of Yr. 2001, Southside Boys and Girls Volunteer 2000, Profession of Yr., Norfolk Fun. Dir. 1998; Kappa Alpha Psi Frat. Save Our Youth 1998.

Offices 7246 Granby St., Norfolk 23505; 757-628-1000; GA Bldg., Rm. 412, Capitol Sq., Richmond 23219; 804-698-1089.

2004 Committees *Privileges and Elections; Science and Technology.*

Election Results

2004 special	Kenneth Alexander	(D)	3,927	100%	$34,278

House Key Votes, 2004

Please see Introduction for more information on bills.

1) Budget Bill	AGN	5) Family Life	FOR	9) Morning After	AGN
2) Feticide	AGN	6) Fire Arms	AGN	10) Legal Aid	AGN
3) Marriage	AGN	7) Open Space	AGN		
4) Abortion	AGN	8) Home School	AGN		

Campaign Contributions 2004 Energy $1,750; Law $1,500; Tech/Communication $1,500; Transportation $1,250; Business/Retail Svs $1,250; Public Employees $1,100; Realty $1,000; Organized Labor $500; Political $500; Finance $500; Mfg $250; Health Care $250; Agriculture $250.

Economic Interests, 2004 *Sal. & Wages,* $10,000+ Metropolitan Funeral Service; *Off. & Dir.,* Metrop. Fun. Serv. Pres., Sec., Treas.; *Sec.,* $10,001-$50,000 Virgini Funeral Service; *Bus. Int.,* $50,000+ ea.: Virginia Funeral Service, Funeral Home rental property; *Pay. for Rep. by You,* $10,001-$50,000 Metrop. Fun. Serv. before city of Norfolk Public Assistance Dept. Soc. Services; *Real Estate,* properties (commercial, open land, residential) some w/others; Gifts: $89 Altria, reception at DNC; $79 Kemper Consulting, dinner; $62 Vectre Corp., dinner; $68 Washingtron Gas, dinner.

HOUSE DISTRICT NINETY-TWO, *Jeion W. Ward (D)*

POLITICAL AND LEGISLATIVE BACKGROUND

House District 92 consists of part of the City of Hampton comprised of the Aberdeen, Bassette, City Hall, Cooper, East Hampton, Lasalle, Lee, Pembroke, Phenix, Phoebus, River, Smith, Jones, Kecoughtan, and Tyler Precincts, and parts of the Buckroe, Fox Hill, Magruder, and Northampton Precincts.

Jeion W. Ward replaced Mary T. Christian in the 2004 election. There are no legislative records.

Delegate HD 92

Jeion W. Ward (D) Member House 2005 - ; b Jan. 6, 2954, Newport News, VA., educ.: Warwick High School (1972); Christopher Newport University (B.A., 1995); married James Addrill Ward, Sr., children: James A, Jr., and Jeremy A.

Middle School Teacher, NAACP, NCNW, Peninsula Central Labor Council, Coalition of Labor Union Women (V.President), American Federation of Teachers Pioneer Award (1997).

Offices: P.O. Box 406, Richmond, Virginia 23218, Rm 508 **Phone:** (804) 698-1092, **Fax:** (804) 786-6310; P.O. Box 7310, Hampton, VA 23666, **Phone:** (757) 827-5921.

2004 Committees Education, General Laws, Transportation

House Key Votes, 2004
Please see Introduction for more information on bills.

1) Budget Bill	AGN	5) Family Life	FOR	9) Morning After	AGN
2) Feticide	AGN	6) Fire Arms	FOR	10) Legal Aid	FOR
3) Marriage	AGN	7) Open Space	FOR		
4) Abortion	AGN	8) Home School	AGN		

Election Results

2004 general	Jeion A.Ward	(D)	9,733	54.2%		$123,939
	Alvin Bryant	(R)	4,657	45.5%		$81,663

Campaign Contributions 2004 Law $2,150; Organized Labor $2,050; Finance $2,000; Transportation $1,680; Energy $1,750; Realty $1,500; Tech/Communications $1,150; Health Care $1,000; Business/Retail Svs $1,000; Agriculture $1,000; Public Employees $860; Political $610; Mfg $250; Candidate Self-financing $100; Defense $100.

Economic Interests, 2004 *Sal. & Wages,* $10,000+ Hampton Federation of Teachers; Northrop Grumman/Newport News shipyard.; Offices and Directorships: Hampton Federation of Teachers, President; Paymts for talks, meetings, and publications: $6,000 Natl Kidney Foundation, conference mtg-travel, registration; Gifts: $100 VA AFL-CIO, Jefferson Jackson Dinner; $89Altria, dinner; $71 Va cable, dinner; $96 Dominion VA, dinner; $59 McGuire Woods Consulting, dinner; $150 MEACC, athletic event tkts; $80 Kemper Consulting, dinner.

THIRD CONGRESSIONAL DISTRICT

HOUSE DISTRICT NINETY-FIVE, Mamye E. BaCote

POLITICAL AND LEGISLATIVE BACKGROUND

House District 95 consists of part of the City of Hampton comprised of the Tarrant, Wythe, Forrest, Kraft, Mallory, and Tucker Capps Precincts and part of Northampton Precinct; and part of the City of Newport News comprised of the Briarfield, Carver, Chestnut, Downtown, Dunbar, Huntington, Jefferson, Magruder, Marshall, New Market, Newsome Park, Reed, Washington, and Wilson Precincts and part of South Morrison Precinct.

Mamye E. BaCote replaced Flora D. Crittenden in the 2004 election. There were no legislative records.

Delegate HD 95

Mamye E. BaCote (D) Member House 2004 - ; b. Feb. 8, 1939, Halifax, VA, educ. VA Union University (AB, 1960), Hampton, Institute (MA 1967), spouse Theodore Edward BaCote, Jr., children: Theodore, III, Derek and Marlon,Roman Catholic.

Professor of Political Science, Women in Municipal Gov't,President, Hampton Roads Regional Jail Authority, V President, Peninsula Airport commission, Vice Chairman, and others. Awards: Invincible Women Award, Political Action Award.

Offices :Suite 1000, 2600 Washington Ave., Newport News, VA 23607,
(757) 244-4415; P.O. Box 406, Richmond, VA 23218, (804) 698-1095,
FAX (804) 786-6310.

2004 Committees General laws, Health, Welfare and Institutions, Transportation.

House Key Votes, 2004

Please see Introduction for more information on bills.

1) Budget Bill	AGN	5) Family Life	FOR	9) Morning After	AGN
2) Feticide	AGN	6) Fire Arms	AGN	10) Legal Aid	FOR
3) Marriage	AGN	7) Open Space	FOR		
4) Abortion	AGN	8) Home School	AGN		

Election Results

2004 general	Mamye E. BaCote	(D)	10,732	64.7%	$77,808
	Ray J. Johnson	(R)	4,562	34.8%	$49,731

Campaign Contributions 2004 Health Care $5,550; Finance $3,500; Transportation $2,639; Realty $2,300; Business/ Retail Svs $2,250; Law $2,100; Energy $1,400; Public Employees $905; Misc $770; Agriculture $750; Political $550; Defense $500; Tech/Communications $500; Organized Labor $350; Undetermined $305; Mfg $250.

Economic Interests, 2004 Personal Liabilities to $50,000: Town Bank, Old Point Natl Bank, loan or finance – VA Educators Credit Union; Gifts: $63 Bon Secours, dinner; $52 Menchville HS Class Reunion, dinner, cruise; $71 VA Cable, dinner; $100 Morton's Steak, 2 gift certificates; $280 Colonial Athletic League, game tks; $150 Norfolk State University, MEAC game tkts; $75 Kemper Consulting, dinner; $96 Dominion Power, dinner; $320 VA Beach Hotel-Motel Assoc, Legislative weekend.

Notes

SENATE DISTRICT THIRTEEN, *Frederick M. Quayle (R)*

POLITICAL AND LEGISLATIVE BACKGROUND
Senate District 13 consists of Surry County; the Isle of Wight County Precincts: Smithfield, Carrolton, Rushmere, Pons, Courthouse, Windsor, Orbit, Walters, Carrsville, and Zuni; the Prince George County Precincts: Templeton, Blackwater, Brandon, Courts Bldg, and Bland; the Southampton County Precincts: Berlin, Ivor, Sebrell, Hunterdale, Courtland, and Sedley; the City of Chesapeake Precincts: Churchland, Jolliff One, Fellowship Baptist Church, Silverwood, Taylor Road Fire Station, Bailey Creek, and Nansemond; the City of Franklin Precincts: 1-1, 2-1, 6-1; the City of Hopewell Precincts Ward 1-5; the City of Portsmouth Precincts: 10, 23-25, 29-36; and the City of Suffolk Precincts: Yeates, Driver, Ebenezer, Chuckatuck, King's Fork, Kilby's Mill, Holland, Lakeside, Elephant's Fork, Nansemond River, and Lake Meade.

Republican Frederick M. Quayle, a Chesapeake lawyer, has represented this district since 1991. New to state politics, Quayle upset the 16 year incumbent, Democrat Johnny S. Joannou by a margin of 493 votes in the newly drawn, heavily Republican district. In 1995, Quayle held onto his seat in a fierce and close re-match, winning by 51.3%. In 1997, Joannou won a seat in House District 79. In the 1999 election, Quayle won by 56.7% over Democrat E. M. Psimas.

During the 2004 session, Quayle sponsored twenty bills, eight passed. Those passed defined a motor vehicle as being screened from view when it was not visable by someone standing at ground level from outside of the property; extended the moratorium on city annexation proceedings; amended the city charter of Franklin to increase the salaries of school board members; and provided guidelines for financial compensation for persons who were wrongfully incarcerated.

Four bills carried over provide for the revocation or suspension of an optometrist's license when practicing in certain locations; authorize sheriffs offices to use unmarked vehicles; provide that real estate appraisers who appraised land, buildings, or structures or improved upon land should have a lien in the land, building, or structure in accordance with the agreed contract price; and provide that comprehensive plans for schools be developed in consultation with the school board and division superintendent in order to meet established levels of service based on future growth.

All four resolutions were successful.

Bills which failed would have allowed the Chesapeake City council to appoint members of the Board of Zoning Appeals; decreased the amount of money a locality paid to compensate a person whose livestock or poultry was killed or injured by a dog; and would have limited to six the number of animals that a person could adopt from a pound.

Senator SD 13

FOURTH CONGRESSIONAL DISTRICT

Frederick MacDonald Quayle (R); Member of Senate: 1992- ; b. Feb. 16, 1936, Suffolk; home, 3925 Point Elizabeth Dr., Chesapeake 23321; educ. Univ. of VA (BA); T.C. Williams Sch. of Law, Univ. Richmond (LLB); married, Brenda Lee Smith; Episcopalian.

Attorney; Assistant Professor in government and public affairs, Christopher Newport University; N. Suffolk Rotary; Chairman Chippoakes Plantation Farm Foundation.

Offices 3808 Poplar Hill Rd., Suite E, Chesapeake 23321-5524; 800-742-8255; GA Bldg., Capitol Sq., Rm. 310, Richmond 23219; 804-698-7513.

2004 Committees *Local Government, Chair; Courts of Justice; Education and Health; Finance; Rules.*

Senate Key Votes, 2004
Please see Introduction for more information on bills.

1) Budget Bill	FOR	5) Family Life	FOR	9)Charter Schools	FOR
2) Feticide	FOR	6) Fire Arms	FOR	10) Legal Aid	FOR
3) Marriage	FOR	7) Open Space	FOR		
4) Child Abuse	FOR	8) Home School	FOR		

Election Results

1999 general	Frederick M. Quayle	(R)	17,789	56.7%	$260,787
	E. M. Psimas	(D)	13,532	43.1%	$145,799

Campaign Contributions 2004 Campaign Contributions 2000-June 30, 2002 Medical $8,350; **Realty/Constr.** $4,050; **Tech./Comm.** $3,800; **Attys.** $2,631; **Finance** $1,250; **Tobacco--PM** $1,000; **Electric** $1,000; **HMOs** $1,000; **Kings Dom.** $1,000; **Transp.** $1,000 (Motorcyclists $250); **Nat. Gas** $500; **Honeywell** $500; **NNShipbldg.** $500; **Billboards** $500; **Serv. Stat./Conv. St.** $250; **Pub. Empl.** $250; **James Hazel** $250.

Economic Interests, 2004 *Pay. for Talks, Mtgs., & Publ.,* $2,554 State, Southern Legislative Conference mtg., expenses), *Gifts,* $79 Hampton Rds Maritime Assoc., dinner; $82 UVA, transportation, dinner, tkt; $192 VA Sheriff Assoc., dinner; $183 Harrison Opera House, tkts; $357McCaulay & Burtch, dinner; $112 McGuire Woods Consulting, dinner; $103 VA Cable, dinner; $113 Dominion Resourses, dinner; $174 VA Agribusiness council, dinner.

SENATE DISTRICT FOURTEEN, *Harry Burne Blevins (R)*

POLITICAL AND LEGISLATIVE BACKGROUND

Senate District 14 includes the City of Chesapeake Precincts: Great Bridge, Bethel, Deep Creek, Greenbrier, Bells Mill, Geneva Park, Gilmerton, B. M. Williams School, Hickory Grove, Indian Creek, Indian River, Norfolk Highlands, Oak Grove, Tanglewood, Westover, Hickory Middle School, Great Bridge Middle School, Bridgetown, Lake Drummond, River Birch, John T. West, Parkways, Pleasant Crossing, Bells Mill II, Green Sea, Grassfield Part 1, Grassfield Part 2; the City of Virginia Beach

FOURTH CONGRESSIONAL DISTRICT

Precincts: Creeds, Blackwater, Timberlake, Green Run, Salem, Glenwood, Dahlia, parts of Courthouse and Rosemont Forest.

Harry B. Blevins, a high school principal and a Republican, is the new Senator for this district, elected in a special September, 2001 election, without opposition. Blevins was the first legislator to run in an election using the newly redistricted senate districts. This Senate seat was opened when the Republican incumbent, Randy Forbes, was elected to Congress during a summer special election, defeating Democrat Louise Lucas (D-18). This was the second time Blevins had followed Forbes into office. In December 1997, Forbes, then a Delegate, won the Senate seat vacated by Mark Earley who had won election as Attorney General. Blevins won the House seat over Democrat A. Robinson Winn in a January 1998 election.

During the 2004 session, Blevins sponsored twelve bills, eight passed. Bills that passed provide that an employer not have to pay benefit charges in unemployment cases caused by a temporary work stoppage due to a disaster which resulted in a state of emergency; mandated the requirement for emergency electrical service for assisted living facilities of over six residents; required that only sheriffs and deputies serve show cause orders; and increased the sheriffs fees for services such as: repossessions, levies, evictions, and sheriff's sales.

Two bills carried over provide that certain maps be excluded from the mandatory disclosure requirement of the Freedom of Information Act (FOIA) and require the Department of Transportation to reimburse the City of Chesapeake for the costs of maintaining and operating draw bridges within its boundaries.

Seven resolutions were successful.

Bills that failed would have allowed the City of Chesapeake to appoint members of the Board of Zoning appeals and provide an exemption from the retail sales tax to non profit organizations that provided services to people with brain-related disorders and disabilities.

Senator SD 14

Harry Burne Blevins (R) Member Senate: 2001- ; Member House 1998- 2001; b. August 22, 1935, Elk Park, NC; address 849 Mt. Pleasant Rd., Chesapeake 23322; educ. E. Carolina Univ. (B.S.), Univ. VA (M.Ed.); married Margie White; Baptist.

High School Principal. Member: Chesapeake Civitan Club (past pres.), Chesapeake Rotary Club (past pres.), Chesapeake Chamber of Comm. (past bd. of dir.); Awards: VA Outstanding Secondary School Principal, Chesapeake First Citizen, VA H.S. League Hall of Fame.

Offices P.O. Box 16207, Chesapeake 23328; 757-546-2435; FAX 757-546-7346; GA Bldg., Rm. 306, Capitol Sq., Richmond 23219; 804-698-7514.

2004 Committees *Agriculture, Conservation and Natural Resources; Courts of Justice; Education and Health; Transportation.*

Senate Key Votes, 2004
Please see Introduction for more information on bills.

1) Budget Bill	FOR	5) Family Life	FOR	9)Charter Schools	FOR
2) Feticide	FOR	6) Fire Arms	FOR	10) Legal Aid	FOR

FOURTH CONGRESSIONAL DISTRICT

3) Marriage   FOR   7) Open Space   FOR
4) Child Abuse   AGN   8) Home School   AGN

Election Results
2001 special   Harry B. Blevins   (R)   3,096   97.9% $20,823

Campaign Contributions 2000-June 30, 2002   **Medical** $8,350; **Realty/Constr.** $4,050; **Tech./Comm.** $3,800; **Attys.** $2,631; **Finance** $1,250; **Tobacco--PM** $1,000; **Electric** $1,000; **HMOs** $1,000; **Kings Dom.** $1,000; **Transp.** $1,000 (Motorcyclists $250); **Nat. Gas** $500; **Honeywell** $500; **NNShipbldg.** $500; **Billboards** $500; **Serv. Stat./Conv. St.** $250; **Pub. Empl.** $250; **James Hazel** $250.

Economic Interests, 2004 *Off. & Dir.*, Bank Hampton Roads, Adv. Board; *Sec.,* $10,001-$50,000 ea.: mutual funds, bonds, stocks: Sprint, United Dom. Realty; Paymts for talks, meetings, publications: $2,008, NCSL meeting; *Gifts,* $158 Hampton Rds Maritime Assoc., dinner; $178 Johnson & Johnson, dinner; $126 Bon Secours, dinner; $136 MCI, dinner; *Real Estate,* 942+ acres timberland, farmland w/others.

SENATE DISTRICT FIFTEEN, *Frank M. Ruff, Jr. (R)*

POLITICAL AND LEGISLATIVE BACKGROUND
Senate District 15 consists of Appomattox, Charlotte, Fluvanna, Halifax, Mecklenburg, and Prince Edward Counties; the Amherst County Precincts: Wright Shop, New Glasgow, and Courthouse Precincts, part of Temperance; the Brunswick County Precincts: Brodnax, Rock Store, Tillman, and Dromgoole; the Buckingham County Precincts: New Canton, White Hall, Curdsville, New Store, Maysville, Wrights, Slate River, and Gold Hill; Cumberland County's Precinct 5 and part of Precinct 4; and the Lunenburg County Precincts: Plymouth, Brown's Store, McCoy Ghee's Store, Arrowhead Gun Club, Pleasant Grove, Reedy Creek, Peoples Community Center, Meherrin Fire Dept, Courthouse.

Frank M. Ruff, Jr., a furniture store owner from Clarksville, and a Republican, has been the Senator for this district since his election in 2000. The seat was opened upon the death of the incumbent, Richard J. Holland, a banker and a Democrat, who had served since 1979. Ruff defeated Democrat Jerry Flowers, who had run against Holland in 1995. In the 1999 election, Holland faced Republican Thomas C. Wright, Jr., a supermarket owner, and although outspent, Holland won with 53.7% of the vote. Wright won Ruff's former seat in House District 61. Ruff himself had lost his first race against Senator Louis Lucas (D-18) in 1991, and later won the House seat in 1993, defeating incumbent Lewis Parker, a Democrat.

During the 2004 session, Ruff sponsored twelve bills, nine passed. These bills abolished the Interagency Coordinating Council on Housing for the Disabled; eliminated the requirement that the Virginia Employment Commission create a workforce plan for use in times of economic recession, natural disaster, or military mobilization; and established the Center for Rural Virginia to maintain economic growth in rural areas.

No bills were carried over to the 2005 session.

Two of the three resolutions were successful.

Bills that failed would have established a Tiered Incentive Program to provide corporate income tax credits to create jobs in economically distressed areas; and financial relief to an injured state employee.

Senator SD 15

Frank Miller Ruff, Jr. (R) Member Senate: 2001- ; Member House: 1994- 2000; b. Bedford, VA, Sept. 22, 1949; home, Rt. 1, Box 24, Clarksville 23927; educ. Univ. of Richmond; married, Jessica T. Bowne; Presbyterian.

Pres., Brentwood Manor Furnishing Store; former member, Mecklenburg County Board of Supervisors; former Chair County's Recycling Comm.; Vice-Chair, Eastern VA, Roanoke River Basin Assn.; Pres., Clarksville Chamber of Commerce; USAR 1971-77); Twin River Masonic Lodge.

Offices P.O. Box 332, Clarksville 23927; 434-372-0551; GA Bldg., Rm. 307, Capitol Sq., Richmond 23219; 804-698-7515.

2004 Committees *Agriculture, Conservation and Natural Resources; Education and Health; General Laws; Local Government.*

Senate Key Votes, 2004
Please see Introduction for more information on bills.

1) Budget Bill	FOR	5) Family Life	FOR	9)Charter Schools	FOR
2) Feticide	FOR	6) Fire Arms	FOR	10) Legal Aid	FOR
3) Marriage	FOR	7) Open Space	AGN		
4) Child Abuse	AGN	8) Home School	FOR		

Election Results

2000 general	Frank M. Ruff	(R)	30,395	51.1%	$388,983
	Jerry B. Flowers III	(D)	28,235	47.5%	$155,815
	A. D. Neill	(I)	826	1.4%	$ None

Campaign Contributions 2004 Campaign Contributions 2000-June 30, 2002 Realty/Constr.
$9,150; **Medical** $8,395; **Repub.** $6,700; **Finance** $4,400; **Individ.** $4,080; **Attys.** $3,800; **Tech./Comm.** $3,250; **Publ. Empl.** $3,150; **Tobacco** $2,900 (Star Sci. $1,000, PM $750); **Insur./HMOs** $2,605; **Paper** $2,600; **Electric** $2,450; **Transp.** $2,250 (Auto Dealers/Manuf. $1,000); **Retail** $1,649; **Lumber** $1,620; **Metals** $1,000; **NNShipbldg.** $1,000; **Coal** $1,000; **Nat. Gas** $750; **Beer** $750; **Farm/Landscape/Food Proc.** $710; **Billboards** $500; **NRA** $500; **Kings Dom.** $500; **Serv. Stat./Conv. St.** $500; **Oil** $350; **Trash** $250; **Funeral** $250; **Misc. Manuf.** $125; **Misc. Defense** $100.

Economic Interests, 2004 *Off. & Dir.*, Brentwood Manor, VP; *Sec.*, $50,000+ ea.: mutual funds (2); $10,001-$50,000 stock Brentwood Manor; *Pay. for Talks, Mtgs., & Publ.*, $445 State, ALEC mtg, travel compensation; $2,504 state, ALEC conference, travel expenses; $200 state, NCSL meeting,

FOURTH CONGRESSIONAL DISTRICT

compensation; $300 state, SCSL meeting, compensation; $750 RUPRI, meeting, travel; $800 RUPRI, SCSL meeting, travel; *Gifts*, $336 Philip Morris (2 dinners, gift box), $172 Glaxo-SmithKline (dinner, show), $95 Sprint (dinner), $70 Geico, dinner; $157 Astra Zeneca, dinner; $65 Sprint, dinner, reception; $150 VA Tech Athletics, game tkts; $200 VA Horse Council, lodging and trail ride; $150 Altria, dinner; $55 VA Cable, dinner; $150 Reynolds, luggage; $60 VA Agribusiness, dinner; Real Estate more than $50,000: rental property, condo.

SENATE DISTRICT EIGHTEEN, *L. Louise Lucas (D)*

POLITICAL AND LEGISLATIVE BACKGROUND

Senate District 18 includes the Counties of Greensville, Nottoway, Sussex; the City of Emporia; Brunswick County Precincts: Edgerton, Fitzhugh, Alberta, Danieltown, Elmore, Seymour, Sturgeon, King's Store, Lawrenceville; the Camps Mill Precinct of the Isle of Wight County; Lunenburg County's Parham's Store and Hound's Creek Precincts; Southampton County Precincts: Boykins, Branchville, Capron, Drewryville, Forks-of-the-River, Blackwater River, Newsoms; City of Chesapeake Precincts: Camelot, Oscar Smith School, E. W. Chittum School, St. Julians, Johnson Park, Sunray I and II, South Norfolk Recreation; City of Franklin Precincts: 3-1, 4-1, and 5-1; City of Portsmouth Precincts: 1, 5, 7, 9, 11, 13, 14, 16, 17, 19, 20-22, 26-28; City of Suffolk Precincts: White Marsh, John F. Kennedy, Cypress Chapel, Airport, Whaleyville, Holy Neck, Olde Towne, Hollywood.

Louise Lucas, a business entrepreneur and a Democrat, has represented this area since 1991. In the redistricting that year, the total picture of the district was changed, and a Senate black majority district (60.17%) was formed. Howard P. Anderson, the Democratic incumbent, chose to resign, having served from 1958-1972 in the House, and from 1972-1991 in the Senate. Lucas, the first African-American woman elected to Portsmouth's City Council, won the Democratic Primary, and then the seat with 52% of the vote over Republican Frank M. Ruff. In 1995, Lucas defeated former Delegate Frank Slayton, who ran as an Independent, and Lucas was unopposed in the 1999 election. Also in 1999, Lucas resigned her position at Norfolk State University to go into business for herself.

During the 2004 session, Lucas sponsored five bills, two passed. Bills that passed authorize school boards to create joint or regional schools with a specialized curriculum and authorized that a physician's assistant who is practicing under the supervision of a physician could pronounce death under specified circumstances; a bill would have required children to wear an approved Coast Guard flotation apparatus on recreational vehicles under twenty-one feet in length was also proposed.

One bill carried over would have established drug treatment courts within the current structure of Virginia's court system.

All six resolutions were successful.

Senator SD 18

FOURTH CONGRESSIONAL DISTRICT

L. Louise Lucas (D), Member of Senate: 1992- ; b. Jan. 22, 1944, Portsmouth; home, Portsmouth; educ. Norfolk State Univ. (BS, MA); Methodist.

Exec. Dir., Lucas Lodge, LLC, Pres. Southside Direct Care Provider; Formerly Assistant Professor/Academic Affairs, Norfolk State Univ.; former mem. Portsmouth City Council, 1984-88; member, NAACP, Natl. Women's Political Caucus, Natl. Political Congress of Black Women; Natl. Council Christians & Jews, Eastern Star; Martin Luther King Leadership Steering Comm.

Offices P.O. Box 700, Portsmouth 23705-0700; 757-397-8200; GA Bldg., Capitol Sq., Rm. 328, Capitol Sq., Richmond 23219; 804-698-7518.

2004 Committees *Courts of Justice; Education and Health; Local Government; Rehabilitation and Social Services.*

Senate Key Votes, 2004
Please see Introduction for more information on bills.

1) Budget Bill	FOR	5) Family Life	FOR	9) Charter Schools	NV
2) Feticide	AGN	6) Fire Arms	FOR	10) Legal Aid	FOR
3) Marriage	AGN	7) Open Space	FOR		
4) Child Abuse	FOR	8) Home School	AGN		

Election Results

1999 general	L. Louise Lucas	(D)	18,592	99.0%	$52,711

Campaign Contributions 2001 Campaign Contributions 2000-June 30, 2002   Medical $4,150; **Realty/Constr.** $2,500; **Tech./Comm.** $1,500; **Tobacco--PM** $1,000; **Dist. Spirits** $250; **Attys.** $150.

Economic Interests, 2004 *Sal. & Wages,* $10,000+ Lucas Lodge, LLC; *Off. & Dir.,* Lucas Lodge, LLC, Exec. Dir.; Southside Direct Care Provider, Pres., Lucus Bonding, President, Natl Employment Agency, President, Portsmouth Day Support Program, President, Southside Direct Care Support, President, Lucas Transportation, President ; *Sec.,* $50,000+ Mutual funds; *Pay. for Talks, Mtgs., & Publ.,* $3,074 state (NCSL travel, per diem); *Gifts,* $63 Bon Secours, reception, dinner; $650 Anheuser-Busch, admission tks; 68 Washington Gas, dinner; $56 Dominion Resources, dinner; $87 Dominion Resources, dinner; *Bus. Int.,* $50,000/less ea.: Lucas Lodge, LLC (group home), Southside Direct Care Provider (adult care res.); *Real Estate,*Twelve prop.

HOUSE DISTRICT FIFTY-SIX, *William Robert "Bill" Janis (R)*

POLITICAL AND LEGISLATIVE BACKGROUND
House District 56 consists of all of Goochland and Louisa Counties; and part of Henrico County comprised of the Lauderdale, Sadler, Causeway, Stoney Run, and West End Precincts.

FOURTH CONGRESSIONAL DISTRICT

W. R. "Bill" Janis, an attorney and a Republican, is the new representative for this district. Although Janis was unopposed in the 2001 November election, other Republicans had sought the chance to run for this seat opened with the retirement of long term incumbent, V. Earl Dickinson, a Democrat and lumber executive.

Dickinson had represented the area since 1972, unopposed in all but three general elections. He was the chairman of the powerful Appropriations Committee, and later with the shift in political power in the House, he shared his chairmanship with Delegate Vincent Callahan (R-34) until the 2001 session.

During the 2004 session, Janis sponsored nineteen bills, ten passed. The bills that passed provide that a copy of a concealed handgun permit will become a defacto permit if the court does not grant or deny the permit within forty-five days of receiving the completed applications; allow the holder of a valid concealed weapons permit to purchase more than one handgun a month; specify that anyone who intentionally drives away without paying for gasoline may be charged with larceny and a civil penalty; and established that DUI is a reportable offense to the Central Criminal Records Exchange.

One bill carried over requires that surplus revenues be refunded to taxpayers when these revenues exceed the amount required to be deposited in the Revenue Stabilization Fund by at least $50 million dollars.

Three out of four resolutions were successful.

Bills that failed provided that assault and battery in the commission of a larceny that results in bodily injury constitutes a crime punishable from two to twenty years in a state prison; that skydiving activity sponsors of skydiving professionals are not liable for the death or injury of a skydiving participant; and exempted manufacturers or sellers from liability for claims of injury due to voluntary use of food products containing obvious dangers.

Delegate HD 56

William Robert "Bill" Janis (R) Member House: 2001-; b. October 15, 1962, Chicago; home, 11404 Maple Hill Place, Glen Allen 23059; educ. VMI (B.A.), Univ. VA Sch. Law (J.D.); married, Rose Ann Hunter; Roman Catholic.

Attorney-at-law; U.S. Navy 1984-1995; Member: St. Benedict's; Knights of Columbus; VFW; Am. Legion; U.S. Navy League; Order of the Arrow; Fed. Society; NRA; Awards: Meritorious Service Medal; Navy Commendation Medal (two awards); Navy Achievement Medal (two awards); Eagle Scout BSA.

Offices P.O. Box 306, Oilville 23129; 804-527-1868; GA Bldg., Rm. 705, Capitol Sq., Richmond 23219; 804-698-1056.

2004 Committees *Courts of Justice; Education; Militia, Police and Public Safety.*

House Key Votes, 2004
Please see Introduction for more information on bills.

1) Budget Bill	FOR	5) Family Life	AGN	9) Morning After	FOR
2) Feticide	FOR	6) Fire Arms	FOR	10) Legal Aid	AGN
3) Marriage	FOR	7) Open Space	AGN		
4) Abortion	FOR	8) Home School	FOR		

Election Results

FOURTH CONGRESSIONAL DISTRICT

2004	general	W. R. "Bill" Janis (R)	17,620	57.8%	$358,161
		Hunter McGuire (D)		42.2%	$338,255

Campaign Contributions 2004 Realty $11,300; Political $10,825; Law $10,600; Transportation $7,700; Energy $5,660;Misc $5,530; Finance $5,420; Business/Retail Svs $5,350; Health Care $3,850; Tech/Communications $2,150; Agriculture $1,800; Mfg $1,700; Public Employees $1,250; Single-Issue Groups $750; Undetermined $250.

Economic Interests, 2004 *Sal. & Wages*, $10,000+ ea.: Robert Half International(spouse); *Off. & Dir.*, New South Investment Corp. (FL), Dir.; *Pers. Liabil.*, $10,001-$50,000 savings inst.; *Sec.*, $50,000+ mutual fund; Business Interests $50,000 or less: W.R. Janis, PLLC,law; Gifts: $130 Altria, dinner; $145 VA Cable, dinner; $135 Kings Dominion, tickets; $295 VA Beach Hotel-Motel Assoc, Legislative weekend; $280 Americans for Tax Reform, lodging; $394 VA Horse Council, trail ride.

HOUSE DISTRICT SIXTY-TWO, *Riley E. Ingram (R)*

POLITICAL AND LEGISLATIVE BACKGROUND
House District 62 consists of part of Chesterfield County comprised of the Enon, Point Of Rocks, and Salem Church Precincts and part of the Bellwood Precinct; part of Henrico County comprised of the Town Hall, Sandston, Seven Pines, Whitlocks, and Dorey Precincts; part of the City of Hopewell comprised of the Ward 3, Ward 4, Ward 5, Ward 7, and Ward 1 Precincts; and part of Prince George County comprised of the Richard Bland College, Templeton, Union Branch, Rives, Blackwater, Brandon, Jefferson Park, and Bland Precincts and part of the Courts Building Precinct.

Riley E. Ingram, a real estate broker, and a Republican, has represented this district since 1992 when he defeated 12-year incumbent and Democrat R. Beasley Jones in the newly drawn district, being the first to challenge Jones since 1982.. Earlier, in 1989, Ingram, former mayor of the city of Hopewell, had lost to Democrat C. Hardaway Marks with 44% of the vote. Ingram has defeated Democratic challenges in 1993 and 1995. He has been unopposed since then. Ingram chairs the Counties, Cities and Towns Committee.

During the 2004 session, Ingram sponsored seventeen bills, nine passed. These bills require state employees who are applying for long-term disability benefits under the Virginia Sickness and Disability Program to also apply for Social Security benefits; provide for compensation for the state's part of the health insurance premiums for law-enforcement officers in the line of duty; allow a local treasurer or tax collector to sell tax delinquent property; and require that when the Virginia Department of Transportation (VDOT) when granted permission for a landfill gas pipeline within any highway right-of-way to also give notice to every county where the pipeline would pass.

One bill carried over would have required the Department of Transportation to submit a conversation plan for approval to the Department of Conservation and Recreation (DCR) for every project that involved land-disturbing activity.

Eleven of twelve resolutions passed.

Bills that failed would have changed the term maternity leave to medical absence due to pregnancy when describing some of several short-term disabilities; provided that mopeds be considered motorcycles when operated on a highway; would have added firefighters of the Virginia National Guard Fire and Rescue to the Virginia Law Officers Retirement system; and allowed the State Forester to collect civil penalties when there is no notification of the commercial harvesting of timber.

Delegate HD 62

Riley Edward Ingram (R); Member House: 1992-; b. Oct. 1, 1941, Halifax County; home, 714 Cedar Level Rd., Hopewell 23860; educ., graduate, Realtor's Institute, Univ. VA Continuing Educ.; married, Mary Ann Brinkley; Church of Nazarene.

Broker; former Mayor, city of Hopewell; member, Crater Planning Dist. Comm.; member, Hopewell Redev. and Housing Auth.; Realtor of the Year - Southside Realtors; member, Hopewell - Prince George Cham. Commerce, Jaycees, Moose Lodge 1472, Am. Legion, Rotary; Mason; NRA; Natl. guard; USA 1960; USAR Band (1962-68); Ducks Unlim.; Sovran Tri-City adv. bd.; Wild Turkey Fed.

Offices 3302 Oaklawn Blvd., Hopewell 23860; 804-458-9873; GA Bldg., Rm. 413, Richmond 23219; 804-698-1062.

2004 Committees *Counties, Cities and Towns, Chair; Appropriations; Privileges and Elections.*

House Key Votes, 2004
Please see Introduction for more information on bills.

1) Budget Bill	FOR	5) Family Life	FOR	9) Morning After	FOR
2) Feticide	FOR	6) Fire Arms	FOR	10) Legal Aid	FOR
3) Marriage	FOR	7) Open Space	FOR		
4) Abortion	FOR	8) Home School	FOR		

Election Results

2004 general	Riley E. Ingram	(R)	14,476	98.7%	$79,010

Campaign Contributions 2004 Realty $6,980; Agriculture $4,728; Finance $4,250; Health Care $3,840; Transportation $3,150; Energy $2,875; Business/Retail Svs $2,855; Law $2,110; Public Employees $1,735; Mfg $1,580; Tech/Communications $1,250.

Economic Interests, 2004 *Sal. & Wages*, $10,000+ ea.: Ingram & Assoc. Real Estate Co., Inc.; Bridgestone-Firestone Tire & Rubber Co. (spouse, retirement); *Off. & Dir.*, Ingram & Assoc. Real Estate, Pres.; Ingram & Assoc. Insur. Agency, Pres.; BB&T Bank (Hopewell), Adv. Bd.; *Pers. Liabil.*, $50,000+ Banks; *Sec.*, $50,000+ ea.: savings cert., stocks in: own realty co., Capitol One, BB&T Bank, realty prtnships (2); $10,001-$50,000 ea.: checking acct., savings cert., realty partnership, stocks in: own insur. co., tires, First Union; *Pay. for Talks, Mtgs., & Pub.*, $325 Am. Legislative Exchange, expenses, per diem), $1,895 state, American Legislative Exchange council mtg; Business Interests More than $50,000:

Ingram & Assoc., rental property, rental apts.,half interest in 58 developed lots; $50,000 or less: Branchester Assoc, land, Charles City Project 1, land, rental bldg., rental house, rental bldgs., two rental houses, vacant lot; Sec. more than $50,000: BB&T bank stock, Ingram & Assoc., Bridgestone-Firestone Tire & Rubber, Capitol One stock, BB&T svgs certificates, partners with Henshaw; land and lot sales.

Gifts, $228 Reynolds, luggage bag; $84 Agri ibusiness, golf tournament; $125 Reynolds, golf outing and ALEC conference; $269 Vectre Crop, Kings Dominion tkts; $109 Altria, dinner; $152 Altria, Kraft Days Reception; $223 Altria, NASCAR Busch race; $346 Altria, NEXTEL Cup race; $163 Altria, NASCAR race; $336 Altria, NESCAR NEXTEL race; $249 Altria, INDY race; $159 Phillip Morris, Open House; Real Estate: 48 houses, 5 commercial bldgs, 10 apts, 9 vacant lots, 10 duplexes.

HOUSE DISTRICT SIXTY-THREE, *Fenton. Lee Bland, Jr. (D)*

POLITICAL AND LEGISLATIVE BACKGROUND

House District 63 consists of all of Dinwiddie County; all of the City of Petersburg; and part of Chesterfield County comprised of the Ettrick and Matoaca Precincts and part of the Branches Precinct.

Fenton. L. Bland, Jr., a mortician, and a former member of the Petersburg City Council, is the representative for this district. Bland, a Democrat, won the 2001 election with 52.5% of the vote over Independent candidate Rosalyn R. Dance, losing only Dinwiddie County to his opponent. The seat was opened with the retirement of Democrat Jay W. DeBoer, an attorney, who had represented the area since 1983, easily defeating all challenges.

Less than three weeks before the Democrats held a caucus in August 2001 to choose between Bland and Christopher T. White to run for the delegate seat, Bland moved his residency to Petersburg where his parents live. His other home, where his wife and children live, is in Prince George County, as is his business. In 2002, four Petersburg residents filed petitions with the city's registrar charging that Bland does not live in Petersburg. Bland had changed his voter's card, driver's license, and other documents to Petersburg, and the registrar dismissed the complaint, according to *The Richmond Free Press*.

During the 2004 session, Bland sponsored four bills, two passed. These authorized the Virginia Employment Commission to convey real property in Petersburg to the City of Petersburg and amended the duties of the Secretary of Commerce and Trade to prepare a report on the status of the urban areas of the Commonwealth in the first year of a governor's administration.

One bill carried over would have permitted those who were entitled to an income tax refund to contribute from $1.00 to the entire refund amount to the Petersburg Public Education Foundation.

Two resolutions were successful.

No bills failed to pass.

FOURTH CONGRESSIONAL DISTRICT

Delegate HD 63

Fenton Lee Bland, Jr. (D) Member House: 2002-; b. (no date given) Petersburg; home, 1103 Booker Circle, Petersburg 23803; educ. VA State Univ. (B.S.), John Tyler Comm. Coll. (A.A.S.); married, Elisabeth Edwards; Baptist.

Mortician; Petersburg City Council 1992-1994; Member: Mt. Olivet Bap. Church; oKappa Alpha Psi; Epsilon Nu Delha Mor.; National Crematin Soc.; Natl. Funeral Directors; John Tyler Comm. Coll. Fndn.; Metrop. Business League; Awards: Top 40 Under 40 - Inside Business Mag. (1999); Metrop. Business League Entrepreneur of the Year.

Offices 1103 Booker Circle, Petersburg 23803; 804-648-8361; GA Bldg., Rm. 407, Capitol Sq., Richmond 23219; 804-698-1063.

2004 Committees *Militia, Police and Public Safety; Privileges and Elections; Science and Technology.*

House Key Votes, 2004

Please see Introduction for more information on bills.

1) Budget Bill	AGN	5) Family Life	FOR	9) Morning After	AGN
2) Feticide	AGN	6) Fire Arms	AGN	10) Legal Aid	FOR
3) Marriage	AGN	7) Open Space	FOR		
4) Abortion	AGN	8) Home School	AGN		

Election Results

2001 general	Fenton. L. Bland, Jr.	(D)	8,774	99.5%	$21,890

Campaign Contributions 2004 Transportation $1,250; Energy $1,250; Law $1,000; Public Employees $750; Agriculture $750; Organized Labor $500; Health Care $500; Finance $500; Tech/Communication $500; Realty $250.

Economic Interests, 2004 *Pers. Liabil.,* $50,000+ ea.: banks (self), (family), savings inst. (self), (family); $10,001-$50,000 loan/finance (self), (family); insur. co. (self), (family); *Sec.,* $10,001-$50,000 stocks in bank; *Bus. Int.,* $50,000+; Consolidated Bk & Trust, stocks; *Real Estate* personal properties w/spouse; Gifts: $400 King's Dominion, general admission; $72 VA Cable, dinner.

HOUSE DISTRICT SIXTY-FOUR, *William K. Barlow (D)*

POLITICAL AND LEGISLATIVE BACKGROUND

House District 64 consists of all of Surry County; all of the City of Williamsburg; part of the City of Franklin comprised of Precinct 1-1; part of Isle of Wight County comprised of the Smithfield, Carrollton, Rushmere, Pons, Courthouse, Windsor, Orbit, Walters, Carrsville, and Zuni Precincts; part of James City County comprised of the Jamestown A, Jamestown B, and Jamestown C Precincts and parts of the Berkeley A, Berkeley B, Powhatan A, Powhatan B, and Roberts A Part 1 Precincts; and part of Southampton County comprised of the Hunterdale and Sedley Precincts.

William K. Barlow, a Smithfield attorney, and a Democrat, has represented the area since 1991. The seat was opened upon the retirement of Democrat C. Hardaway Marks, first elected in 1961. In 1993 and 1995, Barlow defeated Republican Debra E. Quesinberry, was unopposed in 1997, and defeated two candidates in the 1999 election. A *Virginian-Pilot* editorial backed Barlow as "knowledgeable about the fiscal problems of localities" and noted that the Sierra Club had given Barlow a high rating for votes on smart growth and the environment.

FOURTH CONGRESSIONAL DISTRICT

The Republican redistricting plan eliminated an eastern district, and placed Barlow and Delegate George Grayson (D-97) into the same district, making Grayson's 97th House District an "incumbent-free" district. Grayson said he would not challenge Barlow, and considered various options including a move to another district, but ultimately retired after approximately a quarter century of service to his district. In the 2001 election, Barlow trounced Republican Richard E. Hill, Jr., an attorney, winning with 60.6% of the vote. Hill came within 20 votes of capturing James City County, but Barlow led overwhelmingly in all other areas.

During the 2004 session, Barlow sponsored nineteen bills, five passed; five were carried over to the 2005 session. Bills which passed provide for civil penalty for violating a confined animal feeding operation permit that is covered by a Virginia Pollution abatement permit; allowed James City county to regulate illumination levels of property zoned for commercial or business purposes; and amended the charter of the City of Williamsburg to permit underground utility districts after a petition is signed by three-fourths of the landowners in the proposed district.

Five bills carried over provided that decedent in a wrongful death who had a will to have the death award distributed in accordance with the will; set the terms for appointing a guardian or a conservator for mentally retarded individuals; required the owners of water systems and small water utilities to prepare a cost study of an emergency electrical generation system which is filed with the State Corporation Commission; and required the transfer of control from the developer after five years if no significant number of units have been built or are under construction in a time-share program.

One resolution was successful.

Bills which failed would have authorized counties or cities to provide for an instant run off voting method to determine winners for the governing body or the school board; prohibited smoking in public restrooms in restaurants; and allowed governing bodies to make modifications, including addition to official maps without submitting a report to the planning commission or holding a public hearing.

Delegate HD 64

William K. Barlow (D); Member of House: 1992- ; b. March 13, 1936, Isle of Wight County; home, 219 Moonshine Dr., Smithfield 23430; educ. Virginia Tech (BS), Univ. of VA Law School (LLB); married Anne Taylor Rowell; Baptist.

Attorney; member: Smithfield Rotary Club; Smithfield Ruritan; Virginia Tech Alumni Assn. (past Pres.); Smithfield Baptist Church moderator and past chm. Bd. Deacons; USAF (1958-62).

Offices P.O. Box 240, Smithfield 23431; 757-357-9720; GA Bldg., Capitol Sq., Rm. 421, Richmond 23219; 804-698-1064.

2004 Committees *Courts of Justice; General Laws; Militia, Police and Public Safety.*

House Key Votes, 2004
Please see Introduction for more information on bills.

FOURTH CONGRESSIONAL DISTRICT

1) Budget Bill	AGN	5) Family Life	FOR	9) Morning After	AGN
2) Feticide	FOR	6) Fire Arms	FOR	10) Legal Aid	FOR
3) Marriage	FOR	7) Open Space	FOR		
4) Abortion	AGN	8) Home School	AGN		

Election Results

2001 general	William K. Barlow	(D)	13,059	56.6%	$153,853
	Troy Lapetina	(R)	8,463	43.4%	$61,913

Campaign Contributions 2004 Law $3,750; Energy $1,500; Transportation $1,250; Tech/Communications $750; Public Employees $500; Health Care $500; Business/Retail Svs $500; Finance $500; Realty $500; Agriculture $250; Defense $250.

Economic Interests, 2004 *Sal. & Wages*, $10,000+ Suanders Barlow & Riddick Babineau law; *Sec.*, $10,001-$50,000 ea.: mutual fund, stocks in banks (2), GTE; *Bus. Int.*, $50,000/less Barlow & Riddick, P.C.; *Pay. for Rep. Gen.*, $10,001-$50,000 localities; $1,001-$10,000 other; *Real Estate*, Two farms w/family, office bldg.

HOUSE DISTRICT SIXTY-SIX, *M. Kirkland "Kirk" Cox (R)*

POLITICAL AND LEGISLATIVE BACKGROUND

House District 66 consists of all of the City of Colonial Heights; and part of Chesterfield County comprised of the South Chester, North Chester, Harrowgate, Wells, Ecoff, Dutch Gap, Iron Bridge, Winfrees Store, Beach, Winterpock, Walthall, and Bailey Bridge Precincts and part of the Branches Precinct.

M. Kirkland "Kirk" Cox, a Republican and high school government teacher, has represented this area since 1990. Cox upset the incumbent Democrat John "Chip" Dicks in 1989. Dicks later became a lobbyist. Cox has easily defeated Democratic opposition since, and was unopposed in 1993, 1997, 1999, and 2001. Cox co-chaired the Chesapeake and Its Tributaries Committee in 2001, and was appointed to the Joint Legislative Audit and Review Commission. Cox served on the Joint Reapportionment Committee in 2000 to lay the groundwork with the census for drawing up the new district maps.

During the 2004 session, Cox sponsored twenty-one bills, eighteen passed. These bills reduce the maximum number of copies of state publications that must be submitted to the Library of Virginia; abolish the Advisory Committee on Certified Practices; the Board of Military Affairs; combined the boards for the Virginia Industries for the Blind in Charlottesville and Richmond into one state board; and provided for the extension on the expiration date of licenses issued to military or diplomatic personnel.

Seven of eight resolutions carried over. One resolution established a joint subcommittee to study the impact of including electronic records in the state depository system.

Two bills failed that would have amended the emergency protective orders in cases of assault and battery of a family or household member and required the Virginia Department of Social Services to provide information and referral services to non-citizen residents who wish to become citizens.

Delegate HD 66 **Marvin Kirkland "Kirk" Cox (R)** Member House: 1990-; b. Aug. 17, 1957, Petersburg; home, 3236 Longhorn Dr., Colonial Heights 23834; educ. James Madison Univ. (B.S.), Pol. Sci. and Soc. Sci.; married Julia Claire Kirkendall; Baptist.

Teacher, Manchester High School; Manchester High School awards, Time-Life Mag. for org. and leadership, Gov.'s School for the Gifted; mem., Colonial Heights Rotary Club, Jaycees and Jaycee rep. to Colonial Heights Historical Comm.; Pres., Christian Men's Fellowship; Rotary.

Offices 1309 Appomattox Dr., Colonial Heights 23834; 804-526-5135; GA Bldg., Capitol Sq., Rm. 720, Richmond 23219; 804-698-1066.

2004 Committees *Agriculture, Chesapeake and Natural Resources, Chair; Appropriations; General Laws.*

House Key Votes, 2004
Please see Introduction for more information on bills.

1) Budget Bill	FOR	5) Family Life	FOR	9) Morning After	FOR
2) Feticide	FOR	6) Fire Arms	FOR	10) Legal Aid	AGN
3) Marriage	FOR	7) Open Space	FOR		
4) Abortion	FOR	8) Home School	FOR		

Election Results
2004 general   M. Kirkland "Kirk" Cox   (R)   19,077   97.8% $103,244

Campaign Contributions 2004 Health Care $8,400; Finance $7,500; Energy $5,850; Law $5,500; Realty $4,650; Agriculture $4,250; Business/Retail Svs $4,225; Mfg $3,750; Transportation $3,625; Tech/Communications $1,900; Public Employees $600; Political $300; Misc $125.

Economic Interests, 2004 *Sal. & Wages,* $10,000+ ea.: Chesterfield Co. Schools (self), Trustmor Mortgage Co. (spouse); *Pers. Liabil.,* $50,000+ ea.: banks, individ.;Sec. to $50,000: Bank of America, common stock; *Gifts,* $129 Altria, dinner; $180 Kings Dominion, tkts; $80 Ringling Bros. Circus, tkts; 93 Reynolds, golf bag; $82 UVA ball game, dinner; $84 VA AgribusinessCouncil, golf tournament; $305
VA Bch Hotel-Motel Assoc., Legislative weekend; $73 VA Farm Bureau, dinner; 80 VA Tech, football tkts; Real Estate: residence.

HOUSE DISTRICT SEVENTY-FIVE, *J. Paul Councill, Jr. (D)*

POLITICAL AND LEGISLATIVE BACKGROUND
House District 75 consists of all of Greensville and Sussex Counties; all of the City of Emporia; part of Brunswick County comprised of the Edgerton, Fitzhugh, Alberta, Danieltown, Elmore, Seymour, Sturgeon, King's Store, and Lawrenceville Precincts; part of the City of Franklin comprised of Precinct 2-1, Precinct 3-1, Precinct 4-1, Precinct 5-1, and Precinct 6-1; part of Isle of Wight County comprised of the Camps Mill Precinct; part of Lunenburg County comprised of the Parham's Store and Hound's

FOURTH CONGRESSIONAL DISTRICT
Creek Precincts; and part of Southampton County comprised of the Berlin, Ivor, Boykins, Branchville, Capron, Sebrell, Drewryville, Forks-of-the-River, Courtland, Blackwater River, and Newsoms Precincts.

J. Paul Councill, Jr., a farmer, a businessman, and a Democrat, has represented the old 75th House District since 1973. He has been unopposed in general elections since 1982. In the 1991 primary, Alfreda Talton-Harris, challenged Councill, losing by 538 votes. In 2001, Councill again was unopposed. Councill was the co-chair of the Education Committee, until the change of committees in 2002.

During the 2004 session, Councill sponsored three bills, two passed, and one was carried over to the 2005 session. Bills passed amended the Charter of the City of Franklin to increase the salaries of school board members and direct local school boards to award verified units of credit for standard diplomas.

The bills carried over conveyed veterans' land to the Commonwealth as a perpetual memorial park.

The only proposed resolution was successful.

There were no failed bills.

Delegate HD 75

James Paul Councill, Jr. (D) Member House: 1974-; b. Dec. 12, 1921, Norfolk; home, P.O. Box 119, Franklin 23851, educ. Swarthmore Coll.; USAF; married Eugenia Draper; Congregationalist.

Farmer and retail businessman; Tidewater Reg. Health Planning Council (past dir.); Southampton Water Auth. (past sec.; treas.); Dir., Sovran Bk.; Southeast 4-H Educational Center (dir.); Southampton Bd. Sup.; Jaycees; Chamb. of Commerce; Ruritan; YMCA; SW Mental Health Assn. (dir.)

Offices P.O. Box 119, Franklin 23851; 757-562-4283; GA Bldg., Capitol Sq., Rm. 523, Richmond 23219; 804-698-1075.

2004 Committees *Appropriations; Education; Rules.*

House Key Votes, 2004
Please see Introduction for more information on bills.

1) Budget Bill	FOR	5) Family Life	FOR	9) Morning After	AGN
2) Feticide	FOR	6) Fire Arms	FOR	10) Legal Aid	FOR
3) Marriage	FOR	7) Open Space	FOR		
4) Abortion	FOR	8) Home School	FOR		

Election Results

2004 general	J. Paul Councill, Jr.	(D)	12,795	71.3%	$10,967
	John B. Nicholson	(I)		28.7%	$3,952

95

FOURTH CONGRESSIONAL DISTRICT

Campaign Contributions 2004 Agriculture $750; Mfg $500; Finance $500; Energy $500; Health Care $250; Tech/Communication $250.

Economic Interests, 2004 *Sec.*, $50,000+ ea.: mutual fund, stocks in: bank, IBM, Ford, (self); stock in Intl. Paper (spouse); $10,001-$50,000 ea.: stocks in utility, SunTrust; *Gifts*, $217 Philip Morris (dinner, gift box); *Bus. Int.*, $50,000+ ea.: J. P. Councill Co. farming; *Real Estate*, Three prop. (Farm, summer house, office bldg. -spouse); Gifts: $129 Hampton Roads Maritime Assoc., dinner, reception.

HOUSE DISTRICT SEVENTY-SIX, *Steven C. "Chris" Jones (R)*

POLITICAL AND LEGISLATIVE BACKGROUND

House District 76 consists of the City of Chesapeake precincts of Churchland, Gilmerton, Jolliff One, Fellowship Baptist Church, Silverwood, Bailey Creek, Lake Drummond, John T. West, and Nansemond and part of Deep Creek; and the City of Suffolk precincts of Driver, Ebenezer, Chuckatuck, King's Fork, Whaleyville, Kilby's Mill, Holland, Holy Neck, Lakeside, Olde Towne, Elephant's Fork, and Lake Meade Precincts and parts of the Cypress Chapel, Harbour View, and Nansemond River.

Steven "Chris" Jones, a pharmacist and a Republican, has served since his election in 1997. Robert Edward Nelms (R) retired that year after serving since 1992.   Nelms had defeated the veteran incumbent Samuel Glasscock (D) in a newly redrawn district. Glasscock, termed the "conscience of the Assembly" by the media, had served since 1970, and authored the seat belt legislation. Jones defeated two opponents in the 1997 Republican Primary, easily defeated a Democratic opponent, and was unopposed in 1999. Jones won the 2001 election by 70.8% of the vote over Democrat I. M. Steingold.

Jones became a household name among Democratic Delegates in 2001, as the chief author of the redistricting plan, with its new boundaries lumping nine Democrats into four districts, and getting rid of Richard Cranwell (D-14). Delegate Barnie Day (D-10), tossed into the same district with two other Democrats, was quoted by *The Virginian-Pilot*: "He's the perfect face to put on this plan. It's like they went to 'Leave It To Beaver' central casting. And Vance [Wilkins (R-24)] is sitting back ... loving every minute of it. I think everybody understands that Chris is not responsible. He wrote this bill like he wrote the Magna Carta. He's the poster boy for it."

The Republican plan first put Delegate Chip Woodrum (D-16 old, 11 new) and Delegate Vic Thomas (D-17) into the same district, but Republicans announced they had paired Woodrum with Delegate Richard Cranwell (D-14). Woodrum told the media of the mistake. *The Roanoke Times* quoted Jones, "I had no clue where Mr. Cranwell lived until Mr. Woodrum announced to the world we'd missed him, and we fixed the mistake." Later, quoted by *The Washington Post*, Jones said, "Did politics play a part in this? Yes." *The News and Advance* quoted Jones, "The history of redistricting in and of itself is inherently political. Much more could have been done. When you compare what's been done in the past, this plan is much more politically fair. Because this is a process where the majority rules, you have to do the best you can."

During the 2004 session, Jones sponsored thirteen bills, twelve passed. Bills that passed provided that candidates for public office who did not file a final report disclosing their past campaign are required to file reports on an election year schedule in future elections when running for the same office; specified the situations where licensed practical nurse practitioners could sign various forms and certificates; authorized the Cemetery Board to petition the court to appoint a receiver to oversee the cemetery operations when it is necessary to protect the public; and provided for an annual performance review of each local electoral board beginning in 2006.

No bills carried over to the 2005 session. Four of five resolutions were successful.

One bill failed which would have provided that the term certified home inspector not prohibit a licensed engineer or architect from providing services as a home inspector.

Delegate HD 76

Steven Christopher "Chris" Jones (R) Member House: 1998- ; b. June 23, 1958; home, 8978 River Crescent, Suffolk 23433; 757-238-3667; educ. Randolph Macon, MCV Sch. of Pharmacy (B.S.); married, Karen Hope Harrison; Christian.

Pharmacist. Member: Western Tidewater Regional Jail Auth. (Chm.), Forward Hampton Rds. (bd. dir.), Rotary; Mayor Suffolk, V. Mayor Suffolk, city council; Awards: Suffolk Jaycees, Outstanding Young Man of 1989, VA Retail Merch. Assn. VA Retailer of the Year (1995), Sch. Pharmacy MCV Alumni Star Award (1992).

Offices P.O. Box 5059, Suffolk 23435-5059; 757-483-6242; GA Bldg., Capitol Sq., Rm. 707, Richmond 23219; 804-698-1076.

2004 Committees *Appropriations; General Laws; Privileges and Elections.*

House Key Votes, 2004
Please see Introduction for more information on bills.

1) Budget Bill	FOR	5) Family Life	FOR	9) Morning After	AGN
2) Feticide	FOR	6) Fire Arms	FOR	10) Legal Aid	FOR
3) Marriage	FOR	7) Open Space	FOR		
4) Abortion	FOR	8) Home School	FOR		

Election Results

2004 general	S. C. "Chris" Jones	(R)	15,522	99.1%	$110,175

Campaign Contributions 2004 Health Care $30,044; Realty $8,625; Finance $8,400; Law $5,672; Agriculture $3,525; Tech/Communication $3,150; Political $2,250; Business/Retail Svs $1,875; Transportation $1,625; Mfg $1,550; Public Employees $1,500; Energy $1,125; Undetermined $775; Defense $750; Misc $200.

Economic Interests, 2002 *Sal. & Wages,* $10,000+ Bennett's Creek Pharmacy, Inc.; BCP, LLC, EIC, LLC; *Pers. Liabil.,* $10,001-$50,000 ea.: individual, trust; *Sec.,* $50,000+ ea.: Davenport, Bristol Myers; $10,001-$50,000 ea.: mut. funds (2), Davenport, bonds; *Pay. for Talks, Mtgs., & Publ.,* $1,588 state (ALEC, expenses, per diem); $325 ALEC (expenses); *Gifts,* $1,326 Natl. Assn. Chain Drugstores (conf., expenses), $249 Russel L. Polls (sports tickets), $151 GlaxoSmithKline (dinner/theatre), $85 Bon Secours (recep./dinner), $77 Philip Morris (gift box), $56 VA Agribusiness (banquet), $38 El Paso (baseball tickets); *Bus. Int.,* $50,000+ Bennett's Creek Pharmacy, Inc.; rental prop.; $50,000/less rental prop.; *Real Estate,* Three prop. (commercial, residential) some w/others.

HOUSE DISTRICT SEVENTY-SEVEN, *Lionell Spruill, Sr. (D)*

POLITICAL AND LEGISLATIVE BACKGROUND
House District 77 consists of the City of Chesapeake precincts of Camelot, Crestwood, Oscar Smith School, Geneva Park, Georgetown, E. W. Chittum School, St. Julians, Sunray I, South Norfolk Fire Station, Carver School, Providence Church of Christ, Westover, Sunray II, and South Norfolk Recreation and part of Deep Creek Precinct; and the City of Suffolk precincts of White Marsh, John F. Kennedy, Airport, and Hollywood, and part of Cypress Chapel Precinct.

Lionell Spruill, a retired central office technician for Bell Atlantic, and a Democrat, has served in this area since 1993. The seat was opened at that time upon the retirement of V. Thomas Forehand, Jr. a Democrat and an attorney who had served in the House of Delegates since 1980. Spruill won the seat, defeating Eileen Olds in the Democratic primary, and his Independent challenger, Joseph S. Johnson, in the general election. In 1995, Spruill again defeated Johnson, and has been unopposed since then.

During the 2004 session, Spruill sponsored ten bills, one passed. Bills that passed authorized that the Department of Military Affairs and the Virginia National Guard Vehicles when used to perform law enforcement function be equipped with flashing, blinking or alternating colored lights.

The bill carried over would have allowed certain non-conforming lots in Chesapeake City to be developed according to guidelines.

Bills that failed would have exempted from licensing requirements persons who sell items to consumers to be used in connection with a funeral or an alternative to a funeral; required an insurer to disclose the liability limits of an insurance policy to an attorney for the injured policyholder when the request proceeds the filing of a civil action; allowed localities to permit playing basketball using mobile basketball hoops on public streets; and established that state employees called to active military duty would receive a supplemental pay.

Delegate HD 77

Lionell Spruill, Sr. (D) Member House: 1994- ; b. Dec. 28, 1946, South Norfolk (now called Chesapeake), VA; home, 1772 Atlantic Ave., Chesapeake 23324; educ. Norfolk State & Pacific Western Universities; married, Charlene J. Joyner; Methodist.

Retired Central Office Technician, Bell Atlantic; Member Chesapeake City Council; member NAACP; Chesapeake Dem. Party; Knights of Pythagoras (past state dir.); Chesapeake's First Block Security (founder); Chesapeake Forward; Prince Hall Grand Lodge of VA (Most Worshipful Grand Master 1994)

Offices P.O. Box 5403, Chesapeake 23324; 757-545-2573; FAX 757-545-2573; GA Bldg., Rm. 507, Capitol Sq., Richmond 23219; 804-698-1077.

2004 Committees *Appropriations; Counties, Cities and Towns; Health, Welfare and Institutions.*
House Key Votes, 2004
Please see Introduction for more information on bills.
1) Budget Bill   FOR   5) Family Life   FOR   9) Morning After   AGN

2) Feticide	AGN	6) Fire Arms	FOR	10) Legal Aid	FOR
3) Marriage	AGN	7) Open Space	FOR		
4) Abortion	AGN	8) Home School	AGN		

Election Results

| 2004 general | Lionell Spruill, Sr. | (D) | 13,050 | 98.6% | $51,276 |

Campaign Contributions 2004 Realty $8,000; Health Care $5,900; Law $ 4,860; Business/Retail Svs. $2,250; Organized Labor $1,500; Energy $1,500; Tech/Communications $1,250; Finance $1,000; Agriculture $1,000; Transporation $500; Single-Issue Groups $500; Public Employees $500; Political $500; Mfg $250.

Economic Interests, 2004 *Pers. Liabil.*, $50,000+ Banks; *Gifts*, $144 Kings Dom. (dinner), $100 VA Assn. Realtors (post cards sent to realtors to ask them to vote for Spruill), $77 Philip Morris (gift box); *Real Estate*, Two prop.

HOUSE DISTRICT SEVENTY-EIGHT, *John A. "Coz" Cosgrove (R)*

POLITICAL AND LEGISLATIVE BACKGROUND
House District 78 consists of part of the City of Chesapeake comprised of the Great Bridge, Greenbrier, B. M. Williams School, Hickory Grove, Oak Grove, Hickory Middle School, Great Bridge Middle School, Bridgetown, River Birch, Parkways, Pleasant Crossing, and Bells Mill II Precincts.

John A. "Coz" Cosgrove, an electronics engineer and marketing director, is the delegate for this district. Cosgrove, a Republican, won the 2001 election with 65.3% of the vote over Democrat Jo Ann H. Huskey. The seat was opened when incumbent Harry B. Blevins, also a Republican, won a special election to the Senate in September 2001, following the election of Senator Randy Forbes (R) to the Congress. Blevins had served as a Delegate after winning a special election in 1998, when Forbes left this House seat to go to the state Senate.

During the 2004 session, Cosgrove sponsored twenty-two bills, ten passed. Bills that passed provided that the crimes of feticide constitute a Class 2 felony; exempted certain new vehicles from initial safety inspections; prohibited the photographic reproductions of a driver's license temporary or learner's permit issued by the Department of Motor Vehicles (DMV) with the intent to commit an illegal act; and increased the sheriff's fee for repossessions, sheriffs sales and evictions.

Five bills carried over to the 2005 session. Bills carried over would have required the establishment of a public defender's office in the City of Chesapeake; provided an income tax credit to health care practitioners who provide free medical services to persons who are unable to pay for the services; and provided that in awarding contracts of over $500,000 for goods and services that a three percent preference be granted to businesses in Virginia that manufacture, develop, or produce goods or services.

Four out of five resolutions passed.

Bills that failed would have provided for persons failing to stop a motor vehicle after receiving a visible or audible signal from a law enforcement officer; provided that anyone who commits a felony against a person while impersonating a law enforcement officer is guilty of a separate and distinct

Class 6 felony; and allowed cities and counties to impose a fee up to $250,000 on all transactions that are subject to the recordation tax.

Delegate HD 78

John Aloysius "Coz" Cosgrove (R) Member House: 2002- ; b. June 7, 1954, Montgomery, AL; home, 832 Amy Marie Lane, Chesapeake 23322; educ. Tidewater Community Coll. (A.A.S.), Old Dominion Univ. (B.S. E.E. T.); married Sue Ann Culpepper; Baptist.

Electronics Engineer, Marketing Director; U.S. Naval Reserve, Aerospace Engineering Officer 1987-2002; Member: Great Bridge Baptist Church; 4th cong. Dist. GOP Comm., chairman; Chesapeake Rotary Club; South Norfolk Ruritan Club; Fraternal Order of Police Lodge; Graduate, Sorenson Inst.; Chesapeake Crimeline (past member), graduate of Hampton Roads Civil Leadership course.

Offices   P.O. Box 15483, Chesapeake 23328; 757-547-3422; GA Bldg., Rm. 416, Capitol Sq., Richmond 23219; 804-698-1078.

2004 Committees *Privileges and Elections; Science and Technology; Transportation.*

House Key Votes, 2004
Please see Introduction for more information on bills.

1) Budget Bill	FOR	5) Family Life	FOR	9) Morning After	FOR
2) Feticide	FOR	6) Fire Arms	FOR	10) Legal Aid	FOR
3) Marriage	FOR	7) Open Space	FOR		
4) Abortion	FOR	8) Home School	FOR		

Election Results

2004 general	John A. Cosgrove	(R)	12,639	97.5%	$92,519

Campaign Contributions 2004   Realty $9,600; Transportation $5,550; Finance $5,350; Energy $3,150; Law $2,800; Misc $2,650; Mfg $2,600; Business/Retail Svs $2,450; Tech/Communications $2,150; Political $1,950; Health Care $1,200; Public Employees $900; Agriculture $700; Undetermined $575; Candidate Self-Financing $160.

Economic Interests, 2002 *Sal. & Wages*, $10,000+ ea.: City of Chesapeake City Council, Global Technical Systems, USAA (spouse); *Off. & Dir.*, Bank of the Commonwealth, Chairman Chesapeake Adv. Bd.; Sec., $50,000+ ea.: 401K w/US Govt, USAA retirement funds; $10,001-$50,000 401K w/T. Roe Price.

HOUSE DISTRICT SEVENTY-NINE, *Johnny S. Joannou (D)*

POLITICAL AND LEGISLATIVE BACKGROUND

House District 79 consists of part of the City of Chesapeake comprised of the Taylor Road Fire Station Precinct; part of the City of Norfolk comprised of the Larchmont Library and Larchmont Recreation Center Precincts and parts of the Canterbury, Titustown Center, and Zion Grace Precincts; part of the City of Portsmouth comprised of the Ten, Eleven, Twenty-Two, Twenty-Three, Twenty-Four, Twenty-Five, Thirty, Thirty-Three, Thirty-Four, Thirty-Five, Thirty-Six, and Thirty-Seven/Thirty-Eight Precincts; and part of the City of Suffolk comprised of the Yeates Precinct, and parts of the Harbor View and Nansemond River Precincts.

Johnny S. Joannou, an attorney and a Democrat, was elected to serve this district in 1997. Joannou won that election by a comfortable 52.1% or 967 votes. Joannou is no stranger to the General Assembly, having served there as both a Delegate and a Senator. He lost in 1991 to Frederick M. Quayle by 493 votes, losing in a re-match in 1995 by 967 votes. Joannou's past legislative interests included highway
projects, the handicapped, and the environment. The seat was opened when Democrat William "Billy" Moore, who had served since 1984, retired and accepted a judgeship. In the 1999 election, Joannou ran unopposed. In 2001, Joannou defeated opposition from Republican R. W. "Bob" McCreary, Jr., winning with 67.6% of the vote.

During the 2004 session, Joannou sponsored six bills of which two passed. Bills that passed provided that a patient's administrator could obtain copies of a patients health care records when the records are requested in anticipation of litigation and provided that a person serving on jury duty not be penalized by being required to work on the day of jury service.

Two bills carried over would have established a circuit court procedure for persons alleged to have committed abuse, neglect, or exploitation of an adult in order to access adult protective service records when the allegation against the person is believed to have been made in bad fault.

Five resolutions were successful. No bills failed.

Delegate HD 79

Johnny S. Joannou (D) Member House: 1976-84; 1998- ; Member Senate: 1984-91; b. April 22, 1940, Brooklyn, NY; home, 408 Sycamore Rd., Portsmouth 23707; 757-399-8277; educ. VPI (B.S.), UR TC Williams Sch. of Law (LLB); married, Chris Paul Kolantis; Greek Orthodox.

Attorney. Member: State Bd. for Community Colleges, VA State Bar, Portsmouth Dem. Comm., Portsmouth Naval Lodge No. 100 AF&AM, Scottish Rite.

Offices 709 Court St., Portsmouth 23704; 757-399-1700; GA Bldg., Capitol Sq., Rm. 423, Richmond 23219; 804-698-1079.

2004 Committees *Commerce and Labor; Courts of Justice; Finance.*

FOURTH CONGRESSIONAL DISTRICT

House Key Votes, 2004

Please see Introduction for more information on bills.

1) Budget Bill	FOR	5) Family Life	FOR	9) Morning After	AGN
2) Feticide	AGN	6) Fire Arms	FOR	10) Legal Aid	AGN
3) Marriage	FOR	7) Open Space	AGN		
4) Abortion	AGN	8) Home School	FOR		

Election Results

2004 general	Johnny S. Joannou	(D)	12,263	96.8%	$19,455

Campaign Contributions 2004 Finance $7,350; Business/Retail Svs $7,125; Health Care $5,250; Law $5,200; realty $4,450; Energy $3,750; Tech/Communications $2,550; Transportation $2,000; Agriculture $1,800; Organized Labor $1,450; Political $1,150; Public Employees $650; Mfg $500; Misc $455; Defense $150.

Economic Interests, 2004 *Sal. & Wages*, $10,000+ Joannou, Knowles & Associates, P.C.; *Off. & Dir.*, Towne Bank, Adv. Bd.; *Sec.*, $50,000+ ea.: stock law firm, J&C Management Group; $10,001-$50,000 ea.: stock bank, Prof. Respiratory Ser., Reliant Energy (held as custodian for daughter); *Gifts,* $98 VA Trial Lawyers (seminar reg. fees waived), $90 Titan Am. (dinner), $56 VA Agribusiness (banquet); *Bus. Int.*, $50,000+ ea.: J&C Management Group (comm. prop.), J K & R Enterprises (comm. prop.); $50,000/less ea.: Joannou, Knowles & Assoc., Prof. Respiratory Serv., Towne Bank (stock), EDIT Investor Partners; *Real Estate*, Three prop. w/others (commercial, open land).

Notes

FIFTH CONGRESSIONAL DISTRICT

SENATE DISTRICT NINETEEN, *Charles R. Hawkins (R)*

POLITICAL AND LEGISLATIVE BACKGROUND

Senate District 19 consists of Franklin and Pittsylvania Counties; the City of Danville; and the Campbell County Precincts of Courthouse, Morris Church, Brookneal, Gladys, Staunton River, Altavista, Lynch Station, and Yellow Branch, and part of the Evington Precinct.

Charles R. Hawkins, Republican and owner of Thompson's Haberdashery, was first elected to House District 21 in 1981. He prevailed over challenger Louise N. Bryant (D) in 1982 and in the special election of 1983. He was unopposed in the next three elections. On the retirement of Senator W. Onico Barker, Hawkins ran for the Senate seat without opposition. In 1995, Hawkins easily defeated Joyce E. Glaise (D), taking 70.8% of the vote. Hawkins ran unopposed in 1999.

During the 2004 session, Hawkins sponsored twelve bills, ten passed and one was carried over to the 2005 session. These bills require the Department of Transportation to set forth regulations for a comprehensive roadside management program that includes participation by individuals and communities; prohibit the administration of drugs to vertebrate wildlife except with a permit from the Department of Game and Inland Fisheries; establish the positions of Secretary of Agriculture and Forestry; and add Franklin County to provisions that allow certain counties to require connections to their water and sewage systems.

A bill carried over would have required the State Corporation Commission to activate a joint understanding association for any group of health care providers who had been insolvent or could not afford to purchase medical malpractice insurance in the voluntary market.

Two resolutions were successful, one of which provided for the Department of Agriculture and Consumer Services to study ways to enhance the economic development of the horse industry.

No bills failed to pass.

Senator SD 19

Charles Robert Hawkins (R) Member Senate: 1992-; Member House 1982-92; b. Oct. 17, 1943, Danville; home, P.O. Box 818, Chatham 24531; educ., attended U VA; married Sylvia Elaine Spangler; Presbyterian.

Owner, Thompson's Haberdashery; Bd. Dir. Pittsylvania County Chamber of Commerce; Chatham Jaycees; Danville, Pittsylvania County Mental Health Assn.; Nat. Rifle Assn.; Bd. Dir. Central Fidelity Bank; VA Natl. Guard (1963-69).

Offices P.O. Box 818, Chatham 24531-0818; 434-432-9672; GA Bldg., Capitol Sq., Rm. 321, Richmond 23219; 804-698-7519.

2004 Committees *Agriculture, Conservation and Natural Resources, Chair; Finance; General Laws; Privileges and Elections, Rules.*

Senate Key Votes, 2004

Please see Introduction for more information on bills.

1) Budget Bill	FOR	5) Family Life	FOR	9) Charter School	FOR
2) Feticide	FOR	6) Fire Arms	FOR	10) Legal Aid	FOR
3) Marriage	FOR	7) Open Space	FOR		
4) Child Abuse	AGN	8) Home School	FOR		

Election Results

1999 general   Charles R. Hawkins   (R)   17,834   99.9% $62,015

Campaign Contributions 2000-June 30, 2002   Dupont $2,000; **Tobacco--PM** $1,500; **Medical** $1,250; **Coal** $1,000; **Nat. Gas** $850; **Pub. Empl.** $750; **Tech./Comm.** $750; **Individ.** $650; **Honeywell** $500; **Realty/Constr.** $500; **Fishing** $400; **Oil** $300; **VA Automat. Merch.** $250; **Transp.** $250 (VMS); **Republicans** $100.

Economic Interests, 2004 *Sec.*, $10,001-$50,000 ea.: stock in MCI World Com., Norfolk Southern, Cardinal Finan.; *Payments for Talks, Mtgs, & Pub.*, $240 Southeast Compact Commission, mtg, travel expenses; Business Interest $50,000 or less: rental; Real Estate: recreational cabin.

SENATE DISTRICT TWENTY, *William Roscoe Reynolds (D)*

POLITICAL AND LEGISLATIVE BACKGROUND
Senate District 20 consists of Carroll, Floyd, Henry, and Patrick Counties; the Cities of Galax and Martinsville; Grayson County Precincts: Independence, Baywood, Fairview, Oldtown, Providence, Fries Part 1, and Fries Part 2; and Wythe County Precincts: Royal Oak, Rural Retreat, Evansham, Pine Ridge, Spiller, Withers, Fort Chiswell, Max Meadows, Sheffey, Huddle, Zion, and Evergreen.

Democrat William Roscoe Reynolds was elected to the Senate in 1996, having formerly served in the House of Delegates from 1985-1996. Reynolds is an attorney with 16 years experience as Henry County Commonwealth's Attorney. In December, 1996, Reynolds won the open Senate seat after former state Senator Virgil Goode (D-20) was elected to the U.S. House of Representatives in November. Reynolds, opposed in the Senate race by Delegate Allen Dudley (R-9), was endorsed by Goode. Reynolds won with 58.2% of the vote. Reynolds was unopposed in 1999.

During the 2004 session, Reynolds sponsored seventeen bills; nine passed, five were carried over to the 2005 session. Bills passed allow Wythe County to assume the obligation of a public service authority for water and sewage connections; removed the requirement for a certificate of a public need (COPN) for intermediate care facilities for the mentally retarded with fewer than a dozen beds; extended coverage to beekeepers under the damage stamp program; and provide amendments to the State grievance procedure.

Bills which carried over would have provided a one year period of incarceration with no suspension of sentence for every $50,000 misused, misappropriated or unlawfully disposed of by an elected official; required the Virginia Medicaid to increase the eligibility for the elderly and disabled to 100% of the federal poverty lines as allowed by federal laws; and established the Virginia Access Plan to provide health benefits to uninsured and under insured adults.

Eleven of twelve resolutions were successful.

Bills that failed would have set speed limits for non-surface treated roads at 35 miles per hour and provided that an employee or agency that failed to comply with a grievance procedure without just cause would result in a decision against the non-complying party.

Senator SD 20

William Roscoe Reynolds (D)   Member Senate, 1997- ; Member House: 1986-1996; b. May 21, 1942, Martinsville; home, Rt. 3, Box 564, Ridgeway 24148; educ. Duke Univ. (A.B.), Washington & Lee Law Sch.; married Linda Lee Marshall; Methodist.

Lawyer; VA Assn. Commonwealth's Attys. (past pres. & dir.); VA Trial Lawyers; Am. Bar Assn.; Ridgeway Lions Cl. (dir.); past pres. & founder Big Bros. & Big Sisters of Martinsville and Henry County.

Offices   P.O. Box 404, Martinsville 24114-0404; 276-638-2315; GA Bldg., Capitol Sq., Rm. 319, Richmond 23219; 804-698-7520.

2004 Committees   *Agriculture, Conservation and Natural Resources; Courts of Justice; Local Government.*

Senate Key Votes, 2004
Please see Introduction for more information on bills.

1) Budget Bill	FOR	5) Family Life	FOR	9) Charter School	AGN
2) Feticide	FOR	6) Fire Arms	FOR	10) Legal Aid	FOR
3) Marriage	FOR	7) Open Space	FOR		
4) Child Abuse	FOR	8) Home School	AGN		

Election Results

1999 general	W. Roscoe Reynolds	(D) 27,586	99.9%		$86,456

Campaign Contributions 2000-June 30, 2002   Realty/Constr. $6,000; **Medical** $5,250; **Electric** $4,750 (Independent $3,500); **Attys.** $4,325; **Finance** $3,750; **Tech./Comm.** $3,250; **Pub. Empl.** $2,500; **Transp.** $1,584 (Auto Dealers $834, RR $750); **GA Pacific** $1,500; **Insur./HMOs** $1,400; **Tobacco** $1,250 (PM $1,000, Conc. Friends for Tob. $250); **Coal** $1,250; **Dupont** $1,000; **Beer** $900; **Northrup Grumman** $750; **Oil** $550; **VA Automat. Merch**. $250; **Fishing** $150.

Economic Interests, 2004   *Sal. & Wages*, $10,000+ ea.: Stone, Worthy, & Reynolds law; Henry Co. Sch. Bd. (spouse); *Off. & Dir.*, Law firm, Principal officer; *Pers. Liabil.*, $10,001-$50,000 loan or finance co.; *Sec.*, $50,000+ ea.: mut. funds (2), Copeland Co.; $10,001-$50,000 stock Blue Ridge Invest. Club; *Bus. Int.*, $50,000/less Law firm; *Pay. for Rep. & Other Services Gen.*, $1,000-$10,000: banks: *Real Estate*, Open land (w/others); Gifts: $71 Geico, dinner; $130 Altria, dinner; $80 VA Trial Lawyers Assoc, Seminar registration fee.

HOUSE DISTRICT NINE, *Allen W. Dudley (R)*

FIFTH CONGRESSIONAL DISTRICT
POLITICAL AND LEGISLATIVE BACKGROUND

House District 9 consists of all of Floyd and Franklin Counties; and part of Pittsylvania County comprised of the Callands, Sandy Level, West Chatham, Gretna, and Bearskin Precincts.

Republican Allen W. Dudley, a banker, was elected in 1993. In his first race for state office, Dudley won the seat held by Democrat Willard Finney, who retired after serving since 1982. Dudley defeated Democrat Wesley W. Naff III by a slim margin of 111 votes. Dudley has easily defeated Democratic and Independent challengers in 1995, 1997, and 1999. Following the 1996 election of state Senator Virgil H. Goode, Jr. to the U.S. Congress, a special December election was held between Dudley and Roscoe Reynolds (D-10). Reynolds won that election with 58.2% of the vote.

Dudley won the 2001 election in a re-match with Independent opponent D. F. "Whitey" Taylor, winning with 83.5% of the vote.

In the 2004 session, Dudley sponsored ten bills; fifteen passed. Bills that passed restrict the use of one's date of birth as a condition for accepting checks; funding for juveniles placed in treatment programs and clarification of the roles of attorneys regarding juveniles in detention centers. Bills passed require the public water supply to be tested for methyl tertiary-butyl annually instead of quarterly; regulations were determined regarding no discharge zones to control the discharge of raw sewage from boat and vessels. Additionally a bill passed that allows wineries and farm wineries to receive deliveries for other wineries located inside and outside the Commonwealth.

Bills that were carried over modify the states requirement for podiatrists to perform surgery under general anesthesia in hospitals and ambulatory surgery centers; the increase in funds for enterprise zones to 18 million cap in the elimination of regulatory jurisdiction of the State Corporation Commission regarding the multiple employer welfare arrangement (MEWA).

Failed bills would have prohibited issuers from refusing to issue or renew a homeowners policy solely on the breed of dog the homeowner owns; repeal of the language that prohibits a majority of community service board members from being elected or appointed officials and the locality form being represented by more than two elected officials on a community service board.

Five of his six resolutions were successful, two were commending.

Delegate IID 9

Allen W. Dudley (R) Member of House: 1994 ; b. Sept 28, 1947, Franklin City, VA; home, Rt. 6, Box 68, Rocky Mount 24151; educ. East Tennessee State Univ., BS, VA Bankers School of Bank Management, graduate 1970, American Institute of Banking; married, Virginia Ann Crigger; Baptist.

Banker; member, VA Jaycees; Jaycee Intl. Senator; Rocky Mt. Moose Lodge; Treas., Industrialized Housing Assn. of VA; Bd. Member, Developmental Center, Franklin County; Am. Cancer Soc. (past dir., co-chm.); Muscular Dystrophy (past chm.); Bank Admin. Inst. (past pres.).

Offices 1521 Altice Mill Rd., Rocky Mount 24151; 540-489-8989; GA Bldg., Rm. 511, Capitol Sq., Richmond 23219; 804-698-1009.

2004 Committees *Appropriations; Commerce and Labor; Counties, Cities and Towns.*

House Key Votes, 2004
Please see Introduction for more information on bills.

FIFTH CONGRESSIONAL DISTRICT

1) Budget Bill	FOR	5) Family Life	FOR	9) Morning After	FOR
2) Feticide	FOR	6) Fire Arms	FOR	10) Legal Aid	AGN
3) Marriage	FOR	7) Open Space	AGN		
4) Abortion	FOR	8) Home School	FOR		

Election Results

2004 general	Allen W. Dudley	(R)	15,418	58.5%	$73,104
	Mark Newbill	(D)	3,039	41.5%	$96,559

Campaign Contributions 2004 Finance $3,930; Realty $3,000; Law $2,000; Energy $1,950; Health Care $1,750; Tech/Communications $1,750; Agriculture $750; Transportation $250; Business/Retail Svs $225; Mfg $150.

Economic Interests, 2004 *Sal. & Wages*, $10,000+ ea.: Planters Bank & Trust Co.; *Off. & Dir.*, Planters Bank & Trust Co. , VP; *Pers. Liabil.*, $10,001-$50,000 retired person; *Sec.*, $50,000+ bank stock; *Bus. Int.*, $50,000+ ea.: AJ Enterprises, Burnt Chimney (all rentals); $50,000/less Lake Corp. (rentals); *Real Estate*, "Land"; Gifts: $261 Altria, reception & dinner.

HOUSE DISTRICT TEN, *Ward L. Armstrong (D)*

POLITICAL AND LEGISLATIVE BACKGROUND

House District 10 consists of all of Patrick County; part of Carroll County comprised of the Mount Bethel, St Paul, Lambsburg 103/ Oakland A 104, Hillsville B, Laurel Fork, Gladesboro, Hillsville E, Dugspur, Hillsville D, Oakland A, Fancy Gap, Gladeville, Woodlawn D Part 1, and Woodlawn D Part 2 Precincts; part of Henry County comprised of the Bassett 2, Gunville, Scott's Tanyard, Fieldale, Horsepasture, Spencer, Daniels Creek, Collinsville 2, Bassett 1, Oak Level, and Hillcrest Precincts; and part of the City of Martinsville comprised of Precinct #1 and Precinct #6.

Ward L. Armstrong, an attorney and a Democrat, is the Delegate for this district, following the 2001 redistricting process. Armstrong had been in the 11th House District, elected in 1992 following the death of House Speaker A. L. Philpott. Armstrong, Delegate Barnie Day (D-10), and Delegate Thomas Jackson, Jr. (D-6) were all drawn into the same district by the Republican passed plan. Day had been the delegate for the 10th House District since winning a special election in January 1997. Jackson had served in the 6th since 1988. Day and Jackson agreed to retire from the legislature, and Armstrong ran, winning the 2001 election with 53.1% of the vote over Republican opposition.

During the 2004 session, Armstrong sponsored nineteen bills, five passed and two were carried over to the 2005 session. Bills which passed clarify that a grantor may maintain an action for damages, including tax liability in cases of legal malpractice associated with an irrevocable trust; extended coverage under the damage stamp program to beekeepers; and provided that all of Interstate Route 64 become the Korean War Veterans Memorial Highway, Interstate Route 81 become the World War II Veterans Memorial Highway, and Interstate Route 95, the Vietnam Veterans Memorial Highway.

Bills carried over allowed an enterprise zone to consist of three noncontiguous zones; and expanded the arrest jurisdiction of a law enforcement officer to execute a warrant that is issued in his jurisdiction anywhere in the Commonwealth.

Eight of the eleven resolutions were successful. One proposed that the Council of Higher Education consider establishing a higher educational institution in South Central Virginia.

Bills that failed would have provided estate tax exemption for closely held businesses or working farms; authorized enterprise zones to include sub-zones considered appropriate by the county, city, or town; and repealed the Personal Property Tax Relief Act of 1998.

Delegate HD 10

Ward Lynn Armstrong (D); Member of House, 1992- ; b. June 2, 1956, Roanoke; home, P.O. Box 485, Stanleytown 24168; educ. T. C. Williams School of Law, Univ. of Richmond (LLB), Duke Univ. (BA); married Pamela Akers; Baptist.

Attorney; Citizens Against Family Violence; Chamber of Commerce (Bd. 1984-87); Kiwanis; Office on Youth (Bd. 1989); Bassett Pub. Lib. Bd. 1989-92; Natl. Railway Historical Soc.; VA Museum of Transp.; "Christmas Cheer" Charity (past chm.).

Offices P.O. Box 1431, Martinsville 24114-1431; 276-632-7022; GA Bldg., Rm. 813, Capitol Sq.; Richmond 23219; 804-698-1010.

2004 Committees *Counties, Cities and Towns; Courts of Justice; General Laws.*

House Key Votes, 2004
Please see Introduction for more information on bills.

1) Budget Bill	AGN	5) Family Life	FOR	9) Morning After	FOR
2) Feticide	FOR	6) Fire Arms	FOR	10) Legal Aid	FOR
3) Marriage	FOR	7) Open Space	AGN		
4) Abortion	FOR	8) Home School	AGN		

Election Results

2004 general	Ward L. Armstrong	(D)	10,050	100%	$70,773

Campaign Contributions 2004 Business/Retail Svs. $9,225; Health Care $7,500; Law $5,726; Realty $5,450; Finance $4,103; Mfg $3,950; Agriculture $3,000; Energy $2,300, Tech/Communications $2,250; Transportation $2,000; Misc $1,750; Political $1,125; Public Employees $1,000; Organized Labor $500.

Economic Interests, 2004 *Sal. & Wages*, $10,000+ ea.: Ward Armstrong, Attorney at LawPam Armstrong Marketing Services Corp. (spouse); *Off. & Dir.*, Pam Armstrong Mark. Serv., Pres. (spouse), Sec. (self); *Pers. Liabil.*, $10,001-$50,000 retired relative (self); *Sec.*, $50,000+ ea.: mutual funds (2); $10,001-$50,000 ea.: mut. funds (4); stocks in: Merck, BB&T, Pfizer, Lowe's, Trigon, Walmart; *Bus. Int.*, $50,000+ ea.: Ward L. Armstrong law, Armstrong Prop. (rentals); $50,000/less ea.: Pam Armstrong (int. design/adv./market.), Ward L. Armstrong, L.L.C. (rentals); *Real Estate*, Two prop. (office bldg., condo); Gifts: $259 VA Trial Lawyers, Assoc., seminar fee; 82 UVA, basketball game; $270 UVA, football game; $160 VA Tech, football game; $63 Geico, dinner; $190 NEXTEL Cup Series, tkts; $144 Sprint, race tkts; $69 DuPont, dinner.

HOUSE DISTRICT ELEVEN, *Onzlee Ward (D)*

POLITICAL AND LEGISLATIVE BACKGROUND
House District 11 consists of part of Roanoke County comprised of the North Vinton and South Vinton Precincts and part of the Lindenwood Precinct; and part of the City of Roanoke comprised of

FIFTH CONGRESSIONAL DISTRICT
the Highland 1, Highland 2, Jefferson 1, Jefferson 2, Tinker, Williamson Road 1, Williamson Road 2, Williamson Road 4, Williamson Road 5, Peters Creek, Melrose, Eureka Park, Villa Heights, Washington Heights, Westside, Raleigh Court 1, Wasena, and Williamson Road 3 (12)/ Lincoln Terrace (16) Precincts and part of the South Roanoke 1 Precinct.

Onzlee Ware replaced Clifton A. "Chip" Woodrum in the 2004 election.

During the 2004 session, Ware sponsored four bills, two passed. Bills that passed prohibit the granting of a license to methadone clinics located within a half mile of a public or private day care center or a K-12 school; and allow the baiting of a deer if there was a permit from the Department of Game and Island Fisheries.

Four of five resolutions were successful.

A bill which failed would have allowed Roanoke County to charge a fee for operating a local criminal justice training academy.

Delegate HD 11

Onzlee Ware (D), House Member 2004 - ; b Jan. 4, 1954, Greensboro, NC, educ.: NC Agricultural and Technical University (BA, 1976), NC Central School of Law (JD, 1984), children: Gabrielle Nicole; Presbyterian.

Attorney, Commonwealth Transportation Board, VA State Bar, Roanoke City Bar Assoc., NAACP, Life Member and others.

Offices: P.O. Box 1745, Roanoke, VA 24008, (540) 344-7410; FAX: (540) 344-9780; P.O. Box 406, Richmond, VA 23218, (804) 698-1011; FAX: (804) 786-6310.

2004 Committees: Counties, Cities, Towns, Courts of Justice, Education.

House Key Votes, 2004
Please see Introduction for more information on bills.

1) Budget Bill	FOR	5) Family Life	FOR	9) Morning After	FOR
2) Feticide	FOR	6) Fire Arms	FOR	10) Legal Aid	FOR
3) Marriage	FOR	7) Open Space	FOR		
4) Abortion	FOR	8) Home School	AGN		

NO ELECTION RESULTS FOR 2004

Campaign Contributions 2004 Law $5,200; Energy $2,966; Realty $2,850; Health Care $2,700; Business/Retail Svs $2,250; Candidate Self-Financing $1,887; Finance $1,800; Tech/Communication $1,000; Transportation $899; Agriculture $750; Political $750; Misc $700; Public Employees $400; Mfg $400; Undetermined $400; Organized Labor $250.

Economic Interests, 2004 Ware, Cargill & Hill, PC; Business Interests more than $50,000: Ware, Cargill & Hill, PC. Law firm; Gifts: $55 Kemper Consulting, dinner; $65 American Electric Power, dinner; $60 Titan America, dinner; $75 Davis Consulting, dinner; $65 State Farm Ins., dinner; $75 Carilian Health System, dinner; $170 VA Trial Layers Assoc, annual Convention; $115 VA Auto Dealers Assoc., dinner; $152 Altria, Kraft Days reception; $131 Altria, dinner.

FIFTH CONGRESSIONAL DISTRICT

HOUSE DISTRICT NINETEEN, *Lacey E. Putney (D)*

POLITICAL AND LEGISLATIVE BACKGROUND

House District 19 consists of all of the City of Bedford; part of Bedford County comprised of the Stewartsville, Hardy, Otter Hill, Cove, Big Island, Sedalia, Kelso, Boonsboro, Montvale, Shady Grove, Thaxton, Goode, Liberty High School, and Sign Rock Precincts and parts of the Forest and Jefferson Precincts; and part of Botetourt County comprised of the Amsterdam, Asbury, Town Hall, Blue Ridge, Rainbow Forest, Mill Creek, Roaring Run, Buchanan 301/Springwood 304, Courthouse, Eagle Rock, Glen Wilton, Oriskany, and Troutville Precincts.

Lacey E. Putney, a lawyer and Independent, has represented the area since 1962. Putney is one of the most senior legislators. He has won all races with a nice majority. Unopposed from 1982-1985, he took 71.6% of the vote in 1987 over R. E. Gravatt (I). He was again unopposed in 1989, and then took 70% of the vote in 1991 to again defeat Gravatt turned Democrat. Putney was unopposed in 1993 and in 1995, and defeated Independent Eric D. Thompson in 1997 and 1999. Putney was unopposed again in 2001.

Although Putney refers to himself as an Independent, he joined the Republican caucus in the 1998 session, creating a 50-50 split in the House of Delegates, and held a fund raiser to benefit House Republicans. Putney announced he would become a Republican if he had enough votes to become Speaker. He did not, and Vance Wilkins (R-24) of Amherst was elected Speaker. In the 2000 session, Putney remained a member of the Republican caucus.

In the 2004 session, Putney sponsored eight bills, six passed. Bills which passed provide for a referendum to approve an amendment to expand the list of successors to the Governor in an emergency; clarified that retirees covered by the state optional and alternative retirement plans are eligible for health insurance credits provided to state retirees; provided that school superintendents who retired under the alternative defined contribution plan would receive the same health insurance credit benefits as retired teachers; and authorized James Madison University to begin construction on a building to replace one damaged by a fire.

There were ten successful resolutions.

Bills which failed would have increased the retirement allowance paid to state police officers; and removed the monthly credit cap on health insurance credits for retired state employees.

Delegate HD 19

FIFTH CONGRESSIONAL DISTRICT

Lacey Edward Putney (I) Member House: 1962-; b. June 27, 1928, Big Island; home, Rt. 1, Forest 24551; educ. Washington & Lee Univ. (B.A., LL.B.); married Elizabeth Harlow; Baptist.

Attorney; Masons, Scottish Rite; Loyal Order of Moose; Outstanding Young Men Of Am. (1965); U.S. Air Force; JLARC; VA & Am. Trial Lawyers; Chamber of Commerce (past Dir.); Boy Scouts (past Distr. Dir.); VA Baptist Hospital (past Trustee); Patrick Henry Boys & Girls Plantation (Trustee).

Offices P.O. Box 127, Bedford 24523; 540-586-0080; FAX 540-586-1784; GA Bldg., Capitol Sq., Rm. 948, Richmond 23219; 804-698-1019.

2004 Committees *Privileges and Elections, Chair; Appropriations; Rules.*

House Key Votes, 2004
Please see Introduction for more information on bills.

1) Budget Bill	FOR	5) Family Life	AGN	9) Morning After	FOR
2) Feticide	FOR	6) Fire Arms	FOR	10) Legal Aid	AGN
3) Marriage	FOR	7) Open Space	AGN		
4) Abortion	FOR	8) Home School	FOR		

Election Results

2004 general	Lacey E. Putney (I)	13,285	73.6%	$31,656
	Art Lipscomb (D)		26.5%	$9,350

Campaign Contributions 2004 Mfg $1,000; Finance $500; Energy $500; Agriculture $500; Tech/Communications $400; Transportation $250; Health Care $250.

Economic Interests, 2004 *Sec.*, $50,000+ ea.: bonds (3), Wachovia Bank, stock in Bedford Fed. Savings; $10,001-$50,000 ea.: bonds, bank IRA, bank business account; *Bus. Int.*, $50,000+ law/rental apt. bldg.; $50,000/less Putney law.; *Real Estate*, 11 acres; Gifts: $208 VA Trial Lawyers, Assoc., various seminar registration fees waivered.

HOUSE DISTRICT TWENTY, *Christopher "Chris" Brinker Saxman (R)*

POLITICAL AND LEGISLATIVE BACKGROUND
House District 20 consists of the city of Danville; and the Pittsylvania County precincts of Airport, Keeling, Kentuck, Mount Hermon, and Ringgold.

C. B. "Chris" Saxman, general manager of Shenandoah Valley Water, and a Republican, is the new delegate for this district. Saxman won the 2001 election with 64.7% of the vote over Democrat Tracy C. Pyles, Jr.

The area had been represented by Whittington "Whitt" Clement, a Danville lawyer and a Democrat, who was elected in 1987. Clement ran for Attorney General in a four candidate June 2001 Democratic Primary. He lost that election, but was appointed to be Secretary of Transportation under newly elected Governor Mark Warner.

In the 2004 session, Saxman introduced fifteen bills, eight passed. These bills required public and private schools to post notices that teachers were required to report any child suspected of being

112

abused , neglected, or abandoned; provided that contracts for architectural and professional engineering services be renewable for four additional one-year terms; required the Governor to biannually conduct an examination of the commercial activities of state employees to insure cost efficiency; and restrict certain commercial motor vehicles from using the left-most lane or Interstate Route 81.

Bills carried over would have allowed the Governor to establish enterprise zones in areas where there are established agricultural or forest districts and allowed the superintendent of State Police to establish a one year project to improve safety along Interstate 81.

Three of five resolutions were successful. One established the third Saturday in November as Celebrate Adoption Day.

Bills that failed would have removed the requirement for publications of notices in newspapers of requests for proposals under the Public Procurement Act; and prohibited any user fee for any pilot project under the Public Transportation Act of 1995 if the project uses federal funds.

Delegate HD 20

Christopher "Chris" Brinker Saxman (R) Member House: 2002-; b. October 18, 1965, Pittsburg, PA; home, 107 Fallon St., Staunton 24401; educ. Washington & Lee Univ. (B.A.); married, Michele Lynn Frick; Catholic.

General Manager of Shenandoah Valley Water; Member: St. Francis of Assisi; Blue Ridge Alleg. Food Bank, Bd. member; Guardian Angel Academy, Adv. Bd.; International Bottled Water Assn., Bd. member; Shenandoah Valley Kiwanis; AYSO Soccer, coach; Awards: Greater Augusta Regional Chamber Commerce Business of the Year 2000.

Offices P.O. Box 2517, Staunton 24401; 540-886-8284; GA Bldg., Rm. 506, Capitol Sq., Richmond 23219; 804-698-1020.

2004 Committees *Agriculture, Chesapeake and Natural Resources; General Laws; Transportation.*

House Key Votes, 2004
Please see Introduction for more information on bills.

1) Budget Bill	FOR	5) Family Life	AGN	9) Morning After	FOR
2) Feticide	FOR	6) Fire Arms	FOR	10) Legal Aid	FOR
3) Marriage	FOR	7) Open Space	FOR		
4) Abortion	FOR	8) Home School	FOR		

Election Results

2004 general	C. B. Saxman	(R)	12,683	99.1%	$41,329

Campaign Contributions 2004 Business/Retail Svs. $7,769; Misc. $4,450; Transportation $4,350; Law $2,500; Finance $2,250; Realty $2,150; Energy $2,100; Undetermined $1,650; Agriculture $1,650; Health Care $1,350; Tech/Communications $1,250; Mfg $850; Public Employees $100.

FIFTH CONGRESSIONAL DISTRICT

Economic Interests, 2004 *Sal. & Wages*, $10,000+ ea.: Shenandoah Corp. (self and spouse); *Sec.*, $10,001-$50,000 ING: mutual fund, private stock; *Bus. Int.*, $50,000+ CKE, LLC (rental prop.), Less than $50,000: Shenandoah Corp, Paymts for representation by associates: Bottled water service for UVA, UVA Hospital, VDOT, Radford, VA Tech.; Paymts for representation and other services generally: bottled water for telephone utitlites, water utitlites, cable Television companies, oil or gas, banks, savings institutions, loan or finance companies, life insurance, casualty companies, beer, wine, or liquor distributors, counties, cities, or towns, and other; Gifts: $50 VCPE, gift certificate; 100 VA Auto Dealers Assoc, dinner; $53 VA Cable, dinner; $130 VA Cable, dinner; 104 Old Dominion Hwy Contractors, dinner; $102 Old Dominion Hwy Contractors, dinner; $52 Altria, reception; $60 Mariners Museum, family pass; Real Estate: business, recreational, commercial.

HOUSE DISTRICT FIFTY-SEVEN, *Mitchell Van Yahres (D)*

POLITICAL AND LEGISLATIVE BACKGROUND
House District 57 consists of all of the City of Charlottesville; and part of Albemarle County comprised of the Commonwealth, Branchlands, Jack Jouett, University Hall, Ivy, and Free Bridge Precincts.

Mitchell Van Yahres, a retired tree surgeon and a Democrat, has served this area since winning a special election in January 1981. Former Senator Harry Michael was appointed to a federal judgeship, and Thomas J. Michie, Jr., a Delegate representing the district at that time, won the Senate seat. The special election to replace Michie was a three-way race. Van Yahres' victory meant he joined Delegate James Murray in representing the district. They were opposed by Citizens Party candidate Donald Day in the November 1981 election but were easily re-elected. With single-member districting in 1982, Van Yahres was at first unopposed, but defeated his only challenger, Robert F. FitzSimmons (R) in 1985, taking 66% of the vote. Although a Catholic and personally not in favor of abortion, Van Yahres stated in the campaign that he was against requiring a teenager to receive parental consent before obtaining an abortion. He had been unopposed for several elections until 1993 when he defeated Republican Michael W. D. Brown by 61.9%. Van Yahres originally faced a Republican opponent, Michael Walker, who withdrew early on. There was an orchestrated write-in campaign, netting his opponent 2,209 write in votes, or 16.0%, but Van Yahres garnered 83.6% of the vote. In 1997, Van Yahres won with 68.4% over Republican Donald T. Ubben. Van Yahres was unopposed in 1999 and 2001.

During the 2004 session, Van Yahres sponsored seven bills, one passed. The bill passed added Charlottesville to the list of cities that have authority to place caps on total income to determine real estate tax exemptions for the elderly and disabled.

The bills which carried over to the 2005 session would have required health insurers to provide accident and sickness contacts and HMO's whose policies included prescriptions drugs on an outpatient basis to include coverage of FDA approved contraceptives. This bill is the same as SB254.

Of nineteen proposed resolutions, thirteen passed.

Bills which failed would have increased the cigarette tax to sixty cents per pack to exclusively fund the Medicaid Programs; provided that the results of any Standard of Learning assessments could not be considered in granting standard diplomas until all Commonwealth public schools had attained full accreditation; and clarified that the Virginia Information Technology Agency (VITA) could use free software on the Internet as an option to competitively bid contracts.

David Toscano

Delegate HD 57

~~Mitchell Van Yahres~~ **(D)** Member House: 1981-; b. Oct. 21, 1926, Mineola, NY; home, 408 Altamont Circle, Charlottesville 22902; educ. Cornell Univ. (B.S.); married Elizabeth L. Franklin; Catholic.

Retired Tree surgeon and businessman; served on Charlottesville City Council 8 yrs., mayor 2 terms; U.S. AAF 1944-45; United Way (Bd. Dir.); Adv. Bd.: Ashlawn, Old Dom. Eye Fndn.; Friends of the State Arboretum (bd. mem.); Chippokes Plantation (bd. trustees); Blue Ridge Area Food Bank (bd. mem.)

Offices 223 W. Main Street, Charlottesville 22902; 434-977-7863; GA Bldg., Capitol Sq., Rm. 401, Richmond 23219; 804-698-1057.

2004 Committees *Agriculture, Chesapeake and Natural Resources; Education; Finance.*

House Key Votes, 2004

Please see Introduction for more information on bills.

1) Budget Bill	AGN	5) Family Life	FOR	9) Morning After	AGN
2) Feticide	AGN	6) Fire Arms	AGN	10) Legal Aid	FOR
3) Marriage	AGN	7) Open Space	FOR		
4) Abortion	AGN	8) Home School	AGN		

Election Results

2001 general Mitchell Van Yahres (D) 14,266 97.9% $45,435

Campaign Contributions 2004 Health Care $2,300; Law $2,250; Energy $1,250;Public Employees $750; Tech/Communications $700; Transportation $500; Finance $500; Mfg $250; Agriculture $250.

Economic Interests, 2004 *Off. & Dir.*, Pres. ea.: Mitchell Van Yahres ASCA, CCLT, President; *Pers. Liabil.*, $50,000+ banks (family), $10,001-$50,000 banks (self); *Sec.*, $10,001-$50,000 stock in Prologis (realty), bonds; Business Interests $50,000 or less: MJM, off/shop; *Pay. for Rep. & Other Services Gen.*, $1,001-$10,000 consulting; Gifts: $275 UVA, football games; $80 Sprint, reception, dinner; $80 Broadcasters, dinner; $75 Verizon, dinner; $125Verizon, dinner; $85Verizon, dinner; $71 Geico, dinner; $57 Dominion Resources, dinner.

HOUSE DISTRICT FIFTY-EIGHT, *Robert "Rob" B. Bell (R)*

POLITICAL AND LEGISLATIVE BACKGROUND

House District 58 consists of all of Greene County; part of Albemarle County comprised of the Woodbrook, Agnor-Hurt, East Ivy, Scottsville, Monticello, Cale, Keswick, Stony Point, Hollymead, Free Union, and Earlysville Precincts; part of Fluvanna County comprised of the Palmyra, Cunningham, and Rivanna Precincts; and part of Orange County comprised of the One West Precinct.

FIFTH CONGRESSIONAL DISTRICT

Rob B. Bell, a prosecutor and a Republican, is the delegate for this district. Bell won the 2001 election, defeating Democrat Charles S. Martin, an Albemarle County Supervisor, with 59.9% of the vote in an election costing more than $330,000. The seat was opened with the retirement of incumbent Republican Paul C. Harris, Sr., an attorney, who had served since 1997. Harris was appointed to a position in the federal government. Harris had replaced Peter Way, also a Republican, after his retirement, and Way in his turn had served after George Allen had successfully run for Congress after serving since 1983.

During the 2004 session, Bell sponsored thirty-eight bills; fourteen passed. Bills which passed corrected the wording in the provision making it a crime to use the contents of electronic communications if one knows the information was obtained by interception electronic communications; allowed magistrate and juvenile intake officers to confine those who are 18 years or older in a juvenile detention home if the offense occurred prior to the age of 18; authorized registered nurses, licensed practical nurses, and phlebotomists to take blood samples in DUI cases and DNA samples and provided a penalty for defacing, damaging or removing any street address, sign used for identification with 9-1-1 service.

Bills carried over would have increased the fine for killing or poisoning a companion animal if the intent is to defraud an insurer; clarified that it is illegal for an underage person to consume, purchase, or possess alcoholic beverages; and provided that only a sheriff could be a chairman of a regional jail board.

There were five successful resolutions.

Bills which failed would have clarified that a criminal defendant's bond could be forfeited for failure to meet conditions of his recognizance; eliminated the distinction between married and other individuals in sexual crimes of rape and forcible sodomy; and reinstated the habitual offenders law which applies to those convicted of DUI, driving on a suspended license, and refusing to submit to a blood alcohol test.

Delegate HD 58

Robert "Rob" B. Bell (R) Member House: 2002- ; b. (no date given), Palo Alto, CA; home, 2309 Finch Court, Charlottesville 22911; educ. Univ. VA (B.A., J.D.); married, Jessica Sweeney; Methodist.

Prosecutor; Aldergate Methodist Church; Assistant Scoutmaster Troop 102.

Offices 408 Park St., Charlottesville 22902; 434-245-8900; GA Bldg., Rm. 810, Capitol Sq., Richmond 23219; 804-698-1058.

2004 Committees *Courts of Justice; Education; Health, Welfare and Institutions.*

House Key Votes, 2004
Please see Introduction for more information on bills.

1) Budget Bill	FOR	5) Family Life	AGN	9) Morning After	AGN
2) Feticide	FOR	6) Fire Arms	FOR	10) Legal Aid	AGN
3) Marriage	FOR	7) Open Space	AGN		
4) Abortion	FOR	8) Home School	FOR		

Election Results

2001 general	Rob B. Bell III	(R)	13,627	59.9%	$185,613

116

FIFTH CONGRESSIONAL DISTRICT
Charles S. Martin   (D)   9,088   40.0% $146,639

Campaign Contributions 2004   Realty $11,850; Finance $9,500; Health Care $7,950; Business/Retail Svs $4,075; Misc $4,000; Energy $ 4,000; Agriculture $3,350; Law $3,050; Political $2,850; Undetermined $2,125; Tech/Communications $2,000; Transportation $1,450; Public Employees $575; Mfg $500; Candidate Sef-Financing $437; Defense $350.

Economic Interests, 2004 *Sal. & Wages*, $10,000+ ea.: law firm John Cattano (self), Madison Co. (spouse); *Pers. Liabil.*, $10,001-$50,000 loan/finance co.; *Sec.*, $10,001-$50,000 mutual fund; Paymts for representation and other services generally to $50,000: Casualty insurance companies, legal representation; Gifts: $320 UVA, reception.

HOUSE DISTRICT FIFTY-NINE, *Watkins M. Abbitt, Jr. (I)*

POLITICAL AND LEGISLATIVE BACKGROUND
House District 59 consists of all of Appomattox, Buckingham, Cumberland and Nelson Counties; part of Albemarle County comprised of the North Garden 302/ Batesville 303, Porter's, and Covesville Precincts; part of Fluvanna County comprised of the Columbia and Fork Union Precincts; and part of Prince Edward County comprised of the Prospect Precinct and part of the Buffalo Heights Precinct.

Watkins M. Abbitt, Jr., a realtor and co-owner of an insurance company, has represented the area since 1985. Abbitt traded in his Democratic Party status to be an Independent. An early supporter of the Equal Rights Amendment and equal opportunity, Abbitt won in 1985 over James P. McClellan (R) taking 54% of the vote. Unopposed in 1987, Abbitt ended the race in 1989 with 63% of the vote over Scott Harwood (R), and had no challenger in 1991 or 1993. In 1995, Abbitt faced two opponents, but won with 60.1% of the vote. In 1997, Abbitt won with 65.5% of the vote over Republican Daniel H. Gardner. Abbitt was unopposed in 1999. In the 2001 election, Independent Abbitt won with 63.2% of the vote over Democrat Henry P. Hagenau. His opponent captured Fluvanna and Albemarle Counties, narrowly losing Prince Edward County, but Abbitt cornered the rest.

During the 2004 session, Abbitt sponsored eight bills, six passed. Bills which passed added game wardens under the definition of law-enforcement officer to increase the penalty if they are victims of malicious or unlawful wounding; reduced the number of board members that the Governor and the judge of the Circuit Court could appoint to the Board of the Miller School of Albemarle; codified language relating to Railway Preservation and Department Fund; and exempted applicants for a wine or beer shipper's license from a background check by the ABC Board.

No bills were carried over.

117

FIFTH CONGRESSIONAL DISTRICT

Delegate HD 59

Watkins Moorman Abbitt, Jr. (I) Member House: 1986-; b. Oct. 20, 1944, Lynchburg; home, Box 683, Appomattox 24522; educ. Ferrum Jr. Col., VA Comm. Univ. (B.S.); married, Madeline Ganley; Baptist.

Owner, Insur. Agency; Abbitt Realty; Past pres., Appomattox Chamber of Commerce; V. Chm. State Water Control Bd.; Uranium Admin. Gr.; Natl. Rifle Assn.; VA Farm Bureau; Jaycees (past pres.); Lions; VA Scenic River Trust (pres.); State Water Comm.; Float Fishermen of VA (past pres.)

Offices P.O. Box 683, Appomattox 24522; 434-352-2880; GA Bldg., Rm. 804, Capitol Sq., Richmond 23219; 804-698-1059.

2004 Committees *Commerce and Labor; General Laws; Transportation.*

House Key Votes, 2004
Please see Introduction for more information on bills.

1) Budget Bill	FOR	5) Family Life	FOR	9) Morning After	FOR
2) Feticide	FOR	6) Fire Arms	FOR	10) Legal Aid	FOR
3) Marriage	FOR	7) Open Space	FOR		
4) Abortion	FOR	8) Home School	FOR		

Election Results

2004 general	Watkins M. Abbitt, Jr.	(I)	11,782	67.1%	$111,190
	Allen Hale	(D)	6,829	32.9%	$ 27,628

Campaign Contributions 2004 Energy $5,350; Finance $4,750; Health Care $4,400; Realty $3,800; Transportation $2,600; Tech/Communications $2,400; Law $2,310; Mfg $1,500; Business/Retail Svs. $1,263; Public Employees $1,000; Agriculture $250.

Economic Interests, 2004 *Sal. & Wages,* $10,000+ ea.: W. M. Abbitt, Jr. Ins. Agency, Inc.; Tiba Corp. (spouse); *Off. & Dir.,* W. M. Abbitt, Jr. Ins., Pres./Owner; Abbitt Realty, Ptn.; Farmers Bank, Dir.; *Sec.,* $50,000+ ea.: mutual funds (7) stocks in: Abbitt Ins., Abbitt Realty, banks (2), 1/4 int. Stanley Park Partnership; $10,001-$50,000 ea.: stocks in Philip Morris, Kraft, DiMon (tobacco), bank, McDonalds; *Bus. Int.,* $50,000+ ea.: rental prop. & farm, Stanley Park Partnership (rentals), Tiba Corp.; $50,000/less ea.: W. M. Abbitt, Jr. Ins., Abbitt Realty, farm, investment prop.; *Pay. for Rep. by Assoc.,* spouse's Tiba Co. is lobbying firm; partner in Stanley Park is George Murphy a lobbyist; *Real Estate,* Farms in 2 counties, timber, investment, rentals, recreation; *Real Estate Contracts with State Governmental Agencies,* 1/4 int. in Stanley Park sub-division leased 62 units to Longwood College $916,800/yr; Gifts: $147 Altria, dinner; $60 Jewell Smokeless Coal, dinner; $ 2,521 VA Sheriffs Assoc., Bear hunt; $180 American Insurance Assoc., Washington Redskins tkts.

HOUSE DISTRICT SIXTY, *Clarke Noble Hogan (R)*

POLITICAL AND LEGISLATIVE BACKGROUND
House District 60 consists of all of Charlotte and Halifax Counties; part of Nottoway County comprised of Precinct 1-1 and Precinct 3-1 Part 2; and part of Prince Edward County comprised of the Farmville, Lockett, Leigh, Hampden, Darlington Heights, West End, and Center Precincts and part of the Buffalo Heights Precinct.

FIFTH CONGRESSIONAL DISTRICT

Clarke N. Hogan is the delegate for this district. Hogan is the general manager and president of Ontario Hardwood, and a Republican. Hogan defeated Democrat Brad J. Wike, a power company linesman, with 58.2% of the vote in a race costing in excess of $218,000. Wike carried Nottoway County, but Hogan captured the rest of the district.

The seat was opened with the retirement of Democrat W. W. Bennett, Jr., an attorney and farmer, who had helped Democrats to take control of the area which they had lost to Mark Hagood (R) in 1987. Bennett ran as an insider with full Democratic support and won the seat in 1989 taking 65% of the vote. He was unopposed in 1991. In 1993 he defeated Independent challenger Kenneth B. Chambers with 83.7% of the vote, and was unopposed after that time. Bennett said he had been considering retirement to give more time to his family.

During the 2004 session, Hogan sponsored twelve bills; five passed. Bills that passed provide that continuing education courses for dental hygienists would be handled by the Board of Dentistry's regulations; added the chairman of the state and local advisory team to the State Executive Council for At-Risk Youth and Families; and required that health insurance be offered to all part-time state employees who paid the total cost of such insurance coverage.

Two bills were carried over which would have created the Department of Workforce Development under the secretary of Commerce and Trade and allowed the establishment of an inpatient hospice under a hospice license in a facility that had a preexisting license to operate a hospital or nursing home.

Three resolutions were successful.

Bills that failed would have clarified that the term "trailer" did not include a modular building; established the Youth Smoking Penalty Fund; and tightened the requirements for service on a petit jury.

Delegate HD 60

Clarke N. Hogan (R) Member House: 2002-; b. July 21, 1969, Roanoke Rapids, NC; home, 1617 Irish St., South Boston 24592; educ. Univ. of the South at Sewanee TN (B.A.); married, Ellen Gray Maybank; Episcopal.

General Manager, Pres., Ontario Hardwood; Member: Halifax Co. Chamber of Commerce, Sr. Executive Roundtable; Halifax Education Fndn., co-chair, Buildings & Grounds; Halifax Co. - South Boston Museum Bd. of Directors.

Offices 455 Short St., Suite 204, South Boston 24592; 434-575-0000; GA Bldg., Rm. 805, Capitol Sq., Richmond 23219; 804-698-1060.

2004 Committees *Agriculture, Chesapeake and Natural Resources; Health, Welfare and Institutions; Militia, Police and Public Safety.*

House Key Votes, 2004

Please see Introduction for more information on bills.

1) Budget Bill	FOR	5) Family Life	FOR	9) Morning After	FOR
2) Feticide	FOR	6) Fire Arms	FOR	10) Legal Aid	FOR
3) Marriage	FOR	7) Open Space	AGN		

4) Abortion   FOR   8) Home School   FOR

Election Results
2004   general   Clarke N. Hogan   (R)   10,241   66.4% $135,195
                       Brad Wike   (D)   7,338   33.6% $ 17,539

Campaign Contributions 2004 Health Care $3,000; Undetermined $2,500; Transportation $1,950; Agriculture $1,925; Finance $1,750; Energy $1,750; Tech/ Communication $1,000; Law $750; Realty $750; Mfg $250; Business/Retail Svs $225; Political $150.

Economic Interests, 2004 *Sal. & Wages*, $10,000+ Ontario Hardware Co., Inc.; *Sec.*, $50,000+ mutual funds; $10,001-$50,000 ea.: mutual funds, stock in banks (2); *Bus. Int.*, $50,000+ Ontario Hardwood Co., Inc. (lumber business); Gifts: $55 VCTA, dinner; *Real Estate*, 128 acres timber land.

HOUSE DISTRICT SIXTY-ONE, *Thomas C. "Tommy" Wright, Jr.. (R)*

POLITICAL AND LEGISLATIVE BACKGROUND
House District 61 consists of all of Amelia and Mecklenburg Counties; part of Brunswick County comprised of the Brodnax, Rock Store, Tillman, and Dromgoole Precincts; part of Lunenburg County comprised of the Plymouth, Brown's Store, McCoy Ghee's Store, Arrowhead Gun Club, Pleasant Grove, Reedy Creek, Peoples Community Center, Meherrin Fire Dept, and Courthouse Precincts; and part of Nottoway County comprised of Precinct 1-2, Precinct 2-1, Precinct 2-2, Precinct 3-2, Precinct 4-1, Precinct 4-2, Precinct 5-1, and Precinct 3-1 Part 1.

Thomas "Tommy" C. Wright, Jr., a supermarket owner, and a Republican, has served as the representative for this district since his election in a special December 2000 election. The seat was opened when Republican Frank M. Ruff, who had served since his election in 1993, was elected to fill the Senate seat of Richard Holland (D-15) who had died earlier in the year.

Wright had run against Holland for the Senate seat in 1999, outspending Holland, who defeated Wright with 53.7% of the vote. The seat had been held by Democrat Lewis Parker since 1973, until Ruff's successful challenge. In the 2000 special election, Wright defeated Frank W. Bacon, winning with 54.8% of the vote. In the 2001 general election, Wright won with 59.6% of the vote over Democrat W. E. "Bill" Keel.

During the 2004 session, Wright sponsored three bills, one passed. Bills that passed provide a penalty for non-citizens and those who are not legally in the U.S. for possessing a firearm.

A bill carried over would have provided that using a false discount coupon to obtain money or property constituted larceny.

One resolution was successful.

A billed that failed would have included in damages for injury to property any necessary costs to restore or replace property to the position it would have been in without neglect.

FIFTH CONGRESSIONAL DISTRICT

Delegate HD 61

Thomas C. Wright (R) Member of House: 2001- ; b. April 27, 1948, Richmond, VA; home, P.O. Box 1323, Victoria 23974; educ. Old Dominion Univ. (B.A.); married, Frances Rose Abernathy; Christian.

Grocer; member: Victoria Christian Church (trustee and elder), Victoria H.S. Pres. Fndn. (bd. dir.), Lunenburg Crime Solvers Assn. (charter mem.), Lunenburg Co. Rotary Club, Victoria Chamber Comm., Lunenburg Co. Bd. Supervisors (1993-; ch. 1995-97); Regional Econ. Dev. Adv. Council; Work Force Investment Bd. (bus. rep. 2000-), Ft. Picket Local Reuse Auth. (Lunenburg Co. rep.), Southside Bus. & Educ. Comm., Crossroads Community Serv. Bd. (2000-).

Offices   P.O. Box 1323, Victoria 23974; 434-696-3061; GA Bldg., Rm. 410, Capitol Sq., Richmond 23219; 804-698-1061.

2004 Committees   *Agriculture, Chesapeake and Natural Resources; General Laws; Militia, Police and Public Safety.*

House Key Votes, 2004
Please see Introduction for more information on bills.

1) Budget Bill	FOR	5) Family Life	FOR	9) Morning After	FOR
2) Feticide	FOR	6) Fire Arms	FOR	10) Legal Aid	FOR
3) Marriage	FOR	7) Open Space	FOR		
4) Abortion	FOR	8) Home School	FOR		

Election Results

2004 general	T. C. "Tommy" Wright, Jr. (R)	10,529	99.7%	$13,567

Campaign Contributions 2004   Agriculture $5,500; Business/Retail Svs $1,725; Realty $1,500; Finance $1,250; Energy $750; Transportation $500; Health Care $450; Mfg $250.

Economic Interests, 2004   *Sal. & Wages,* $10,000+ ea.: Wright's Supermarket, Luneneburg Co. Sch. Bd.; *Sec.,* $10,001-$50,000 ea.: mutual funds (2), stocks in: Philip Morris, Norfolk Southern, BMC Software, Bank America, Supervalue, Coca Cola, Wal Mart; *Bus. Int.,* $50,000/less Wright's Supermarket. (grocery).

SENATE DISTRICT TWENTY-ONE, *John S. Edwards (D)*

POLITICAL AND LEGISLATIVE BACKGROUND
Senate District 21 consists of Craig and Giles Counties; the City of Roanoke; the Montgomery County Precincts of A-1, 2, 3; B-1, E-1, 2; F-1, 2; G-1, 2; Pulaski County's Belspring Precinct; and the Roanoke County Precincts of Catawba, Mason Valley, Northside, Peters Creek, Bennett Springs, Botetourt Springs, and Woodlands.

Democrat John Edwards, a Roanoke attorney, has served in the Senate since 1995. Edwards won by 54.6% of the vote over one term Republican incumbent J. Brandon Bell who had served since his win over Democrat J. Granger Macfarlane. In 1999, Edwards defeated Republican William Fralin. In 2001, Edwards, backed by a host of groups and legislators, including Delegate Viola Baskerville (D-71) who applauded his positive stance on women's issues, faced three other candidates in the June Democratic Primary for Attorney General, but lost to Don McEachin (D-74).

During the 2004 session, Edwards sponsored twenty-four bills, ten passed and four were carried over. Four of the bills that passed exempted emergency regional medical service councils from consumer affairs registration requirements; specified adoption requirements for agencies outside the state provided that courthouses and courtroom security fee funds be used for equipment; and specified that the duties of the Council of Education include facilitation agreements between two and four year institutions.

Bills continued amended the charter of the city of Roanoke and provided for the hospitalization of mentally ill defendants.

Failed bills would have regulated dance halls; and changed the membership and powers of the Rail Transportation Development Authority.

Senator SD 21

John S. Edwards (D); Member Senate: 1996-; b. Oct. 6, 1943, Roanoke; home, 3745 Forest Road, SW, Roanoke 24015; educ. Princeton Univ., Union Theological seminary, UVA Law Sch.; married, Catherine Dabney Edwards; Lutheran.

Attorney; Roanoke City Council (1993-1995); Vice Mayor (1994-95); U.S. Attorney for Western District of VA (1980-81); Captain, U.S.M.C. (1971-73); Chairman: VA Lutheran Homes, Inc., Roanoke Civic Center Commission (1989-91), VA Bar Assn.'s Criminal Law Comm./Section (1987-91); author several law articles.

Offices P.O. Box 1179, Roanoke 24006-1179; 540-985-8690; FAX 540-345-9950; GA Bldg., Capitol Sq., Rm. 309, Richmond 23219; 804-698-7521.

2004 Committees *Commerce and Labor; Courts of Justice; Education and Health.*

Senate Key Votes, 2004
Please see Introduction for more information on bills.

1) Budget Bill	FOR	5) Family Life	FOR	9) Charter School	AGN
2) Feticide	FOR	6) Fire Arms	FOR	10) Legal Aid	FOR
3) Marriage	AGN	7) Open Space	FOR		

4) Child Abuse   FOR   8) Home School   AGN

Election Results

1999 general	John S. Edwards	(D)	23,091	58.9%	$488,009
	W. H. Fralin, Jr.	(R)	16,133	41.1%	$480,290

Campaign Contributions 2000-June 30, 2002   Medical $7,650; **Attys.** $3,200; **AFL CIO** $3,000; **Finance** $2,750; **Electric** $2,550; **Realty/Constr.** $2,200; **Tech./Comm.** $2,100; **Insur./HMOs** $1,600; **Transp.** $1,000 (Auto Dealers $750, RR $250); **Kings Dom.** $750; **Pub. Empl.** $600; **Tobacco--PM** $500; **Beer** $250; **Farmer** $200; **Individ.** $150.

Economic Interests, 2004   *Sal. & Wages*, $10,000+ Law firm; *Off. & Dir.*, Atty.; *Sec.*, $50,000+ mutual funds; $10,001-$50,000 ea.: mutual funds (2), market index fund, stocks in: America Online, Coca-Cola; *Pay. for Talks, Mtgs., & Pub.*, $2,675 Senate (NCSL, expenses); *Bus. Int.*, $50,000+ Law; *Pay. for Rep. & Other Serv. Gen.*, legal services to $10,001: Factory 324, Dolce, retail companies, and other ; *Real Estate*, One prop. w/family, recreational; Gifts: $152 Altria, reception; $85 Altria, dinner; $82 UVA, trip to basketball game; $76 Geico, dinner.

SENATE DISTRICT TWENTY-TWO, *J. Brandon Bell, II (R)*

POLITICAL AND LEGISLATIVE BACKGROUND

Senate District 22 includes Botetourt County; the Cities of Radford and Salem; the Montgomery County Precincts of B-2, B-3, C-1, C-2, C-3, C-4, D-1, D-2, D-3 Part 1, D-4, and D-5; the Roanoke County Precincts of Glenvar, Green Hill, Plantation, Burlington, Mountain View, Bonsack, Hollins, Bent Mountain, Poages Mill, Windsor Hills, Garst Mill, Oak Grove 304/Castle Rock 305, North Vinton, South Vinton, Lindenwood, Mount Pleasant, Cotton Hill, Penn Forest, Cave Spring, Odgen, Clearbrook, Mount Vernon, Hunting Hills; and Montgomery A.

Republican J. Brandon Bell, II replaced Malfourd W. Trumbo in the 2004 election.

During the 2004 session, Bell sponsored two bills, one passed. The bill that passed regulated the use of store profits for pre release and post-release reentry and transition services for those at correctional facilities.

A bill to license Methadone clinics was incorporated into another bill.

Two resolutions were successful. One provided for a Joint Commission on Health Care to study improving services and reducing Health Care costs to Medicaid recipients through public-private partnerships.

SIXTH CONGRESSIONAL DISTRICT

Senator SD 22   **J. Brandon Bell, II (R)** Member Senate: 1992-96, 2004 - ; b Dec. 20, 1958, Charlottesville, VA, educ.: Mississippi State University (BA Business Administration 1980), spouse: Debbie H. Bell; Methodist.

Financial Consultant, President, Bell Wealth Management.

Offices: P.O. Box 21485, Roanoke, VA 24018, (540) 777-1541; FAX: (540) 772-0178; P.O. Box 396, Richmond, VA 23218, (804) 698-7522, FAX: (804) 698-7651.

2004 Committees: General Laws, Priveleges and Elections, Rehabilitation and Social Services, Transportation.

Senate Key Votes, 2004
Please see Introduction for more information on bills.

1) Budget Bill	AGN	5) Family Life	FOR	9) Charter Schools	FOR
2) Feticide	FOR	6) Fire Arms	FOR	10) Legal Aid	FOR
3) Marriage	FOR	7) Open Space	FOR		
4) Child Abuse	AGN	8) Home School	FOR		

Election Results
1999 general	J. Brandon Bell, III (R) 27,378	99.9%	$75,466

Campaign Contributions 2000-June 30, 2002 Attys. $3,000; **Medical** $2,000; **Pub. Empl.** $2,000; **Transp.** $1,300 (Auto Manuf. $1,100); **Electric** $1,300; **Tech./Comm.** $1,250; **Realty/Constr.** $1,200; **Tobacco--PM** $1,000; **HMOs** $1,000; **Serv. Stat./Conv. St.** $1,000; **Beer/Dist. Spirits** $750; **Coal** $500; **Credit Unions** $500; **Oil** $300.

Economic Interests, 2004 *Sal. & Wages,* $10,000+ ea.: Bell, Wealth Management; Personal Liabilities to $50,000: other loan or finance companies; Sec. to $50,000: Roth IRA, note; Bus. Interest $50,000+: Bell Wealth Management; Gifts: $192 VA Sheriffs Assoc., dinner; $91 VA Sheriffs Assoc., dinner; $76 State Farm, dinner; $74 Carillion Health Systems, dinner; $147 Altria, dinner.

SENATE DISTRICT TWENTY-THREE, *Stephen D. "Steve" Newman (R)*

POLITICAL AND LEGISLATIVE BACKGROUND
Senate District 23 consists of Bedford County; the Cities of Bedford and Lynchburg; the Amherst County Precincts of Coolwell, Monroe, Elon, Pleasant View, Amelon, Madison, and part of Temperance; and the Campbell County Precincts of Brookville, New London, White's Church, Bedford Springs, Walker, Concord, Kings, Airport, Spring Hill, and part of Evington.

Stephen Newman, a direct mail company owner and a Republican, has been the Senator for this district since his election in 1995. Newman had been a Delegate since 1992, and ran for the Senate seat following the retirement of Democrat Elliiot Schewel, who had served since 1976. Schewel was known for his concern with education, health issues, and poverty. Newman easily won re-election in 1999 over Democratic opposition. *The Richmond Times-Dispatch* reported ethical discussions over Newman's lobbying of fellow legislators on behalf of his work with Barr Laboratories, a pharmaceutical company, and in appearances before state regulators. Newman called it a "partisan" issue. A religious conservative, Newman draws support from Jerry Falwell's constituency.

During the 2004 session, Newman sponsored seven bills, five passed. The bills that passed granted to child care center a religious exemption from license requirements; required reporting of test results; the Standards of Learning Test; and authorized the construction of Route 20 bypasses around cities.

A bill failed would have revised the provision of the Department of Medical Assistance Services and provided for a waiver to allow for consumer-directed personal care services.

Senator SD 23

Stephen D. "Steve" Newman (R), Member Senate: 1996- ; Member House 1992-1995; b. Oct. 15, 1964, Stuart, VA; home, 2052 Indian Hill Rd., Lynchburg 24503; educ., Lynchburg Christian Acad., Central VA Community Coll., Lynchburg Coll.; married Kimberley Ann Newman; Baptist.

Direct Mail Co. owner; former broadcaster, program dir. for Inland Broadcasting Co.; Lynchburg City Council, 1988-91; member Lynchburg Transp. Safety Com.; mem. Central VA Planning Commission; VA Municipal League; Am. Cancer Soc.

Offices P.O. Box 2209, Lynchburg 24501-0209; 434-385-1065; GA Bldg., Rm. 303, Capitol Square, Richmond 23219; 804-698-7523.

2004 Committees *Education and Health; Local Government; Rehabilitation and Social Services; Transportation.*

Senate Key Votes, 2004
Please see Introduction for more information on bills.

1) Budget Bill	AGN	5) Family Life	FOR	9) Charter Schools	FOR
2) Feticide	FOR	6) Fire Arms	FOR	10) Legal Aid	FOR
3) Marriage	FOR	7) Open Space	AGN		
4) Child Abuse	AGN	8) Home School	FOR		

Election Results

1999 general	Stephen D. Newman	(R)	23,052	66.2%	$231,829
	John C. Campbell, Sr.	(D)	11,255	32.3%	$ 90,476
	"Schwartz" Trent	(I)	529	1.5%	None

Campaign Contributions 2000-June 30, 2002   Medical $7,350; **Finance** $5,000; **Insur./HMOs** $4,000; **Realty/Constr.** $3,000; **Tranps.** $2,500 (Auto Dealers $1,250); **Attys.** $2,450; **Tech./Comm.** $2,400; **GA Pacific** $1,500; **Electric** $1,500; **Tobacco** $1,250 (PM $1,000, RJR $250); **Kings Dom.** $500; **Retail** $500; **Pub. Empl.** $350; **Northrup Grumman** $250.

Economic Interests, 2004 *Sal. & Wages,* $10,000+ ea.: S.D.N. Company, Centra Health; *Off. & Dir.,* S.D.N. Co., owner; *Sec.,* $10,001-$50,000 ea.: mut. fund, stocks: E-Trade, Barr Lab., Nokiz Corp.; *Bus. Int.,* $50,000+: S.D.N. Co. (consulting - Barr Lab.).

SENATE DISTRICT TWENTY-FOUR, *Emmett W. Hanger, Jr. (R)*

POLITICAL AND LEGISLATIVE BACKGROUND
Senate District 24 contains the counties of Augusta, Greene, and Highland; the Cities of Lexington, Staunton, and Waynesboro; the Albemarle County Precincts of Crozet and Free Union; the Rockbridge County Precincts of Highland Belle, Vo-Tech, Goshen, Meadowview, Rockbridge Baths, and Rockbridge; the Rockingham County Precincts of Keezletown, Mill Creek, Massanetta Springs, Montezuma, Mt. Crawford, Grottoes, North River, Elkton, Swift Run, McGaheysville, and South Fork.

Emmett W. Hanger, Jr., a realtor and a Republican, has been the Senator for this area since 1995. In that year, Hanger defeated Democrat Frank Nolen, an incumbent since 1975, by 50.9%. Hanger had served in
the House from 1983-1991, until defeated by Creigh Deeds (D-18) following redistricting. Hanger was unopposed in 1999. Hanger chairs the Rehabilitation and Social Services Committee.

During the 2004 session, Hanger sponsored twenty bills, nine passed and three were carried over. Bills that passed allowed the Governor to sell and convey Staunton Correctional Center; amended the Charter of Lexington; established a Watershed Coordination Program; provided for additional details on procedures for postponing an election due to the governor's order of a state of emergency; and gave localities flexibility in defining an inoperable motor vehicle.

Bills continued to bring the Commonwealth's sales and tax laws into conformity with the Streamlined Sales and Use Tax Agreement; and limited land preservation tax credits.

Senator SD 24

Emmett W. Hanger, Jr. (R) Member Senate: 1996- ; Member House 1983-1992; b. Aug. 2, 1948, Staunton; home, P.O. Box 2, Mount Solon 22843; educ. James Madison Univ. (B.S) Management and Economics; M.B.A.); married Sharon Hanger; Church of the Brethren.

Real Estate; Former Business school owner; Captain, Army/Natl. Guard (1972-1983); member, Sangerville Towers Ruritan Club; Bd. of Dir.: Frontier Museum, Augusta County Fair; Former Commissioner of the Revenue of Augusta County.

Offices P.O. Box 2, Mount Solon 22843-0002; 540-885-6898; GA Bldg., Rm. 431, Capitol Sq., Richmond 23219; 804-698-7524.

2004 Committees *Rehabilitation and Social Services, Chair; Agriculture, Conservation and Natural Resources; Local Government; Privileges and Elections; Rules.*

Senate Key Votes, 2004
Please see Introduction for more information on bills.

1) Budget Bill	FOR	5) Family Life	FOR	9) Charter Schools	FOR
2) Feticide	FOR	6) Fire Arms	FOR	10) Legal Aid	FOR
3) Marriage	FOR	7) Open Space	FOR		
4) Child Abuse	AGN	8) Home School	FOR		

Election Results

1999 general   Emmett Hanger, Jr.   (R)   20,373   99.5% $21,784

Campaign Contributions 2000-June 30, 2002   Medical $2,600; **Tech./Comm.** $1,750; **Dupont** $1,500; **Tobacco--PM** $1,000; **Pub. Empl.** $500; **Electric** $500; **Oil** $300; **Trash** $250; **Dist. Spirits** $250; **Attys.** $250; **Realty/Constr.** $250; **Fishing** $150.

Economic Interests, 2004 *Sal. & Wages*, $10,000+ ea.: Hanger & Associates, Augusta Co. Schools (spouse); *Pers. Liabil.*, $10,001-$50,000 Banks; *Sec.*, $50,000+ (note) ea.: Dominion Business School, Virginia College (Jr. Coll.); Business Interests $50,000 +: Hanger & Assoc; *Pay. for Talks, Mtgs., & Pub.*, $400 state, Bay Commission, expenses; $1.025 state, NCSL Denver, expenses; $367 NCSL Washington, expenses; $200 state, NCSL Salt Lake City, expenses; $2,319; $400 Bay Comm. Harrisonburg, expenses; Gifts: $150 Colonial Williamsburg, session, meals; $275 VA Beach, events, lodging; $352 Kings Dominion, tkts; $200 BA Horse Council, Trail Ride.

HOUSE DISTRICT EIGHT, *H. Morgan Griffith (R)*

POLITICAL AND LEGISLATIVE BACKGROUND

House District 8 consists of all of the City of Salem; and part of Roanoke County comprised of the Catawba, Mason Valley, Glenvar, Northside, Peters Creek, Green Hill, Bennett Springs, Botetourt Springs, Woodlands, Bent Mountain, Poages Mill, Windsor Hills, Garst Mill, Oak Grove 304/Castle Rock 305, Cotton Hill, Penn Forest, Cave Spring, and Mount Vernon Precincts.

Morgan Griffith, a criminal lawyer and a Republican, has represented the area since 1993 when he easily defeated Democratic opposition to win the open seat. G. Steven Agee had resigned to run for the Republican nomination for Attorney General against James S. Gilmore III, but lost. Seven years later, in 2000, Agee was named to the Virginia Court of Appeals. Griffith was unopposed until 2001, when he defeated Democrat Dana Martin, a business consultant, with 69.7% of the vote.

Griffith is the Majority Leader in the House. In the 2001 session, Griffith aligned himself firmly with Gilmore and the Speaker, Vance Wilkins (R 24), defending Gilmore's budget plans against the Senate's pleas to reduce the 70% increase in the car tax cut to 55% to avoid cutting vital public services. That session ended in a historic budget impasse.

During the 2004 session, Griffith sponsored thirty-three bills, thirteen passed and five were carried over. The bills that passed allocated construction funds for "smart roads"; established registration procedures for sex offenders; required training of personnel to handle domestic violence, sexual assault, stalking and violation of protection orders; created a Domestic Violence Victim Fund; and exempted certain meetings of the General Assembly from the Freedom of Information Acts.

Bills continued provided for reasonable efforts to be made to reunite children with parents under foster care plans; penalties for persons who entice another to violate a protective order; and the creation of a Child Support Guidelines Review Panel in the legislative branch of government.

Failed bills would have required school buses to comply with federal regulations; create a Health Security Act; required vehicle inspections by trailer dealers; provided for evidence of unlawful discriminatory practices under the Fair Housing Law; and set standards for awarding reasonable attorney's fees in cases of violation of the Motor Vehicle Warranty Enforcement Act.

Delegate HD 8

H. Morgan Griffith (R) Member House: 1994- ; b. March 15, 1958, Philadelphia, PA; home, 320 Pennsylvania Ave., Salem 24153; educ. Emory & Henry College (B.A.), Washington & Lee Univ. Sch. of Law (J.D.); married, Mary Frances Dyess; Episcopalian.

Attorney; Past Director, Legal Aid Society of Roanoke Valley; VA State Bar; Salem Lions Club; Blue Ridge Mtns. Council, Boy Scouts of America; Lions Club; Stonegate Swim Club (Dir.); Award, Catawba Dist. Boy Scouts of Am. Silver Beaver (1994).

Offices P.O. Box 1250, Salem 24153; 540-389-4498; GA Bldg., Rm. 607, Capitol Sq., Richmond 23219; 804-698-1008.

2004 Committees *Commerce and Labor; Courts of Justice; Militia, Police and Public Safety; Rules.*

House Key Votes, 2004
Please see Introduction for more information on bills.

1) Budget Bill	FOR	5) Family Life	FOR	9) Morning After	AGN
2) Feticide	FOR	6) Fire Arms	FOR	10) Legal Aid	AGN
3) Marriage	FOR	7) Open Space	FOR		
4) Abortion	FOR	8) Home School	FOR		

Election Results

2004 general	H. Morgan Griffith	(R)	17,401	59.3%	$393,245
	Mark Emick	(D)	7,581	40.8%	$128,834

Campaign Contributions 2004 Law $17,100; Health Care $12,050; Energy $11,000; Finance $10,200; Realty $8,550; Tech/Communications $7,500; Business/Retail Svs $5,678; Transportation $5,000; Mfg $3,800; Agriculture $4,650; Public Employees $1,700; Political $405; Misc $300; Single-Issue Groups $300; Undetermined $250.

Economic Interests, 2004 *Off. & Dir.*,FNB Corp., Dir.; Stonegate Swim Club, Dir.; *Pers. Liabil.*, $10,001-$50,000 retired indiv.; *Sec.*, $10,001-$50,000 ea.: stock in Stonegate Swim Club, FNB Corp. stock; Business Interest $50,000+ ea.: H. Morgan Griffith law; Stonegate Swim Club (swim & tennis); *Real Estate*, One office/apt. bldg.; Gifts: $98 VSA Trial Lawyers Assoc, seminar; $4,314 Taipei Economic and Cultural Repr. Office, trip to Taiwan, expenses; $152 Altria, Kraft Days reception.

HOUSE DISTRICT FOURTEEN, *Daniel "Danny" Webster Marshall III (R)*

POLITICAL AND LEGISLATIVE BACKGROUND
House District 14 consists of all of the City of Danville; part of Henry County comprised of the Irisburg, Mount Olivet, Fontaine, and Ridgeway Precincts; and part of Pittsylvania County comprised of the Airport, Ringgold, Brosville, Bachelors Hall, and Ferry Road Precincts.

Danny W. Marshall III, the president of Marshall Concrete Products, and a Republican, is the new representative for this district. Marshall won with 60.4% of the vote over Democratic challenger Joyce E. Glaise, a school teacher.

Democrat C. Richard Cranwell, an attorney, had served since 1971, and had been the House Majority Leader from 1992 until Republicans tipped the power to their side. Then Cranwell was the Minority

Leader. A powerful figure, loved by some and feared by many, with his fingers in many legislative pies, Cranwell was redistricted into the same district with Delegate Chip Woodrum (D-16 old, 11 new). Unable to oust Cranwell through election challenges, the Republicans succeeded in removing him at last by changing the boundaries.

During the 2004 session, Marshall sponsored eight bills, five passed and three were carried over. Bills that passed increased the membership of the Advanced Learning and Research Institute; designated the Advanced Learning and Research Institute an educational institution; and created a transportation district within Charlottesville City and Albemarle County.

A bill continued provided for a moratorium on new health insurance mandates and strengthens the requirements for reporting on students' truancy.

Delegate HD 14

Danny W. Marshall III (R) Member House: 2002- ; b. January 20, 1952, Danville; home, 183 Acorn Lane, Danville 24541; educ. Danville Community College; married, Deborah Kaye Hardy; Baptist.

President, Marshall Concrete Products; Danville City Council 2000-01; Member: West Main Baptist; Pittsylvania Chamber, past pres.; Pittsylvania Economic Develop.; Dan River Regional Vision; National Concrete Masonry, past chair; VA Concrete Masonry, past chair; VA Masonry Council, past chair.

Offices   1088 Industrial Ave., Danville 24541; 434-797-5861 GA Bldg., Rm. 809, Capitol Sq., Richmond 23219; 804-698-1014.

2004 Committees   *Counties, Cities and Towns; General Laws; Science and Technology.*

House Key Votes, 2004
Please see Introduction for more information on bills.

1) Budget Bill	FOR	5) Family Life	AGN	9) Morning After	FOR
2) Feticide	FOR	6) Fire Arms	FOR	10) Legal Aid	FOR
3) Marriage	FOR	7) Open Space	FOR		
4) Abortion	FOR	8) Home School	FOR		

Election Results

2004 general	Danny W. Marshall III	(R)	11,652	99.9%	$26,269

Campaign Contributions 2004   Agriculture $4,425; Health Care $3,250, Tech/ Communications $2,250; Finance $1,750; Realty $1,000; Law $750; Transportation $650; Energy $500; Public Employees $400; Misc $200; Political $150; Business/Retail Svs $125.

Economic Interests, 2004   *Sal. & Wages,* $10,000+ Marshall Concrete Products of Danville, Inc.; *Pers. Liabil.,* $50,000+ ea.: banks, construction material supplier, motor sports team; $10,001-$50,000 insurance co.; *Sec.,* $50,000+ ea.: stocks in: Marshall Con. Prod. Danville, Marshall Con. Prod. Christiansburg, South Central So., G&W Motor parts, Solution (not readable); *Bus. Int.,* $50,000+ ea.: Marshall Con. Prod. Danville, Marshall Con. Prod. Christiansburg. G&W Motorparts (race car shop); $50,000/less South Central Sol., software; *Real Estate:*personal property, farm, investment lot; *Gifts:* $55 VCTA, dinner; $100 VA Auto Dealers, dinner; $275 VA Beach Leg. Weekend.

HOUSE DISTRICT SIXTEEN, *Robert Hurt (R)*

POLITICAL AND LEGISLATIVE BACKGROUND
House District 16 consists of part of Henry County comprised of the Axton, Mountain Valley, Collinsville 1, Mountain View, Figsboro, Stanleytown, and Dyers Store Precincts; part of the City of Martinsville comprised of Precinct #2, Precinct #3, Precinct #4, and Precinct #5; and part of Pittsylvania County comprised of the Mt. Hermon Fire Station, Chatham, Tunstall, Tightsqueeze, West Blairs, Central, Riceville, East Blairs, Mt. Airy, East Gretna, Keeling, Kentuck, Hurt, Motley Sycamore, Renan, Stony Mill, Swansonville, Whitmell, Mt. Hermon, Mt. Cross, and Spring Garden Precincts.

Robert Hurt, an attorney and a Republican, defeated Democratic opponent R. W. Collins with 65% of the vote in the 2001 election. Hurt has served on the Rural Virginia Prosperity Commission.

Before redistricting, this House District comprised the Roanoke area, and was served by Delegate Chip Woodrum, now in House District 11.

During the 2004 session, Hurt sponsored twenty-five bills, thirteen passed, and three were carried over. Bills that passed provided for solicitation and registration as a sex offender in cases of child pornography; a penalty for subsequent correction for criminal street activity in gangs; the distribution of campaign materials at polling places except within forty feet of the entrance; direct schools to include career and technical education curricular; a community based probation program in cases of assault and battery against a family or household member; and allowed an underage alcohol offender to be placed on community-based prohibition.

Bills continued provided free motor vehicle registration to continue for members of volunteer fire departments and rescue squads; and established the definition of a disabled employee under the Line of Duty Act.

Bills that failed would have dismissed one to the dual charges of driving under the influence of alcohol or drugs and reckless driving; provided a tiered program to provide a tax credit for the creation of jobs in economically distressed localities; and provided additional provisions for a speedy trial and speedy sentencing within six months of arraignment.

Delegate HD 16

Robert Hurt (R); Member of House, 2002- ; b. June 16, 1969, New York; home, 216 N. Main St., Chatham 24531; educ. Hampden-Sydney College (B.A.), Mississippi College Sch. of Law (J.D.); married, Kathryn Raine Heithaus; Presbyterian.

Attorney; Member: Chatham Presb. Ch., Elder; Chatham Rotary Club, Pres.-Elect; VA State Bar, Council Rep. for 22nd Jud. Circuit 1998-01; VA Bar Assn.; Rural VA Prosperity Commission.

Offices P.O. Box 2, Chatham 24531; 434-432-3431; GA Bldg., Rm. 812, Capitol Sq.; Richmond 23219; 804-698-1016.

2004 Committees *Counties, Cities and Towns; Courts of Justice; Militia, Police and Public Safety.*

SIXTH CONGRESSIONAL DISTRICT

House Key Votes, 2004

Please see Introduction for more information on bills.

1) Budget Bill	FOR	5) Family Life	AGN	9) Morning After	FOR
2) Feticide	FOR	6) Fire Arms	FOR	10) Legal Aid	FOR
3) Marriage	FOR	7) Open Space	FOR		
4) Abortion	FOR	8) Home School	FOR		

Election Results

2004 general	Robert Hurt	(R)	11,853	61.6%	$122,347
	Kimble Reynolds	(D)	6,382	38.4%	$ 58,623

Campaign Contributions 2004   Health Care $3,500; Law $3,000; Finance $1,750; Tech/Communications $1,750; Agriculture $1,175; Misc $891; Energy $500; Realty $500; Transportation $450;Public Employees $400; Business/Retail Svs $225; Political $150.

Economic Interests, 2004 *Sal. & Wages,* $10,000+ H. Victor Millner, Jr., P.C.; *Sec.,* $50,000+ stock in Wachovia; Gifts: Feld Enterprises, Circus tkts.

HOUSE DISTRICT SEVENTEEN, *William H. Fralin, Jr. (R)*

POLITICAL AND LEGISLATIVE BACKGROUND

House District 17 consists of part of Botetourt County comprised of the Coyner Springs and Cloverdale Precincts; part of Roanoke County comprised of the Plantation, Burlington, Mountain View, Bonsack, Hollins, Mount Pleasant, Ogden, Clearbrook, and Hunting Hills Precincts, and part of the Lindenwood Precinct; and part of the City of Roanoke comprised of the Jefferson-Riverdale, Williamson Road 6, Monterey, Raleigh Court 2, Raleigh Court 3, Raleigh Court 4, Raleigh Court 5, Fishburn Park, Grandin Court, South Roanoke 2, Lee-Hi, and Garden City Precincts, and part of the South Roanoke 1 Precinct.

During the 2004 session, Fralin sponsored six bills, two passed. The bills that passed increased payments of emergency responses such as rescue and emergency medical services expenses to localities in certain serious traffic accidents; provided for a variable toll rate to encourage travel during off-peak hours

One bill was continued which granted credit for toll payments made by owners and operators of commercial vehicles.

Bills failed would have required safety belts to school buses and imposed additional fees to support the Roanoke Law Library.

131

Delegate HD 17

William H. Fralin (R) Member House: 2004 - ; b. Feb. 8, 1963, Alexandria, VA educ.: University of Virginia (BS, History 1985), T.C. Williams School of Law, University of Richmond (JD 1989), spouse: Karen Richmond Buswell, children: William, Clayton and Laney, Episcopal.

Offices: P.O. Box 20363, Roanoke, VA 24018, (540) 772-7600; P.O. Box 406, Richmond, VA 23218, (804) 698-1017, FAX: (804) 786-6310.

2004 Committees: Education, Priveleges and Elections, Transportation.

House Key Votes, 2004
Please see Introduction for more information on bills.

1) Budget Bill	FOR	5) Family Life	AGN	9) Morning After	AGN
2) Feticide	FOR	6) Fire Arms	FOR	10) Legal Aid	FOR
3) Marriage	FOR	7) Open Space	FOR		
4) Abortion	FOR	8) Home School	FOR		

Election Results

2004 general	William Fralin, Jr.	(D)	16,977	62.1%	$223,600
	Linda Wyatt	(D)		31.4%	$51,330

Campaign Contributions 2004 Self-Financing $25,500; HealthCare $7,286; Realty $4,84; Law $4,600; Finance $3,800; Energy $2,750; Business/Retail Svs $2,500; Misc $2,200; Mfg $1,950; Political $1,500; Tech/Communication $1,500; Transportation $1,000; Public Employees $500; Defense $250; Agriculture $250.

Economic Interests, 2004 *Sal. & Wages*, $10,000+ Medical Facilities of America, Inc.; Offices & Directorships: Medical Facilities of America, Inc., Exec. Vice President; Personal Liabilities $50,000 +: Heywood Fralin, Medical Facilities of America, Inc.; Sec. $50,000 +: Med. Facilities of VA I, II & III; $10,000 to $50,000: Aarondale Limited Partnership, Baylake Limited Partnership, Medical Facilities of VA IV, F &W Office Park II, Meadow Creek Lane Care Center, Carolina Health Care Center of Cumberland Co. and Burke; Business Interests$50,000 +: Medical Facilities of VA II; $50,000 or less: Medical Facilities of VA I, III, IV, Aarondale Limited Partnership, Baylake Limited Partenship, Carolinaa Health Care Center of Burke, F & W Office Park II, Carolina Health Care Center of Cumberland Co.; Paymts for representation by you to $10,000: Medical Facilities of America, Inc.; Paymts other $100,000 to $250,000: nursing homes, assisted living facilities and retirement centers; Gifts: $66 American Electric Power, dinner ; Real Estate: residential.

HOUSE DISTRICT EIGHTEEN, *Clifford Lynwood "Clay" Athey, Jr. (R)*

POLITICAL AND LEGISLATIVE BACKGROUND
House District 18 consists of all of Warren County; part of Fauquier County comprised of the Warrenton, Marshall, Leeds, Waterloo, Upperville, The Plains, and Broad Run Precincts and part of

the Baldwin Ridge Precinct; and part of Frederick County comprised of the Cedar Creek, Stephens City, and Middletown Precincts.

C. L. "Clay" Athey, Jr. won the 2001 election with 54.3% of the vote over Democratic challenger Peter B. Schwartz and Independent candidate Jerry M. Wood in this seat opened with redistricting. Kay Hayes lost the Republican nomination to Athey.

Athey is an attorney and a Republican. He was a member of the Front Royal Council, and the Mayor of Front Royal.

During the 2004 session, Athey sponsored twenty-five bills, eight passed, four were carried over. Bills that passed abolished the Disabled Interagency Coordination Council on Housing; abolished the advisory Committee on Certified Practices concerning licensees of sex offender treatment providers; established reciprocal agreements for concealed hand gun permits with other states; established mandatory minimum fines for a first offense for driving under the influence of alcohol or drugs; and established the Amber Alert system.

Bills carried over allowed for a choice of pharmacies under health insurance plans; provided for a flat tax on individual and corporate income; and repealed individual income tax and increases in sales and use taxes.

Bills that failed would have abolished the Advisory Board of Rehabilitation Providers; abolished the Board of Military Affairs, and relating to insurance on rental vehicles when used as a substitute for a vehicle being repaired or serviced.

Delegate HD 18

Clifford Lynwood "Clay" Athey, Jr. (R); Member House: 2002- ; born September 1, 1960, Front Royal, VA; home, 112 Shenandoah Ave., Front Royal 22630; educ. Lord Fairfax Community College (A.A.), VCU (B.A.), Univ. of Dayton School of Law (J.D.); married, Stacey Lynne Knox; Methodist.

Attorney; Front Royal Town Council 1996-2000; Front Royal Mayor 2000-2002; Member: Front Royal United Methodist Church; Front Royal Rotary Club; Front Royal Elks Lodge; Chamber of Commerce.

Offices 35 North Royal Ave., Front Royal 22630; 540-635-7917; GA Bldg., Rm. 510, Capitol Sq., Richmond 23219; 804-698-1018.

2004 Committees *Courts of Justice; Health, Welfare and Institutions; Militia, Police and Public Safety*

House Key Votes, 2004
Please see Introduction for more information on bills.

1) Budget Bill	FOR	5) Family Life	AGN	9) Morning After	AGN
2) Feticide	FOR	6) Fire Arms	FOR	10) Legal Aid	FOR
3) Marriage	FOR	7) Open Space	FOR		
4) Abortion	FOR	8) Home School	FOR		

Election Results   NO ELECTION RESULTS FOR 2004

SIXTH CONGRESSIONAL DISTRICT

Campaign Contributions 2004   Health Care $4,900; Law $3,500; Energy $2,150; Finance $2,050; Political $1,750; Undetermined $1,550; Realty $1,300; Transportation $1,150; Business/Retail Svs $1,150; Agriculture $1,000; Mfg $750; Tech/ Communications $750; Public Employees $650; Misc $600.

Economic Interests, 2004   *Sal. & Wages*, $10,000+ ea.: Napier, Pond, Athey & Athey, PC, Warren Co. Public Sch.; *Pers. Liabil.*, $10,001-$50,000 ea.: banks (self), banks (family); *Bus. Int.*, $50,000+ Napier, Pond, Athey & Athey, PC; $50,000/less Athey Family Partnership (rental prop.); *Pay. for Representation & Other Services Generally*, legal services $10,001-$50,000 ea.: casualty insur. co., localities; $1,001-$10,000 ea.:   oil/gas retail, banks, savings, loan/finance; *Real Estate*, Four properties w/others (2 rentals); Gifts: $370 Altria, dinner; $50 GlaxoSmithKline, dinner; $243 VADA, convention.

HOUSE DISTRICT TWENTY-TWO, *Kathy J. Byron (R)*

POLITICAL AND LEGISLATIVE BACKGROUND
House District 22 consists of all of Campbell County; and part of Bedford County comprised of the Chamblissburg, Staunton River, Moneta, Mountain View, New London, Walton's Store, White House, and Huddleston Precincts, and parts of the Forest and Jefferson Precincts.

Kathy J. Byron, who heads her own telemarketing firm of B & B Presentations, has served since her election in 1997.   The seat was opened upon the retirement of Joyce K. Crouch (R) who had served since 1990, winning the seat held for many years by her husband, Joseph Crouch, until his death. Byron, a Republican, won with 59.0% of the vote over Democrat Kaye Sweeney Lipscomb.   In 1999, Byron defeated Democratic newcomer Jason Campbell with 63.9% of the vote.   Byron won the 2001 election
with 56.3% of the vote over Independent challenger W. Shelton Miles, III, a pastor.   Miles garnered far more votes than do Independent candidates generally.

During the 2004 session, Byron sponsored fourteen bills, nine passed, one was carried over. Bills that passed provided for penalties when assault and battery were committed against family or household members; expanded the types of activities that principles must report to local law enforcement officers regarding persons illegally carrying a firearm on school property; established a penalty for those who knowingly are infected with a sexually transmitted disease or hepatitis B engaging in sexual activity with the intent to transmit the infection to another person; required parental consent for minors to use the morning after pill, and provided that extend health insurance coverage for dependent children.

A bill continued which provided that hearsay statements by children age seven and younger are admissible in civil abuse and neglect cases.

A successful resolution established a joint subcommittee to study issuing smart driver's licenses and identification.

Bills that failed would have established procedures for hearings prior to issuing a warrant for arrest and authorized respiratory care practitioners to administer controlled substances within the scope of their practice.

Delegate, HD 22

SIXTH CONGRESSIONAL DISTRICT
Kathy J. Byron (R) Member House 1998- ; b. September 5, 1953, Abingdon, PA; home, 516 Bent Oak Ct., Lynchburg 24502; 804-582-1592; married, John "Jack" T. Byron; Baptist.

CEO B&B Presentations, Inc.; Member: Republican Women's Club; Greater Lynchburg Chamber of Commerce.

Offices 523 Leesville Rd., Lynchburg 24502; 434-582-1592; FAX 804-522-1591; GA Bldg., Rm. 414, Capitol Sq., Richmond 23219; 804-698-1022.

2004 Committees *Agriculture, Chesapeake and Natural Resources; Commerce and Labor; Finance; Science and Technology.*

House Key Votes, 2004
Please see Introduction for more information on bills.

1) Budget Bill	FOR	5) Family Life	AGN	9) Morning After	FOR
2) Feticide	FOR	6) Fire Arms	FOR	10) Legal Aid	AGN
3) Marriage	FOR	7) Open Space	AGN		
4) Abortion	FOR	8) Home School	FOR		

Election Results
2004 general	Kathy J. Byron	(R)	11,564	100%	$24,195

Campaign Contributions 2004 Finance $4,500; Health Care $2,961; Tech/Communications $2,500; Energy $2,000; Law $1,600; Transportation $1,318; Agriculture $1,250; Mfg $1,200; Realty $1,000; Busines/Retail Svs $750.

Economic Interests, 2004 *Sal. & Wages,* $10,000+ B&B Presentations, Inc.; *Off. & Dir.,* B&B Presentations, Pres.; *Pay. for Talks, Mtgs., & Pub.,* $300 state (ALEC, expenses, per diem), $1,959 House of Delegates, Conference (expenses); *Gifts,* $70 Geico, dinner; *Bus. Int.,* $50,000+ ea.: B&B Presentations (telemark.), Windy Bush (realty); *Pay. for Rep. & Other Services Generally$50,000 - $100,000*: trade associations, marketing direct mail, other; Real Estate: recreational land.

HOUSE DISTRICT TWENTY-THREE, *L. Preston Bryant, Jr. (R)*

POLITICAL AND LEGISLATIVE BACKGROUND
House District 23 consists of all of the City of Lynchburg; and part of Amherst County comprised of the Wright Shop and Coolwell Precincts.

L. Preston Bryant, Jr., an executive with a civil engineering firm, and a Republican, has served this district since 1995. The seat opened with the election of Republican Steve Newman to Senate District 23. Bryant narrowly defeated Democrat Gilliam "Gibb" Cobbs, who had lost to Newman in 1993, by 777 votes. Bryant easily won in 1997 over Democratic challenger James B. "Jim" Feinman, and he was unopposed in 1999 and 2001. During 2002, *The Roanoke Times* began a regular feature of columns by Bryant and by former Delegate Barnie Day (D).

During the 2004 session, Bryant sponsored seventeen bills, thirteen passed, two were carried over. Bills that passed granted powers to the Assistive Technology Loan Fund Authority to borrow money; proposed taxation changes in telecommunication services; increased the pay back period for in energy performance-based contacts; provided for vaccinations for residents of nursing homes and the development of long-term care insurance for state employees.

The only bill that was continued provided for a voluntary contributor to the Dr. Martin Luther King, Jr. Commission Fund under the state income tax.

Delegate HD 23

L. Preston Bryant, Jr. (R), Member House: 1996-; b. June 5, 1964, Lynchburg; home, 1403 Oakwood Ct., Lynchburg 24503; educ. Randolph-Macon Col. (B.A.), Univ. Richmond (M. Hum.), Univ. of London (M.A.); married, Elizabeth Southworth Walker; Episcopal.

Vice President, Hurt & Proffitt, Inc. (engineering, planning, surveying); Member, Lynchburg City Council (1994-95), Kiwanis Club; Bd. member: Central VA Community Services (1994-95), Randolph-Macon Col. Bd. of Assoc. (1994-), VA Fndn. for Humanities and Public Policy (1994-); award "Clean Water Legislator of the Year, 1998" VA Assn Municipal Wastewater Agencies.

Offices P.O. Box 3589, Lynchburg 24503; 434-528-1097; GA Bldg., Rm. 706, Capitol Square, Richmond 23219; 804-698-1023.

2004 Committees *Appropriations; Commerce and Labor; Counties, Cities and Towns.*

House Key Votes, 2004
Please see Introduction for more information on bills.

1) Budget Bill	FOR	5) Family Life	AGN	9) Morning After	FOR
2) Feticide	FOR	6) Fire Arms	FOR	10) Legal Aid	FOR
3) Marriage	FOR	7) Open Space	FOR		
4) Abortion	FOR	8) Home School	FOR		

Election Results

2004 general	L. Preston Bryant, Jr.	(R)	13,396	97.1%	$46,228

Campaign Contributions 2004 Health Care $33,331; Law $9,044; Energy $8,725; Finance $6,975; Tech/Communications $5,750; Realty $4,250; Public Employees $4,000; Political $3,000; Mfg $2,300; Business/Retail Svs $1,650; Transportation $1,500; Misc $975; Defense $750; Agriculture 750; Undetermined $250.

Economic Interests, 2004 *Sal. & Wages*, $10,000+ ea.: Hurt & Proffitt, Inc.; WSET TV; *Off. & Dir.*, Hurt & Proffitt, VP; *Sec.*, $10,001-$50,000 ea.: mutual funds (2), annuity, stock in own co.; *Pay. for Talks, Mtgs., & Publ.*, $804 state (Sothern Regional Educ. Board, expenses, per diem); *Bus. Int.*, $50,000+ rental prop.; $50,000/less Hurt & Proffitt (engineering); *Pay. for Rep. by Associates*, Hurt & Proffitt (consulting eng.) for clients before DOT, DEQ, Health, Cons. & Rec., VA Tech, Central VA Comm. College, UVA, Longwood, VA Comm. College System, VA Museum Nat. History; *Pay. for Rep. & Other Services Generally*, engineering services $250,001+ ea.: water utilities, manuf., localities; $100,001-$250,000 ea.: electric, banks, savings, loan/finance; $50,001-$100,000 ea.: gas util., tel., life insur.; *Real Estate*, duplex residential, rental townhouse; Gifts: $169 VA Sheriffs Assoc. annual mtg., expenses; $114 VA Sheriffs Assoc, plaque; $67 McGuire Woods Consulting, dinner.

HOUSE DISTRICT TWENTY-FOUR, *Benjamin L. Cline (R)*

POLITICAL AND LEGISLATIVE BACKGROUND

The House District 24 consists of all of Rockbridge County; all of the Cities of Buena Vista and Lexington; part of Amherst County comprised of the New Glasgow, Courthouse, Temperance, Monroe, Elon, Pleasant View, Amelon, and Madison Precincts; and part of Augusta County comprised of the Middlebrook, Spottswood, White Hill, and Sherando Precincts.

Benjamin L. Cline is the new Delegate for House District 24. A Republican and former staff member for U.S. Congressman Robert Goodlatte, Cline won the November 2002 election, defeating Mime Elrond, Democrat and director of Summer Scholars at Washington & Lee University, with 57.4% of the vote. An editorial in Lynchburg's *News & Advance* noted that Cline "owns a condo in Washington, DC, and was campaigning out of his parents' house in Lexington. The fact that Cline didn't live or work in the district didn't make much difference to a majority of those who voted. Neither did the fact that he failed to vote in three of the last four elections." Furthermore, "He ran on a staunchly conservative ticket that seemed to resonate with the district's voters. The district drawn by [former Delegate and House Speaker Vance] Wilkins is about as Republican as they come." Cline expressed interest in beginning a technology related company, as he had to resign from his position with Goodlatte in order to assume his House duties. Quoted in Shenandoah's *The News Leader*, Cline said his top priority in the 2003 session would be a bill to make prescription drugs more affordable for the elderly.

During the 2004 session, Cline sponsored ten bills, three passed. The bills that passed authorized the development of a single application form for pharmaceutical assistance programs and purchasing discount cards; amended the Charter of the Town of Glasgow; and granted that retired law enforcement officers could carry concealed weapons.

All twenty resolutions were successful. One joint resolution instructed the Transportation Board and Department of Transportation to review ways to address congestion and safety problems on interstate Route 81.

Delegate HD 24

Benjamin L. Cline (R) Member House: 2002- ; b. Feb. 29, 1972, Stillwater, OK; home Amherst; educ. Bates Coll. (B.A.); Roman Catholic.

Self-Employed; Member St. Patrick's Church.

Offices P.O. Box 1405, Amherst 24521; 434-946-9908; GA Bldg., Rm. 719, Capitol Sq., Richmond 23219; 804-698-1024.

2004 Committees *Agriculture, Chesapeake and Natural Resources; Counties, Cities and Towns, Militia, Police and Public Safety.*

House Key Votes, 2004

SIXTH CONGRESSIONAL DISTRICT
Please see Introduction for more information on bills.

1) Budget Bill	FOR	5) Family Life	AGN	9) Morning After	FOR
2) Feticide	FOR	6) Fire Arms	FOR	10) Legal Aid	AGN
3) Marriage	FOR	7) Open Space	FOR		
4) Abortion	FOR	8) Home School	FOR		

Election Results

2004 general	Benjamin L. Cline	(R)	10,176	69.2%	$67,411
	Eric Sheffield	(I)	7,538	30.8%	$13,146

Campaign Contributions 2004: Tech/Communications $2,500; Health Care $2,000; Transportation $1,750; Energy $1,750; Law $1,650; Mfg $1,000; Political $1,000; Business $1,000; Finance $1,000; Realty $1,000; Agriculture $950; Public Employees $750; Misc $250; Undetermined $200.

Economical Interests 2004: Offices & Directorships: New Dominion Solutions, LLC., President; Business Interests $50,000 or less: New Dominion Solutions, LLC; Gifts: $76 Mc Guire Woods, Consulting, dinner; $118 DuPont Govt Affairs, dinner; $130 VA Cable, dinner; $100 VA Auto Dealers Assoc., dinner.

HOUSE DISTRICT TWENTY-FIVE, *R. Steven "Steve" Landes (R)*

POLITICAL AND LEGISLATIVE BACKGROUND
House District 25 consists of all of the City of Waynesboro; part of Albemarle County comprised of the Crozet Precinct; part of Augusta County comprised of the Verona, Crimora, New Hope, Weyers Cave, Fort Defiance, Lyndhurst, Dooms, Fishersville, and Wilson Precincts; and part of Rockingham County comprised of the Mill Creek, Grottoes, Elkton, McGaheysville, and South Fork Precincts.

Republican R. Steven Landes, a life insurance agent, has served since 1995. The seat was opened with the retirement of Republican Pete Giesen, who had served almost continuously since 1964. Landes, who had been a legislative assistant to Giesen and others, defeated Democratic opposition in that year, and overcame Independent challenges in 1997 and 1999. Landes was unopposed in 2001.

During the 2004 session, Landes sponsored twenty-one bills, fourteen passed and four carried over. Bills that passed abolished the Rudee Inlet Authority; abolished the establishment of bird sanctuaries in Roanoke County and the town of Culpeper; established the Office of Secretary of Agriculture and Forestry; created the Center for Rural Virginia; and created the Wine Board within the Department of Agriculture and Wine Promotion Fund and abolishes the Winegrowers Advisory Board.

Carried over bills that granted income tax credit for long-term care insurances; provided health insurance coverage and treatment inborn errors of metabolism; and established that health analysis was admissible in cases of driving under the influence of alcohol or drugs.

Sixteen resolutions were successful. They provided for a joint subcommittee to study the balance of power between the execution and legislative branches if the governor could serve two terms; a Joint Legislative Audit and Review Commission to study the social services system; and a resolution to rescind and withdraw all past resolutions which applied to Congress calling a convention to amend the U.S. Constitution.

Bills that failed would have abolished the establishement of a bird sanctuary in Roanoke Coaunty; and included special agents of the Department of Corrections under the Law Officer's Retirement system.

SIXTH CONGRESSIONAL DISTRICT

Delegate HD 25

R. Steven "Steve" Landes (R) Member House: 1996; b. Nov. 15, 1959, Staunton; home, Rte. 1, Box 606, Weyers Cave 24486; educ. VA Commonwealth Univ. (B.S.); married, Angela Beth Hochmeister; United Church of Christ.

Life Insur. Agent; Member: Frontier Culture Museum (Bd. Trust.), Ruritan Club, Chamb. Comm., Model Gen. Assem. (past adv.), Shenandoah Valley Priv. Ind. Council (past VCh.); Outstanding Young Men of Am. (1988-89, 1992); 1992 Rep. Natl. Conv.

Offices   P.O. Box 42, Weyers Cave 24486; 540-245-5540; GA Bldg., Rm. 528, Capitol Sq., Richmond 23219; 804-698-1025.

2004 Committees   *Appropriations; Education; Health, Welfare and Institutions.*

House Key Votes, 2004

Please see Introduction for more information on bills.

1) Budget Bill	FOR	5) Family Life	AGN	9) Morning After	FOR
2) Feticide	FOR	6) Fire Arms	FOR	10) Legal Aid	FOR
3) Marriage	FOR	7) Open Space	FOR		
4) Abortion	FOR	8) Home School	FOR		

Election Results

2004 general   R. Steven "Steve" Landes   (R)   16,196   99.0% $36,322

Campaign Contributions 2004 Health Care $8,000; Tech/Communicatons $3,250; Law $3,000; Finance $2,700; Realty $2,250; Transportation $2,000; Energy $1,500; Agriculture $1,250; Business/Retail Svs $955; Misc $500; Mfg $500.

Economic Interests, 2004 *Sal. & Wages,* $10,000+ ea.: NewBiz Virginia, Exec. Dir. (self), Atty. & Legal Specialist, Central Shenandoah Criminal Justice Training Academy; Assist. Commonwealth's Atty. Augusta Co. (spouse); *Sec.,* $10,001-$50,000 ea.: mut. funds (2); money market SunTrust Bank, stock in bank holding co.; Gifts: $75 VA Agribusiness, dinner; $157 Astra Zeneca, dinner; $102 Old Dominion Hwy contractors, dinner; $130 VA Cable, dinner; $296 DuPont, dinner; $64 Mathew Bender Co., dinner; $100 VA Auto Dealers Assoc., dinner; $272 VA Horse Council, trail ride; $75 Shenandoah Valley Tech Council, dinner; VA Tech, football tkts; $80 UVACommonwealth Day; $100 Mantel USA, box of flower bulbs; Real Estate: farm land.

SENATE DISTRICT TEN, *John C. Watkins (R)*

POLITICAL AND LEGISLATIVE BACKGROUND
Senate District 10 contains the counties of Amelia and Powhatan; the Chesterfield County Precincts of Skinquarter, Tomahawk, Evergreen, Woolridge, Brandermill, Smoketree, Monacan, Reams, Huguenot, Crestwood, Midlothian, Robious, Bon Air, Greenfield, Salisbury, Cranbeck, Sycamore, Shenandoah, Beaufont, Watkins, and Belgrade 508/Black Heath 511; the Cumberland County Precincts 1-1, 1-2, 2, and 3, and part of Precinct 4; the Goochland County Precincts of Fife, Hadensville, Three Square, Sandy Hook, and Goochland Court House; Henrico County's Monument Hills Precinct; and the City of Richmond Precincts of 101-106, 111-114, 203, 204, 207, 409-411, 413.

John C. Watkins, head of his own plant nursery, and a Republican, is the senator for this district. First elected to the House in 1981, Watkins ran unopposed in a special senate election in early 1998 when the seat was opened after Governor-elect James Gilmore (R) appointed then Senator Joseph Benedetti (R) to be director of the Department of Criminal Justice Services. Watkins easily won re-election in 1999. He introduced the Republican congressional redistricting plan in the summer 2001 sessions.

During the 2004 session, Watkins sponsored twenty-six bills, fifteen passed; four were carried over to the 2005 session. All four of his resolutions passed. The bills that passed provide for filing annual reports of public service corporations; amended the City Charter of Richmond; provided the location and testing of water wells in Goochland County; created the Virginia-North Carolina Interstate High-Speed Rail Compact; provided penalties for late filing for unemployment compensation; placed the Migrant and Seasonal Farm Worker's Board and Migrant Worker Policy Committee under the auspices of the Employment Commission; assessed permit application fees and annual fees to generate funding for air, water and waste permit programs; required certain electric suppliers to pay a minimum tax rather than a corporate tax, when their minimum tax liability is greater than the corporate tax liability.

Bills continued provided transportation impact fees in certain counties for new residential development; and eliminated offsets for Social Security on Railroad Retirement Act benefits when the unemployment trust fund has a solvency lend of 50 percent or more.

A resolution passed requiring the Department of Health to study statewide response to victims of sexual assault.

Failed bills would have limited the rate imposed by localities on generating equipment reported to the State Corporation Commission by electric suppliers; and provided for an additional one percent occupancy tax for any two contiguous counties trying to attract convention business to the region. ;

Senate SD 10

John Chewning Watkins (R) Member Senate: 1998- ; Member House: 1982-1998; b. March 1, 1947, Petersburg; home, 15610 Midlothian Tnpk., Midlothian 23113; educ. VPI & SU (B.S.); married Kathryn Ann Clawson; Lutheran.

Pres. Watkins Nurseries; VA, Southern/Am. Nurserymen's Assns.; Am. Soc. Landscape Archs./Landscape Contrac. Am.; Rotary; Jaycees; Am. Legion; J. S. Reynolds Comm. Coll. fac.; Chesterfield Hist. Soc.; Ch. Bd. Zoning Appeals 1977-81; Army 1970-71.

Offices P.O. Box 159, Midlothian 23113-0159; 804-379-2063; GA Bldg., Capitol Sq., Rm. 316, Richmond 23219; 804-698-7510.

SEVENTH CONGRESSIONAL DISTRICT

2004 Committees *Agriculture, Conservation and Natural Resources; Commerce and Labor; Local Government; Transportation.*

Senate Key Votes, 2004
Please see Introduction for more information on bills.

1) Budget Bill	FOR	5) Family Life	FOR	9) Charter School	FOR
2) Feticide	FOR	6) Fire Arms	FOR	10) Legal Aid	AGN
3) Marriage	FOR	7) Open Space	AGN		
4) Child Abuse	AGN	8) Home School	FOR		

Election Results

1999 general	John C. Watkins	(R)	21,366	69.9%	$217,809
	Alexander McMurtrie	(I)	9,164	30.0%	$526,693

Campaign Contributions 2000-June 30, 2002 Realty/Constr. $27,600; **Finance** $13,600; **Medical** $12,200; **Tech./Comm.** $10,600; **Attys.** $10,425; **Electric** $9,450; **Insur./HMOs** $8,650; **Transp.** $5,150 (Auto Dealers/Manuf. $2,900); **Retail** $4,075 (Grocery $3,050); **Nat. Gas** $3,550; **Tobacco** $2,600 (PM $1,300, Smokeless $1,300); **Pub. Empl.** $2,450; **Chem./Plastics** $2,000; **NNShipbldg.** $1,500; **Oil** $1,150; **Coal** $1,000; **Kings Dom.** $1,000; **Funeral** $900; **Individ.** $848; **Columbia Energy** $780; **Billboards** $750; **Honeywell** $750; **Beer** $550; **Quarries** $500; **Trash** $400; **Serv. Stat./Conv. St.** $300; **Village Turf** $150; **Koch** $150.

Economic Interests, 2002 *Sal. & Wages,* $10,000 + ea.: Watkins Nursery (WN); Chesterfield Sch.; *Off. & Dir.,* WN, Pres.; Chippenham/Johnston Willis Hospital, Dir.; Bank Powhatan, Dir.; Watkins Land (WL), Manager; TransCommunity Financial, Bd of Directors.; *Pers. Liabil.,* $50,000+ banks (self), other loan/finance co. (family); $10,001 $50,000 banks (fam.); *Sec.,* $50,000+ ea.: stock WN, Wat. Land, Wat. Amelia, Wat. Carolina, Bank of Am.; $10,001-$50,000 ea.: mutual fund, stock in: Dry Bridge Ptnship., Motorola, Gillette, Rocky Oak ltd. liability, WL Powhatan, Fighting Creek Ptnship, Bank Powhatan; *Pay. for Talks, Mtgs., & Pub.,* $6,089 state (SLC, NCSL, SSEB, VA-NC Interstate High-Speed Comm., expenses, per diem); *Gifts,* $89 VA Agribusiness Council, reception, banquet; $152 Altria, Kraft Days Reception; $147 Altria, dinner; $346 Altria, NASCAR Nextel race; $336 Altria, NASCAR race; $159 Altria, PMUSA Open House, $105 Property Casualty Insurers Assoc., dinner; $63 Bon Secours, reception, dinner; $76 State Farm Ins., dinner; $395 Dominion, VA Tech football game tkts, transportation and food; *Bus. Int.,* (all realty except nursery) $50,000+ ea.: WN, WL, Watkins Amelia; $50,000/less ea.: Dry Bridge, Watkins Carolina; WL of Powhatan, Rocky Oak; *Pay. for Rep. & Other Serv. Gen.,* $250,001+ ea.: Retail Companies, Counties, cities, or towns, other residential, plant material, landscaping service; $50,000 to $100,000 ea.: banks, localities; *Real Estate,* business office, forest, nursery product, land lease sales, options, land purchase in Chesterfield County, Powhatan County and Amelia County ; *Real Estate Contracts W/State Govt. Agencies.,* 2 prop., WN/WL, VDOT, condemna./dedica. complete.

SENATE DISTRICT ELEVEN, *Stephen H. Martin (R)*

POLITICAL AND LEGISLATIVE BACKGROUND
Senate District 11 contains the City of Colonial Heights; and the Chesterfield County Precincts of South Chester, North Chester, Harrowgate, Wells, Ecoff, Iron Bridge, Gates, Beulah, Bird, Jacobs, Falling Creek, Belmont, Chippenham, Meadowbrook, Salem Church, Five Forks, Ettrick, Deer Run, Matoaca, Winfrees Store, Beach, Winterpock, Walthall, Branches, Bailey Bridge, Spring Run, Pocahontas 307/Crenshaw 308, Genito, Providence, Lyndale, Manchester, Wagstaff, Davis, and Harbour Pointe 401/Swift Creek 411.

Stephen H. Martin, an insurance and financial consultant, and a Republican, has been in the Senate since 1994, and served as a Delegate from 1988-1994. The Senate seat opened with the resignation of

Robert E. Russell, Sr. (R) after his 1993 conviction for embezzling money from a nonprofit organization for which he was treasurer. Russell had served since 1982 when he defeated incumbent Alexander

McMurtrie, Jr. (D), and again in 1991. Martin easily won 74% of the vote from two Independent challengers and McMurtrie. Martin, unopposed in 1995, comfortably won re-election in 1999. Martin is a leader in the anti-abortion rights movement.

During the 2004 session, Martin sponsored twenty-four bills, fourteen passed; three were carried over to the 2005 session. Six of his eight resolutions passed. The bills that passed established the membership and meetings of the Out-of-Family Investigations Advocacy committee; reduced the number of publications submitted to the State Library; abolished special funds that are dormant; eliminates the reporting requirement of the Department of Housing and Community Development regarding housing funds along with medical and psychological practices audit committees; changed the distribution of annual and biennial copies of the state agency reports; permitted Chesterfield County to supplement salaries and expenses of state and local Health Department employees; allowed toll-free use of Richmond Metropolitan Authority toll facilities to quadriplegic drivers; specified the duties of members of the Child Abuse and Neglect Advisory Board; provided that the Richmond Metropolitan Authority grant free use of toll facilities quadriplegics; provided that the Transportation commissioner would maintain and repair billboard signs; and specified the condition of appointment of voting registrars; and defined non-legislature citizen member of legislation appointments.

Bills continued provide coverage of booking technicians in the Line of Duty Act; established business and real property investment tax credits in Enterprise Zones; and established a joint subcommittee to study the appointment, responsibilities, and oversight of general registrars.

A resolution failed to establish a joint subcommittee to study the Public Records Act.

Failed bills would have exempted certain martial arts programs from licensure as a day care center; provided health insurance coverage for biologically based mental illness, provided licenses for ultra light aircraft; voter registration based on political party affiliation in primary election; staffing authority for a Joint Commission or Health Care; and created a Consumer Benefits Plan.

Senator SD 11

Stephen Holliday Martin (R) Member House: 1988-1994; Senate 1994- ; b. June 15, 1956, Chesterfield County; home, 8831 Reams Rd., Richmond 23236; educ. Lynchburg Christian Acad., graduate; married Sharon Christine Wiley; Baptist.

Insurance Consultant and Securities Dealer, Principal in Martin Financial Services; Am. Legislative Exchange Council; Richmond Assn. of Life Underwriters; Life Underwriters Training Fellow; Natl. Assn. of Security Dealers; Chesterfield CSB; Chesterfield Bus. Council; Chesterfield Alternatives, Pres., Chm. Bd.; Chesterfield Emergency Planning Comm.

Offices P.O. Box 700, Chesterfield 23832; 804-648-9073; GA Bldg., Capitol Sq., Rm. 302, Richmond 23219; 804-698-7511.

2004 Committees *Education and Health; General Laws, Local Government; Privileges and Elections.*

Senate Key Votes, 2004
Please see Introduction for more information on bills.

1) Budget Bill	AGN	5) Family Life	FOR	9) Charter School	FOR
2) Feticide	FOR	6) Fire Arms	FOR	10) Legal Aid	FOR
3) Marriage	FOR	7) Open Space	FOR		
4) Child Abuse	AGN	8) Home School	FOR		

Election Results

1999	Stephen Martin	(R)	17,716	64.5%	$261,287
	W. S. Hastings, Jr.	(D)	9,689	35.3%	$ 28,205

Campaign Contributions 2000-June 30, 2002 **Medical** $11,400; **Insur./HMOs** $7,850; **Realty/Constr.** $7,350; **Transp.** $6,383 (Auto Dealers/Manuf./Rep. $4,833); **Finance** $5,075; **Attys.** $5,000; **Tobacco** $3,800 (PM $1,800, Universal $1,500, RJR $500); **Dupont** $3,000; **Pub. Empl.** $2,275; **Tech./Comm.** $2,250; **Electric** $2,250; **Kings Dom.** $2,000; **Day Care** $1,500; **Republicans** $1,500; **Honeywell** $1,000; **Individ.** $850; **Retail/Consult.** $750; **Serv. Stat./Conv. St.** $750; **NNShipbldg.** $500; **Oil** $250; **Billboards** $250; **VA Automat. Merch.** $250; **Natl. Fed. Ind. Bus.** $200; **Beer** $200.

Economic Interests, 2004 *Sal. & Wages*, $10,000+ ea.: Martin Financial Services, SCN L.L.C. (w/spouse), New York Life (spouse); *Personal Liability* $50,000 + ea: Credit Union; *Business Interests* $50,000 less: Martin Financial Services, SCN, vending; *Pay. for Talks, Mtgs., & Pub.*, $826 State (ALEC, conf. expenses, per diem); $904 state, ALEC annual mtg, expenses; $200 state, ALEC SNIP, per diem; *Gifts*, $263 Kings Dominion, six tkts; $85 Altria, dinner; $147 Altria, dinner; $163 Altria, NASCAR race; *Pay. for Rep. & Other Services Generally*, insurance, consulting $1,001-$10,000 ea.: oil or gas companies, insurance sales and services, mfg companies, life insurance companies, Dept of Professional Occupational Regulations; $10,000 to $50,000: higher education institution, legal; churches, legal.

SENATE DISTRICT TWELVE, *Walter A. Stosch (R)*

POLITICAL AND LEGISLATIVE BACKGROUND

Senate District 12 consists of Goochland County Precincts of Centerville and Manakin; Henrico County Precincts of Dumbarton, Glen Allen, Glenside, Greendale, Hermitage, Hilliard, Hunton, Johnson, Lakeside, Longan, Maude Trevvett, Moody, Staples Mill, Stratford Hall, Summit Court, Bloomingdale, Canterbury, Randolph, Chipplegate, Cardinal, Coalpit, Crestview, Freeman, Innsbrook, Jackson Davis, Lauderdale, Ridge, Sadler, Cedarfield, Skipwith, Three Chopt, Tucker, Westwood, Causeway, Stoney Run, Byrd, Lakewood, Derbyshire, Gayton, Godwin, Maybeury, Mooreland, Pemberton, Pinchbeck, Ridgefield, Rollingwood, Spottswood, Tuckahoe, and West End; and City of Richmond's 309 Precinct.

Walter A. Stosch, a CPA and a Republican, was elected to the 73rd House District in 1983 and to the Senate in 1991. With the retirement in 1991 of Senator Edwina Dalton Phillips (R), Stosch easily won the Senate seat over Democrat Charlotte Armstrong, retained it in 1995 against Independent Murray L. Steinberg, and had no opposition in 1999. Stosch has been the Senate Majority Leader since 1998.

SEVENTH CONGRESSIONAL DISTRICT
The Motorola site in eastern Henrico has traded hands more than once, being built on former state land which Stosch quietly helped to have designated as surplus land for economic development by the county, avoiding public hearings, according to a letter Stosch wrote to Gov. George Allen. Efforts by several environmental groups - including Alliance for the Chesapeake Bay, Audubon Society, Chickahominy Watershed Alliance, James River Association, The Nature Conservancy, Native Plant Society, Sierra Club, Varina Environmental Protection Group - to have a state owned, permanently protected preservation area of fragile and rare plants on 700 acres, near that industrial park, continue to be blocked by Henrico and Stosch, despite offers of private landowners to give hundreds of acres to such a preserve.

During the 2004 session, Stosch sponsored fifteen bills, three were continued, two were commending. They extend provisions for certain media-related businesses; issued funding agreements; created the Securities Facilitation Act; amended defined contributions of the retirement system; established a procedure when employer defaults the retirement system; reporting requirements in street maintenance in Arlington and Henrico Counties.

Continued bills would provide road impact fees; corporate income tax credit against cigarette manufactured and exported to a foreign county; changed Securities Act to Uniform Securities Act; and joint subcommittee to study public funding.

Senator SD 12

Walter Allen Stosch (R) Member Senate: 1992-; Member House 1983-92; b. Aug. 18, 1936, Fredericksburg; home, 12101 Country Hills Way, Glen Allen 23059; educ. U Richmond (B.S. Acct.), (M.B.A.); married Eleanor Herbert; Baptist.

Certified Public Accountant; Sr. partner Gary, Stosch, Walls, & Co.; Bd. Dir., VA Soc. CPA; Outstanding CPA VA 1980; Richmond Jaycees; Am. Legion; Lions; U.S. Army 1953-56; Richmond Area Heart Assn. (past Chm.); Dominion Club (founding bd. member).

Offices 4551 Cox Road, Suite 110, Richmond 23060-6740; 804-527-7780; FAX 527-7740; GA Bldg., Capitol Sq., Rm. 621, Richmond 23219; 804-698-7512.

2004 Committees *General Laws, Chair; Commerce and Labor; Finance; Rules; Transportation.*

Senate Key Votes, 2004
Please see Introduction for more information on bills.

1) Budget Bill	FOR	5) Family Life	FOR	9) Charter Schools	FOR
2) Feticide	FOR	6) Fire Arms	FOR	10) Legal Aid	FOR
3) Marriage	FOR	7) Open Space	FOR		
4) Child Abuse	FOR	8) Home School	FOR		

Election Results

1999 general	Walter A. Stosch	(R)	24,451	98.7%	$346,618

Campaign Contributions 2000-June 30, 2002 Republicans $135,740; **Finance** $4,300 (CPAs $2,500); **Tech./Comm.** $4,000; **Medical** $3,500; **Tobacco--PM** $2,000; **Attys.** $1,250; **Realty/Constr.** $1,200; **Serv. Stat./Conv. St.** $1,000; **Dupont** $1,000; **Cobb Office Prod.** $900; **Honeywell** $750; **Horse/Trainers** $750; **Transp.** $650; **Nat. Gas** $500; **Electric** $500; **VA Nat. Resources** $500.

Economic Interests, 2004 *Sal. & Wages,* $10,000+ ea.: Stosch, Dacey & George, P.C.(SDG); *Off. & Dir.,* Stockholder & Dir. in: SDG; Universal Corp.; *Pers. Liabil.,* $50,000+ banks; *Sec.,* $50,000+

ea.: mut. funds (3), Wilmington Trust retire., United Dominion Retire., Centerpoint Prop. Ptnship, Ace, Anh. Busch, Berkshire Hathaway, Cincinn. Finan., Markel, XL Capital, Martin Marietta, Clayton Homes, Carmax Group; $10,001-$50,000 ea.: mut. funds (3), RLI Corp., Cedar Fair Ptnship, Albemarle Corp., Hillenbrand Ind., Servicemaster, Dominion Res., Brown Forman, Universal Corp., International Speedway, Circuit City, Albertsons, Am. Express, Ford Motor, Walt Disney, Harrah's Entertainment; *Gifts:$176 Reynolds, briefcase; $84 VA Agribusiness council, golf tournament; $159 Altria, open house*; Business Interests: $50,000/less ea.: 5 investment partnerships: Fairlane/Greenville (SC), Southern Pines/Tanglewood (NC), Elizabeth City/Southgate (NC), Brookbury Gr. (Richmond); Stosch Group, rental farm; *Pay. for Rep. by You*, $10,000+ tax indiv. & bus. excess of $10,000, tax returns, VEC; *Pay. for Rep. by Assoc.*, CPA firm at Dept. Tax., VEC, state courts, SCC, "etc."; *Pay. for Rep. & Other Serv. Gen.*, $100,001-$250,000 manuf. co.; $50,001-$100,000 retail co.; $1,001-$10,000 electric, telephone util.; *Real Estate*, Two prop. (land, farm) w/others. **Please note:** Senator Stosch for several years has not listed any amounts of money received for representation or services rendered before state agencies, only giving a blanket letter that he occasionally helps with tax returns, and that details cannot be disclosed.

SENATE DISTRICT TWENTY-FIVE, *R. Creigh Deeds (D)*

POLITICAL AND LEGISLATIVE BACKGROUND
Senate District 25 contains the counties of Alleghany, Bath, and Nelson; the Cities of Buena Vista, Charlottesville, Clifton Forge, and Covington; Albemarle County's Precincts of Woodbrook, Commonwealth, Branchlands, Agnor-Hurt, Jack Jouett, University Hall, Ivy, East Ivy, North Garden 302/Batesville 303, Scottsville, Monticello, Porter's, Covesville, Cale, Keswick, Stony Point, Hollymead, Free Bridge, and Earlysville; Buckingham County's Glenmore Precinct; and the Rockbridge County Precincts of Airport, Ben Salem, Fancy Hill, Effinger, Collierstown, Glasgow, Natural Bridge, Fairfield, Mountain View, and Vesuvius.

R. Creigh Deeds, an attorney and a Democrat, is the new senator for this district. Deeds, who had served in the House since 1992, was re-elected to the House in November 2001. Redistricting moved Deeds from the old House District 18 to the new House District 12, which Delegate James Shuler (D) had represented. Then, in December 2001, and following the tragic death of Senator Emily Couric (D) from pancreatic cancer, Deeds won the special senate election for that seat. Couric, a published author, had been seen as a formidable candidate for Lt. Governor. She had served since 1995, focusing on education, health care reform, and environmental protections. Couric served as head of the Democratic Party in her last year. Couric had overturned first term senator Edgar Robb (R) with 50.1% of the vote in a four candidate race. Robb had, four years earlier, scored a 644 vote (0.6%) victory over 20 year veteran legislator Thomas J. Michie, Jr. (D), respected for his strong stand for the rights of women and for his landmark Indoor Clean Air Act. Deeds defeated Republican Jane S. Maddux in the December 18th special election with 68.7% of the vote, as Couric had done in 1999.

During the 2004 session, Deeds sponsored twenty-six bills, nine passed and nine were carried over to the 2005 session. Nine of ten resolutions were successful. Bills that passed designate Route 220 as Sam Snead Memorial Highway; imposed a utility tax on consumers in the Town of Irongate; exempted certain people receiving transportation services from the Freedom of Information Act; regulated the posting of signs at yard sales and auctions; placed restrictions on using bicycles and mopeds on roadways; created the Rivanna River Basin Commission; and regulated the filing of title insurance documents with circuit court clerks.

Bills continued specified a procurement preference for U.S. made goods; a deferred real estate tax for certain disabled military veterans; abolished the prohibition against duck blind hunting in certain localities. Provided that spousal support agreements are subject to revision by the court and that spousal support terminates upon cohabitation. The imposition of a transient occupancy tax in Nelson County; and the creation of an annual report on the effectiveness of the prescription drug payment assistance programs; and agreements for spousal support, modification and enforcement in divorce decrees.

Failed bills would have stipulated no penalty if parties engaged in wire electronic, or oral communications had previously consented to interception; and assessment for the State Police Training and Relations Fund; a tax waiver if parties seeking a marriage license have received prior counseling; and created a Natural and Historic Resource Fund and Commission.

Senator SD 25

Robert Creigh Deeds (D); Member Senate: 2002- ; Member House: 1992-2001; b. Jan. 4, 1958, Richmond; home, P.O. Box 266, Millboro 24460; educ. Concord Col. (BA), Wake Forest Univ. (JD); married Pamela Kay Miller; Presbyterian.

Attorney; member, Am. & VA State Bar, VA Trial Lawyers, Ruritans, Lions; Deputy Commissioner Bath; former chair, House Democratic Caucus.

Offices P.O. Drawer D, Hot Springs 24445; 540-839-2473; P.O. Box 5462 Charlottesville 22905-5462; 434-296-5491; GA Bldg., Rm. 308, Capitol Sq., Richmond 23219; 804-698-7525.

2004 Committees   *Agriculture, Conservation and Natural Resources; Privileges and Elections; Transportation.*

Senate Key Votes, 2004
Please see Introduction for more information on bills.

1) Budget Bill	FOR	5) Family Life	FOR	9) Charter Schools	AGN
2) Feticide	FOR	6) Fire Arms	FOR	10) Legal Aid	FOR
3) Marriage	AGN	7) Open Space	FOR		
4) Child Abuse	FOR	8) Home School	FOR		

Election Results

2001 special	R. Creigh Deeds	(D)	20,093	68.7%	$220,929
	Jane S. Maddux	(R)	9,117	31.2%	$173,935

Campaign Contributions 2000-June 30, 2002   **Medical** $3,400; **Finance** $2,500; **Democrats** $2,500; **Attys.** $2,275; **Tech./Comm.** $1,750; **Realty/Constr.** $1,500; **GA Pacific** $1,000; **Insur.** $1,000; **Beer/Wine** $850; **Serv. St./Conv. St.** $750; **Oil** $550; **Auto Dealers** $500; **Electric** $500; **Tobacco--PM** $500; **Restau.** $350; **Individ.** $300; **Planned Par. Blue Ridge PAC** $300; **Farmer** $200.

Economic Interests, 2004   *Sal. & Wages,* $10,000+ R. Creigh Deeds law; *Pers. Liabil.,* $10,001-$50,000 Banks; *Sec.,* $10,001-$50,000 ea.: mutual funds (2), stock in BB&T bank; Gifts: $170 VA Trial Lawyers Assoc, convention fee waived; $145 UVA, tkts to two pre-games, refreshments; $88 Reynolds, attache case; Real Estate: 2 residential, agricultural properties, forest land.

SENATE DISTRICT TWENTY-SIX, *Mark D. Obershain (R)*

POLITICAL AND LEGISLATIVE BACKGROUND

SEVENTH CONGRESSIONAL DISTRICT

Senate District 26 consists of the counties of Page, Rappahannock, Shenandoah, and Warren; the City of Harrisonburg; the Rockingham County Precincts of Broadway, Timberville, Fulks Run, Bergton, Lacey Spring, Singers Glen, Edom, Melrose, Tenth Legion, Dayton, Turner Ashby (Silver Lake), Ottobine, Mt. Clinton, and Bridgewater.

Mark Obershain replaced Kevin Miller in the 2004 election. There were no legislative records.

Senator SD 26

Mark D. Obershain (R) Member Senate: 2004 -; b Jun. 11, 1962, Richmond, VA; educ. Virginia Tech (BA, 1984); Washington and Lee University School of Law (JD 1987); married, Suzanne Speas Obenshain; Presbyterian.

Attorney

P.O. Box 555. Harrisonburg, VA 22803, (540) 437-3126, FAX (540) 437-3134; P.O. Box 396, Richmond, VA 23218, (804) 698-7526, FAX (804) 698-7651.

2004 Committees Agriculture, Conservation and Natural Resources, Courts of Justice, Local Government, Privileges and Elections.

House Key Votes, 2004   Obanshain was not in office for Key Votes in 2004
Please see Introduction for more information on bills.

1) Budget Bill	5) Family Life	9) Morning After
2) Feticide	6) Fire Arms	10) Legal Aid
3) Marriage	7) Open Space	
4) Abortion	8) Home School	

Election Results

2004 general	Mark Obenshain	(R)	27,366	67.9%	$211,695
	Rodney Eagle	(I)		31.9%	$61,863

Economic Interests, 2004 Salary or Wages: Keeler Obenshain PC; Sec. to $50,000: 4 mutual funds, more than $50,000: one mutual fund; Paymts for representation by associates: Motor Vehicle & Trailer Dealers, commercial landowners, various employers, Business Interests $50,000 +: Keeler Obanshain, PC; Paymts for representation and other services generally: legal services to cable television companies, Inter and Intra state transportation, oil or gas, banks, mfg, casualty companies, retail, beer, wine or liquor companies, counties, cities, towns, other; Gifts: $382 VA Tech, football tkts; $88 Ringling Bros Circus, tkts; $ 100 VA Auto Dealers Assoc, dinner; $130 VA Cable, dinner; Real Estate: open land, rental property.

SEVENTH CONGRESSIONAL DISTRICT
HOUSE DISTRICT TWENTY-SEVEN, *Samuel A. Nixon, Jr. (R)*

POLITICAL AND LEGISLATIVE BACKGROUND
House District 27 consists of part of Chesterfield County comprised of the Gates, Beulah, Bird, Jacobs, Falling Creek, Chippenham, Meadowbrook, Five Forks, Deer Run, Spring Run, Pocahontas 307/ Crenshaw 308, Genito, Providence, and Lyndale Precincts, and part of the Manchester Precinct.

Samuel A. Nixon, Jr., President of Strategic Information Systems, and a Republican, has represented the area since 1994. In that year, Nixon won a special election on March 8, 1994, was sworn into office on the 10th, and the session adjourned on the 12th. Republican Stephen Martin had served in the House since 1988, but ran for and won the 11th Senate District seat vacated by Republican Senator Robert Russell after a conviction for embezzlement. Nixon won the expensive two week campaign in which he outspent Democrat Marjorie M. Clark. Nixon took 81.0% of the vote in this Republican stronghold. Nixon was unopposed in 1997. In 1995 and 1999 Nixon defeated Independent Bradley E. Evans who had run unsuccessfully against Stephen Martin twice before. In 2001, Nixon again was unopposed.

During the 2004 session, Nixon sponsored thirteen bills, eight passed and two were carried over to the 2005 session. Bills that passed created online auctions under the Public Procurement Act; abolished non-profit debt counseling agencies; provided for deposits to be made by self insurers into worker's compensation; provided for the issuance of motorcycle's learners permits; provided for exemption of the University of Virginia Medical Center on information and telecommunications procurements; and provided for special education for children with disabilities who are placed across jurisdiction lines.

Bills continued established a penalty for providing remote access without written certification of compatibility in land records.

Failed bills would have created the use of Internet filters in libraries to protect against child pornography; required a driver's license for young motorcycle operators.

Delegate HD 27

Samuel A. Nixon, Jr. (R) Member House 1994- ; b. Nov. 9, 1958, Martinsville; home, 7412 Barkbridge Road, Chesterfield 23832; educ. James Madison Univ. (BBA, Marketing); married Carol A. Gibbs Nixon; Methodist.

Information Systems Pres.; Member Chesterfield Jaycees (past treas., dir.), VA Jaycees (past Govt. Affairs Prog. Manag.), Bd. of John Tyler Comm. College, Data Proc. Mgt. Assn.; awarded Outstanding Young Men of America (1983-86, 1988); Who's Who in the South and Southeast; VA Tech Ten Legislator (1995).

Offices P.O. Box 34908, Richmond 23234; 804-745-4335; GA Bldg., Capitol Sq., Rm. 503, Richmond 23219; 804-698-1027.

2003 Committees *Commerce and Labor; Finance; Health, Welfare and Institutions; Science and Technology*

House Key Votes, 2004
Please see Introduction for more information on bills.

1) Budget Bill	FOR	5) Family Life	AGN	9) Morning After	FOR
2) Feticide	FOR	6) Fire Arms	FOR	10) Legal Aid	AGN

148

| 3) Marriage | FOR | 7) Open Space | AGN |
| 4) Abortion | FOR | 8) Home School | FOR |

Election Results

2001 general   Samuel A. Nixon, Jr.   (R) 16,012   98.2% $18,739

Campaign Contributions 2004 Tech/Communications $5,000; Health Care $4,950; Finance $4,750; Law $3,175; Realty $2,875; Agriculture $2,250; Energy $2,000; Transportation $1,750; Busainess/retail Svs $1,625; Mfg $1,200; Misc $150; Candidate Self-Financing $125.

Economic Interests, 2004 *Sal. & Wages*, $10,000+ The Computer Solution Company, Inc.; *Sec.*, $10,001-$50,000 ea.: 401K, mut. funds (3), stock in UNISYS; Paymts for representation, and other services generally $10,000 to $50,000: computer services to electric utilites, Inter and Inra state transportation companies, banks, loan and finance, mfg, life insurance, casualty, other; Gifts: $180 VA Internatl, Grand Am. Event, hotel; $100 Kings Dominion, tkts; $150 Altria, Kraft Days, reception; $109 Altria, dinner; $249 Altria, Indy car race; $336 Altria, NASCAR race; $50 William Mullens, dinner; $50 Richmond Region, book; $250 Home Depot, Nascar race.

HOUSE DISTRICT THIRTY, *Edward T. "Ed" Scott (R)*

POLITICAL AND LEGISLATIVE BACKGROUND

House District 30 consists of all of Culpeper and Madison Counties; and part of Orange County comprised of the One East, Two West, Two East, Three, Four, Locust Grove, and Lake of the Woods Precincts.

Edward T. Scott replaced George Broman in the 2004 election.

During the 2004 session, Scott sponsored five bills, all of which passed. The bills that passed allow victim statements in cases where a person pleads guilty to a felony; extended sunset provisions for free textbook distribution to professors; designated the qualifications for the using state funds by professional librarians; required the Department of Accounts to conduct recovery of state contracts; and established fee for licenses for wine or beer shippers.

Delegate HD 3   Ed Scott , House Member 2004 - ; b. Aug. 6, 1965, Culpeper, VA, educ.; Culpeper HS (1983), Va Polytechnic Institute and State University (BS Animal Science, 1987), spouse Pauline Cecil, children:Danielle; Episcopal.

Manager   Agriculture   Operations; Distinguished Young Alumni Citation (1994).

Offices: 206 S. Main Street, Suite 203, Culpeper, VA   22701, (540) 825-6400, FAX: (540) 825-6649; P.O. Box 406, Richmond, VA 23218, (804) 698-1030, FAX: (804) 786-6310.

2004 Committees   Agriculture Chesapeke and Natural Resources, Science and Technology, Transportation.

House Key Votes, 2004
Please see Introduction for more information on bills.

1) Budget Bill	FOR	5) Family Life	FOR	9) Morning After	AGN
2) Feticide	FOR	6) Fire Arms	FOR	10) Legal Aid	FOR
3) Marriage	FOR	7) Open Space	FOR		
4) Abortion	FOR	8) Home School	FOR		

Election Results

2004 general	Ed Scott	(R)	13,343	87.4%	$98,409

Campaign Contributions 2004   Candidate Self-Financing $3,000; Realty $2,600; Transportation $2,520; Finance $2,250; Law $2,100; Health Care $2,000; Energy $1,850; Political $1,750; Business/Retail Svs $1,750;Public Employees $1,700, Misc $1,350; Mfg $1,250; Agriculture $1,250; Tech/Communications $950.

Economic Interests, 2004   Salary & Wages: Culpeper Farmer's Cooperative, Inc.; Business Interests $50,000 less: Picca Enterprises, Inc, farming; Sec. to $50,000: stocks, mutual fund, 401K's; Gifts: $84 VA Agribusiness Council, golf tournament; $152 Altria, reception; $131 Altria, dinner; $102 Old Dominion Hwy Contractors, dinner; $100 VA Auto Dealers Assoc., dinner.

HOUSE DISTRICT SIXTY-FIVE, R. Lee Ware, Jr. (R)

POLITICAL AND LEGISLATIVE BACKGROUND
House District sixty-five consists of all of Powhatan County: and part of Chesterfield County comprised of the Skinquarter, Tomahawk, Evergreen, Woolridge, Brandermill, Smoketree, Monacan, Harbour Pointe 401/Swift Creek 411, Midlothian, Salisbury, Sycamore, and Watkins Precincts.

Robert Lee Ware, Jr., a history and government teacher form Powhatan County, and a Republican, was elected in 1998. The seat was opened by then Lt. Governor elect John Hager and Attorney General Richard Cullen, while Johnson was backed by his soon-to-be boss, Attorney General elect Mark Earley.   A fierce battle ensued between Ware and Democrat Edward Barber, a popular supervisor on the Chesterfield Board. Ware emerged the winner by 65.4% . Ware defeated two opponents in the 2001 election, winning with 74.9% of the vote.

During the 2004 session, Ware sponsored twelve bills, seven passed, three were carried over. The bills that passed authorized the Commissioner of Revenue to compromise and settle tax assessments prior to the exhaustion of all administrative and judicial review; authorized donations by localities to organizations providing recreational or day care to senior citizens; and established a real estate assessment depart in Powhatan County.

Bills continued provided for health insurance coverage for anorexia nervosa and bulimia nervosa; changes in the provisions of the Prisoner Litigation Reform Act; indexing of personal exemptions of the state income tax.

A failed bill would have allowed school board employees who earned $15,000 or less to subtract $15,000 from their income when filing their income tax.

Delegate   HD 65
R. Lee Ware, Jr. House Member 1998 – b. Aug. 20, 1952, Fitchburg, MA., educ.: Wheaton College, IL (BA,   1974), VA Commonwealth

University (Continuing Educ.),   spouse Kathleen Ann, children: Karen , Thomas, and Jeboman Catholic.

History and Government teacher; Powhattan County Board of Supervisors (1988-96 former Chairman), VA State Board of Educ. (1995-97); John Marshall Foundation Award for Excellence in teaching US Constitution.

Offices: P.O. Box 689, Powhatan, VA 23139, (804) 598-6696, P.O. Box 406, Richmond, VA 23218, (804) 698-1065, FAX: (804) 786-6310

2004 Committees: Agriculture Cheseapke and Natural Resources, Commerce and Labor, Finance.

House Key Votes, 2004
Please see Introduction for more information on bills.

1) Budget Bill	AGN	5) Family Life	FOR	9) Morning After	AGN
2) Feticide	FOR	6) Fire Arms	FOR	10) Legal Aid	FOR
3) Marriage	FOR	7) Open Space	FOR		
4) Abortion	FOR	8) Home School	FOR		

Election Results

2004 general	R. Lee Ware, Jr.	(R)	13,343	75.1%	$76,549
	Rob Williams	(D)		24.9%	$11,092

Campaign Contributions 2004   Realty $5,750; Finance $4,550; Law $3,200; Health Care $3,050; Energy $2,400; Tech/Communications $2,000; Misc $1,500; Public Employees $1,200; Political $1,000; Agriculture $750; Business/Retail Svs $650; Transportation $500; Undetermined $250.

Economic Interests 2004: Salary & Wages: Blessed Sacrament Huguenot, Thomas V. Smith, CPA.

HOUSE DISTRICT SIXTY-EIGHT, *Bradley P. "Brad" Marrs (R)*

POLITICAL AND LEGISLATIVE BACKGROUND
House District 68 consists of Chesterfield County precincts of Reams, Wagstaff, Huguenot, Crestwood, Robious, Bon Air, Greenfield, Cranbeck, Shenandoah, and Belgrade 508/ Black Heath 511; and part of the City of Richmond comprised of the 101-106, 112- 114, 204, 410, 411, and 413 Precincts.

Bradley P. "Brad" Marrs, a lawyer and a Republican, was elected in 2001. Marrs defeated two candidates, winning with 41.1% of the vote over Democrat Ed Barber and Independent Republican John A. Conrad. This election cost in excess of $560,000 in the power struggle.

SEVENTH CONGRESSIONAL DISTRICT

During the 2004 session, Marrs sponsored thirteen bills, six passed, three were carried over to the 2005 session. Two of his resolutions were successful. Bills passed allow teachers to purchase computers on state contracts for use outside the classroom; concerned the conversion of papers of circuit court clerks to use electronic format for archiving records; established that in cases of child support guidelines not include income forms a second job or payment of medical expenses; established policies concerning developing student policies involving self defense; amended the charter of Chesterfield County and enforced compulsory school attendance.

Bills continued covered funding for additional deputies for circuit court clerks and considered the applicability of mental incapacity and physical helplessness of the complaining witnesses in sexual assault cases.

A successful resolution pertaining to setting standards for licensing Child Day Care Centers provided that the Joint legislation Audit and Review Commission study the potential impact on providers, parents and children.

A failed bill would have amended the City Charter of Richmond.

Delegate HD 68

Bradley P. "Brad" Marrs (R); Member House: 2002- ; b. (no date given), Evansville, IN; home, 2824 Robys Way, Midlothian 23113; educ. William & Mary (A.B.), Univ. VA (J.D.); married, Elizabeth G. K.; Southern Baptist.

Lawyer; VA Child Day-Care Council 1995-01; Member: Bon Air Baptist; VA State Bar; Richmond Bar Assn.; VA Trial Lawyers Assn.; Huguenot Little League; Awards: Inside Business, Richmond, "Top 40 Under 40" Dec. 1997; Certificate of Recognition, Bradley P. Marrs Day, 1997, per Gov. Allen.

Offices P.O. Box 3941, Richmond 23235-9998; 804-323-1454; GA Bldg., Room. 509, Capitol Sq., Richmond 23219; 804-698-1068.

2004Committees *Counties, Cities and Towns; Courts of Justice; Health, Welfare and Institutions.*

House Key Votes, 2004
Please see Introduction for more information on bills.

1) Budget Bill	FOR	5) Family Life	FOR	9) Morning After	FOR
2) Feticide	FOR	6) Fire Arms	FOR	10) Legal Aid	AGN
3) Marriage	FOR	7) Open Space	AGN		
4) Abortion	FOR	8) Home School	FOR		

Election Results

2004 general	Bradley P. Marrs	(R) 10,788	98.5%		$136,285

Campaign Contributions 2004 Law $21,478; Realty $6,250; Health Care $4,050; Business/Retail Svs. $4,000; Finance $3,000; Energy $1,750; Agriculture $1,650;Transportation $750; Tech/Communications $750; Political $650; Public Employees $150.

Economic Interests, 2004 *Sal. & Wages*, $10,000+ Meyer, Goergen & Marrs, P.C. (self), Chesterfield Co. Public Schools (spouse); *Pers. Liabil.*, $10,001-$50,000 other loan/finance Co.; *Sec.*, $50,000+ ea.: mutual fund, stock in Capital One; $10,001-$50,000 stock Wachovia; *Gifts:* $85Altria, dinner; $75 BonSecour, dinner; $80 DeFoggi, church pageant tkts; $80 David Horner, dinner; $50 Mortons Steakhouse, gift certificate; $116 Richmond Ballet, tiks; $200 Sorenson Institute, tkts and dinner; $182 UVA tkts, transportation to game; $120 VA tech, tkts to football game and brunch; $50 William and Mary, tkts to football game and brunch; $55 VA Optometric Assoc., dinner ; Paymt for talks, mtgs and publications: $515 VA Trial Lawyers Assoc, panelist at annual seminar, hotel expenses; Pay. for Rep. & Other Services Generally, legal $250,001+ loan/finance co.; $50,001-$100,000 ea.: banks, savings instit.; $10,001-$50,000 ea.: oil/gas retail store fixtures; $1,001-$10,000 ea.: interstate & intrastate transportation; Paymt for representation by you to $10,000: Godsey & Sons, legal services.

HOUSE DISTRICT SIXTY-NINE, *Franklin P. "Frank" Hall (D)*

POLITICAL AND LEGISLATIVE BACKGROUND
House District 69 consists of part of Chesterfield County comprised of the Belmont, Davis, and Beaufont Precincts and part of the Manchester Precinct; and City of Richmond Precincts 404, 412, 501-504, 509, 510, 610, 802, 807, 810, 902, 908-911, and parts of the 402 and 609 Precincts.

Frank Hall, an attorney and a Democrat, has served since 1975 when the Richmond delegation was elected at large. Hall practices law with his wife, Phoebe, and is Chairman of the Board of the Commonwealth Bank. Hall lost a special Senate election in August 1986, after the death of Senator Edward E. Willey (D), to Delegate Joseph B. Benedetti (R) in a three-week campaign costing more than $100,000 each. Hall has defeated all House opponents, running unopposed in 1983, 1985, 1991, 1997, 1999, and 2001. Hall became chairman of the powerful Counties, Cities and Towns Committee in 1992, and with the split in political power had co-chaired it since 1999 with Delegate Riley Ingram (R-62). During 2000, this committee held public hearings across the state on growth control issues. Hall lost his place as a budget conferee and membership on the Assembly watchdog, the Joint Legislative Audit and Review Commission. In 2002, the Republicans assumed chairmanship of all committees.

During the 2004 session, Hall sponsored two of his three bills, one was carried over to the 2005 session. The two bills passed provide for the use of tinting films on limousine windows and issuing revenue bonds of community development authorities.

A bill was carried over which provides for voluntary contributions for cancer research when filing the state income tax.

Delegate HD 69

Franklin "Frank" Perkins Hall (D) Member House: 1976-; b. Dec. 13, 1938, Amelia Courthouse; home, 9006 Cherokee Rd., Richmond 23235; educ. Lynchburg Coll. (B.S.), Am. Univ. (M.B.A.), and Am. Univ. (J.D.); married Phoebe A. Poulterer; Presbyterian.

Attorney and Businessman; Commonwealth Bank, Chm; Natl. Municipal League; Richmond City Strategy Team; VA State & Richmond Bar; VA Trial Lawyers; VA Jaycees; VA Mental Health Assn.; Church Hill Model Neigh. Pol. Bd.; Blue Key Natl. Honor Frat.; Richmond Area Young Dem. past pres.; 3rd District VA Young Dem.; Dean's Award, Wash. College of Law; 1997 received Davenport Award from Home Builders Asss. of VA.

Offices P.O. Box 3407, Richmond 23235; GA Bldg., Rm. 614, Capitol Sq., Richmond 23219; 698-1069.
2004 Committees *Appropriations; Counties, Cities and Towns; Rules.*

House Key Votes, 2004
Please see Introduction for more information on bills.

1) Budget Bill	AGN	5) Family Life	FOR	9) Morning After	AGN
2) Feticide	AGN	6) Fire Arms	AGN	10) Legal Aid	FOR
3) Marriage	NV	7) Open Space	FOR		
4) Abortion	AGN	8) Home School	AGN		

Election Results
2004 general   Franklin P. "Frank" Hall   (D)   10,413   99.4% $176,518

Campaign Contributions 2004   Health Care $20,725; Energy $17,750; Finance $14,650; Realty $14,200; Transportation $13,275; Tech/Communications $12,250; Law $10,750;Business/Retail Svs $6,725; Agriculture $6,400; Public Employees $5,075; Misc $1,350; Defense $1,000; Mfg $800; Organized Labor $500; Single-Issue Groups $500; Political $380.
Economic Interests, 2004 *Sal. & Wages,* $10,000+ Hall & Hall law, First Community Bank; *Off. & Dir.,* Partner: Hall & Hall, Family Law Firm of VA; First Community Bank, Dir./Chair. Bd.; Director of:
Kellerher Corp., VCU Hospital Authority; FPH Enterprises, Partner; *Pers. Liabil.,* $50,000+ ea.: Banks: self, family; $10,001-$50,000 ea.: insur. co.: self, family; *Sec.,* $50,000+ ea.: mutual fund, stock in bank; $10,001-$50,000 mutual fund;Business Interests $50,000 or less: Family Law Firm, More than $50,000: Hall & Hall, Hall Tree Farm, FPH Enterprises, Patterson , Baldwin Realty; Fidelity Group; *Pay. for Rep. by You,* $10,001-$50,00: Bd of Directors, banks; $1,001-$10,000 oil or gas companies; *Real Estate,* Four prop. w/others (commercial, residential, tree farm); Gifts: $89 Altria, reception; $336 Altria, NASCAR tkts; $159 Altria, PM Open House; $193 VA Trial Lawyers Assoc., convention fees; $98 VA Trial Lawyers Assoc, CLE charges; $205 VA Cable, dinner; $7,500 State Leg. Leaders Federation, trip to Ukraine; $6,000 Taipei Economic & Cultural Office, trip to Taipei.
HOUSE DISTRICT SEVENTY-TWO, *John S. "Jack" Reid (R)*

POLITICAL AND LEGISLATIVE BACKGROUND
House District 72 consists of part of Henrico County comprised of the Glen Allen, Hunton, Longan, Coalpit, Innsbrook, Jackson Davis, Cedarfield, Tucker, Byrd, Lakewood, Gayton, Godwin, Maybeury, Mooreland, Pemberton, Pinchbeck, and Ridgefield Precincts.

John S. "Jack" Reid, a public school administrator, and a conservative Republican, has been a Delegate since 1990. The seat was opened when veteran legislator and Democrat Ralph L. Axselle, Jr. retired from the House. Axselle later became a lobbyist. Archibald Wallace III (D), an attorney, challenged Reid for the seat, but Reid won with 62.4% of the vote. Unopposed until 1995, Reid defeated Democrat Nancy Finch and Independent Eriks Goodwin with 57.6% of the vote. In 1997, Reid defeated Independent Shelby McCurrin with 71.6% of the vote. In 1999, Reid defeated Libertarian Party candidate John H. Girardeau III with 83% of the vote. Reid was unopposed in the 2001 election. The Republican Caucus selected Reid to be the House party whip.

During the 2004 session, Reid sponsored twelve bills, four passed and four were carried over to the 2005 session.   Bills passed prohibited nudist camps for juveniles; regulated the filing of death certificates; and enforced school and corrective action plans.

Bills continued would specify causes for revocation or suspension of optometrist's licenses; provide for voluntary contributions to the Office of Commonwealth Preparedness Fund; and reduce emissions through a clean smoke stack provision.

SEVENTH CONGRESSIONAL DISTRICT

A successful resolution proposed a Joint Legislation Audit and Review Commission to study the impact and demand for services by the aging population.

A bill to regulate and license abortion clinics failed.

Delegate HD 72

John Spence "Jack" Reid (R) Member House: 1989-; Party Whip 2000; b. Aug. 1, 1942, Norfolk; home, 1619 Swansbury Dr., Richmond 23233; educ. Woffard Coll., U VA (M.Ed.); married Julia "Judi" Goodridge; Episcopalian.

Public School Administrator, Chesterfield Co.; Bd. Dir. West Richmond Kiwanis; Pres. Carver Elem. Sch. PTA; Chm. Rep. Comm. Third Cong. Dist. 1980-82; Pres. Tuckahoe Village Civic Assn. 1978; Tuckahoe Lodge #347, A F & A M; Shrine; Phi Delta Kappa.

Offices P.O. Box 29566, Richmond 23242; 804-741-2927; GA Bldg., Capitol Sq., Rm. 703, Richmond 23219; 804-698-1072.

2004 Committees *General Laws, Chair; Appropriations; Education.*

House Key Votes, 2004
Please see Introduction for more information on bills.

1) Budget Bill	FOR	5) Family Life	AGN	9) Morning After	FOR
2) Feticide	FOR	6) Fire Arms	FOR	10) Legal Aid	FOR
3) Marriage	FOR	7) Open Space	AGN		
4) Abortion	FOR	8) Home School	FOR		

Election Results

2004 general	John S. "Jack" Reid	(R)	19,902	93.1%	$64,582

Campaign Contributions 2004 Law $4,500; Realty $3,800; Business/ Retail Svs $3,650; Finance $2,700; Transportation $2,450; Tech/Communications $1,650; Health Care $1,500; Energy $1,250; Agriculture $1,250; Mfg $1,000.

Economic Interests, 2004 *Sal. & Wages,* $10,000+ Chesterfield Co. Pub. Sch.; *Sec.,* $50,000+ ea.: half interest in trusts at Bank of America w/stocks/funds totalling more than $2 million and including: AT&T, Bank AM., Citigroup, Dom. res., Du Pont, Exxon Mobil, GE, SBC Comm., Verizon, Pepsico, JP Morgan, AOL Time Warner, Johnson & Johnson, Medtronic, Pfizer, Wal Mart, Home Depot, EMC Corp., Cisco, Nortel, Intel, Microsoft, Calpine, Duke Energy; Paymt for talks, mtgs and publications: $750 - $1,000 Education Comm of States, Steering Committee mtg, expenses; $750-$1,000 Education Comm. Of States, attended annual conference as steering committee, three nights expenses; Gifts: 350 Colonial Athletic Assoc., basketball tournament; $60 Dominion Power, dinner; $50 VA Bankers Assoc, dinner; $147 Altria, dinner; $100 VA Motor Speedway, dinner; Real Estate: recreational.

SEVENTH CONGRESSIONAL DISTRICT
HOUSE DISTRICT SEVENTY-THREE, *John M. O'Bannon III (R)*

POLITICAL AND LEGISLATIVE BACKGROUND
House District 73 consists of part of Henrico County comprised of the Brookland, Dumbarton, Glenside, Greendale, Hermitage, Johnson, Lakeside, Maude Trevvett, Moody, Staples Mill, Cardinal, Crestview, Freeman, Monument Hills, Ridge, Skipwith, Three Chopt, Westwood, Derbyshire, Rollingwood, Spottswood, and Tuckahoe Precincts; and the 111 and 409 Precincts of the City of Richmond.

John M. O'Bannon III was elected in a special December 2000 election, having won the Republican caucus nomination over five candidates, and defeated Independent Sterling W. Hening. The seat was opened with Eric Cantor's election to Congress to fill Thomas Bliley's seat, following his retirement. O'Bannon, a neurologist who accepted campaign dollars from both tobacco and beer companies, is married to Pat O'Bannon, a Henrico County Supervisor. In 2001, O'Bannon ran unopposed.

During the 2004 session, O'Bannon sponsored twenty-two bills, sixteen passed, four were carried over to the 2005 session. Bills passed provided for a standard of conduct for directors of Charitable Corporations; permitted dentists to practice in certain dental clinics; required ambulance permits to be consistent with federal requirements; provided an explanation of benefits to those enrolled in health maintenance organizations; made it unlawful to assist individuals in procuring prescription drugs from a pharmacy or other source; provided for a multi-state license privileges for nurses; granted regulatory exceptions to assisted living facilities with Alzheimer's units; provided for disclosure of mental health information to the patient granted access to health records to guardians ad litem and attorneys who are representing minors; and established procedures for quarantine for public heath threats of communicable diseases.

Bills continued regulated the penalty for mauling by doges; the penalty for cruelty to animals; and coverage for fire department chaplains in the line of duty.

Delegate HD 73

John M. O'Bannon III (R) Member House: 2000- ; b. Feb. 14, 1948, Richmond; home, 8111 Rose Hill Road, Richmond; educ. Hargrave Military Academy, Univ. of Richmond (B.S.), MCV (M.D.); married, Patricia Anne Steinmetz; Baptist.

Physician, Neurological Associates; member: River Road Baptist Church Bd. of Deacons, Phi Beta Kappa, Alpha Omega Alpha, Richmond Acad. Med. (pres.), Med. Soc. VA (leg. ch.), Rich. Metro. Hosp. (former chief of staff), Rotary Club West Rich., Hargrave Mil. Acad. (bd. trustees, vice ch.), Henrico Doctors Hosp. (bd. trustees, former chief staff), Am. Med. Assn., Council for Ethical & Judicial Affairs; award: Caravati Service Award, MCV Alumni Assn.

Offices P.O. Box 70365, Richmond 23255-0365; 804-282-8640; GA Bldg., Capitol Sq., Rm. 518, Richmond 23219; 804-698-1073.

2004 Committees *Finance; Health, Welfare and Institutions; Science and Technology.*

House Key Votes, 2004

Please see Introduction for more information on bills.

1) Budget Bill	FOR	5) Family Life	FOR	9) Morning After	FOR
2) Feticide	FOR	6) Fire Arms	FOR	10) Legal Aid	FOR
3) Marriage	FOR	7) Open Space	FOR		
4) Abortion	FOR	8) Home School	FOR		

Election Results

2004 general	J. M. O'Bannon III	(R)	19,624	98.7%	$93,692

Campaign Contributions 2004 Health Care $22,775; Business/Retail Svs $6,000; Law $4,250; Realty $4,250; Finance $4,000; Energy $3,250; Transportation $1,000; Tech/Communications $1,000; Agriculture $1,000; Misc $750; Mfg $750.

Economic Interests, 2004 *Sal. & Wages*, $10,000+ Neurological Assoc.; *Pers. Liabil.*, $50,000+ Insur. co.; Offices & Directorships: Henrico Doctors Hospital, Director, VA Health Quality Center, Director, (wife) *Sec.*, $50,000+ ea.: Neur. Assoc.; money pur. plan; *Bus. Int.*, $50,000+ ea.: Neur. Assoc., O'Bannon Prop.(farming); Paymts for talks, mtgs, and publications: $306 American Society of Medical Association Counsel, CLE speaker; Gifts: $152 Altria, reception; $158 Altria, Open House; $89 Sepracor, Inc, dinner; $50 VA Thoroughbred Assoc., baseball cap; $50 VA Agribusiness Council, banquet; *Real Estate,* Two prop. w/spouse (river house, 53 acres in mountains).

EIGHTH CONGRESSIONAL DISTRICT

SENATE DISTRICT THIRTY, *Patricia S. "Patsy" Ticer (D)*

POLITICAL AND LEGISLATIVE BACKGROUND

Senate District 30 contains the Arlington County Precincts of Arlington, Aurora Hills, Crystal City, Hume, Columbia, Fairlington, Virginia Highlands, Abingdon, Fillmore, Claremont, Glebe, Oakridge, Arlington View, and Shirlington; the Fairfax County Precincts of Mount Eagle, Belle Haven, Belleview, Huntington, Marlan, and Grosvenor, and parts of the Groveton and Hayfield 406/Woodlawn 412/Fairfield 413 Precincts; and the City of Alexandria Precincts of Annie B. Rose House, City Hall, Lyles Crouch School, Jefferson Houston School, Lee Center, Cora Kelly Center, Mt. Vernon Recreation Center, George Washington School, George Mason School, Agudas Achim Synagogue, Temple Beth El Synagogue, Maury School 201/Blessed Sacrament Church 204, and Second Presbyterian 205/Howard 9th Grade Center 206.

Democrat Patricia S. "Patsy" Ticer is the senator for this district. She was elected in 1995 in a major upset for the Republicans, by 57.6% against two term incumbent Robert Calhoun, Republican. In this expensive race, Calhoun outspent Ticer., the first woman Mayor of Alexandria, and a member of the city council for nine years. In the 1999 election, Ticer defeated independent C. W. Levy.

During the 2004 session, Ticer sponsored fourteen bills and five resolutions. Four of the bills and four of the resolutions passed. Five bills failed, three were carried over and two were incorporated into other bills.

Local elected officials receiving large campaign contributions from a single donor must report the contribution within five days of receipt under SB 470. This law applies to contributions greater than $500 received in non-election years. Another bill that passed provided local governments in Northern Virginia with greater authority to regulate the parking of certain vehicles in residential districts. A charter amendment bill authorized the City of Alexandria to provide grants up to $5000 to city employees to purchase or rent residences within the City.

Sen. Ticer's fourth bill to pass modified the law on criminal background checks for foster parents. Provided that a child-placing agency may approve as a foster parent an applicant convicted of statutory burglary if 25 years have passed since the conviction and the person has had his civil rights restored by the Governor.

A bill relating to parole revocation stated that a prisoner would receive credit for good time if parole violation was technical and did not involve a new and subsequent charge was incorporated into another bill. A second bill that was incorporated required that a portion of the profits from inmate stores or canteens be used for employment and housing assistance for inmate's pre-and post-release. Currently the profits must be used for educational and recreational purposes.

Of her bills that failed, one would have modified the Hate Crime law to include sexual orientation. Another bill would have prohibited the use of cell phones while driving. One failed resolution advocated the position that the proposed Equal Rights Amendment to the U.S. Constitution remains viable and should be ratified despite the expiration of the ten year ratification period in the proposed ERA as adopted by the Congress.

Senator SD 30

Patricia S. "Patsy" Ticer (D) Member Senate: 1996-; b. Jan. 6, 1935, Washington, D.C.; home, home, 512 Prince St., Alexandria 22314; educ., Sweet Briar College (B.A. Govt.); married, John T. Ticer; Episcopal.

Former Mayor of Alexandria; Member: Metrop. Wash. Council of Govts. (past chair), Nor. VA Transp. Comm. (past chair), VA Transp. Coord. Council, Nor. VA Planning District Commission (past chair), Nor. VA Housing Coalition (founding member), Gov. Council on Child Day Care and Early Childhood Programs (Past vice chair), SCAN; Awards: Scull Award, 1993 Public Policy Award Nor. VA Assn. Educ. of Young Children.

Offices Room 2007, City Hall, 301 King St., Alexandria 22314-3211; 703-549-5770; FAX 703-739-6761; GA Bldg., Capitol Sq., Rm. 429, Richmond 23219; 804-698-7530.

2004 Committees *Agriculture, Conservation and Natural Resources; Local Government; Rehabilitation and Social Services.*

Senate Key Votes, 2004
Please see Introduction for more information on bills.

1) Budget Bill	FOR	5) Family Life	FOR	9) Charter School	AGN
2) Feticide	AGN	6) Fire Arms	AGN	10) Legal Aid	FOR
3) Marriage	AGN	7) Open Space	FOR		
4) Child Abuse	FOR	8) Home School	AGN		

Election Results

1999 general	Patricia S. "Patsy" Ticer	(D)	17,846	80.8%	$89,803
	C. W. Levy	(I)	3,938	17.8%	$ 233

Campaign Contributions 2000-June 30, 2002 **Restaurants** $11,000; **Attys.** $6,900; **Tech./Comm.** $6,900; **Individ.** $6,815; **Realty/Constr.** $5,850; **Finance** $4,350; **Pub. Empl.** $2,915; **Org. Labor** $2,500 (AFL CIO $2,150); **Transp.** $2,100 (Auto Dealers $750); **Medical** $1,500; **Consult.** $1,300; **Rec./Amuse. Pk.** $1,250; **Electric** $1,250; **Beer/Wine/Dist. Spirits** $1,000; **Soft Drink** $750; **Shipbldg.** $750; **Democrats** $600; **Retail./Business** $550; **Advert.** $500; **Fishing** $450; **Funeral** $100; **Trash** $100.

Economic Interests, 2004 *Sec.*, $50,000+ annuity; $10,001-$50,000 ea.: mut. fds. (10); bonds, money funds (2), annuity, stock in Burke & Herbert Bank; *Pay. for Talks, Mtgs., & Pub.*, $1,185 Commission on Accreditation for Law Enforcement Agencies, meeting expenses; $984 mtg expenses for Buffalo; $1,342 mtg expenses for Austin, TX; $2,058 senate, NCSL mtg expenses; Gifts: $102 VA Mtg Brokers Assoc., dinner; $62 Metro Airport Authority, dinner; $300 NUBIA, gala; $130 Altria, dinner; $77 Geico, dinner; $400 Washington Gas, Family Services Gala; $50 Vinfera Winegrowers Assoc., dinner; $68 MCI, dinner; $89 Domion Power, dinner; Real Estate: single family residence.

SENATE DISTRICT THIRTY-ONE, *Mary Margaret Whipple (D)*

POLITICAL AND LEGISLATIVE BACKGROUND
Senate District 31 includes the City of Falls Church; the Arlington County Precincts of Ashton Heights, Ballston, Barcroft, Cherrydale, Wilson, East Falls Church, Glen Carlyn, Clarendon, Lyon Park, Lyon
Village, Overlee Knolls, Park Lane, Rosslyn, Thrifton, Westover, Woodlawn, Arlington Forest, Jefferson, Dominion Hills, Lexington, Rock Spring, Yorktown, Madison, Marshall, Nottingham, Ashlawn, Virginia Square, and Woodbury; and the Fairfax County Precincts of Baileys, Barcroft, Glen Forest, Holmes, Ravenwood, Willston, Skyline, and Fort Buffalo.

Mary Margaret Whipple, a Democrat, has served since 1995, handily defeating Republican opposition then and again in the 1999 election. Whipple previously served on the Arlington County Board. The Senate seat was opened with the retirement of Democrat Edward M. Holland who had served in the Senate since 1971. Holland co-sponsored the bill abolishing parole in Virginia and worked on legislation to create a separate family court for domestic issues. Whipple was selected in 2000 as chair of the Senate Democratic Caucus. With redistricting, Whipple and Senator Leslie Byrne (D) were thrown into the same district, and only one can run in the next election for this seat.

During the 2004 session, Whipple sponsored nineteen bills and nine resolutions. Seven of the nine resolutions passed. Nine bills passed, three failed, two were incorporated into other bills, and five were continued.

Amendments to the Falls Church City charter gave the City greater flexibility to deal with personnel and other matters. Another bill that passed provided for the implementation of the Help America Vote Act. SB 454 authorized the Department of Environmental Quality to collect penalty fees from stationary sources in severe nonattainment areas that do not attain air quality standards set by the Federal Clean Air Act. The fees collected would be used for air quality monitoring and evaluation and for measures to improve air quality in severe nonattainment areas.

A bill affecting school closing clarifies the circumstance when state aid will be reduced due to severe weather conditions or emergency situations. The bill allows makeup days and permit's the Board of Education to waive the need for makeup days under a declared state of emergency without reductions in funding.

Several resolutions commending individuals passed as did a memorial remembering local historian Ann Rourke "Nan" Netherton.

Bills that Whipple introduced and that were carried over included bills relating to Standards of Learning assessment; the creation of a Special Advisor to the Governor on Workforce Education; a bill on pollution loading allocations for nitrogen and phosphorous levels in the Chesapeake Bay, and a bill to define contraception methods as not subject to the abortion laws.

Among Whipple's bills that failed to pass were two tax measures. One would have equalized taxing authority between cities and counties by granting counties the same taxing authority as cities. A second bill would have increased the sales tax on fuels from two to four percent for those jurisdictions in the Northern Virginia Transportation District. A proposed constitutional amendment to establish a Redistricting Committee to redraw Congressional and Legislative districts also failed.

Senator SD 31

Mary Margaret Whipple (D) Member Senate: 1996-; b. May 26, 1940, Watseka, Illinois; home, 3556 N. Valley St., Arlington 22207; educ. Rice Univ., The American Univ. (B.A. English), George Washington Univ. (M.A.); married, Thomas S. Whipple; Presbyterian.

Member: Arlington Co. Bd. (Vice Chair), Wash. Metro Area Transit Authority, Nor. VA Transp. Commission (Chair), VA Assn. of Counties (Exec. Bd.), Gov. Comm. Nor VA Potomac River Basin (1985-1990), Jt. Leg. Comm. to Study Implementation of the Clean Air Act in VA (1991), Council of Govts., Pres. Arlington Branch AAUW 1989-1990, Chair Arlington Co. School Bd. 1978-1979, Arlington BPW, Arlington LWV; Leg. of Yr. 1998 Chesapeake Bay Fndn.

Offices 3556 N. Valley St., Arlington 22207-4445; 703-538-4097; GA Bldg., Capitol Sq., Rm. 430, Richmond 23219; 804-698-7531.

2004 Committees *Agriculture, Conservation and Natural Resources; Education and Health; Local Government; Rules.*

Senate Key Votes, 2004
Please see Introduction for more information on bills.

1) Budget Bill	FOR	5) Family Life	FOR	9) Charter Schools	AGN
2) Feticide	AGN	6) Fire Arms	AGN	10) Legal Aid	FOR
3) Marriage	AGN	7) Open Space	FOR		
4) Child Abuse	FOR	8) Home School	AGN		

Election Results

1999 general	Mary Margaret Whipple	(D)	22,873	70.3%	$55,022
	S. C. Tate	(R)	9,656	29.7%	$12,749

Campaign Contributions 2000-June 30, 2002 **Tech./Comm.** $8,250; **Transp.** $4,450; **Attys.** $4,450; **Realty/Constr.** $3,745; **Individ.** $3,025; **Finance** $2,850; **Medical** $1,250; **Pub. Empl.** $1,250; **Democrats** $1,100; **Retail/Business** $900; **Insur.** $500; **Trash** $500; **Electric** $500; **Owens-Illinois** $500; **Northrup Grumman** $500; **Greater Wash. Bd. Trade** $500; **Advert.** $100; **Fishing** $100.

Economic Interests, 2004 *Sal. & Wages*, $10,000+ U.S. Govt. ret.; *Sec.*, $50,000+ Merrill Lynch portfolio including in $10,000-$50,000 range: Advance PCS, Advent Software, Affil. Comp., Alliant ind., Alteria Corp., Amerisource Bergen, Apollo Group, Applera CP, Avon, Barr Labs, Bed Bath & Beyond, FJ Serv., Brocade Comm., Cabot, Cephalon, Check Point Software, Citrix, City Natl.. Computer Sci., Concord EFS, Copart, Edwareds JD, Enzon, First Health, Flextronics, Franklin Res., Genzyme, Global Santa Fe, Guidant, Harley Davidson, Human Genome Sci., Icos, Intermune, Intersil, Invitrogen, Jacobs Engine, Jones Apparel, Juinper Netwks., Kin Pharmaceuticals, KLA Tencor, L-3 Comm., Macromedia, Manor Care, Medimune, Moody's, Netwk. App., Novellus Sys., Nivida, Peoplesoft, Pepsi Bot., Peregrine Sys., Quest Diagn., RF Micro., Ross Stores, Sanmina, Sicor, starbucks, Stryker, Sungard Data, Symantec, Tiffany, TJX, Univision, USA Educ., Valero Energy, Verisgn, Williams Sonoma, Yahoo; $10,001-$50,000 ea.: realty partnerships (2); *Pay. for Talks, Mtgs., & Publ.*, $1,738 State (NCSL, Annual mtg., expenses; *Gifts*, $75 Washington Gas, dinner; $118 Loudoun Healthcare, dinner; *Bus. Int.*, $50,000/less IL farm; *Real Estate*, One prop. Canada (w/spouse); Business Interests $50,000 or less: farming; Real Estate: summer cottage in Canada.

SENATE DISTRICT THIRTY-SIX, *Linda T. "Toddy" Puller (D)*

POLITICAL AND LEGISLATIVE BACKGROUND
Senate District 36 covers the Fairfax County Precincts of Virginia Hills, Villages, Bucknell, Fort Hunt, Hollin Hall, Kirkside, Sherwood, Stratford, Waynewood, Westgate, Whitman, Woodley, Gunston, Belvoir, and Pohick Run, and parts of Groveton and Hayfield 406/Woodlawn 412/Fairfield 413; and the Prince William County Precincts of Lodge, Potomac, Henderson, Occoquan, Bethel, Chinn, Dale, Neabsco, Godwin, Civic Center, Minnieville, Bel Air, Belmont, Library, Lynn, Featherstone, Potomac View, Rippon, and Kilby.

Linda T. "Toddy" Puller, a consultant and a Democrat, was elected to the Senate in 1999, having previously served in the House since 1992. Puller, a former school teacher, is the president of Puller and Associates, a political and government relations consulting firm. Having suffered a stroke a few years ago, her health rose as an election issue, but the voters gave her 52.4% of the vote in the expensive race. The seat had opened with the retirement of Democrat Joseph Gartlan who had represented the district since 1972. One of the most influential members of the Virginia Senate, Gartlan had been in the forefront of environmental issues, human rights protections, and ethics and campaign finance reform. Gartlan was the force behind the establishment of the tri-state Chesapeake Bay Commission.

During the 2004 session, Puller sponsored nineteen bills and ten resolutions. Seven bills passed, seven failed, two were incorporated into other bills and three were continued. Seven of her ten resolutions were passed.

Successful bills included two relating to the marriage laws: one that required court authorization before a conservator for an incapacitated person could seek a divorce; a second bill changed the factors the court is to consider when it determines the division or transfer of marital property, debts or awards. Another bill permits localities to prohibit the feeding of migratory and no migratory waterfowl in heavily populated areas where that feeding would be a threat to public health or the environment.

SB 381 established the Virginia Disability Commission within the legislative branch chaired by the Lt. Governor and consisting of twelve members. The purpose of the commission is to identify and recommend legislative priorities and policies relating to services and funding of programs for Virginians with disabilities. The bill provides that the commission's authority will sunset in three years. Another bill modifies the criteria by which medical care facilities will be relocated to include consideration of the accessibility of the site and the facility. The bill requires public and governmental notification and the solicitation of comments on the proposed relocation of the medical facility.

Several bills relating to the issuance of special and personalized license plates passed or were incorporated into other bills. Several of Senator Puller's resolutions were passed that commended certain individuals and expressed sorrow at the passing of Jack Knowles and Emily Myatt.

Two resolutions that failed involved the creation of study committees: one would have created a subcommittee to review the educational technology funding options recommended by JLARC to the

General Assembly. The second requested the Department of Veterans Services to study the need for and cost of additional veterans care centers.

Of the bills that failed, the one that received the most attention was a bill to amend the election law to permit the sale of refreshments by nonprofit, nonpartisan groups within 40 feet of a polling place. This bill was introduced when PTA and Scouting groups attempted to sell refreshments on election days and were denied permission by election officials.

Another failed bill would have authorized the Virginia Public School Authority to issue bonds in the amount of $1 billion to pay the costs of school construction, renovation and other infrastructure for local schools.

Senator SD 36

Linda T. "Toddy" Puller (D) Member Senate: 2000- ; Member House: 1992-1999 ; b. Jan. 19, 1945, Cedar Rapids, Iowa; home, 1805 Windmill Lane, Alexandria 22307; educ., Mary Washington College (BA); widow; Episcopalian.

Consultant; member, Lee & Mt. Vernon Chamber of Commerce; Bd. of Dir., Campagna Center; Bd. of Dir., Fairfax Affordable Housing; Fairfax County Transp. Adv. Commission; member, Dem. State Central Comm.; Mt. Vernon-Lee Chamber of Commerce; VA Dept. for Children (Adv. Bd.); United Community Ministries; Youth Service Award.

Offices P.O. Box 73, Mt. Vernon 22121-0073; 703-765-1150; GA Bldg., Rm. 314, Capitol Sq., Richmond 23219; 804-698-7536.

2004 Committees *Courts of Justice; Local Government; Rehabilitation and Social Services.*
Senate Key Votes, 2004
Please see Introduction for more information on bills.

1) Budget Bill	FOR	5) Family Life	FOR	9) Charter Schools	AGN
2) Feticide	AGN	6) Fire Arms	AGN	10) Legal Aid	FOR
3) Marriage	FOR	7) Open Space	FOR		
4) Child Abuse	FOR	8) Home School	AGN		

Election Results

1999 general	Linda T. Puller	(D)	17,363	52.4%	$302,417
	Daniel F. Rinzel	(R)	15,757	47.6%	$235,115

Campaign Contributions 2000-June 30, 2002 **Realty/Constr.** $29,475; **Medical** $11,590; **Tech./Comm.** $7,820; **Beer/Wine/Dist. Spirits** $7,560; **Attys.** $6,235; **Individuals** $6,189; **Electric** $6,105; **Finance** $5,265; **Pub. Empl.** $4,430; **Org. Labor** $4,390; **Transp.** $3,950 (Auto Dealers $2,750); **Democrats** $2,564; **Serv. Stat./Conv. St.** $2,000; **Recycling** $1,500; **Env. Eng.** $1,120; **Insur.** $1,040; **Soft Drink** $1,000; **Consult.** $1,000; **Rec./Amuse. Pk.** $850; **Defense/Shipbldg.** $750; **Retail/Business** $650; **Nat. Gas** $540; **Greater Wash. Bd. Trade** $500; **Oil** $300; **Tobacco--PM** $250; **Billboards** $250; **Advert.** $250; **Veterin./Landscape** $200.

Economic Interests, 2004 *Sal. & Wages,* $10,000+ U.S. Govt. Veterans Admin.; *Sec.,* $50,000+ deferred comp. state, mutual funds (2); $10,001-$50,000 ea.: mutual funds (3), Timber Ridge ltd prtnship, stock in: Kanisa, All Bases Covered invest.; *Pay. for Talks, Mtgs., & Publ.*, $1,195 Senate, expenses; $1,021 senate, NCSL , expenses; Real Estate: apartment, land; Gifts: $62 Metro Washington Airport Authority, dinner; $68 MCI, dinner; $63 Geico, dinner; $59 Glaxo SmithKline, dinner; $102 Old Dominion Hwy Contractors, dinner;

HOUSE DISTRICT THIRTY-FOUR, *Vincent F. Callahan, Jr. (R)*

POLITICAL AND LEGISLATIVE BACKGROUND
The 34th District consists of part of Fairfax County comprised of the Colvin, Chain Bridge, Chesterbrook, Churchill, Cooper, El Nido, Great Falls, Kenmore, Langley, Salona, Clearview, Forestville, Shouse, Sugarland, Hickory, Seneca, Magarity, and Tysons Precincts.

Vincent F. Callahan, Jr., writer, publisher, and Republican, has served since his election in 1966. In 1987, he was one of three Republican candidates endorsed by the Virginia AFL-CIO. Unopposed in 1989 and
1991, he beat two Independents in 1993, and won over a Democratic challenge in 1995. In 1997 and 1999, Callahan handily defeated Democrat Carole L. Herrick, vastly outspending her. In the 2001 election, Callahan won with 60.1% of the vote over Democrat Dale A. Evans. Callahan chairs the Appropriations Committee.

During the 2004 election, Callahan sponsored twenty-one bills and resolutions. Thirteen bills and resolutions passed, five failed and three were continued. Callahan's principle role in the legislature is service as Chairman of the House Finance Committee and he is primarily responsible for managing the state's budget bills.

In addition to the budget bills, Callahan measures that passed included a bond bill for institutions of higher education; changes in the retirement rules for state employees; to improve transportation in Fairfax County, and for credit assistance revenue bonds for mass transit in the Dulles Corridor. Measures that failed include changes in retirement plans for state police officers, law enforcement officials and certain state employees. Four resolutions recognizing individuals who had recently died all passed along with one resolution relating to expenses and salaries of members of the House of Delegates.

Delegate HD 34

Vincent Francis Callahan, Jr. (R) Member House: 1968-; b. Oct. 30, 1931, Washington, D.C.; home, 6220 Nelway Dr., McLean 22101; educ. Georgetown Univ. (B.S.); married Dorothy H. Budge; Catholic.

Publisher, Pres., Callahan Publications; member, Natl. Press Club; Adv. Comm. on Intergovt. relations (chm.); Metro Wash. COG (past dir.); Independent Newsletters Assn.; Izaak Walton League; Rep. candidate for Lt. Gov. 1965; Rep. candidate for Congress 1976; Cham. Commerce; USMC, USCGR; Minority Floor Leader 1982-85; Nor. VA Comm. Col. Fd. (Dir.); Kiwanis (past Pres.); WNVT (Adv. Bd.); United Way; Mental Health Assn. of Northern VA; JLARC.

Offices P.O. Box 1173, McLean 22101; 703-356-1925; GA Bldg., Capitol Sq., Rm. 947, Richmond 23219; 804-698-1034.

2004 Committees *Appropriations, Chair; Commerce and Labor; Rules.*

House Key Votes, 2004

Please see Introduction for more information on bills.

1) Budget Bill	FOR	5) Family Life	FOR	9) Morning After	FOR
2) Feticide	FOR	6) Fire Arms	FOR	10) Legal Aid	FOR
3) Marriage	FOR	7) Open Space	FOR		
4) Abortion	FOR	8) Home School	FOR		

Election Results

2004 general	Vincent F. Callahan, Jr.	(R)	14,113	99.7%	$196,084

Campaign Contributions 2004 Realty/Constr. $28,000; Health Care $10,550; Tech/Communications $10,250; Finance $9,250; Energy $8,000; Business/Retail Svs $6,921; Public Employees $6,250; Law $5,700; Defense $5,000; Agriculture $3,500; Misc $3,400; Political $2,950; Transportation $2,350; Mfg $950; Undetermined $500; Single-Issue Groups $250.

Economic Interests, 2004 *Sal. & Wages*, $10,000+ ea.: Callahan Publications (self); Kaiser Fndn. Health Plan, Inc. (spouse, retired); *Gifts*, $62 Metro Washington Airport Authority, dinner; $88 VA Power, dinner.

HOUSE DISTRICT FORTY-TWO, *David B. Albo (R)*

POLITICAL AND LEGISLATIVE BACKGROUND
The 42nd House District consists of part of Fairfax County comprised of the Gunston, Lorton, Newington, Delong, Cardinal, Keene Mill, Valley, Irving, Saratoga, Hunt, Silverbrook, and West Springfield Precincts and parts of the Pohick Run, Sangster, and Woodyard Precincts.

David B. Albo, an attorney and a Republican, has represented this area since 1993. Albo was legislative aide to his predecessor, former Delegate Robert K. Cunningham (R) who had held the district seat from 1984-1993. When Cunningham announced his retirement, Albo made a bid against Democrat Laurie Frost and won with 53.1% of the vote. In 1995 and 1997, Albo defeated Democratic opposition and ran unopposed in 1999. In the 2001 election, Albo defeated Democrat D. B. Collins with 61.1% of the vote.

During the 2004 session, Albo sponsored forty-nine bills and resolutions of which twenty-four passed, six were tabled, three were stricken, eight were continued, six were incorporated, one was passed-by indefinitely, and one was left in committee.

Several of the passed or incorporated bills made changes in the criminal law relating to gangs, mob crimes, the obstruction of justice, and to amend the concealed weapons law to include the carrying of a machete as a prohibited items. Two of the bills related to the operations and management of the state Lottery. One bill passed would permit the opening of state ABC stores on Sunday in Fairfax County and other urban areas; a second bill on ABC Sunday operations was stricken.

Two bills relating to revisions in criminal penalties and computer trespass were continued as was a proposed constitutional amendment relating to the use of the Transportation Trust fund. A measure on school board employee compensation was left in committee. Measures that were tabled included changes in the funding formula for the Standards of Quality in public schools, and two proposed changes in criminal law.

Delegate HD 42

David B. Albo (R) Member House: 1994- ; b. April 18, 1962, Flushing, NY; home, 8313 Garfield Ct., Springfield 22152; educ. Univ. of VA (B.A., Economics), Univ. of Richmond (J.D.); Episcopalian.

Attorney, Albo & Anderson; member, Fairfax County Chamber of Commerce Leg. Comm.; Trans. Subcom. (chm.).

Offices P.O. Box 6405, Springfield 22152; 703-451-3555; GA Bldg., Rm. 527, Capitol Sq., Richmond, 23219; 804-698-1042.

2004 Committees *Agriculture, Chesapeake and Natural Resources; Courts of Justice; General Laws; Privileges and Elections.*

House Key Votes, 2004
Please see Introduction for more information on bills.

1) Budget Bill	FOR	5) Family Life	AGN	9) Morning After	AGN
2) Feticide	FOR	6) Fire Arms	FOR	10) Legal Aid	FOR
3) Marriage	FOR	7) Open Space	FOR		
4) Abortion	FOR	8) Home School	FOR		

Election Results
2004 general   David B. Albo   (R) 11,258   99.3% $101,635

Campaign Contributions 2004 Business/Retail Svs $23,050; Law $6, 450; Tech/Communications $4,900; Realty $4,750; Health Care $4,000; Finance $2,750; Agriculture $2,600; Mfg $2,250; Energy $1,750; Transportation $1,500; undetermined $750; Public Employees $650; Political $250.

Economic Interests, 2004 *Sal. & Wages*, $10,000+ Albo & Oblon, L.L.P.; *Sec.*, $50,000+ funds w/broker; $10,001-$50,000 ea.: 2 accts broker, Albo Ltd. Ptnship stock, stock in Bristol Meyer Squibb (spouse's employer); Sec. to $50,000: Ferris-Baker-Watts, SEP-IRA; general accts; Paymts for talks, meetings, and publications: $1,271 American Legislative Exchange Council, expenses; Business Interests $50,000+ Albo & Oblou, LLP; $50,000 or less: Albo Limited Partnership; Paymts for representation and other services generally $250,000+: Other, general legal services; from $1,000 to $50,000: general legal services to professional assoc.; Gifts: $182 Dominion, redskin tks; $140 Nissan Pavillian, concert tkts; $120 Reynolds, golf bag; $147 Altria, dinner; $106 Altria, dinner; $336 Altria, NEXTEL race; $147 Dominion Power ,dinner; $156 Dominion Power, Wolf Trap & Dinner.

HOUSE DISTRICT FORTY-THREE, Mark D. Sickles *(D)*

POLITICAL AND LEGISLATIVE BACKGROUND
House District 43 consists of the Fairfax County Precincts of Bush Hill, Franconia, Pioneer, Rose Hill, Virginia Hills, Beulah, Villages, Kingstowne, Van Dorn, and Belvoir Precincts and parts of the Cameron, Groveton, Hayfield 406/ Woodlawn 412/ Fairfield 413, Mount Eagle, and Pohick Run.

Mark D. Sickles defeated Tom Bolvin in the 2004 election.,

EIGHTH CONGRESSIONAL DISTRICT

During the 2004 session, Sickles sponsored twelve bills and resolutions. Five bills and resolutions passed, five were continued and two failed.

One bill that passed required the notification to electric utilities of the location of all nursing homes and assisted living facilities in the state so that the utilities might facilitate the restoration of power and set service priorities during widespread power outages. Another bill requires that draft minutes of Property Owners Associations be available for inspection and copying within 60 days of a meeting or when the minutes are distributed to board members in anticipation of a board meeting. A bill to expand the persons who may be covered by local government liability insurance to include certain police, fire, emergency service and medical officials and employees. A resolution commending a high school student; and INOVA Health System for seatbelt usage and awareness activities was passed.

A bill continued would have increased the tree canopy requirements for local governments adopting tree conservation and replacement ordinances, and allow for exceptions to the requirements in certain cases. A proposed increase in state aid to local libraries in densely populated areas was carried over.

Another continued bill would permit individuals to check their eligibility, with the Department of State Police, to possess or transport a firearm outside of the context of the purchase of a firearm. A second bill relating to the qualifications for obtaining a concealed weapons permit was passed-by indefinitely.

Delegate HD 43

Mark D. Sickles (D) Member House 2004 - ; b. Feb. 18, 1957, Arlington, VA; educ. Clemson University, SC (BS Forest Management, 1981), Georgia Institute of Technology (MS, Industrial Management, 1984), Georgia Institute of Technology (MS, Technical and Science Policy, 1986); Presbyterian.

Government and Public Affairs consultant; Fairfax County Library (former Chairman), Southeast Health Planning Task Force, Northern VA Democratic Business Council and others; Lord Fairfax Award, 1999.

Offices : P.O. Box 10628, Alexandria, VA 22310, (703) 922-6440, FAX: (703) 922-6880; P.O. Box 406, Richmond, VA 23218, (804) 698-1043, FAX: (804) 786 6310.

2004 Committees: Health Welfare and Institutions, Privileges and Elections.

House Key Votes, 2004

Please see Introduction for more information on bills.

1) Budget Bill	AGN	5) Family Life	FOR	9) Morning After	AGN
2) Feticide	AGN	6) Fire Arms	FOR	10) Legal Aid	FOR
3) Marriage	AGN	7) Open Space	FOR		
4) Abortion	AGN	8) Home School	AGN		

Election Results

2004 general	Mark D. Sickles	(D)	9,550	53.8%	$297,109
	Thomas Bolvin	(R)		46.1%	$193,113

Campaign Contributions 2004 Law $11,650; Realty $6,900; Health Care $6,750; Business/Retail Svs $6,443; Transportation $6,175; Public Employees $5,346; Energy $5,250; Finance $4,550; Organized Labor $3,350; Political $2,725; Tech/Communications $2,650; Misc $1,950; Single-Issue Groups $1,250; Agriculture $1,250; Undetermined $1,150; Mfg $525; Defense $350.

EIGHTH CONGRESSIONAL DISTRICT

Economic Interests, 2004 *Sal. or Wages*, $10,000+ ea.: Mark Sickles Public Affairs, Principal; Sec. $50,000+: mutual funds: Morgan StanleyDean Witter; Lincoln Financial Group; Less than $50,000: stocks and mutual funds; Paymts for representation and other services generally $100,000 to $250,000: Trade associations, Federal Gov't relations; Gifts: $115 VA Auto Dealers Assoc, dinner; $126 Dominion Resources, dinners; $101 Northern VA Technology Council, Fall banquet.

HOUSE DISTRICT FORTY-FOUR, *Kristen "Kris" J. Amundson (D)*

POLITICAL AND LEGISLATIVE BACKGROUND
House District 44 consists of part of Fairfax County comprised of the Belle Haven, Bucknell, Fort Hunt, Hollin Hall, Huntington, Sherwood, Stratford, Waynewood, Westgate, Whitman, and Woodley Precincts and parts of the Groveton, Hayfield 406/ Woodlawn 412/ Fairfield 413, and Mount Eagle Precincts.

Kristen J. Amundson, a writer and a Democrat, was first elected in 1999. The seat opened when former Delegate Linda "Toddy" Puller ran for Senate. Amundson defeated Republican Scott T. Klein with 51.2% of the vote, with the candidates spending a total of a half million dollars to win the votes from the less than
14,000 people who decided the election. In the 2001 election, Amundson faced a re-match with Klein, narrowly winning with 50.9% of the vote, or with a margin of 353 votes in a race that cost over $400,000.

During the 2004 session, Amundson sponsored twenty-four bills and resolutions; five bills were passed, ten failed and two were continued. Four resolutions passed, two failed and one was incorporated.

Of the bills that passed, one eliminated the obsolete and duplicative statutory reporting requirements on many state agencies, and another eliminated the Committee on Early Intervention whose work had been taken over by the Departments of Health and Education. Another bill modifies the criteria by which medical care facilities will be relocated to include consideration of the accessibility of the site and the facility. The bill requires public and governmental notification and the solicitation of comments on the proposed relocation of the medical facility. All four resolutions commending or memorializing individuals passed.

Five of the failed bills related to public education funding, school construction funding, Standards of Quality, and efficiency reviews of a school division's central operations. Another bill would have set standards for health and family life education instructional materials. A change in the allocation of Electoral College votes from the current winner takes all statewide vote total to one based on the popular votes cast in each congressional district did not pass.

A bill to amend the competency standards for Nurse Practitioners was carried over as was a bill relating to the sale of violent video or computer games.

EIGHTH CONGRESSIONAL DISTRICT

Delegate HD 44

Kristen "Kris" Jane Amundson (D) Member House: 2000 - ; b. Dec. 3, 1949, Brainerd, MN; home, P.O. Box 7073, Alexandria 22307; educ. Malcalester College (BA), Am. Univ. (MA); divorced; Episcopal.

Writer; Member: PTA; Virginia School Boards Assn. (Past Pres.); Westgrove Citizens Assn. (Pres.); West Potomac Civic Assn. (Pres.); New Hope Housing, formerly Route One Corridor Housing (Pres.); Mount Vernon-Lee Chamber Comm.; Commission on Future Pub. Educ. VA; VA Comm. Educ. Accountability; Fairfax Co. Sch. Bd. (Member, Mount Vernon District) 1991-99 and Chairman (2 years); Author of *School Violence: Safeguarding Our Children*; Who's Who of American Women.

Offices P.O. Box 143, Mt. Vernon 22121; 703-619-0444; GA Bldg., Rm. 709, Capitol Sq., Richmond 23219; 804-698-1044.

204 Committees *Agriculture, Chesapeake and Natural Resources; Counties, Cities and Towns.*

House Key Votes, 2004
Please see Introduction for more information on bills.

1) Budget Bill	AGN	5) Family Life	FOR	9) Morning After	AGN
2) Feticide	AGN	6) Fire Arms	AGN	10) Legal Aid	FOR
3) Marriage	AGN	7) Open Space	FOR		
4) Abortion	AGN	8) Home School	AGN		

Election Results

2004 general	Kristen Amundson	(D)	9,684	55.9%	$257,925
	David Kennedy	(R)	9,331	44.1%	$63,711

Campaign Contributions 2004 Realty $8,980; Law $7,025; Public Employees $6,305; Organized Labor $5,805; Tech/Communications $5,270; Energy $4,310; Misc $3,110; Business/Retail Svs $2,813; Health Care $2,710; Transportation $2,500; Finance $2,210; Agriculture $950; Defense $905; single-Issue Groups $700; Mfg $650; Political $500; Undetermined $155.

Economic Interests, 2004 *Sal. or Wages,* $10,000+ KJA Communications; *Off. & Dir.,* KJA Commun., Pres.; *Sec.,* $10,001-$50,000 IRA stocks all less than $10,000; *Gifts,* $200 Washington Gas, Gala; $101 Northern VA Tech Council, dinner; $62 Metro Washington Airport Authority, dinner; Business Interest $50,000+: KJA Communications, writing; *Pay. for Rep. & Other Services Generally,* $50,001-$100,000 pub. co.; $1,001-$10,000 communications co.

HOUSE DISTRICT FORTY-FIVE, *Marian A. Van Landingham (D)*

POLITICAL AND LEGISLATIVE BACKGROUND
House District 45 consists of part of the City of Alexandria comprised of the Annie B. Rose House, City Hall, Lyles Crouch School, Jefferson Houston School, Lee Center, George Washington School, George Mason School, Agudas Achim Synagogue, Maury School 201/ Blessed Sacrament Church 204, and Second Presbyterian 205/ Howard 9th Grade Center 206 Precincts; the Arlington County

EIGHTH CONGRESSIONAL DISTRICT

Precincts of Fairlington, Abingdon, and Shirlington; and part of Fairfax County comprised of the Belleview, Kirkside, Marlan, and Grosvenor Precincts and parts of the Cameron and Mount Eagle Precincts.

Marian A. Van Landingham, a professional artist and a Democrat, has represented the area since 1982. In 1981, she scored a surprise victory over Republican Delegate David Speck, considered one of the most promising rookies in the 1980 session. In 1988, she challenged Republican Robert Calhoun in a special election for the 30th District Senate seat. She won the city, but lost to Calhoun in the Fairfax County precincts. She has defeated all opposition for the House since 1991, running unopposed in 1995, and again in 2001. Van Landingham is creator and first director of the Torpedo Factory, an Art Center. She chaired the Privileges and Elections Committee, and with the power split in the House became a co-chair, until the 2002 session when the Republicans assumed control of all committees.

During the 2004 session, Van Landingham sponsored eight bills, one resolution commending Robert Bloxom, retired from the 100th district. Van Landingham was people-oriented and introduced legislation covering disabilities, alert and warning systems., affordable learning, and school terms. Her bills that passed created a disability commission that will report; an alert and warning system in case of an emergency, and provided for affordable housing in the City of Alexandria; provision for a comprehensive plan for the city to individuals accessible housing was continued.

Failed bills was her bill to give credit for prior service for substitute teachers.

Van Landingham will not run for her seat in 2005. it is generally known and accepted that Van Landing ham gave considered and thoughtful service to her constituents during her long service repeatedly to the city of Alexandria.

Delegate HD 45

Marian A. Van Landingham (D) Member House: 1982-; b. Sept. 10, 1937, Albany, GA; home, 1100 Camerons St., Alexandria 22314; educ. Emory Univ. (B.A., M.A.); Methodist.

Professional Artist; Past Pres., Upper King St. Neighborhood Assn.; Torpedo Factory Artists Assn.; Cultural Alliance of Greater Washington; Alexandria Chamber of Commerce; Alexandria Dem. Com.; NAACP; VA Water Resources Research Cntr.; Washingtonian of the Yr. 1974; George Washington Community Service Award 1986; Legislator of the Year 1993, VA Interfaith Center; Gov.'s Award, Fighting Drugs.

Offices City Hall, 301 King St., Alexandria 22314; 703-549-2511; GA Bldg., Capitol Sq., Rm. 402, Richmond 23219; 804-698-1045.

2004 Committees *Appropriations; Militia, Police and Public Safety; Privileges and Elections.*

House Key Votes, 2004
Please see Introduction for more information on bills.

1) Budget Bill	FOR	5) Family Life	FOR	9) Morning After	AGN
2) Feticide	AGN	6) Fire Arms	AGN	10) Legal Aid	FOR
3) Marriage	AGN	7) Open Space	FOR		

EIGHTH CONGRESSIONAL DISTRICT

4) Abortion   AGN   8) Home School   AGN

Election Results

2004 general   Marian Van Landingham   (D)   20,022   63.0% $49,978

                    Jay R. Test   (R)   36.9% $55,732

Campaign Contributions 2004 Law $2,600; Energy $2,000; Health Care $1,500; Finance $1,500; Misc $1,400; Public Employees $1,400; Political $1,000; Realty $700; Business/Retail Svs $550; Transportation $500; Undetermined $400; organized Labor $400; Tech/Communication $400.

Economic Interests, 2004 *Pers. Liabil.*, $10,001-$50,000 bank mortgage 2nd home Richmond; *Sec.*, $50,000+ ea.: GE, annuity; $10,001-$50,000 ea.: mutual funds (2), bonds (2), stock in: Atlanta Gas Lt., Ameren, Citigroup, Exxon, FPL, Ford Motor, Heilig Meyers, Sara Lee, Sierra Pac. Res.; *Gifts*, $62 Metropolitan Washington Airport Authority, dinner; Business Interests $50,000 or less: Van Landingham Enterprises, art studio; Real Estate: residential and timberland in Ga.

HOUSE DISTRICT FORTY-SIX, *Brian J. Moran (D)*

POLITICAL AND LEGISLATIVE BACKGROUND

House District 46 consists of the City of Alexandria Precincts of the Temple Beth El Synagogue, Hermitage, Southern Towers Stratford, James K. Polk School, Patrick Henry School, Landmark Center, Charles E. Beatley Jr. Library, John Adams School, William Ramsay School, and South Port; and the Skyline Precinct of Fairfax County.

Democrat Brian J. Moran has represented the area since his election in 1995. In that election and in the 1997 election, he easily defeated Republican challengers. He was unopposed in 1999. Moran, an assistant Commonwealth Attorney in Arlington, continues the family political tradition, as his brother, James Moran, was mayor of Alexandria before being elected to the U.S. House of Representatives. The state seat opened on the retirement of Democrat Bernard S. Cohen, who had served since 1980, and who was widely known as a champion of the people in his fight for smoke-free places, the right to "death with dignity," workers' rights laws, and marital sexual assault statutes.

Moran has established himself as a strong force, a supporter of issues of importance to women and the family, and in the 2002 session, he was the Minority Floor Leader.

Brian Moran was very prodigious during the 2004 session, introducing twenty-two bills and eight resolutions. Eleven of his bills passed and five his resolutions. His resolutions establishing a redistricting commission was incorpated in another commission.

His passed bills establish an alternative work schedule and telecommunicating policy; provide penalty for third conviction of driving under the influence of alcohol or drugs; the Board of Education Development is to develop community-based program fro adults and provide distribution of property for those licensed. Crossed over bills to individuals under the Freedom of Information Act meetings of public bodies and a constitutional amendment to establish a redistricting commission to redraw the boundaries of congressional and legislative districts. His House Joint Resolutions record sorrow upon the dealth of Patricia Ann Krantz and Charles E. Chuck, Jr. commended were Arlen Roger and Stepler Ridout and the Alexandria Bar Association commemorating their 75th anniversary.

Failed bills were bills to compensate teachers according to national average and to provide that special funds not be used for any other purpose.

Delegate HD 46

Brian J. Moran (D) Member House: 1996-; b. Sept. 9, 1959, Natick, Mass.; home, 49 Fendall Ave., Alexandria 22304; educ. Univ. of Mass., Framingham State Col. (B.A.), Catholic Univ. (J.D.), Suffolk Univ. (grad. program); married Karyn Patricia Kranz.

Attorney; Assistant Commonwealth Attorney, Arlington; Faculty Advisor, Natl. College of District Attorneys; Member: VA Bar and MD Bar Assns.; Alexandria Chamber of Commerce, Alexandria United Way, Stop Child Abuse Now (Bd. member), George Wash. Pkwy Classic (Chm.), Alexandria Jaycees; Budget and Fiscal Affairs Adv. Comm. (chm.).

Offices 4154 Duke St., Alexandria 22304; 703-370-4154; GA Bldg., Capitol Sq.. Rm. 712, Richmond 23219; 804-698-1046.

2004 Committees *Courts of Justice; Health, Welfare and Institutions; Transportation.*

House Key Votes, 2004
Please see Introduction for more information on bills.

1) Budget Bill	AGN	5) Family Life	FOR	9) Morning After	AGN
2) Feticide	AGN	6) Fire Arms	FOR	10) Legal Aid	FOR
3) Marriage	AGN	7) Open Space	FOR		
4) Abortion	AGN	8) Home School	AGN		

Election Results

2004 general	Brian J. Moran	(D)	10,011	93.7%	$138,922

Campaign Contributions 2004 Law $17,550; Realty $14,246; Health Care $11,625; Finance $9,400; Energy $8,750; Defense $7,250; Transportation $6,870; Tech./Communication $6,000; Business/Retail Svs $4,225; Agriculture $2,500; Organized Labor $2,500; Public Employees $2,275; Misc $1,760; Single-Issue Groups $1,000; Political $1,000; Mfg $750.

Economic Interests, 2004 *Off. & Dir.*, Brian Moran, P.C., Pres.; *Pers. Liabil.*, $10,001-$50,000 banks; *Sec.*, $50,000+ stocks, mutual funds; *Bus. Int.*, $50,000+ ea.: Brian J. Moran, law; Alexandria Legal Pad LLC (rental prop.); $50,000/less Mango Mike's Restaurant; Paymts for talks, mtgs and publications: $326 VA Women Attorneys Assoc., Annual conference, expenses; Business Interests: Alexandria Legal Pad, rental property; Gifts: 1,224 VA Trial Lawyers, Seminar; $63 Geico, dinner; $62 Metro Washington Airport Authority, dinner; $147 Altria, dinner; $89 Altria, reception at Natl convention; $130 VA Auto Dealers Assoc, dinner; $250 Va Commerce Bank, Alexandria Scholarship Gala; $500 INOVA Health System, gala; $101 Northern VA Tech Council, Fall Banquet; $450 VA Horse Council, trail ride; $189 Greater Washington Bd of Trade, dinner; Real Estate: vacation home in Shenandoah county, VA.

HOUSE DISTRICT FORTY-SEVEN, *Akbert C. Eisenberg (D)*

POLITICAL AND LEGISLATIVE BACKGROUND
House District 47 consists of part of Arlington County comprised of the Ashton Heights, Ballston, Clarendon, Lyon Park, Overlee Knolls, Westover, Arlington Forest, Fillmore, Jefferson, Dominion Hills, Lexington, Arlington View, Ashlawn, Virginia Square, and Woodbury Precincts, and parts of the Barcroft and Glen Carlyn Precincts.

Albert C. Eisenberg replaced James F. Almand in the 2004 election. There were no legislative records.

Delegate HD 47

Albert C. Eisenberg (D) Member House: 2004 - ; b Oct. 15, 1946, Jersey City, NJ; educ. University of Virginia (BA History 1968), Hampton Institute (MA Education 1971), wife Sharon Eileen Davis; children: Mathew and Alex; Jewish.

Principal, EBT Strategy Group, LLC.

Offices: P.O. Box 1511, Arlington, VA 22210, (703) 276-9414, FAX (703) 276-9414; P.O. Box 406, Richmond, VA 23218, Rm 817, (804) 698-1047, FAX (804) 786-6310.

2004 Committees Agriculture Chesapeake and Natural Resources, Science and Technology.

House Key Votes, 2004
Please see Introduction for more information on bills.

1) Budget Bill	AGN	5) Family Life	FOR	9) Morning After	AGN
2) Feticide	NV	6) Fire Arms	AGN	10) Legal Aid	FOR
3) Marriage	AGN	7) Open Space	FOR		
4) Abortion	AGN	8) Home School	AGN		

Election Results

2004 general	Albert Eisenberg	(D)	13,494	65.5%	$34,329
	Christian Hoff	(R)		34.4%	$69,447

Campaign Contributions 2004 Transportation $2,150; Tech/Communications $1,250; Law $1,000; Health Care $1,000; Finance $1,000; Political $750; Business/Retail Svs $700; Public Employees $600; Realty $500; Energy $350; Organized Labor $250; Agriculture $250; Misc $70.

Economic Interests, 2004 Salary/Wages $10,000+: EBT Strategy Group, LLC; Sec.$10,000 to $50,000: mutual funds, Vanguard, less than $50,000: mutual funds and bonds; Gifts: $225 Washington Gas, Chamber winter gala event; $81 Washington Gas, dinner; $110 VA Bankers Assoc., dinner; Real Estate: second home.

HOUSE DISTRICT FORTY-EIGHT, *Robert H. Brink (D)*

4) Abortion   AGN   8) Home School   AGN

Election Results

2004 general	Robert H. Brink	(D)	14,652	60.9%	$61,339
	Steve Sass	(R)		39.0%	$31,544

Campaign Contributions 2004 Law $3,875; Health Care $3,746; Finance $1,750; Energy $1,750; Tech/Communications $1,500; Public Employees $1,350; Transportation $1,000; Realty $700; Mfg $700; Organized Labor $600; Political $500;Business/Retail Svs $250; Agriculture $250; Undetermined $125; Misc $100.

Economic Interests, 2004 *Sal. & Wages*, $10,000+ ea.: EB&T Strategy Group, Brink & Associates (spouse); *Pers. Liabil.*, $10,001-$50,000 ea.: Loan or finance co. (self, family), banks (family); *Sec.*, $50,000+ ea.: mutual funds (2); $10,001-$50,000 stock in Profile Tech.; *Bus. Int.*, $50,000+ Brink & Associates (marketing, communications consultants); Paymts for talks, mtgs, and publications: Office of the Clerk, NCSL mtg, registration; $1,127 Office of the Clerk, travel, lodging; $835 Nat'l Govenors Assoc., travel, lodging; Paymts for representation, and other services generally to $10,000: consulting for other; Gifts: $175 VA Foundation for the Humanities, dinner and lodging; $150 VA YMCA, dinner,lodging; $115 VA Auto Dealers Assoc., reception; $65 GlaxcoSmithKline, dinner;Real Estate: recreational.

HOUSE DISTRICT FORTY-NINE, *Adam P. Ebbin (D)*

POLITICAL AND LEGISLATIVE BACKGROUND

House District 49 consists of part of the City of Alexandria comprised of the Cora Kelly Center and Mt. Vernon Recreation Center Precincts; part of Arlington County comprised of the Arlington, Columbia, Claremont, Glebe, and Oakridge Precincts, and parts of the Barcroft and Glen Carlyn Precincts; part of Fairfax County comprised of the Baileys Precinct and parts of the Glen Forest and Holmes Precincts.

Adam P. Ebbin replaced L. Karen Damer in the 2004 election.
Ebbin, in his first session sponsored eight bills; two passed, four failed and two were carried over.

His bill the change the boundaries in Arlington County and one undo adult protective services the provisions in its department to report some aspects of adult abuse, neglect and exploitation.

Failed were his bills regarding in-state eligibility for alien students prohibiting possession of firearms, following or stalking or sexual battery convictions; and abolishing sales tax on foods.

EIGHTH CONGRESSIONAL DISTRICT

Delegate HD 49   **Adam P. Ebbin (D)** Member House: 2004 - ; b. Nov. 10, 1963, Huntington, NY, educ. American University (BA 1985) , Jewish.

Marketing Consultant.

Offices: P.O. Box 41827, Arlington, VA 22204, (703) 549-8253, FAX (703) 739-6761; P.O. Box 406, Richmond, VA 23218, (804) 698-1049, FAX (8040 786-6310.

2004 Committees *Education; Health, Welfare and Institutions; Transportation.*

House Key Votes, 2004
Please see Introduction for more information on bills.

1) Budget Bill	AGN	5) Family Life	FOR	9) Morning After	AGN
2) Feticide	AGN	6) Fire Arms	AGN	10) Legal Aid	FOR
3) Marriage	AGN	7) Open Space	FOR		
4) Abortion	AGN	8) Home School	AGN		

Election Results

2004 general	Adam P. Ebbin	(D)	7,529	97.0%	$114,992

Campaign Contributions 2004 Energy $5,679; Health Care $5,200; Law $5,175; Political $4,200; Transportation $4,179; Realty $4,155; Public Employees $4,150; Business/Retail Svs $3,850; Undetermined $2,897; Tech/Communications $2,500; Finance $450; Misc $2,066; Single-Issue Groups $1,000; Agriculture $750; Mfg $400; Organized Labor $250.

Economic Interests, 2004 *Sal. & Wages,* $10,000+ : 21st Century Democrats; Sec.to $50,000: mutual funds, stocks; Paymts for talks, mtgs, and publications: $3,087 American Council of Young Political Leaders, expenses in Study Tour of Nicaragua & El Salvador; Gifts: $62 Dominion Resources, dinner; $115 VA Auto Dealers Assoc., dinner; $150 Arlington Chamber of Commerce, Gala at Ritz Carlton; $75 Washington Gas, ABBIE Awards; $75 Washington Gas, ALEX Luncheon; $65 Washington Metro Airport Authority, dinner; $$150 Northern VA Bldg Industries Assoc., Presidents Ball.

EIGHTH CONGRESSIONAL DISTRICT

POLITICAL AND LEGISLATIVE BACKGROUND

House District 48 consists of part of Arlington County comprised of the Aurora Hills, Crystal City, Cherrydale, Hume, Wilson, East Falls Church, Lyon Village, Park Lane, Rosslyn, Thrifton, Virginia Highlands, Woodlawn, Rock Spring, Yorktown, Madison, Marshall, and Nottingham Precincts.

Robert H. Brink, a legislative consultant and a Democrat, has served since his election in 1997. The seat was opened with the retirement of Democrat Julia Connally, who had served since 1992, filling the seat vacated by Democrat Mary Marshall. Marshall retired after 22 years of service. Brink served as legislative counsel to Lt. Gov. Donald S. Beyer for the 1997 session. Brink has a long history of civic leadership in the Arlington community. In 1997, Brink defeated two candidates, and in 1999, Brink handily defeated Republican S. John Massoud with 62.8% of the vote. In the 2001 election, Brink trounced Republican Victor K. Williams, winning with 64.5% of the vote.

During the 2004 session, Brink sponsored eleven bills and two resolutions. His successful bills provided for expense and reimbursement to the school board in Arlington County; made changes in election laws for voters equipment and technology; and regulations by the Department of Motor Vehicle of Drivers Improvement Clinics; and provided that organizations be stated under campaign finance disclosure.

His two resolutions establish on Inspector General to study the need for the Joint Legislature and Review Commission and a Joint commission to study pain management in long term care.

Delegate HD 48

Robert "Bob" Hendricks Brink (D), Member House: 1998- ; b. Nov. 17, 1946, Chicago, IL; home, 2670 Marley Rd., Arlington 22207; educ. Monmoth College, IL (B.A.), College William & Mary (J.D.); married, Deborah Harrison Schanck Brink; Christian.

Legislative Consultant; U.S. Army 1969-71, Vietnam 1970-71; Leg. counsel to Lt. Gov. Donald S. Beyer 1997; Counsel, Committee on Government Operations, U.S. House of Rep. (1978-89); Dep. Assist. Atty. Gen. for leg. affairs, U.S. Dept. Justice (1993-97); Dep. Gen. Counsel, Committee on the Judiciary, U.S. House of Repres. (1989-93); Member: Arlington Sch. Bonds Campaign (Man. 1988; Gen. Coord. 1996); Arlington Co. Transp. Comm. (1996-97); Arlington Co. Fiscal Aff. Adv. Comm. (1983-1985, chair 1984-85); Nor. VA Hotline, Vol. Listener (1972-75), Adv. Bd. (1985-93); Award: Honored Citizen Award for Outstanding Serv., Arlington Sch. Bd., 1991.

Offices 2670 Marcey Rd., Arlington 22207-5234; 703-243-5778; GA Bldg., Capitol Sq., Rm. 817, Richmond 23219; 804-698-1048.

2004 Committees *Privileges and Elections; Science and Technology.*

House Key Votes, 2004

Please see Introduction for more information on bills.

1) Budget Bill	AGN	5) Family Life	FOR	9) Morning After	AGN
2) Feticide	AGN	6) Fire Arms	AGN	10) Legal Aid	FOR
3) Marriage	AGN	7) Open Space	FOR		

Notes

NINTH CONGRESSIONAL DISTRICT
SENATE DISTRICT THIRTY-EIGHT, *Phillip P. Puckett (D)*

POLITICAL AND LEGISLATIVE BACKGROUND
Senate District 38 consists of the counties of Bland, Buchanan, Dickinson, Russell, and Tazewell; the Pulaski County Precincts of New River, West Cloyd, Draper, South Pulaski, Newbern, Dublin, Hiwasee 302/Snowville 304, Massie, Walker, and Robinson; the Smyth County Precincts of Saltville and Rich Valley; the Wise County Precincts of Appalachia, Dorchester, Guest River, West Pound, East Pound, and St. Paul; and Wythe County's Jackson Memorial Precinct.

Phillip Puckett was elected in a special election December 15, 1998, to replace Democrat Jackson Reasor. Reasor resigned his seat November 30, 1998, to become chief executive officer of the Old Dominion Electric Cooperative. Puckett, a Democrat and insurance agent from Russell County won with 55% of the vote over two challengers. In the 1999 election, Puckett faced Republican Barnes Lee "Barney" Kidd of Tazewell, who had served one term as the Delegate representing District Five in the 1994-1995 session. Puckett was re-elected with 69% of the vote.

During the 2004 session, Puckett sponsored nineteen bills, seven passed, including Worker's Compensation for food stamp recipients. Seven of the eight resolutions were successful, five commending. Food stamp recipients are now eligible for medical costs from covered injuries. Buchanan County Tourists Train Development Authority increased in membership to 33 members and is permitted to borrow money and accept contributions, grants, and other financial assistance. Cities, counties and towns are now exempt from the consumer utility tax. Utilities consumed on church or non-profit properties are exempt from local property taxes. Civil immunity is granted to officials who participate in programs for probationers and persons in community service. Revenues generated by the Coal and Gas Road Improvement Tax; and designated for local water or sewage projects shall be distributed to the local public service authority rather than the local governing body.

Included in the failed bills were those that allowed members of the Breaks Interstate Park Commission's Retirement system to switch to the Virginia Retirement System and for the Virginia state health insurance to cover infertility.

Senator SD 38

Phillip P. Puckett (D) Member Senate 1998- ; b. Russell Co., VA, August 10, 1947; home, P.O. Box 2440, Lebanon 24266; educ. Univ. Tennessee (B.S.), VPI & SU (M.A.); married Jeanette Griffith.

Pres., Lebanon Insurance Agency, Inc.; Member: Lebanon Community Fellowship; Russell Co. Chamber Commerce; Lebanon Little League (Dist. Treas.); Lebanon Vol. Fire; VA Fire Services Bd. (former member); Fireman of the Year 1986.

Offices P.O. Box 924, Tazewell 24651-0924; 276-979-8181; GA Bldg., Rm. 318, Capitol Sq., Richmond 23219; 804-698-7538.

2004 Committees *Agriculture, Conservation and Natural Resources; Local Government; Transportation.*

Senate Key Votes, 2004
Please see Introduction for more information on bills.

1) Budget Bill	FOR	5) Family Life	FOR	9) Charter School	FOR
2) Feticide	FOR	6) Fire Arms	FOR	10) Legal Aid	FOR

3) Marriage   FOR   7) Open Space   FOR
4) Child Abuse   FOR   8) Home School   FOR

Election Results

1999 general	Phillip P. Puckett	(D)	29,120	70.3%	$86,180
	Barney L. Kidd	(R)	12,269	29.6%	$12,259

Campaign Contributions 2000-June 30, 2002   Medical $6,875; **Coal** $4,900; **Finance** $4,175; **Transp.** $4,115 (Auto Dealers $1,740); **Tech./Comm.** $4,000; **Attys.** $3,235; **Realty/Constr.** $2,450; **Oil** $2,175 (Oil co. $1,550, fuel distrib. $625); **Electric** $1,800; **Insurance** $1,600; **Nat. Gas** $1,500; **AFL CIO** $1,500; **EMATS** $1,290; **Tobacco** $1,000 (PM $750, RJR $250); **GA Pacific** $1,000; **Pub. Empl.** $625; **Beer** $625; **Quarries** $500; **Billboards** $500; **Metals** $375; **Individ.** $375; **Trash** $250; **VA Automat. Merchan.** $250; **Advert.** $240; **Soft Drink** $125.

Economic Interests, 2002   *Sal. & Wages,* $10,000+ Lebanon Insur. Agency, Inc.; *Off. & Dir.,* Lebanon Ins. Agency, Pres.; *Pers. Liabil.,* $10,001-$50,000 banks; *Gifts,* $132 Jewell Resources (coat, light, dinner), $77 Philip Morris (gift box), $56 VA Agribusiness (recep./banquet); *Bus. Int.,* $50,000+ Lebanon Ins.; *Pay. for Rep. & Other Services Generally,* $50,001-$100,000 insurance to "other."

SENATE DISTRICT THIRTY-NINE, *James K. "Jay" O'Brien, Jr. (R)*

POLITICAL AND LEGISLATIVE BACKGROUND

Senate District 39 has vastly changed from southwestern Virginia to northern Virginia. The new district consists of the Fairfax County Precincts of Bush Hill, Cameron, Franconia, Pioneer, Rose Hill, Crestwood, Garfield, Lynbrook, Beulah, Kingstowne, Van Dorn, Lorton, Newington, Delong, Cardinal, Clifton, Fairfax Station, Keene Mill, Woodyard, Irving, Saratoga, Hunt, Silverbrook, West Springfield, and Newgate; and the Prince William County Precincts of Buckhall, McCoart, Springwoods, Westridge, Lake Ridge, Old Bridge, Rockledge, and Mohican.

The former district was largely rural, including the counties of Grayson, Smyth, going east taking the northern part of Carroll County, southern section of Pulaski County, and all of Montgomery County. It contained the cities of Independence, Galax, Christiansburg, and Radford.

James K. O'Brien, Jr. was elected to Senate District 39 in Virginia in the November 2002 election, defeating Democrat Rosemary M. Lynch with 56.6% of the vote in an election decided by 45.3% of the registered voters. A businessman and a Republican, O'Brien had served as a delegate in House District 40 since his election in 1991.

During the 2004 session, O'Brien sponsored twenty-nine bills, eleven passed, and seven were carried over.

He introduced seven resolutions, four passed with one commending.

Bills that passed included a constitutional amendment to revise provisions concerning the effective date and implementation of decennial redistricting measures; the establishment of a pilot program for local law enforcement; the provision that a person may only have his name on one office unless in the case of a special election; the exemption of law enforcements numbers for cell phones, pagers, etc. from the Freedom of Information Act; the addition of the Department of Homeland Security to the list of those who are the conservators of the peace; the division of Engineers and Building to establish and report on performance of use of the states real properties.

Additional bills that passed included authorization of state and local entities to enter into cooperative procurement agreement with any federal agency; and the creation of the position of Special Advisory to the Governor for Workforce Development. Bills requiring person 80 years or older take vision exam to obtain a drivers licence; and juveniles convicted of criminal gang related felonies quality for Serious or Habitual Offender comprehensive Action Program (SHOCAP), also passed.

Bills carried over dealt with changes in provisions of "living wages", towing a vehicle, and medical malpractice joint underwriting. Bills dealing with eminent domain requiring condemned property be put to public use after 10 years or offered for sale to the previous parental placement for adoptions; and schools, designation of shop or salon prior to issuance of license and day care centers to provide information to noncustodial parents were also continued.

Failed bills would have dealt with the exception of retired U.S. Marshalls service officers; from permit fees, the requirement of emergency electrical systems for hospitals,nursing homes, ect.; the creation of the Government Fee Disclosure Act; and the acceptance of foreign personal identification cards. Also a bill requiring helath insurance issuers provide written notification 30 days prior to a change in rates or fees failed.

Resolutions regarding the support and recognition of the National Guard and Reserve members by conducting awarness programs; and a constitutional amendment regarding the effective dates of legislative and congressional redistricting passed. A resolution regarding consititutional amendment providing the permanence of the Transportation Trust Fund failed along with a resolution regarding the naming of an athletic field at Mountain View School.

Senator SD 39

James K. "Jay" O'Brien, Jr. (R); Member Senate 2003- ; Member House, 1992-2002; b. Dec. 10, 1951, Nuremberg, Germany; home, 7903 Clifton Hunt Ct., Clifton 20124; educ., U.S. Military, West Point (BS), Univ. of Oklahoma (MA); married Grace Staves; Catholic.

Self-Employed, Office Furniture; USAR Infantry Officer; Reserve Officers Assn.; Rotary; Jaycees; Izaak Walton League; American Legion; Fairfax Co. Rep. Com.; West Point Assn. of Grads.; Fairfax County Chamber of Commerce; Knights of Columbus; Dept. of Health, Human Services Sec. Award.

Offices P.O. Box 7202, Fairfax Station 22039; 703-750-0936; FAX 703-750-1183; GA Bldg., Rm. 322, Capitol Sq., Richmond 23219; 804-698-7539.

2004 Committees *General Laws; Privileges and Elections; Rehabilitation and Social Services.*

Senate Key Votes, 2004
Please see Introduction for more information on bills.

1) Budget Bill	AGN	5) Family Life	FOR	9) Charter Schools	FOR
2) Feticide	FOR	6) Fire Arms	FOR	10) Legal Aid	FOR
3) Marriage	FOR	7) Open Space	AGN		
4) Child Abuse	FOR	8) Home School	FOR		

NINTH CONGRESSIONAL DISTRICT

Election Results

2002 general	Jay O'Brien	(R)	27,935	56.64%	$173,408
	R. M. Lynch	(D)	21,364	43.31%	$135,647

Campaign Contributions 2002   Republicans $68,381; **VA Conservative Action PAC** $7,500; **Transp.** $7,250; (Auto Dealers $3,250); **Realty/Constr.** $7,000; **Beer/Wine** $6,500; **Medical** $6,450; **Attys.** $3,700; **Tech./Comm.** $2,850; **Finance** $2,800; **Sugar Plum Tent Co.** $2,750; **Soft Drink** $2,600; **State Empl. Rts.** $2,500; **Individ.** $2,050; **Trash** $2,000; **Insurance** $1,900; **Pub. Empl.** $1,850; **Serv. Stat./Conv. St.** $1,750; **Retail/Business** $1,355; **Electric** $1,000; **Coal** $1,000; **GSW Inc.** $1,000; **VA Bingo Group PAC** $500; **Kings Dom.** $500; **VA Hospitality & Travel** $250; **Landscape** $250; **Oil** $200.

Economic Interests, 2004 *Sal. & Wages*, $10,000+ ea.: Krug Furniture, Softcare Innovations, HAG Seating; *Off. & Dir.*, Sevea Staves Ent., Sales; *Pers. Liabil.*, $50,000+ banks; *Bus. Int.*, $50,000+ Sevea Staves Enterprises (office furniture); *Pay. for Rep. Gen.*, $100,001-$250,000 man. rep./office furniture; Gifts: $190 Mc Guire Woods, dinner; $62 Metro Wash Airport Athority, dinner; $75 MCI, dinner; $102 Old Dominion Hwy Contractors, dinner; $108 Altria, dinner; $449 Kings Dominion, tkts.

SENATE DISTRICT FORTY, *William C. Wampler (R)*

POLITICAL AND LEGISLATIVE BACKGROUND
Senate District 40 consists of the counties of Lee, Scott, and Washington; the Cities of Bristol and Norton; the Grayson County Precincts of Bridle Creek, Flatridge, Grant, Mouth Of Wilson, Mount Rogers, Rugby, Troutdale, Comers Rock, and Elk Creek; the Smyth County Precincts of Seven Mile Ford, Chilhowie, St. Clair, East Park, West Park, Atkins, Wassona, Royal Oak East, Royal Oak West, Adwolfe, Sugar Grove, and Konnarock; and the Wise County Precincts of North Coeburn, Wise, Big Stone Gap, East Stone Gap, Clinch Valley, and South Coeburn Precincts.

William C. Wampler, Jr., who works with insurance and real estate, and is a Republican, was first elected in 1987 to Senate District 39. winning by 27 votes. Redistricting in 1991 placed two Senate incumbents in the same district. Senator John D. Buchanan (D) had served this area for many years before his death in 1991. A special election for this seat was won by former Delegate J. Jack Kennedy (D). Redistricting threw Kennedy and Wampler together in the same district. In a bitter campaign, Wampler took 52% of the vote in the 1991 general election. Wampler was unopposed in 1995 and 1999.

During the 2004 session, Wampler sponsored fifteen bills, eight succeeded. The bills that passed included a reduction of tuition to University of Virginia's college at Wise. All three of his resolutions were successful. These included two nominations to state commissions. The Coalfield Economic Development Authority was authorized to engage in economic development marketing and business attraction activities. The Virginia Economic Development Partnership Authority increases its membership from 13 to 18 members. Bills also passed prohibiting licensor for methadone clinics located one half mile from a K-12 school and the requirement of the courts to report active duty members guilty of assault and battery to family advocacy representatives of the United States armed forces. Colonialist bills that passed repeal the statute that requires the Commission of Health to report on the status of telemedicine by agencies of the Commonwealth and the requirement of the state to mow the grass and remove weeds on property acquired for the construction of a transportation project.

NINTH CONGRESSIONAL DISTRICT

Bills that were carried over dealt with telephone companies filing a cost allocation manual and the Line of Duty Act which provides the continued funding of health insurance and death payment to eligible persons.

Bills that failed would have prohibited the use of video or audio signals generated by the senate for political or commercial use, legislation defining a "non-legislative member"; and the creation of the Virginia Cultural Economic Development Fund. Also a bill increasing personal exemptions regarding state income tax failed.

According to the Richmond Times Dispatch, Wampler's name appeared on a rumored "hit-list" of five Republican state senators to be targeted by conservative Republicans in primaries in 2003. All of them fought former Governor Jim Gilmore over the repeal of the car tax. "Virginians for Responsible Government", a political action committee, headed by the chairman of Universal Corp., formed in response to the rumors, held a fund-raiser in July 2003 to assemble a high-profile list of supporters and a formidable war chest to "make it difficult" to any newcomers to mount a challenge to any of the five senators. The others John Chichester (R-28), Walter Stosch (R-12), Thomas Norment, Jr. (R-3), and Ken Stolle (R-8).

Wampler voted against the Equal Rightrs Amendment with failed by one vote in the Senate Privileges and Elections Committee.

Senator SD 40

William C. Wampler, Jr. (R) Member Senate: 1988-; b. Sept. 9, 1959, Bristol, TN; home, 3 Long Crescent Dr., Bristol, VA 24201; educ. Univ. Tenn. (B.A.); married Mary B. Thurmond; Episcopalian.

Insurance; Bd. Trustees Forward SW VA; U.S. Army Reserves, Maj.; Meritorious Service Medal; Jaycees; Southwest VA Higher Educ. Cntr. (Chm.); Powell River Project Adv. Bd.

Offices 510 Cumberland St. #308, Bristol, VA 24201-4387; 276-669-7515; GA Bldg., Capitol Sq., Rm. 301, Richmond 23219; 804-698-7540.

2004 Committees *Commerce and Labor, Chair; Finance; General Laws; Privileges and Elections; Rules.*

Senate Key Votes, 2004
Please see Introduction for more information on bills.

1) Budget Bill	FOR	5) Family Life	FOR	9) Charter Schools	FOR
2) Feticide	FOR	6) Fire Arms	FOR	10) Legal Aid	FOR
3) Marriage	FOR	7) Open Space	FOR		
4) Child Abuse	FOR	8) Home School	FOR		

Election Results

1999 general   William C. Wampler, Jr.   (R)   28,326   99.9% $134,263

Campaign Contributions 2000-June 30, 2002   Medical $11,500; **Coal** $9,500; **Tech./Comm.** $8,750; **Attys.** $6,950; **Insur./HMOs** $6,500; **Realty/Constr.** $5,250; **Nat. Gas** $5,000; **Republicans** $4,645; **Electric** $4,000; **Finance** $2,650; **Pub. Empl.** $2,500; **Transp.** $1,500 (Auto Dealers $1,000, RR $500); **Beer/Wine** $750; **Tobacco--PM** $500; **Billboards** $500; **Individ.** $500; **Oil** $250; **VA Automat. Merchan.** $250.

NINTH CONGRESSIONAL DISTRICT
Economic Interests, 2004 *Sal. & Wages,* $10,000+ ea.: Nash & Powers Insur. Co., U.S. Army (self), Penn Stuart (spouse); *Off. & Dir.,* Member of: WSM Development LLC, WB LLC, Wampler Consulting Group LLC; Bassett Furnture, Dir.; *Pers. Liabil.,* $50,000+ VHDA; *Sec.,* $50,000+ stocks in insur. co.; $10,001-$50,000 ea.: stock in Dominion Res., King Pharmaceutical; *Pay. for Talks, Mtgs., & Publ.,* $453 VA Assn. Counties (annual mtg, expenses), $300 VA Rehab. Assoc.(mtg., exp.); *Bus. Int.,* $50,000/less ea.: Wampler Consulting Gr. (rental prop.), WSM (rental), WB (rental); *Pay. for Rep. & Other Services Generally* $10,001-$50,000 NVI, VA markets; $1,001-$10,000 ea.: gas util., gas retail, manuf., mining, life insur., casualty ins., other ins., retail, alcoholic bev./distrib., trade assn., prof. assn., localities, other; *Real Estate,*rental property and land; *Real Estate Contracts with State Govt. Agencies,* WB LLC and Wampler Consulting Group, LLC $9,550 VHDA lender.; Gifts: $65 Carillion, dinner mtg; $72 Carillion, dinner mtg; $240 Food City/KVAT, race tkts; $53 GlaxoSmithKline, dinner mtg; $130 Kings Dominion, tkts; $1,623 CSX, White Silver Springs; $1,931 KBR, fishing trip; $611 Dominion Resources, hunting trip; $1,831KBR, hunting trip; $400 Cumberland Resources, travel; $54 Dominion Resources, dinner mtg; $66 Dominion Resources, dinner mtg.

HOUSE DISTRICT ONE, *Terry G. Kilgore (R)*
POLITICAL AND LEGISLATIVE BACKGROUND
The First House District consists of all of Lee and Scott Counties; part of Washington County comprised of the Burson Place, Mendota, Valley Institute, Wallace Part 3, and Wallace Part 1 Precincts and part of the Greendale Precinct; and part of Wise County comprised of the Big Stone Gap, East Stone Gap, and Clinch Valley Precincts.

Terry Kilgore, an attorney and a Republican, has represented the area since 1993. The seat was opened on the retirement of Ford C. Quillen, a Democrat and an attorney from Gate City who had served since 1969. He was Chairman of the Privileges and Elections Committee, and was known for his legislative concerns with the miners in Southwest Virginia and the mining industry, conservation, and recycling. Kilgore's twin brother, Jerry, served in Governor Allen's cabinet, became a lobbyist, and in 2001 was elected the state's Attorney General. Terry Kilgore defeated Democratic opposition in 1993 and 1997, and was unopposed in 1995, 1999, and 2001.

During the 2004 session, Kilgore sponsored thirty bills, eleven passed. Nine of ten resolutions passed, three were commending. Successful bills created the Drug Treatment Act, funding for legal aid societies; and the Judicial Council's Standing Committee be given civil immunity in the investigation of the Commission of Accounts. Bills passed eliminating the requirement of the court to act "upon petition" to issue a capias for nonsupport; a special rate was created for filing fees in custody and visitation proceedings; and extended authority to petition the court to name a standby guardian for an incapacitated person to the child or children of an incapacitated person.

Bills that were carried over were regarding contributions to legal aid societies, physicians who are summoned as witness will have the cost associated with health care services that were cancelled or rescheduled paid for by the party issuing the summons, and IRA benefits being exempt from creditors.

One of Kilgore sponsored bills would have provided that is a Class 4 felony to willfully deliberately and unlawfully terminate the life of a fetus to be guilty of a Class 2 felony. Bills also failed requiring disclosure of liability limits to an attorney for an injured person prior to filing of a civil action for personal injuries due to a motor vehicle accident; provisions that any one over the age of 18, including a spouse or blood relative of the declarant, to serve as a witness for the advanced directive; and the provision of creditable compensation of teacher for retirement purposes including compensation that is not pursuant to a contract for teaching.

Additional bills that failed clarified the subrogation to lien for medical cost regarding personal injury, implementation of uniform language regarding the release of escrow funds to cigarette manufacturers that are not under the Master Settlement Agreement, and the Department of Transportation to maintain property for construction thereof. Also bills that would make it unlawful to obstruct for contaminate flood ways or floodplains, use copper and copper alloys kettles to make apple butter and molasses, and compensation to be set a 75 percent of the compensation in United States Federal Courts for state court appointed failed.

Delegate HD 1

Terry G. Kilgore (R) Member House: 1994- ; b. Aug. 23, 1961, Kingsport, TN; home, Rt. 1, Box 474-B, Gate City 24251; educ. Univ. VA, Clinch Valley College (UVA College at Wise) (B.A.), William & Mary Sch. of Law (J.D.); married, Debbie Sue Wright; United Methodist.

Attorney; Commonwealth Attorney, Scott County, 1987-94.

Offices P.O. Box 669, Gate City 24251; 276-386-7701; GA Bldg., Rm. 714, Capitol Sq., Richmond 23219; 804-698-1001.

2004 Committees *Commerce and Labor; Courts of Justice; Militia, Police and Public Safety; Rules.*
House Key Votes, 2004
Please see Introduction for more information on bills.

1) Budget Bill	FOR	5) Family Life	AGN	9) Morning After	FOR
2) Feticide	FOR	6) Fire Arms	FOR	10) Legal Aid	FOR
3) Marriage	FOR	7) Open Space	AGN		
4) Abortion	FOR	8) Home School	FOR		

Election Results

2004 general	Terry G. Kilgore	(R)	12,777	100%	$71,283

Campaign Contributions 2004 Energy $5,550; Law $5,350; Realty $3,200; Finance $2,650; Health Care $2,000; Business/Retail Svs $1,665; Tech/ Communications $1,500; Transportation $1,200; Mfg $1,000; Agriculture $1,000; Public Employees $550; Undetermined $500.

Economic Interests, 2004 *Sal. & Wages*, $10,000+ ea.: Wolfe, Farmer, Williams & Rutherford, attorneys (self), Scott Co. School Bd. (spouse); *Pers. Liabil.*, $10,001-$50,000 ea.: banks (self), (family); Sec. to $50,000: ABA Retirement Act, mutual funds; *Pay. for Talks, Mtgs., & Publ.*, $1,753 VA Trial Lawyers Assoc, speaker at annual mtg., expenses, $500 VA Trial Lawyers Assoc., speaker at annual mtg, lodging; $1,782 state, ALEC travel to Seattle, expenses; *Pay. for Rep. & Other Services Generally*, legal services $1,001-$10,000 ea.: water utilities, interstate transp., oil/gas retail, banks, retail co., localities; *Real Estate*, One prop. (law bldg.); Gifts: $63 Old Dominion Hwy Contractors, dinner; $50 VA Agribusiness, dinner.

HOUSE DISTRICT TWO, *Clarence E. "Bud" Phillips (D)*

NINTH CONGRESSIONAL DISTRICT

POLITICAL AND LEGISLATIVE BACKGROUND

The Second House District consists of all of Dickenson County; all of the City of Norton; part of Russell County comprised of the Copper Creek, Moccasin, South Castlewood, Cleveland, Dante, North Castlewood, Cooks Mill, Daughertys, Elk Garden, and Lebanon Precincts and part of the Honaker Precinct; and part of Wise County comprised of the Appalachia, Dorchester, Guest River, West Pound, North Coeburn, Wise, East Pound, South Coeburn, and St. Paul Precincts.

Clarence "Bud" Phillips, a lawyer and a Democrat, was first elected to the old House District 3 in 1989. In a low key, low budget campaign, he won over Roy Smith (R) by 1,121 votes. His predecessor, William F. Green, retired after 10 years of working for legislation relative to the coal industry, mining, and safety. Phillips had no challenges in House District 2 from 1991-1997. In 1999, he defeated a challenge from Republican Erick A. Bowman with 76% of the vote. Phillips was unopposed in the 2001 election.

During the 2004 session, Phillips sponsored eighteen bills and three resolutions. Ten bills were successful, along with all three resolutions, two were commending. Successful legislation requires criminal history record checks for all persons elected by the General assembly as justices, judges, etc. and all persons appointed by the circuit courts as magistrates or substitute judges and also prohibits the appointment of persons with certain criminal backgrounds, the requirement that each motor vehicle safety station to have garages liability insurance of at least $500,000. Highway in southwest Virginia as designated "Virginia's Heritage Music Trail: The Crooked Road" and portions of US 23 is designated "Country Music Highway". Convenience stores and gas stations with less than 15 seats that serve food and are not part of a national or regional restaurant chain are exempt from the Department of Health regulations. Natural gas companies can make direct sales to certain public schools in the Commonwealth that are not located in a territory for which a certificate to provide gas service was issued by the State Corporation Commission. Water and sewage authories that meet certain conditions are permitted to install, own or lease pipes or conduits for carrying fiber optic cable. Revenues generated by the coal and gas road improvement tax designated for local water projects to be distributed to the local public service authority instead of the local governing body.

Failed legislature would have allowed special license plates issued to supporters of the Boy Scouts of America; logging and skid roads to be reseeded, and members of the Breaks Interstate Park Commission's Retirement System to switch to the Virginia Retirement System. Additional bills that failed would have modified the sentencing guidelines for anyone convicted of multiple drug convictions shall not include a recommendation for probation, absentee ballots shall not be rejected solely because of an error or omission made by the voter in his residence address as long as the record can be verified by the Virginia voter registration system; and the capping of worker's compensation for the surface and underground coal classifications for voluntary markets at existing levels.

Phillips voted to ratify the Equal Rights Amendment which failed by six votes in the House of Privileges and Election Committee.

Delegate HD 2

Clarence Edward "Bud" Phillips (D) Member House: 1990-; b. April 8, 1950, Clintwood; home, Rt. HC 05, Box 596, Coeburn 24230; educ. Clinch Valley Col. (UVA College at Wise) (B.A.) History, East Tenn. State Univ. (M.A.) Admin. Sup., (J.D.); married Teresa Eileen Grizzle; Baptist.

Lawyer, Teacher; former principal; VA State Bar; VA Trial Lawyers; Stone Mt. Health Care Clinic; Pinnacle Park Comm.

Offices P.O. Box 36, Castlewood 24224; 276-762-9758; GA Bldg., Rm. 803, Capitol Sq., Richmond 23219; 804-698-1002.

2004 Committees *Appropriations; General Laws; Privileges and Elections.*

House Key Votes, 2004
Please see Introduction for more information on bills.

1) Budget Bill	FOR	5) Family Life	FOR	9) Morning After	FOR
2) Feticide	FOR	6) Fire Arms	FOR	10) Legal Aid	FOR
3) Marriage	FOR	7) Open Space	FOR		
4) Abortion	FOR	8) Home School	AGN		

Election Results

2004 general	Clarence E. Phillips	(D)	11,330	99.7%	$9,232

Campaign Contributions 2004 Realty $1,500; Health Care $1,250; Transportation $500; Finance $500; Tech/Communications $500; Agriculture $500; Business/Retail Svs $250.

Economic Interests, 2004 *Sal. & Wages,* $10,000+ Clarence E. Phillips P.C.; *Pers. Liabil.,* $50,000+ banks (family, loan secured by cert. dep.); *Sec.,* $50,000+ mutual funds (insur.); *Bus. Int.,* $50,000+ Clarence E. Phillips law; *Pay. for Rep. by You,* $1,001-$10,000: Mfg, chemical, water utitilies, retail companies, professional associates, counties, cities, or towns, legal services; *Pay. for Rep. & Other Services Generally,* legal each $100,00-$250,000 ea.: Wolkers Comp, legal services ; $1,001-$10,000 prof. assn.; *Real Estate,* Two prop. (farm, recreation): Gifts: $63 Bon Secours, dinner; $88 Dominion Power, dinner.

HOUSE DISTRICT THREE, *Jackie T. Stump (D)*

POLITICAL AND LEGISLATIVE BACKGROUND
The Third House District consists of all of Buchanan County; part of Russell County comprised of the Drill and Swords Creek Precincts and part of the Honaker Precinct; and part of Tazewell County comprised of the Tip Top, Amonate, Bishop, Adria, Gap Store, Bandy, Abbs Valley 101/Boissevain 103/Falls Mills 104/Pocahontas 106, Burkes Garden, Clear Fork, Freestone, Jeffersonville, Thompson Valley, Cedar Bluff, Baptist Valley, Wardell, Pounding Mill, Richlands, Jewell Ridge, and Raven Precincts.

Jackie T. Stump, a retired United Mine Workers leader, and a Democrat, has served since his first election to the old House District 4 in 1989 as a write-in candidate. As an Independent, he took 67% of the vote over incumbent Democrat Donald A. McGlothlin. The union, the miners, and the people responded to a Democratic administration which sent troopers to break the picket lines. The Pittston coal strike lasted 11 months. Stump ran as a Democrat in 1991 and 1993 with no opposition. In

1995, Stump was outspent by $26,000, but easily defeated Republican Thomas R. Scott, Jr., a Grundy attorney, by 63.9%. Stump has been unopposed since that time.

During the 2004 session, Stump sponsored twelve bills and two resolutions. Seven bills were successful, along with both of his resolutions, one was commending. The Department of Motor Vehicles now provides licensure for motorcycle rider safety training centers, instructions, etc. The Buchanan County Tourist Train Development Authority increased its membership from 8 to 22 members and is permitted to borrow money and accept contributions; civil immunity is granted to officials who participate in programs for probationers and persons on community service. The hunting stamp was established; cities and towns are now exempt from the consumer utility tax, utilities consumed on church properties exempt from local property taxes. The Coalfield Economic Development Authority is authorized to engage in economic development marketing and business attraction activities.

Failed bills would have authorized that vehicles owned by regional jail authorities be "local government" vehicles and therefore have the registration provided for and increased state portion of the sales and use tax from 3.5 percent to 5.5 percent.

Carry over bills would require state health plans to cover annual mammograms for persons over 40 and screening for ovarian cancer using the CA125 blood test for high risk individuals and repeals the requirements for notifying cities and towns of tort claims against them.

Delegate HD 3

Jackie Thomas Stump (D) Member House: 1990-; b. Jan. 13, 1948, Lebanon, VA; home, P.O. Box 8, Council 24260; educ. Honaker High School, Garden High School; married Linda Gail Addair; Pentecostal.

Miner, retired; United Mine Workers of Am. (UMWA) District 28; VA Coal Council; VA State Exec. Bd. AFL-CIO; U.S. Air Force 1967-71, Medal, Oak Leaf; American Legion.

Offices P.O. Box 429, Oakwood 24631; phone/FAX 276-498-7207; GA Bldg., Capitol Sq., Rm. 513, Richmond 23219; 804 698 1003.

2004 Committees *Appropriations; Counties, Cities and Towns; Transportation.*

House Key Votes, 2004
Please see Introduction for more information on bills.

1) Budget Bill	FOR	5) Family Life	FOR	9) Morning After	FOR
2) Feticide	FOR	6) Fire Arms	FOR	10) Legal Aid	FOR
3) Marriage	FOR	7) Open Space	FOR		
4) Abortion	FOR	8) Home School	FOR		

Election Results

2004 general	Jackie T. Stump	(D)	10,184	100%	$52,569

Campaign Contributions 2004 Energy $11,250; Realty $10,250; Transportation $3,550; Undetermined $1,705; Tech/Communications $1,650; Finance $1,375; Health Care $1,275; Law

NINTH CONGRESSIONAL DISTRICT
$895; Agriculture $875; Organized Labor $800; Public Employees $750; Business/Retail Svs $395; Mfg $150; Single-Issue Groups $100.

Economic Interests, 2004 *Sal. & Wages*, $10,000+ ea.: United Mine Workers of America (retired), JTS Research Co.; *Off. & Dir.*, JTS Res., Pres., Seamore Travel, Pres.; *Bus. Int.*, $50,000+ ; JTS Res., $50,000 or less: Seamore Travel; Payments for representation and other services to $50,000: Interstate transportation companies, mining companies, consulting; *Real Estate*, house and land, recreational; Gifts: $102 Old Dominion Hwy Contractors, dinner; $110 VA Aggregates Assoc., golf tournament.

HOUSE DISTRICT FOUR, *Joseph P. Johnson, Jr. (D)*

POLITICAL AND LEGISLATIVE BACKGROUND
The Fourth House District includes all of the City of Bristol; the Smyth County Precincts of Saltville, Chilhowie, St. Clair, and Konnarock; and the Washington County Precincts of East Abingdon, West Abingdon, Clinchburg, Hayter's Gap, Watauga, South Abingdon, Glade Spring, Meadowview, Rhea 501/ Damascus 502/ Green Cove 503, High Point 701/ John Battle 703, and Wallace Part 2, and part of Greendale.

Joseph P. Johnson, Jr., a Democrat, lawyer, and native of Washington County, formerly served in House District Six. He was elected to that position in 1965, re-elected in 1966, and then left the House for family and business reasons. Johnson entered politics again in the 1989 election, soundly defeating Chandall Lowe (R). He has run unopposed since that time.

During the 2004 session, Johnson sponsored three bills. Of his five resolutions, two are commending. His successful bill allows the department of taxation to appoint local government treasurers to collect delinquent state taxes in the same manner they collect delinquent local taxes. Resolutions passed regarding the support and recognition of the national guard and reserve members by conducting awareness programs and commemorating the Washington County Service Authority 50th anniversary.

Johnson had one billed carried over regarding martial communications being completely privileged from disclosure unless either spouse is charge with a crime or tort against each other or a child of either spouse.

Johnsons failed bill would have authorized that vehicles owned by regional jail authorities be "local government" vehicles and therefor have the registration provided for.

NINTH CONGRESSIONAL DISTRICT

Delegate HD 4

Joseph Pickett Johnson, Jr. (D) Member House: 1990-; 1965-69; b. Dec. 12, 1931, Hayter's Gap; home, 19562 Jonesboro Rd., Abingdon 24210; educ. Emory & Henry Col., Univ. Richmond Law Sch.; married Mary Ann Allison; Baptist.

Attorney, Johnson, Scyphers & Austin; Wash. County Bar Assn.; VA State Bar; VA Trial Lawyers Assn.; former sub. judge, 28th Gen. District Court; U.S. Air Force serving in Korea; Vet. Foreign Wars; Am. Legion; Masons; Bd. Govs., Emory & Henry; Bd. Dir. First VA Bank, Damascus; Abingdon Civitan Club; Abingdon Jaycees Award.

Offices 164 E. Valley St., Abingdon 24210; 276-628-9940; GA Bldg., Rm. 811, Capitol Sq., Richmond 23219; 804-698-1004.

2004 Committees *Commerce and Labor; Courts of Justice; Finance.*

House Key Votes, 2004
Please see Introduction for more information on bills.

1) Budget Bill	AGN	5) Family Life	FOR	9) Morning After	FOR
2) Feticide	FOR	6) Fire Arms	FOR	10) Legal Aid	FOR
3) Marriage	FOR	7) Open Space	AGN		
4) Abortion	FOR	8) Home School	FOR		

Election Results

2004 general	Joseph P. Johnson, Jr	(D)	12,671	99.8%	$12,338

Campaign Contributions 2004 Energy $1,500; Health Care $1,250; Organized Labor $500; Business/Retail Svs $500; Tech/Communications $500; Agriculture $500; Finance $250.

Economic Interests, 2004 *Sal. & Wages,* $10,000+ Johnson & Johnson P.C. (law practice); *Off. & Dir.,* BB&T, Bd. Dir.; *Sec.,* $50,000+ ea.: mutual funds, stocks in: New York Life, Exxon, CLC (realty), banks (3); $10,001-$50,000 ea.: mutual funds (3); *Bus. Int.,* $50,000+ ea.: Johnson & Johnson, P.C. law; realty, Bowers Property ; *Pay. for Rep. Gen.,* $1,001-$10,000 legal serv. for bank; *Real Estate,* Four prop. (2 open land, 2 commercial all w/others): Gifts: $296 VA Polytech Inst. & State University, tkts to VPI football game; $50 VA Agribusiness Council, banquet; $80 Sprint, reception, dinner; $78 State Farm, dinner.

HOUSE DISTRICT FIVE, *Charles William "Bill" Carrico, Sr. (R)*
POLITICAL AND LEGISLATIVE BACKGROUND
House District 5 consists of all of Grayson County; all of the City of Galax; the Carroll County Precincts of Hillsville C, Sylvatus, Vaughn, Woodlawn E, and Laurel; the Smyth County Precincts of Seven Mile Ford, Rich Valley, East Park, West Park, Atkins, Wassona, Royal Oak East, Royal Oak West, Adwolfe, and Sugar Grove; and the Wythe County Precincts of Rural Retreat, Fort Chiswell, Jackson Memorial, Sheffey, Huddle, and Zion, and part of the Evergreen Precinct.

C. W. "Bill" Carrico, Sr., an in-school suspension supervisor, a retired state trooper, and a Republican, is the delegate for this district. In a 2001 election upset, Carrico defeated incumbent Democrat, John Tate, with 58.9% of the vote in the November general election. Carrico, who was injured in a car accident while working as a state trooper, retired from that position in 2000.

NINTH CONGRESSIONAL DISTRICT

John Tate, a Democrat and an attorney had served the area since his election in 1995. Tate won by 867 votes over incumbent Republican Barnes "Barney" Lee Kidd, who had served one term in the House. Only two years earlier, Kidd himself had captured the seat in an upset victory over G. C. Jennings, a Democrat who had held the seat since 1981. Tate won a tough re-match in 1997 with Kidd, and in 1999, defeated Republican Jack S. "Chip" Hurley, Jr.

During the 2004 session, Carrico sponsored twelve bills; four passed; five failed, three were continued; and three were commending. Bills passed reduce new employer thresholds to receive major business facility job tax credit; provide for development and use in higher educational institutions; protection of job security of military reservists; provide insured with claims experience or medical costs.

Continued bills dealt with DUI or drug penalties while having drugs in the blood; health coverage for infertility; and definition of law enforcement officer; and entitlement to consel during investigation.

Bills that failed would have created State Police Training and Retention Fund; salary increase for State Police officers; and use fees collected by circuit court clerks.

Delegate HD 5

Charles William "Bill" Carrico, Sr. (R) Member House: 2002- ; b. Nov. 6, 1961, Marion, VA; home, 1139 Turkey Knob Rd., Fries 24330; educ., VA Highlands Community College; VA State Police Academy; married, Paula Denise Sweet; Pentecostal.

In-School Suspension Supervisor; VA State Trooper , retired 2000; Member: Cliffview Church of God; Church and Pastor Council; Youth Leadership Council; Grayson Republican Party, Treas.; VA State Police Assn.

Offices   578 B East Main St., PO Box 188, Independence 24348; 276-773-9600; GA Bldg., Rm. 713, Capitol Sq., Richmond 23219; 804-698-1005.

2004 Committees   *Education; Militia, Police and Public Safety; Transportation.*

House Key Votes, 2004

Please see Introduction for more information on bills.

1) Budget Bill	FOR	5) Family Life	AGN	9) Morning After	FOR
2) Feticide	FOR	6) Fire Arms	FOR	10) Legal Aid	FOR
3) Marriage	FOR	7) Open Space	FOR		
4) Abortion	FOR	8) Home School	FOR		

Election Results

2004 general	C. W. "Bill" Carrico, Sr.	(R)	11,561	54.9%	$ 138,981
	Thomas Graham	(D)		45.1%	$210,972

Campaign Contributions 2004 Energy $4,400; Public Employess $3,650; Transportation $3,400; Law $3,300; Health Care $3,000; Agriculture $3,000; Realty $2,883; Tech/Communications $1,950; Business/Retail Svs $1,761; Political $1,500; Finance $1,250; Mfg $650; Defense $250.

Economic Interests, 2004 *Sal. & Wages,* $10,000+ Managed Care Innovation LLC (Workers' Comp. payment due to an injury on the job), Social Sec. (disability payment due to accident while working as

190

State Trooper); *Off. & Dir.*, Mountain Side Pools, Sole Proprietor; *Pers. Liabil*, $50,000+ ea.: banks: self, family; *Real Estate*, One prop. (30 acres farm land) w/spouse.

HOUSE DISTRICT SIX, *W. B. "Benny" Keister (D)*

POLITICAL AND LEGISLATIVE BACKGROUND

The Sixth House District consists of all of Bland County; part of Giles County comprised of the Glen Lyn, Rich Creek, Narrows, Pearisburg, Staffordsville, White Gate, Sugar Run, Eggleston, Pembroke, and Hatfield Precincts; part of Pulaski County comprised of the Belspring, New River, West Cloyd, Draper, South Pulaski, Newbern, Massie, Walker, and Robinson Precincts; part of Tazewell County comprised of the Springville and Graham Precincts; and part of Wythe County comprised of the Royal Oak, Evansham, Pine Ridge, Spiller, Withers, and Max Meadows Precincts and part of the Evergreen Precinct.

W. B. "Benny" Keister, a counselor for the New River Regional Jail, and a Democrat, was first elected to the former House District 7 in 1999. Keister is also known in the region for his position as a NASCAR racing official. That House seat had opened with the retirement of Republican Thomas G. Baker, Jr., who served 10 years in the House, first elected to the old House District 12 in 1989. In the 2001 election, Keister defeated Republican opposition from Billy B. Ashworth, a bank account manager, with 54.2% of the vote. Redistricting in 2001 put several delegates into the same district. Thomas M. Jackson, who had been the delegate for this area since his election in 1987, retired. Jackson had been the minority whip in the House, and was respected on both sides of the aisle.

During the 2004 session, Keister sponsored six bills, three passed., one resolution failed. Bills that passed gave greater flexibility to facilities owned by the Regional Industrial Facility Authority to direct tax revenues collected and also added district 1 and 2 to the current planning districts, broadens the use of fees collected by the courts to be used to fund equipment and other property for courthouse security; and allows the retiring officers of the Department of Forestry and Department of Conservation and Recreation to purchase their handguns.

Failed bills would have included the increase in the amount of wages that a recipient of unemployment could earn, without having such benefits offset by the amount of wages from $25 to $100, requirement of the local Social Services Agency 24 to notify the local government and the Attorney of the Commonwealth and make available to them record of neglect; and the prohibition of the use of a vehicle sound amplification system that can be heard within 50 feet from the vehicle.

Delegate HD 6

Walter Benjamin "Benny" Keister (D) Member House: 2000- ; b. March 13, 1941, Radford; home, 628 Hudson Dr., Dublin 24084; educ. Lees-McRae Col., E. Tenn. State Univ. (B.S.), Radford Univ (M.S.); divorced; Christian.

Programs Director, New River Regional Jail; retired teacher; Pulaski Co. Lifesaving Crew; Pulaski Co. Chamber of Commerce; Va.'s First Industrial Dev. Auth.; Regional Emergency Medical Service Board; New River Valley Economic Alliance; Wal-Mart Hometown Leadership Award.

Offices P.O. Box 1023, Dublin 24084; 540-994-0800; GA Bldg., Rm. 819, Capitol Sq., Richmond 23219; 804-698-1006.

2004 Committees *Agriculture, Chesapeake and Natural Resources; Education; Health, Welfare and Institutions.*

House Key Votes, 2004
Please see Introduction for more information on bills.

1) Budget Bill	AGN	5) Family Life	FOR	9) Morning After	AGN
2) Feticide	AGN	6) Fire Arms	FOR	10) Legal Aid	FOR
3) Marriage	FOR	7) Open Space	FOR		
4) Abortion	AGN	8) Home School	AGN		

Election Results

2004 general	W. B. Keister	(D)	10,247	50.6%	$168,352
	Morgan Morris	(R)		49.4%	$55,204

Campaign Contributions 2004 Health Care $3,950; Energy $3,850; Law $1,950; Realty $1,500; Business/Retail Svs $1,450; Tech/Communications $1,350; Public Employees $1,058; Transportation $1,050; Organized Labor $800; Finance $750; Mfg $250.

Economic Interests, 2004 *Sal. & Wages*, $10,000+ ea.: VA Retire. System, New River Valley Reg. Jail Authority; *Off. & Dir.*, First National Bank of Christiansburg, Member, Adv. Bd. Dublin; *Pers. Liabil.*, $10,001-$50,000 banks; *Gifts*, $1,000 Motor Mile Speedway, season tkts; $370 VA Tech , football tkts.

HOUSE DISTRICT SEVEN, *David Ashley "Dave" Nutter (R)*

POLITICAL AND LEGISLATIVE BACKGROUND
The Seventh House District consists of all of the City of Radford; part of Montgomery County comprised of the B-2, B-3, C-1, C-2, C-3, C-4, D-1, D-2, D-3 Part 1, D-4, D-5, E-1, and E-2 Precincts; part of Pulaski County comprised of Dublin and Hiwasee 302/Snowville 304 Precincts; and Montgomery A.

David A. "Dave" Nutter, the Director of College and Media Relations at Virginia Tech, is the Delegate for this district. In a major upset in 2001, Nutter defeated Democratic incumbent James Shuler with 52.4% of the vote. Shuler had served in the former House District 12. Shuler, however, won back the

NINTH CONGRESSIONAL DISTRICT

12th House District in a special January 2002 election, when it opened after R. Creig Deeds (D) won a Senate seat.
House District 7 had been the district served by Benny Keister. With redistricting, several Democratic incumbents were tossed together.

During the 2004 session, Nutter sponsored eighteen bills, eight passed including the elimination of restrictions on the number of unfunded graduate and undergraduate scholarships. However, the total value
of all such scholarships remains. He also introduced two resolutions, one passed. The allowance of out-of-state concealed weapons permits in the Commonwealth as long as the holder is at least 21 years old for a handgun or lower age if another state allows it for weapons other than handgun. Two bills passed regarding the Neighborhood Assistance Act, one gives an extension for the sunset date for tax credits from the close of 2004 to 2009, and the other stipulates that not just health clinics that donate services but health care professionals too, can receive allocations of tax credits from the Commissioner of the Department of Social Services. The charter for the City of Radford was amended regarding the city's boundary description and the town of Christiansburg was amended stating that neither the Mayor nor any other council member be eligible during his tenure to hold any office, position, or employment with the Town. Additionally, a bill exempts an owner of a dog or cat who uses reasonable force in when they are attacked by another dog or cat of intentional animal cruelty.

Legislation carried over to the 2004 session included the Public Procurement Act regarding preference for goods made in the United States; the duties of the Virginia Economic Development Partnership Authority, and the prohibition of insurers from imposing pharmacies terms and conditions that are not equally required from all pharmacies in the Commonwealth.

Failed bills would have increased the retirement allowance for certain state employees and law enforcement officers, provided state employees with 12 months of additional retirement service credits for each year the state does not provide a general salary increase; and the allowance of the sale and purchase of firearms outside of the Commonwealth in noncontiguous states; also failed was a resolution for the Council of Higher Education to examine the methodology for establishing faculty salary structure.

Delegate HD 7

David Ashley "Dave" Nutter (R) Member House: 2001- ; b. April 2, 1955, Clarksburg, W VA; home, 2729 Old Fort Rd , Blacksburg 24060; educ. VA Tech (B.A.); married, Jackie Gale Sheffield; Methodist.

Director of College and Media Relations, VA Tech; Member: Christiansburg/ Mont. Chamber Commerce, Educa. Comm. (1996-99), chair Govt. Relations (2000-01); New River District Boy Scouts; Mont. Co. GOP, chair comm. 1995-2000; Mont. Co. Bush for Pres. Campaign.

Offices P.O. Box 1344, Christiansburg 24068; 540-382-7731; GA Bldg., Rm. 806, Capitol Sq., Richmond 23219; 804-698-1007.

2004 Committees *Agriculture, Chesapeake and Natural Resources; Militia, Police and Public Safety; Science and Technology.*

NINTH CONGRESSIONAL DISTRICT

House Key Votes, 2004
Please see Introduction for more information on bills.

1) Budget Bill	FOR	5) Family Life	FOR	9) Morning After	FOR
2) Feticide	FOR	6) Fire Arms	FOR	10) Legal Aid	FOR
3) Marriage	FOR	7) Open Space	FOR		
4) Abortion	FOR	8) Home School	FOR		

Election Results

2004 general   David A. Nutter   (R)   8,603   99.8% $42,469

Campaign Contributions 2004 Health Care $4,000; Political $2,650; Realty $2,400; Energy $2,250; Law $2,050; Finance $1,500; Tech/Communications $1,250; Public Employees $1,150; Business/Retail Svs $1,000; Agriculture $1,000; Transportation $500; Mfg $500; Misc $250; Defense $250.

Economic Interests, 2004 Gifts: $50 GlaxoSmithKline, dinner; $160 VA Tech, football game tkts; $80 VA Tech, football game tkts; $120 VA Tech, football game tkts; $86 American Electric Power, dinner.

HOUSE DISTRICT TWELVE, *James M. Shuler (D)*

POLITICAL AND LEGISLATIVE BACKGROUND
House District 12 consists of all of Alleghany, Bath, and Craig Counties; all of the Cities of Clifton Forge and Covington; part of Giles County comprised of the Newport Precinct; and part of Montgomery County comprised of the A-1, A-2, A-3, B-1, F-1, F-2, G-1, and G-2 Precincts.

James M. "Jim" Shuler, a Blacksburg veterinarian and a Democrat, survived redistricting in 2001, moved to a new district and lost the November 2001 election, then moved back to his old district and won his former seat in January 2002. With redistricting, Shuler and Creigh Deeds were placed in the same district. Shuler, who had property in more than one district, moved and lost to a Republican challenger. Deeds won the 12th seat. But with the death of Senator Emily Couric (D-25) from pancreatic cancer, a December election was held for the Senate seat, which Deeds won. Shuler moved back, then ran for and won the 12th House District seat in a January 8, 2002 special election, winning with 70.8% of the vote over Republican candidate Larry J. Linkous in a special election decided by 26.4% of the registered voters. Shuler has represented the area since 1993 and the retirement of Democrat Joan H. Munford.

During the 2004 session, Shuler sponsored eleven bills. One bill passed, five failed, two were carried over, and two were incorporated. The bills that passed allow medical assistance services to include marriage and family therapists.

Carried over bills increased guidelines for tuitions; and prisoner's participation in residential community programs prior to release.

Failed bills would have regulated dance halls; prohibited hunting with duck blinds in certain localities; give health insurance credits to retired teachers; increased retail and use tax for education; and increased the personal property tax on qualifying vehicles.

Delegate HD 121

James M. "Jim" Shuler (D) Member House: 1994- ; b. Dec. 31, 1943, Rockingham County, VA; home, 3000 Wakefield Dr., Blacksburg 24060; educ. VPI & SU (B.S.), Univ. GA (D.V.M.); married, Margaret Sue Flippin; Baptist.

Veterinarian; Blacksburg Town Council; Natl. Bank Blacksburg, VA Veterinary Medical Assn.; Kiwanis (past pres.); State Board of Health (past member).

Offices 1480 South Main St., Blacksburg 24060; 540-953-1103; GA Bldg., Rm. 822, Capitol Sq., Richmond 23219; 804-698-1012.

2004 Committees *Agriculture, Chesapeake and Natural Resources; Militia, Police and Public Safety.*

House Key Votes, 2004
Please see Introduction for more information on bills.

1) Budget Bill	AGN	5) Family Life	FOR	9) Morning After	AGN
2) Feticide	AGN	6) Fire Arms	FOR	10) Legal Aid	FOR
3) Marriage	NV	7) Open Space	FOR		
4) Abortion	AGN	8) Home School	AGN		

Election Results

2004 general	James M. Shuler	(D)	7,284	99.9%	$69,764

Campaign Contributions 2004 Finance $8,600; Energy $5,700; Health Care $4,332; Realty $3,250; Transportation $2,350; Tech/Communication $2,300; Agriculture $2,050; Business/Retail Svc $2,025; Public Employees $1,650; Law $1,500; Organized Labor $1,300; Misc $700; Defense $500, Mfg $450; Political $300; Single-Issue Groups $200.

Economic Interests, 2004 Offices & Directorships: National Bankshares, Dir., National Bank, Blacksburg, Dir.; *Pers. Liabil.,* $50,000+ banks; *Sec.,* $50,000+ stocks NBB; $10,001-$50,000 ea.; mutual funds, stocks in AT&T, Fund. Investors, Lucent, Lib. Funds Trust, AOL, Cardinal Bankshares; *Pay. for Talks, Mtgs., & Publ.*to $50,000: Banks; *Gifts,* $ 210 Altria, gift; $228 Reynold, gift; $78 State Farm Ins. Dinner; $152 Altria, reception; $109 Altria, dinner; $158 Altria, dinner; $336 Altria, NASCAR NEXTEL race.

TENTH CONGRESSIONAL DISTRICT

SENATE DISTRICT TWENTY-SEVEN, *Harry Russell "Russ" Potts, Jr. (R)*

POLITICAL AND LEGISLATIVE BACKGROUND

Senate District 27 consists of the counties of Clarke and Frederick; the City of Winchester; the Fauquier County Precincts of Kettle Run, Casanova, Warrenton, Baldwin Ridge, Remington, Opal, Marshall, Leeds, Waterloo, Upperville, The Plains, New Baltimore, and Broad Run; and the Loudoun County Precincts of Middleburg, St. Louis, Purcellville, Round Hill, Hillsboro, Hamilton, Philomont, Lovettsville, Waterford, Lucketts, Between the Hills, Greenway, Dry Mill, and part of Aldie.

H. Russell "Russ" Potts, Jr., a businessman and a Republican, was elected over three opponents in 1991 following the retirement of Sen. William Truban (R), who had served since 1971. In 1995, Potts won by 65.2% over Democrat Thomas Lewis. Potts ran unopposed in 1999.

During the 2004 session, Potts sponsored twenty-nine bills and resolutions. Ten of his eleven resolutions passed. Eight bills passed, three were incorporated into other bills, two were carried over and five bills failed.

Several of the bills that passed were health related. One bill changed the requirements for Athletic Trainers from certification to licensure and required the Board of Medicine to issue regulations; another bill required that information on pharmaceutical benefits under Medicare be provided and that senior citizen volunteers be trained to help provide this information. Another bill defined the doctor-patient relationship for persons treated in emergency rooms as ending upon the discharge of the patient. A bill established a regulatory system for dental plan organizations.

A bill on political sign regulation passed; a bill to rename the Rt. 340 bridge in Clark County also passed. Bills that were incorporated included limitations on medical malpractice recovery, the definition of a disabled employee under the Line of Duty Act; and a tax increase on cigarettes to be used for specific purposes.

Bills that failed included a proposal to require political parties to nominate statewide candidates for Governor, Lt. Governor and Attorney General by primary election; a bill on employer responsibility for parental leave for school involvement; a bill to amend the membership of the Charitable Gaming Board; and a bill on salaries for state police officer.

Most of the resolutions that passed commended individuals, local sports teams or expressing sorrow at the passing of local citizens. A resolution asking for a study of companion animals by the state veterinarian failed.

Senator SD 27

H. Russell "Russ" Potts, Jr. (R) Member Senate: 1992-; b. March 4, 1939, Richmond; address, 210 Handley Blvd., Winchester 22601; educ. Univ. MD (BS, Journalism), married, Emily Strite Potts; Methodist.

Pres., Sports Productions, Inc.; Shenandoah Apple Blossom Festival Bd.; member, Handley High Sch. Bd. Trustees, Grafton Sch. Bd.; Henry and William Evans Children's home; Winchester Reg. Health System Bd., Boy Scouts of America Bd.; USAR; Who's Who in Am.

Offices 14 N. Braddock St., Winchester 22601-4120; 540-665-2092; GA Bldg., Rm. 330, Capitol Sq., Richmond 23219; 804-698-7527.

TENTH CONGRESSIONAL DISTRICT

2004 Committees *Education and Health, Chair; Commerce and Labor; Finance; Privileges and Elections; Rules.*

Senate Key Votes, 2004
Please see Introduction for more information on bills.

1) Budget Bill	FOR	5) Family Life	FOR	9) Charter Schools	FOR
2) Feticide	FOR	6) Fire Arms	FOR	10) Legal Aid	FOR
3) Marriage	FOR	7) Open Space	FOR		
4) Child Abuse	FOR	8) Home School	FOR		

Election Results
1999 general   H. R. "Russ" Potts, Jr.   (R)   26,276   99.2% $279,121

Campaign Contributions 2000-June 30, 2002 **Medical** $8,200; **Realty/Constr.** $8,175; **Individ.** $5,100; **Insur./HMOs** $4,000; **Finance** $3,450; **Environ.** $3,100 (Piedmont Defense $3,000); **Farms/Horse Farms** $3,000; **Tech./Comm.** $2,755; **Attys.** $2,655; **Chem./Plastics** $2,350; **Pub. Empl.** $2,250; **Electric** $2,200; **Beer/Wine** $2,100; **Transp.** $1,700 (Auto Dealers $1,100); **Exec. Recruit.** $1,000; **Coal** $1,000; **Retaur.** $800; **AFL CIO** $500; **Food Proc.** $500; **Sec./Detective** $500; **Retail/Consult.** $500; **Tobacco--PM** $500; **Republicans** $450; **Nat. Gas** $300; **Shipbldg.** $250.

Economic Interests 2004 *Sal. & Wages*, $10,000+ ea.: Russ Potts Productions, NTELOS; *Off. & Dir.*, Russ Potts Prod., Pres.; *Pers. Liabil.*, $50,000+ banks; *Sec.*, $10,001-$50,000 ea.: stock in: AT&T, Western Union, NTELOS; Paymts for talks, mtgs,and publications: $1,268 VA Medical PAC, reception; Pymts for representation and other: Telephone utilities, marketing;*Gifts*, $157 Capital Strategies, dinner; $76 State Farm Companies, dinner; $52 Vectre Corp., dinner; $102VA Sheriffs Assoc, dinnr; $192 VA Sheriffs Assoc, dinner; $91 VA Sheriffs Assoc, dinner; *Bus. Int.*, $50,000/less Russ Potts Prod. (sports event marketing).

SENATE DISTRICT TWENTY-NINE, *Charles J. Colgan III (D)*

POLITICAL AND LEGISLATIVE BACKGROUND
Senate District 29 consists of the cities of Manassas and Manassas Park, the Prince William County Precincts of Brentsville, Armory, Nokesville, Parkside, Jackson, Linton Hall, Woodbine, Park, Saunders, Enterprise, Coles, King, Dumfries, Graham Park, Pattie, Washington-Reid, Montclair, Evergreen, Haymarket, Loch Lomond, Sinclair, Stonewall, Sudley, Westgate, Catharpin, Bull Run, Plantation, Mullen, and Kerrydale, and part of Quantico.

Charles Colgan, the founder of Colgan Airways and a Democrat, was first elected in 1975 over Byrd Democrat A. Selwyn Smith. In the 1975 election, Colgan ran a consumer-oriented campaign, supporting fair utility rates, posting of drug prices, and mass transit. After winning that primary he won the general election against Republican Lawrence Randall. Colgan had considered running for Congress from the old Eighth District against J. Kenneth Robinson (R) but decided against it. He had been unopposed in the last several elections, until 1995, when he defeated Republican James S. Long with a comfortable 58.1% of the vote. In 1999, Colgan defeated R. S. Fitzsimmonds III with 58.2% of the vote. Colgan served as a Senate negotiator in budget-reconciliation talks with delegates. With the shift to Republican power, Colgan lost the co-chairmanship of the Commerce and Labor Committee. Colgan was one of three Democrats appointed to the eight member Joint Reapportionment Committee to oversee redistricting, noting, "It's going to be one of the most political things we've done."

During the 2004 session, Colgan sponsored twenty bills and one resolution. Twelve bills passed, four were carried over, two were incorporated into another bill and two failed. A resolution commending the 71st Infantry Division Association passed.

Several of the Senator's bills related to taxes and tax information. Of the bills that passed, one bill provided for the release of information to help collect unpaid taxes and another allowed release of information to help find holders of unclaimed property. A bill relating to real estate taxes and exemptions for elderly or disabled persons in Northern Virginia passed. Exemptions and revisions to the sales tax for churches and youth sports related nonprofit organizations.

Other passed bills include: issuance of disabled parking license plates to parents and guardians of persons with disabilities; rules relating to the confinement of persons who committed crimes while juveniles; a provision requiring notice to schools of prohibited gang participation by intake officer; and a bill permitting the increase in salary for Manassas City School Board. Two bills relating to special license plates and the motor fuel tax were incorporated into other bills.

Senator SD 29

Charles Joseph Colgan (D) Member Senate: 1976-; b. Sept. 25, 1926, Frostburg, MD; home, 14206 Vint Hill Rd., Nokesville 20181; educ. Aviation, technical, accounting, and management courses; widower; Roman Catholic Church.

Founder, Colgan Airways Corporation (1965), Natl. Capital Airways (1991); served U.S. Army & Air Force; Prince William County Bd. Sup.; Washington Metro. Council of Governments; Lions; Knights of Columbus; VA Aviation Trades Assn. Hall of Fame 1980.

Offices 10677 Aviation Lane, Manassas 20110-2701; 703-368-0300; GA Bldg., Capitol Sq., Rm. 432, Richmond 23219; 804-698-7529.

2004 Committees *Commerce and Labor; Finance; General Laws; Privileges and Elections; Rules.*

Senate Key Votes, 2004
Please see Introduction for more information on bills.

1) Budget Bill	FOR	5) Family Life	FOR	9) Charter Schools	FOR
2) Feticide	FOR	6) Fire Arms	FOR	10) Legal Aid	FOR
3) Marriage	FOR	7) Open Space	FOR		
4) Child Abuse	FOR	8) Home School	AGN		

Election Results

1999 general	Charles J. Colgan	(D)	16,865	58.2%	$196,024
	R. S. Fitzsimmonds III	(R)	12,087	41.7%	$ 70,040

Campaign Contributions 2000-June 30, 2002 **Colgan/Parrish Golf Tourn. PAC** $15,709; **Tech./Comm.** $2,750; **Medical** $2,175; **Pub. Empl.** $1,850; **Hotel/Tour** $1,500; **Realty/Constr.** $850; **Attys.** $750; **Nat. Gas** $600; **Oil** $550; **Finance** $550; **Tobacco--PM** $500; **Transp.** $400; **Coal** $250; **VA Automat. Merch.** $250.

TENTH CONGRESSIONAL DISTRICT

Economic Interests 2004 *Sal. & Wages*, $10,000+ ea.: Colgan Air, Inc.; *Off. & Dir.*, Colgan Air, Chairman Bd. Dir.; *Sec.*, $50,000+ stock Colgan Air; *Gifts*, $283 VA Manuf. Assn. (lodging Homestead), $77 Philip Morris (gift box); *Bus. Int.*, $50,000+/less Capital Aviation & Instrument Corp. (aircraft radio & instr. repair & installation); *Pay. for Rep. & Other Services Generally*, $50,001-$100,000 airline service - interstate transp.; Real Estate: condominium for personal use, condo for rental..

SENATE DISTRICT THIRTY-THREE, *William C. "Bill" Mims (R)*

POLITICAL AND LEGISLATIVE BACKGROUND

Senate District 33 consists of the Fairfax County Precincts of Fox Mill, Floris 203/Frying Pan 235, Franklin, Kinross, Navy, and Lees Corner; and the Loudoun County Precincts of Sanders Corner, Ashburn Farm, Guilford, Forest Ridge, Simpson, Arcola, Balls Bluff, West Leesburg, East Leesburg, Oakcrest, Sugarland North, Sugarland South, Seneca, Lowes Island, Sully, Park View, Rolling Ridge, Farmwell Station, Algonkian, Ashburn Village, Potomac, Cascades, and part of Aldie.

Attorney and Republican William C. "Bill" Mims was elected Senator in a 1998 special election. Beginning that session as a Delegate, Mims ended it as a Senator, winning with 61.8% of the vote over two challengers. Mims had served as a Delegate in House District 32 since 1991. In 1997, Governor-elect Gilmore appointed Senator Charles Waddell (D-33), who had served since 1971, as Deputy Secretary of Transportation. In 1999, Mims easily defeated an Independent challenger.

During the 2004 session, Mims sponsored forty-one bills and resolutions. Sixteen bills passed, four failed, seven were carried-over and four were incorporated into other bills. Nine resolutions passed and one failed.

Several of Senator Mim's bills related to law enforcement and crime. Of the bills that passed one established a presumption against bail for gang related activity; another relates to the procedure for detention and arrest of illegal aliens; another established penalties and restitution requirements for persons damaging cemeteries; an increase in fines for jurors failure to appear; and a bill increasing penalties for persons repeatedly violating the HOV (carpool) lane restrictions on highways in Northern Virginia. Four bills relating to driving under the influence of alcohol or drugs were incorporated into other bills. A bill on deferred disposition in criminal trials failed as did a bill on confidential communications in cases of domestic violence or sexual assault.

Other bills that passed included rules relating to the practice of Podiatry; the use of retroactive child support payments; definitions of a passenger carrying microbus; wetlands mitigation on islands in the Potomac River, changes in the time for filing suit on foreclosure of liens under the Condominium and Property Owners Association act, and two bills relating to deeds of trust.

Bills relating to electronic tax returns, detention of mentally incapacitated persons, educational Standards of Quality, and changes in the Child Custody and Enforcement Act were carried over.

Two tax related bills failed. One bill on the transient occupancy tax in Fairfax County and a bill to cap the personal property tax rate on motor homes.

Several resolutions commending individuals and organizations passed as did a resolution relating to services to offenders with mental illness or substance abuse. A resolution to study the future of higher education in Virginia failed.

Senator SD 33

William C. Mims (R); Member House: 1992- ; b. June 20, 1957, Harrisonburg; home, 11 Crisswell Ct., Sterling 20165; educ. College of William & Mary (BA), Georgetown Univ. Law Center (JD, LLM); Episcopalian; married Jane Rehme.

Lawyer; Trial Attorney, Hazel & Thomas; Dir., Marshall Home Preservation Fund, Christian Legal Soc., VA Inst. for Pol. Leadership (adv. bd.); Kiwanis; VA Campus GWU (adv. bd.); Dulles Area Tran. Assn. (Dir.); Youth for Tomorrow (Trustee); Tech Ten Award (Nor. VA Tech. Council) 2000.

Offices P.O. Box 741, Leesburg 20178-0741; 703-779-1888; FAX 703-777-4001; GA Bldg., Rm. 320, Capitol Sq., Richmond 23219; 804-698-7533.

2004 Committees *Courts of Justice; Education and Health; Local Government; Transportation.*

Senate Key Votes, 2004

Please see Introduction for more information on bills.

1) Budget Bill	FOR	5) Family Life	FOR	9) Charter Schools	FOR
2) Feticide	FOR	6) Fire Arms	FOR	10) Legal Aid	FOR
3) Marriage	FOR	7) Open Space	FOR		
4) Child Abuse	FOR	8) Home School	FOR		

Election Results

1999 general	William C. "Bill" Mims	(R)	30,472	77.2%	$75,332
	G. C. Myers	(I)	8,869	22.5%	$ 4,333

Campaign Contributions 2000-June 30, 2002 **Realty/Constr.** $18,950; **Attys.** $13,250; **Tech./Comm.** $7,475; **Medical** $6,800; **Finance** $6,000; **Beer/Wine/Dist. Spirits** $4,750; **Insur./HMOs** $3,800; **Republicans** $3,050; **Transp.** $2,950 (Air Transp. $1,000); **Individ.** $2,750; **Electric** $2,700; **Pub. Empl.** $1,750; **Forestry/Lumber** $1,000; **Soft Drink** $750; **Retail/Grocery** $750; **Greater Wash. Bd. Trade** $500; **Furniture** $500; **Food Proc.** $500; **Trash** $500; **Serv. Stat./Conv. St.** $500; **Quarries** $500; **Coal** $500; **Nat. Gas** $250.

Economic Interests 2004 *Sal. & Wages,* $10,000+ ea.: Mims & Atwill & Leigh, P.C. law; Faith Christian School (spouse); *Off. & Dir.,* John Carr House L.L.C, Member; Mims & Atwill & Leighm P.C., Dir./V-P; *Pers. Liabil.,* $10,001-$50,000 loan or finance co.; *Sec.,* $50,000+ John Carr House

TENTH CONGRESSIONAL DISTRICT

(ltd. liability co.); $10,001-$50,000 ea.: mutual funds, stock; VA college savings plan, stocks in law firm; *Pay. for Talks, Mtgs., & Pub.*, $1,677 VA Trial Lawyers Assoc, presentation at annual mtg, expenses; $1,038 Commonwealth of VA, Identity Theft presentation at annual mtg, expenses; $700 Council of State Govt's, Identity Theft presentation at annual mtg, expenses; *Gifts*, $62 Metro Airports Authority, dinner; $60 Fairfax Chamber of Commerce, gift basket; $75 Lexis-Nexis Publications, dinner; $100 Loudoun Healthcare, dinner; $74 Dominion, concert, $75 Access Point Public Affairs, dinner; $100 Wolf Trap Foundation, dinner, concert; $60 VA Tech, football game; *Pay. for Rep. & Other Services Generally*, $100,001-$250,000 incl. all three attys. billing all other clients; $10,001-$50,000 ea.: electronics, concrete, retail co.; $1,001-$10,000 banks; *Real Estate*, Two prop. (commercial w/others).

SENATE DISTRICT THIRTY-SEVEN, *Kenneth Cuccinelli (R)*

POLITICAL AND LEGISLATIVE BACKGROUND
Senate District 37 contains the Fairfax County Precincts of Fairview, Sideburn, Bonnie Brae, Burke, Pohick, Valley, Orange, Cherry Run, Terra Centre, White Oaks, Burke Centre, Sangster, Popes Head, Parkway, Centre Ridge, Chantilly, Dulles, Greenbriar East, Greenbriar West, Leehigh, London Towne, Rocky Run, Virginia Run, Centreville, Green Trails, Deer Park, Willow Springs, and Cub Run 903/Stone 917.

Kenneth Cuccinelli, a Republican, was elected to fill the seat left open by the resignation of Senator Warren E. Barry. Cuccinelli won the special August 2002 election with 55.0% of the vote over Democrat C. Belter in an election decided by 16.4% of the voters of that area.

Cuccinelli was a leader in the successful fight in Northern Virginia against the referendum for that area that proposed an increase in sales tax to fund transportation improvements. This proposal was defeated at the ballot box in November 2002.

During the 2004 session, Cuccinelli sponsored twenty-five bills and five resolutions. Six bills passed, four were carried over, one was incorporated into another bill, and fourteen failed. Three resolutions passed and two failed.

Of the bills that passed two were transportation related. One bill required the consideration of HOV toll lanes as part of any study to improve traffic conditions on Interstate 66 in Northern Virginia and a second bill provided that a court order is required for release of any personal information on data collected by automated toll collection systems. A bill modified teacher disciplinary procedures involving hearings and recommendations for dismissal and revocation of license passed. Disclosure rules for members of local governments or board involved in land use proceedings in Fairfax were amended to report gifts in excess of $100 annually. A bill regulating voting procedures at polling places was incorporated into another bill.

Bills that failed relating to taxes, budget and finance included: a bill relating to local excise, transient, tobacco and real estate tax rates; a bill to limit growth in actual real estate taxes paid; amendments to the Budget Reform Act of 2004; and a proposal to create an Office of State Inspector General.

Other failed bills included: a proposal to regulate abortions performed after the first trimester; provisions relating to permits to sell firearms; to prohibit geographic discrimination in admissions policies at state colleges and universities; and to permit the representation by Virginia law students of persons at involuntary commitment hearings.

A resolution urging Congress to propose a constitutional amendment protecting marriage passed and a proposed Virginia constitutional amendment limiting appropriations failed. Two resolutions commending local organizations passed.

Senator SD 37

Kenneth T. Cuccinelli II (R) Member Senate: 2002-; b. July 30, 1968 Edison, NJ; home, 6801 Mt. Olive Ct., Centreville 20121; educ. UVA (B.S.M.E.), George Mason Univ. (M.A., J.D.); married Alice Monteiro Cuccinelli; Roman Catholic.

Patent attorney; Member: Virginia State Bar; Fairfax Bar Association.

Offices P.O. Box 684, Centreville 20122; 703-766-0635; GA Bldg., Capitol Sq., Rm. 313, Richmond 23219; 804-698-7537.

2004 Committees *Agriculture, Conservation and Natural Resources; Courts of Justice; Local Government; Rehabilitation and Social Services.*

Senate Key Votes, 2004
Please see Introduction for more information on bills.

1) Budget Bill	AGN	5) Family Life	FOR	9)Charter Schools	FOR
2) Feticide	FOR	6) Fire Arms	FOR	10) Legal Aid	AGN
3) Marriage	FOR	7) Open Space	AGN		
4) Child Abuse	AGN	8) Home School	FOR		

Election Results

2002 special	Ken Cuccinelli	(R)	10,041	55.01%	$119,885
	Cathy A. Belter	(D)	8,193	44.89%	$ 83,868

Campaign Contributions 2002 Republicans $69,739; **Tech./Comm.** $28,887; **Conserv./Anti-Choice** $10,250 (VA Conserv. Action $6,500, Am.'s Fndn. $1,000); **Individuals** $7,520; **Attys.** $5,834; **Realty/Constr.** $4,850; **Pub. Empl.** $4,129; **Finance** $2,700; **Transp.** $2,500; **Medical** $2,450; **Beer/Wine** $2,400; **Consult.** $2,100; **Insurance** $1,400; **Club for Growth PAC** $1,000; **Trash** $1,000; **Lumber** $1,000; **Nat. Gas** $600; **Veterin./Landscape** $450; **Misc. Defense** $400; **Advert.** $300; **Natl. Fed. Independ. Business** $250; **Grocery St.** $250; **Oil** $100.

Economic Interests 2004 *Sal. & Wages,* $10,000+ Quest Fore, Inc.; Business Interest $50,000 +: Gura & Day, LLC, law; Paymts for representation and other services generally $10,000 to $50,000: HVAC business, Radio Syndacation, political consulting, services rendered –law; $1,000 to $10,000: towing, mechanical mfg, and catering, services rendered – law; Paymts for representation by you for $1,000 to $10,000: VEC unemployment claim JRM Enterprises, Real Estate: residential; Gifts: $4,544 Friedrich Naumann Foundation, trip – transatlantic exchange to Germany; $73 VA Dominion Power, dinner, $105 McGuire Woods Consulting, dinner.

HOUSE DISTRICT THIRTEEN, *Robert G. "Bob" Marshall (R)*

TENTH CONGRESSIONAL DISTRICT

POLITICAL AND LEGISLATIVE BACKGROUND

The 13th House District consists of part of Loudoun County comprised of the Middleburg and Aldie Precincts and parts of the Arcola, Cascades, and Forest Ridge Precincts; and part of Prince William County comprised of the Brentsville, Armory, Buckhall, Nokesville, Jackson, Linton Hall, Woodbine, Evergreen, Haymarket, Catharpin, Bull Run, and Mullen Precincts and part of the Sinclair Precinct.

Robert G. Marshall, a Republican, has served in this area since his election in 1991. In that year, redistricting created a new seat by moving the 13th House District from southwest Virginia to Fairfax County. Marshall defeated Democratic opposition then and again in 1993, won over Independents in 1995 and 1997, and in 1999, defeated Democrat Denise M. Oppenhagen. In the 2001 election, Marshall won with 62.7% of the vote over attorney and Democrat Lou R. Brooks, Jr.

During the 2004 session, Marshall sponsored thirty-four bills and resolutions. Two bills passed, eleven bills were carried-over and ten bills failed. Five joint resolutions failed and two were carried over. Three resolutions asking the Governor and state agencies to provide budget information passed.

A bill stating that marriage or civil unions between same sex people or performed in other states is not valid or recognized in Virginia passed. A bill to permit cooperative procurement activities between Virginia and the federal government passed.

A bill to permit designation of university student fees was carried over. Three bills relating to development and the cost of public services such as law enforcement, sewage systems, and impact fees were carried over.

Two bills to regulate abortion procedures failed as did a proposal to prohibit state university health clinics from dispensing the so-called morning after pill. Standards to prevent conflicts of interest for guardians involved with end of life decisions failed. Two measures relating to the election of mayors in cities failed.

Three resolutions relating to stem cell research and reproductive technology failed. One resolution on the operations and escalating costs of the health care system was carried over and one failed. A resolution for a constitutional amendment on the Highway trust fund was carried over.

Delegate HD 13

Robert Gerard Marshall (R); Member House: 1992- ; b. May 3, 1944, Takoma Park, MD; home, 7930 Willow Pond Ct., Manassas 20111-8013; educ. Belmont Abby College (BA), CA State Univ. (MA); married, Catherine Ann Fonseca; Catholic.

Shenandoah Electronic Intelligence; Dir. of Congressional Inf., American Life League; member, Committee of 100, Cub Scouts, and Little League; Prince William & Greater Manassas Chamber of Commerce; Republican Committee.

Offices P.O. Box 421, Manassas 20108-0421; 703-361-5416; GA Bldg., Capitol Sq., Rm. 522, Richmond 23219; 804-698-1013.

2004 Committees *Counties, Cities and Towns; Privileges and Elections; Science and Technology.*

House Key Votes, 2004
Please see Introduction for more information on bills.

1) Budget Bill	AGN	5) Family Life	AGN	9) Morning After	FOR
2) Feticide	FOR	6) Fire Arms	FOR	10) Legal Aid	FOR
3) Marriage	FOR	7) Open Space	FOR		
4) Abortion	FOR	8) Home School	FOR		

Election Results

2004 general	Robert G. "Bob" Marshall (R)	11,551	99.0%	$35,910

Campaign Contributions 2004 Tech./Comm. $6,533; Single-Issue Groups $2,250; Misc $1,500; Realty $1,500; Finance $1,200; Energy $1,200; Law $750; Public Employees $650; Agriculture $500; Transportation $450; Undetermined $400; Mfg $250; Political $250; Business/Retail Svs $250.

Economic Interests, 2004 *Sal. & Wages*, $10,000+ ea.: Shenandoah Electronic Intelligence (self), Grimberg Construction (spouse); *Gifts*, $78 UVA, football tkts; $421 Dominion Power, Redskin tkts, transportation; $73 T Farms, Christmas tree plants; $180 Ken Mims, adjust.

HOUSE DISTRICT FIFTEEN, *Allen L. Louderback (R)*

POLITICAL AND LEGISLATIVE BACKGROUND
House District 15 consists of all of Page, Rappahannock, and Shenandoah Counties; and part of Rockingham County comprised of the Swift Run Precinct.

Allen L. Louderback, a real estate investor and a Republican, was first elected in 1999. The seat was opened with the retirement of Republican Raymond "Andy" Guest, who had served since 1971. Guest, a farmer, was known for his efforts to legalize and regulate horse-race gambling in Virginia. The party meeting selected Louderback out of four candidates. In the 2001 election, Louderback defeated opposition from Independent candidate Bradley G. Pollack with 63% of the vote.

During the 2004 election, Louderback sponsored nine bills and three resolutions. Two bills and all three resolutions passed. Four bills failed and three were carried over.

A bill to create the Luray-Page County airport authority passed as did a measure to permit a referendum on the election of the Chairman of the Page County Board of Supervisors.

Carried over proposals included one to permit the establishment of retail ABC franchises and to prohibit the opening of new government ABC stores. A bill making numerous changes to state income, sales & use, and estate taxes was carried over.

A bill to require driver's licenses to contain licensee's residential address failed as did a proposed fee on cigarette manufacturers not participating in the Master Settlement agreement.

Two resolutions commending Page County High School teams passed as did a resolution urging Congress to enact the proposed State Waste Empowerment and Enforcement Act.

TENTH CONGRESSIONAL DISTRICT

Delegate HD 15

Allen Lee Louderback (R) Member House: 2000-; b. March 12, 1948, Luray; home, 1131 Old Farms Rd., Luray 22835; educ. VPI (B.S./Bus. Admin.); married Nadia Laura Farrag; United Church of Christ.

Self-employed businessman; Second District of Page Co. (Sup., 2 terms); Luray Rotary (Pres.); Page Co. Republican Party (Past Chair.); Luray Little League (Past Dir. and Assist. Coach).

Offices 1131 Old Farms Road, Luray 22835, 540-743-7644; GA Bldg., Capitol Sq., Rm. 408, Richmond 23219; 804-698-1015.

2004 Committees *Agriculture, Chesapeake and Natural Resources; Courts of Justice; Finance.*

House Key Votes, 2004
Please see Introduction for more information on bills.

1) Budget Bill	FOR	5) Family Life	AGN	9) Morning After	FOR
2) Feticide	FOR	6) Fire Arms	FOR	10) Legal Aid	AGN
3) Marriage	FOR	7) Open Space	FOR		
4) Abortion	FOR	8) Home School	FOR		

Election Results

2004 general	Allen Louderback	(R)	12,429	63.1%	$79,057
	Thomas Lewis	(D)	7,242	36.8%	$4,980

Campaign Contributions 2004 Business/Retail Svs $5,035; Agriculture $2,900; Tech/Communication $2,090; Transportation $2,000; Energy $1,760; Realty $1,720; Law $1,000; Finance $890; Misc $630; Public Employees $500; Mfg $250; Political $250; Health Care $250; Undetermined $130.

Economic Interests, 2004 *Sal. & Wages,* $10,000+ Valley View Mobile Home Court (partnership); Business Interests more than $50,000: Center Plaza Coin Laundry, Valley View Mobile Home Courts; $50,000 or less: three trailer courts in Luray as rental property; *Gifts:* $93 Reynolds, golf bag.

HOUSE DISTRICT TWENTY-SIX, *Glenn M. Weatherholtz (R)*

POLITICAL AND LEGISLATIVE BACKGROUND

House District 26 consists of all of the City of Harrisonburg; and part of Rockingham County comprised of the Broadway, Timberville, Fulks Run, Bergton, Lacey Spring, Singers Glen, Edom, Melrose, Keezletown, Tenth Legion, Dayton, Turner Ashby (Silver Lake), and Mt. Clinton Precincts.

Glenn M. Weatherholtz, a Republican, was elected in 1995. The seat was opened with the retirement of Clinton Miller (R) who had served since 1972. Weatherholtz defeated Democratic challengers that year and again in 1997. In 1999 and 2001, Weatherholtz ran unopposed. Weatherholtz had previously been elected as Rockingham County Sheriff in 1971, after serving with the Virginia State Police for over 10 years.

During the 2004 session, Weatherholtz sponsored thirteen bills and two resolutions. Six bills passed, five were carried-over and two failed. Both his resolutions passed.

Weatherholtz, a retired sheriff, sponsored several law enforcement related measures. Of the adopted measures: one bill changed the requirements for certification as a crime prevention specialist; one provided for a waiver of the law enforcement certification exam based on previous experience; a third allows private colleges and universities to enter into reciprocal mutual aid agreements with outside localities. Two proposals relating to use of fees by Criminal Justice Services Department and the Law Officers Retirement System failed. A proposal on election of benefits in the Law Officers Retirement System was carried over.

A measure amending the Harrisonburg city charter passed as did a measure requiring moped operators to have identification. A bill to limit damages in suits from public transportation operators was carried over. A bill on foreclosure of real property sold at auction was also carried over.

Delegate HD 26

Glenn M. Weatherholtz (R) Member House: 1996-; b. July 5, 1936, Shenandoah County; home, 104 Belmont Dr., Harrisonburg 22801; educ. Triplett H.S., Massanutten Military Academy, Adv. Police and Col. courses; married, Blanche V. Gordon; United Church of Christ.

Sheriff; Member: Virginia Sheriffs' Assn., FBI Natl. and VA Academies, Harrisonburg Kiwanis Club, Elkton Masonic Lodge, Crime Solvers (Bd. of Dir.), Hazardous Materials Comm., Elks Lodge; Awards: Commonwealth Award, James Madison Univ. (1995); Outstanding Law Enforcement Officer of the Year, Harrisonburg Moose Lodge; Outstanding Lawman of the Year, Harrisonburg Kiwanis Club; Law Enforcement Commendation Medal, Sons of the Am. Rev.; U.S. Army (1955-57).

Offices 737 A East Main St., Harrisonburg 22801; 540-574-3225; GA Bldg., Rm. 716, Capitol Sq., Richmond 23219; 804-698-1026.

2004 Committees *Agriculture, Chesapeake and Natural Resources; Counties, Cities and Towns; Courts of Justice; Militia, Police and Public Safety.*

House Key Votes, 2004
Please see Introduction for more information on bills.

1) Budget Bill	FOR	5) Family Life	AGN	9) Morning After	FOR
2) Feticide	FOR	6) Fire Arms	FOR	10) Legal Aid	FOR
3) Marriage	FOR	7) Open Space	FOR		
4) Abortion	FOR	8) Home School	FOR		

Election Results

2004 general	Glenn M. Weatherholtz	(R)	11,479	54.5%	$93,275
	Lowell Fulk	(D)		45.4%	$91,192

Campaign Contributions 2004 Energy $1,000; Agriculture $750; Law $500; Business/Retail Svs $475; Realty $250.

Economic Interests, 2004 *Sec.*, $50,000+ ea.: Mutual funds (6); $10,001-$50,000 ea.: mutual funds (3), stock in Coca Cola, Cracker Barrel, Merck, CVS, Vectren, BP Amoco; *Gifts,* $152 Altria, Kraft

Days Reception; $147 Altria, legislative dinner; $259 VA Cable, dinner; $282 Geico, dinner;$108 VA Sheriffs Assoc., dinner; $160 Omega Proteins, dinner.

HOUSE DISTRICT TWENTY-NINE, *Beverly J. Sherwood (R)*

POLITICAL AND LEGISLATIVE BACKGROUND
House District 29 consists of all of the City of Winchester; and the Frederick County Precincts of Russells, Gore, Kernstown, Gainesboro, Albin, Clearbrook, Neffstown, Carpers Valley, and Shenandoah.

Beverly J. Sherwood, was first elected in 1993. A Republican, Sherwood won handily in a district that had been represented from 1974 until his retirement by Democrat Al Smith. Sherwood defeated Democratic opponents in that year and in 1995. She was unopposed in the 1997 and 1999 elections. In 2001, Sherwood defeated Independent challenger Paul D. Blaker with 77.6% of the vote.

Sherwood owns and runs the Sherwood Christmas Tree Farm, and works as an office manager for medical consultants in Winchester. In 2002 , with the restructuring of House committees, Sherwood became the chair of the Militia, Police and Public Safety Committee.

During the 2004 session, Sherwood sponsored nine bills and one resolution. Seven bills passed and one failed. Her resolution passed.

The passed bills covered a number of different topics. Two transportation bills limited speeds on dirt roads in certain counties and another amended the rules for the use of a restricted license after a conviction for driving under the influence. The size of the Winchester school board was increased to four from three. The Freedom of Information Act was amended to exempt certain park and recreation records. The excise tax on apples was repealed.

A bill relating to SCHEV approval of certain degree programs at higher educational institutions failed.

Delegate HD 29

Beverly J. Sherwood (R) Member House: 1994- ; b. May 29, 1947, Ossining, NY; home, 180 Quaker Lane, Winchester 22603; educ. Ossining High School, graduate; married, Frank Vincent Sherwood; Baptist.

Owner/Manager Sherwood Christmas Tree Farm; First woman, Gainsboro Ruritan Club; member, Frederick County Bd. of Supervisors; VA Christmas Tree Growers Assn.

Offices P.O. Box 2014, Winchester 22604; 540-667-8947; GA Bldg, Rm. 512, Capitol Sq., Richmond 23219; 804-698-1029.

2004 Committees *Militia, Police and Public Safety, Chair; Agriculture, Chesapeake and Natural Resources; Appropriations.*

House Key Votes, 2004

TENTH CONGRESSIONAL DISTRICT

Please see Introduction for more information on bills.

1) Budget Bill	FOR	5) Family Life	FOR	9) Morning After	FOR
2) Feticide	FOR	6) Fire Arms	FOR	10) Legal Aid	FOR
3) Marriage	FOR	7) Open Space	FOR		
4) Abortion	FOR	8) Home School	FOR		

Election Results

2004 general	Beverly J. Sherwood	(R)	13,897	99.3%	$39,576

Campaign Contributions 2004 Tech/Commuications $1,750; Law $1,550; Energy $1,500; Finance $1,250; Realty $1,250; Agriculture $1,250; Transportation $1,000; Political $1,000; Mfg $900; Business/Retail Svs $750; Health Care $250.

Economic Interests, 2004 *Sal. & Wages*, $10,000+ Westvaco; *Gifts*, $73 VA Farm Bureau Federation, dinner; $152 Altria, Kraft Days Reception; $109 Altria, dinner; $52 Old Dominion Hwy Contractors, dinner; Real Estate: 10 acres recreational.

HOUSE DISTRICT THIRTY-ONE, *Lee Scott Lingamfelter (R)*

POLITICAL AND LEGISLATIVE BACKGROUND
House District 31 consists of part of Fauquier County comprised of the Kettle Run, Catlett, Casanova, and New Baltimore Precincts and part of the Baldwin Ridge Precinct; and part of Prince William County comprised of the Park, Saunders, Enterprise, Coles, King, Lodge, Dale, Neabsco, Godwin, Minnieville, and Bel Air Precincts and parts of the Quantico and Washington-Reid Precincts.

Scott Lingamfelter, a retired Army colonel and a Republican, is the new delegate for this district. Lingamfelter won this open seat, first defeating two other Republicans in the August 2001 Republican Primary, in an expensive primary with 53.5% of the vote over Dell P. Ennis and G.E. B. Waters, in an election decided by 6.4% of the registered voters. In the November general election, Lingamfelter won with 55.8% of the vote over Democrat Mickie D. Krause, with the two opponents neck in neck in Prince William County, while Lingamfelter overwhelmingly carried Fauquier County.

During the 2004 session, Lingamfelter sponsored twenty-nine bills and five resolutions. Eight bills passed, four were incorporated into other bills, four were carried over, and thirteen failed.

Bills passed included one to prohibit mobile infrared transmitters used to change traffic signals. A bill grants residency status to members of the armed forces stationed in Virginia for the purpose of purchasing a firearm. Another permits the protection of social security numbers of concealed handgun permit holders from public release. Regulation of pneumatic BB and paintball guns by local governments was allowed under certain conditions. A bill requires ready access to proffer cash payments and expenditures reports in local zoning records.

A bill to include property forfeiture used in connection with criminal gang behavior was incorporated into another bill as was a bill regarding confidentiality of state settlement agreements. A special license plate issued to members of the American Legion was also incorporated.

Two bills relating to health care treatment for minors – reporting, parental notification and record keeping failed. A proposal to test drug offenders for sexually transmitted and other reportable diseases failed. Political party identification for voter registration failed. A proposed Commonwealth Vehicle Board to advise the DMV and a change in the motorcycle helmet law also failed.

Four resolutions commending or memorializing individuals passed as did a resolution asking JLARC to study tax practices in other states.

Delegate HD 31

Lee Scott Lingamfelter (R) Member House: 2001- ; b. March 27, 1951, New York; home, 5420 Lomax Way, Woodbridge 22193; educ. VMI (B.A.), U VA (M.A.); married, Shelley Elizabeth Glick; Episcopalian.

Retired Army Colonel; U.S. Army 1973-2001; Member: Christ Our Lord Church; Lake Ridge Rotary Club; Assn. of the U.S. Army Vets. of Foreign Wars; American Legion; Soc. of the 1st Div.; Prince William Chamber Commerce; Awards: Defense Superior Service Medal 2001; Legion of Merit 1997, 1999; Bronze Star Medal 1992; Virginia Family Foundation Citizen of the Year, 2000.

Offices 5420 Lomas Way, Woodbridge 22193; 703 580 1294; GA Bldg., Rm. 417, Capitol Sq., Richmond 23219; 804-698-1031.

2004 Committees *Education; Finance; Militia, Police and Public Safety.*

House Key Votes, 2004
Please see Introduction for more information on bills.

1) Budget Bill	FOR	5) Family Life	FOR	9) Morning After	FOR
2) Feticide	FOR	6) Fire Arms	FOR	10) Legal Aid	FOR
3) Marriage	FOR	7) Open Space	FOR		
4) Abortion	FOR	8) Home School	FOR		

Election Results

2004 general	L. Scott Lingamfelter	(R)	8,572	55.0%	$230,604
	David Brickley	(D)	6,783	45.0%	$ 198,673

Campaign Contributions 2004 Realty $7,550; Business/Retail Svs $5,025; Energy $3,750; Finance $3,600; Law $3,250; Transportation $3,150; Political $2,559; Tech/Communication $2,300; Agriculture $2,010; Defense $2,000; Health Care $1,350; Public Employees $1,250; Misc $1,060; Mfg $750; Single-Issue Groups $500; Undetermined $50.

Economic Interests, 2004 Officers & Directorships: Commonwealth Consulting & Technology, LLC, President; *Sec.*, $50,000+ ea.: mutual funds (2); $10,001-$50,000 stocks Branch Cabell; Gifts: $130 Altria, dinner; $93 Reynolds, golf bag; *Real Estate*, vacation home.

HOUSE DISTRICT THIRTY-TWO, *Richard Hayden "Dick" Black (R)*

TENTH CONGRESSIONAL DISTRICT

POLITICAL AND LEGISLATIVE BACKGROUND

House District 32 consists of part of Loudoun County comprised of the Sanders Corner, Ashburn Farm, Sugarland North, Sugarland South, Seneca, Lowes Island, Farmwell Station, Algonkian, Ashburn Village, and Potomac Precincts and part of the Cascades Precinct.

Dick Black, a retired military Colonel, a trial attorney, and a Republican, is the delegate for House District 32, first elected in a special February, 1998 election. The seat was opened when then Delegate William C. Mims won a Senate seat. Black defeated Democratic opposition that year, in the 1999 election, and again in 2001, when he won with 57.7% of the vote over Patricia H. Morrissey.

During the 2004 session, Black sponsored fourteen bills and two resolutions. One resolution passed, four bills were incorporated into other measures, two bills were carried over, and eight bills failed.

A bill requiring public libraries to filter or otherwise protect juveniles Internet access was incorporated. Two bills relating to abortion and the murder of an unborn child were incorporated. The inclusion of chiropractors in health maintenance organizations was carried over as was a provision on the registration of military vehicles.

Allocation of state highway funds by vehicle miles traveled failed. A provision on standardized testing by public schools of home schooled children failed as did a measure on the apportionment of funds under the Standards of Quality for public schools. A bill to permit the distribution of health information to applicants for marriage licenses failed. A resolution urging Congress to preserve state sovereignty in matters relating to religious faith failed.

Delegate H.D. 32

Richard H. "Dick" Black (R) Member House: 1998- ; b. May 15, 1944 Baltimore; home, 20978 Flatboat Ct., Sterling 20165; educ. Univ. FL (BSBA; JD); married, Barbara Jean Hale Black; Roman Catholic.

Attorney; U.S. Marines 1963-1970 (Viet Nam); U.S. Army 1976-1994, pilot and flight instructor; Member: Fairfax and Loudoun Co. Rep. Comm.; Trustee Loudoun Co. Library Bd. 1997; Law Enforcement Alliance of Am., VA Soc. for Human Life, VA Right to Life; member Bar in VA, FL, and D.C.; Awards: Legion of Merit, Purple Heart, Presidential Unit Citation, several military awards.

Offices 20978 Flatboat Ct., Sterling, VA 20165; 703-406-2951; GA Bldg., Capitol Sq., Rm. 517, Richmond 23219; 804-698-1032.

2004 Committees *Courts of Justice; Education; Privileges and Elections; Transportation.*

House Key Votes, 2004
Please see Introduction for more information on bills.

1) Budget Bill	FOR	5) Family Life	AGN	9) Morning After	FOR
2) Feticide	FOR	6) Fire Arms	FOR	10) Legal Aid	AGN
3) Marriage	FOR	7) Open Space	AGN		
4) Abortion	FOR	8) Home School	FOR		

Election Results

210

2004 general	R. H. "Dick" Black	(R)	10,272	52.1%	$231,154
	David McWatters	(I)	7,524	11.3%	$16,175
	Patricia Morrissey	(D)		36.5%	$230,204

Campaign Contributions 2004 Realty/Constr. $80,250; Finance $19,250; Tech/Communications $10,605; Health Care $10,500; Business/Retail Svs $10,500; Misc $6,350; Undetermined $4,000; Agriculture $3,750; Energy $3,500; Transportation $3,500; Political $3,000; Law $2,075; Single-Issue Groups $1,140; Defense $1,000; Mfg $250; Public Employees $250.

Economic Interests, 2004 *Sec.*, $50,000+ stock insurance co.; $10,001-$50,000 ea.: mutual fund, stocks in Merck, Golden West Fin., Diamonds Trust, Berkshire Hathaway, Am. Intnl.; Business Interests $50,000 or less: Richard H. Black, Attorney at Law; Gifts: $118 Access Point Public Affairs, dinner; $147 Altria, dinner; $102 Old Dominion Hwy Contractors, dinner; $90 Kings Dominion, tkts;$62 Metro Airport Authority, dinner.

HOUSE DISTRICT THIRTY-THREE, *Joe T. May (R)*

POLITICAL AND LEGISLATIVE BACKGROUND

House District 33 consists of all of Clarke County; and part of Loudoun County comprised of the Simpson, St Louis, Purcellville, Round Hill, Hillsboro, Hamilton, Philomont, Lovettsville, Waterford, Lucketts, Between The Hills, Greenway, Balls Bluff, West Leesburg, East Leesburg, Dry Mill, and Oakcrest Precincts.

Joe May, a Republican, has served in the House since 1993. In that year, May won with 51.9% of the vote against two challengers. May succeeded Republican Linda Wallace (formerly Linda Rollins) who chose to retire after serving since 1988. May founded his own company which designs, manufactures, and distributes electronic products around the world. In 1995 and 1997, May defeated challengers, and ran unopposed in 1999 and 2001. May chairs the Science and Technology Committee.

During the 2004 session, May sponsored twenty-one bills and three resolutions. Thirteen bills passed, two were carried-over and six failed. Two resolutions passed and one was carried-over.

Several of Delegate May's bills related to technology, education and commerce. A bill passed limiting the information that may be displayed on credit card receipts. The study of integrated research and academic campuses will be continued by the Research and Technology Advisory Commission. The Secretary of Technology will monitor and report on trends in broadband communications technology. Changes were made in the Uniform Computer Information Transactions Act. A resolution to identify opportunities in nanotechnology research and economic development passed. Related bills that failed included a proposed "Virginia is for Technology" marketing campaign and a proposed entrepreneurial support network.

In other areas exemptions from the Freedom of Information Act for cell phone and pagers numbers of law enforcement personnel were adopted as was a measure to limit the use of unique identifying numbers on public records. Open space preservation fees for distribution to Outdoors Foundation passed.

Proposed public use impact fees were carried over as was a measure restricting use of social security numbers. A bill relating to seatbelt usage and the prohibition of a vehicle search for a seatbelt violation failed.

Delegate HD 33

Joe T. May (R) Member House: 1994- ; b. June 8, 1937, Broadway, VA; home, 40354 Foxfield Ln., Leesburg 20175; educ. VPI & SU (B.B.E.E.); married, Roberta Compton Downs; Church of Brethren.

Business Owner, Holds 13 patents; AOPA; George Mason Bank (adv. bd.); 4-H Educ. Cntr.; VA Tech Eng. Com. of 100; Loudoun Civil War Roundtable; Sons of Confederate Veterans; VA Employment Comm. Outstanding Employee 1990.

Offices P.O. Box 4104, Leesburg 20177; 703-777-1191; GA Bldg., Rm. 514, Capitol Sq., Richmond 23219; 804-698-1033.

2004 Committees *Science and Technology, Chair; Appropriations; Transportation.*

House Key Votes, 2004
Please see Introduction for more information on bills.

1) Budget Bill	FOR	5) Family Life	AGN	9) Morning After	FOR
2) Feticide	FOR	6) Fire Arms	FOR	10) Legal Aid	FOR
3) Marriage	FOR	7) Open Space	FOR		
4) Abortion	FOR	8) Home School	FOR		

Election Results

2004 general	Joe T. May	(R)	17,107	98.5%	$70,800

Campaign Contributions 2004 Tech./Comm. $7,750; Health Care $5,000; Transportation $4,500; Finance $3,250; Energy $1,750; Business/Retail Svs $1,000; Realty $1,000; Law $700; Public Employees $500; Defense $500; Agriculture $500; Mfg $250.

Economic Interests, 2004 *Off. & Dir.*, EIT, Pres.; *Pers. Liabil.*, $50,000+ ea.: banks (self) (family), other loan or fin. (self) (family); *Sec.*, $50,000+ ea.: money market, stock in own corp.; $10,001-$50,000 ea.: money markets (2), stock in bank; *Pay. for Talks, Mtgs., & Publ.*, $1,237 state, NCSL mtg, expenses; *Gifts*, $56 Ringling Bros. circus, tkts; $81 Washington Gas, dinner; $62 Metro Airport Authority, dinner; $152 Altria, Kraft Days Reception; $147 Altria, dinner; $101 Northern VA Tech Council, fall banquet; $203 Loudoun Health Care, dinner; *Bus. Int.*, $50,000+ ea.: EIT, Inc. (manuf.); *Real Estate*, One prop. (farmland).

HOUSE DISTRICT FORTY, *Timothy D. Hugo (R)*

POLITICAL AND LEGISLATIVE BACKGROUND

TENTH CONGRESSIONAL DISTRICT

House District 40 consists of part of Fairfax County comprised of the Clifton, Fairfax Station, Popes Head, Centre Ridge, Newgate, Virginia Run, Centreville, Green Trails, Deer Park, and Willow Springs Precincts and part of the London Towne Precinct.

Timothy Hugo was elected to the Virginia House of Delegates in a special election held on December 17, 2002. He replaced James K. ("Jay") O'Brien, Jr., who was elected to the state Senate in the redrawn senate district following the retirement of Senator Madison Marye (D).

Hugo is the executive director of CapNet, a national technology industry association that lobbies lawmakers on Capitol Hill. Hugo defeated Democrat Carol Hawn with 67.4% of the vote to her 30.3%. Two Independents also ran: Mark A. Calhoun and Joseph P. Oddo garnering about 2% of the vote.

During the 2004 session, Hugo sponsored twenty-five bills and resolutions. Of his twenty-one bills; eleven passed, five were carried-over and five failed. Four resolutions passed and one was carried over.

Two bills passed designating roads in Fairfax County as Virginia byways. A bill defined racing a motor vehicle that results in serious bodily harm as a felony. A transient occupancy tax was authorized for Fairfax County with funds to be spent on tourism promotion and a visitor's bureau. A bill to facilitate transfer of credits and admissions between state two and four year colleges passed. Voting equipment at polling places must remain in plain view of election officers.

A bill relating to electronic voting was carried over. The proposal to require repeat drunk driving offenders to use a special colored license plate was carried over. Certain proposed exemptions from the sales and use tax for certain contractors was carried over.

The designation of political parties on election ballots and voter registration by party failed. A proposed new limited banquet and mixed beverage license failed . Prohibition of geographic discrimination by state colleges and universities failed.

A resolution on the study of voting equipment certification passed as did a study of remote sales tax collection. A proposed constitutional amendment relating to the highway trust fund was carried over.

Delegate HD 40

Timothy D. Hugo (R) Member House: 2003- ; b. Jan. 7, 1963, Norfolk; home, Centreville; educ. William & Mary; St. Andrews Church; married, Paula Mary Goggin.

Technology Government Relations; USAR (1990-1998); Member: Burke Rotary, American Legion, Clifton Lions.

Offices P.O. Box 893, Centreville 20122; GA Bldg., Capitol Sq., Rm. 818, Richmond 23219; 804-698-1040.

2004 Committees *Education; Privileges and Elections; Transportation.*

House Key Votes, 2004
Please see Introduction for more information on bills.

| 1) Budget Bill | AGN | 5) Family Life | AGN | 9) Morning After | FOR |

213

TENTH CONGRESSIONAL DISTRICT

2) Feticide	FOR	6) Fire Arms	AGN	10) Legal Aid	FOR
3) Marriage	FOR	7) Open Space	FOR		
4) Abortion	FOR	8) Home School	FOR		

Election Results

2004 general	Timothy D. Hugo	(R)	2,927	99.8%	$218,140

Campaign Contributions 2004   Tech/Communications $12,901; Transportation $11,779; Business/Retail Svs $11.091; Political $10,350; :aw $10,098; Finance $7,500; Energy $5,500; Realty $4,750; Undetermined $4,000; Candidate Self-Financing $1,000; Public Employees $750; Agriculture $750; Health Care $500; Misc $250.

Economic Interests, 2004   Offices & Directorships: CapNet, President, The Tim Hugo Group, President; Paymt for talks, mtgs, and publications: $602 state, ALEC mtgs, expenses; 700 time Warner, flight to Seattle; *Bus. Int.*, $50,000/less Timothy D. Hugo sole proprietorship (consulting); Paymts for representation and other generally from $100,000 to $250,000: gov't affairs; Gifts: $152 Altria, Kraft Days Reception; $194 Old Dominion Contractors Assoc., dinner; $73 Dominion VA Power, dinner; $225 Kings Dominion, tkts; @101 NVTC, Fall Banquet tkt; $109 Fairfax Co. Chamber of Commerce, gift basket.

HOUSE DISTRICT FIFTY, *Harry J. Parrish (R)*

POLITICAL AND LEGISLATIVE BACKGROUND
House District 50 consists of all of the Cities of Manassas and Manassas Park; and part of Prince William County comprised of the Parkside, Loch Lomond, Stonewall, Sudley, Westgate, and Plantation Precincts and part of the Sinclair Precinct.

Republican Harry J. Parrish was first elected in 1981.   After the 1991 redistricting he is still representing roughly the same area. Parrish, with 30 years municipal service in Manassas is also president of his
father's business, Manassas Ice and Fuel Company.   During his service in the Virginia General Assembly he has been opposed only twice, in 1982 and 1987. Parrish chairs the Finance Committee.

Delegate Parrish is one of the most senior members of the House and is Chairman of the Finance Committee. During the 2004 session, he sponsored fifteen bills and one resolution. Six bills passed, two were incorporated into other bills, and seven failed. A resolution commending R.B. Thomas passed.

A number of the bills related to taxes and finance. A change in the reporting requirements for motor fuels tax passed as did a measure to establish penalties for interstate motor carriers operating in Virginia without proper identification and registration in violation of the International Fuels Tax Agreement. Provisions relating to property tax exemptions were changed for certain charitable organizations. Two measures relating to the income tax and for general tax reform failed. A bill to close income tax loopholes was incorporated into another bill.

Operating certificates for electric generating facilities were extended for two years. A bill requiring notice to schools of gang related activity passed as did a change in the salary of school board officials in the City of Manassas Park.

A proposed increase in the membership of the State Corporation Commission failed. A proposed change in eligibility for in-state tuition for certain people domiciled out the state failed.

214

Delegate HD 50

Harry Jacob Parrish (R) Member House: 1982-; b. Feb. 19, 1922, Fairfax County; home, 8898 Bond Ct., Manassas 20110-4327; educ. Wofford Coll., Spartansburg, SC; VPI; married Mattie Hooe Cannon; Methodist.

Chm. of Bd., Manassas Ice & Fuel Co.; VA Petroleum Jobbers (past Pres.); VA Oil Men's Assn.; Natl. Oil Jobbers Coun.; Kiwanis; VA Munic. League; Boy Scouts; Soc. Presv. Black Heritage; Transp. Coord. Council; Cham. Comm.; Metro Wash. Air Quality Com.; U.S.A.F., Ret. Col.; former Mayor Manassas 1963-81.

Offices 8898 Bond Court, Manassas 20110-4327; 703-367-0505; GA Bldg., Capitol Sq., Rm. 504, Richmond 23219; 804-698-1050.

2004 Committees *Finance, Chair; Commerce and Labor; Rules.*

House Key Votes, 2004
Please see Introduction for more information on bills.

1) Budget Bill	FOR	5) Family Life	FOR	9) Morning After	FOR
2) Feticide	FOR	6) Fire Arms	FOR	10) Legal Aid	FOR
3) Marriage	NV	7) Open Space	FOR		
4) Abortion	FOR	8) Home School	AGN		

Election Results

2004 general	Harry Jacob Parrish	(R)	9,178	99.9%	$13,187

Campaign Contributions 2004 Energy $4,250; Health Care $3,000; :aw $1,750; Transportation $1,500; Public Employees $1,000; Political $1,000; Realty $1,000; Business/Retail Svs $900; Agriculture $625; Finance $500; Tech/Communication $500.

Economic Interests, 2004 *Sal. & Wages,* $10,000+ Manassas Ice & Fuel Co. (MIFCO); *Off. & Dir.,* MIFCO, Chair. Bd., Dir. (self), VP/Dir. (spouse); *Sec.,* $50,000+ ea.: bonds (5), mutual fund, state deferred cont. plan, stocks in: MIFCO, Gasfair (realty), banks (3), Philip Morris, Dominion Resources, Verizon, Exxon, Host Marriott; $10,001-$50,000 ea.: bonds (3), mutual funds, stock in: Trigon, AT&T, Corus (manuf.), banks (2), IBM, Henrico Co. water/sewer, Phillips Petrol., Nextel, Daimler Chrysler, United Dom. Realty, Marriott Intnl., MFS Municipal Trust; Business Interests: Manassas Ice & Fuel Co., Gasfair Co.; *Pay. for Talks, Mtgs., & Publ.,* $1,283 state, Southern Legislative Conference, Little Rock, expenses; $1,675 state, Natl. conference of State Legislators, expenses; *Gifts,* Over $50, dinners from Agribusiness, NOVEC, Williams & Mullins, Washington Bd of Trade, Eli Lilly, Dominion VA Power (5), Norfolk & Southern, Verizon (2), Altria, VA Power, United Airlines, Greater Washington Bd of Trade; $78 State Farm Ins., dinner   ; *Pay. for Rep. Gen.,* $100,001-$250,000 chair of bd. ea.: ice manuf., retail co.

HOUSE DISTRICT SIXTY-SEVEN, *Gary Alan Reese (R)*

POLITICAL AND LEGISLATIVE BACKGROUND
House District 67 consists of part of Fairfax County comprised of the Chantilly, Dulles, Greenbriar East, Greenbriar West, Navy, Rocky Run, Waples Mill, Lees Corner, and Cub Run 903/Stone 917 Precincts and part of the London Towne Precinct; and part of Loudoun County comprised of part of the Arcola Precinct.

TENTH CONGRESSIONAL DISTRICT

Gary Reese, an attorney and a Republican, is the delegate for this district. Reese won the August 2001 Republican Primary over two challengers, with 39.5% of the vote in an election decided by 6.0% of the registered voters. In the November 2001 general election, Reese won with 60.6% of the vote over Democrat Gayla G. Schoenborn, carrying both Fairfax and Loudoun County overwhelmingly. The seat had been opened with the retirement of Republican and attorney Roger J. McClure who had represented this area since 1992, after its creation with redistricting in 1991.

During the 2004 session, Reese sponsored twenty-eight bills and two resolutions. Nineteen bills passed, three were carried over and six failed. Both his resolutions passed.

A number of Reese's bills related to civil procedure and legal processes. Three bills passed relating to jurisdiction in certain civil cases, judgments in settlement and installment orders, and documentation of subpoenas. Circuit courts are allowed to charge fees for remote access to records and two bills passed relating to service of process. A bill on records retention in general district courts was carried over.

Procedures for the consolidation of school districts passed. Two amendments were made to the Residential Landlord-Tenant Act relating to landlord access to correct nonemergency conditions, and the award of attorney's fees in cases of noncompliance.

Bills that failed included definitions of trespass upon church or school property, and a change in the rate of interest for judgments. A proposed increase in the cigarette tax to offset the property tax failed as did a similar proposal to tax cigarettes with revenue going to fund the Standards of Quality. A bill relating to emission standards for electric generating facilities failed.

Delegate HD 67

Gary Alan Reese (R) Member House: 2001-; b. March 11, 1945, San Antonio, TX; home, 11928 Bennett Road, Oak Hill 20171; educ. William & Mary (B.A.), U VA Sch. Law (J.D.); married, Carol Sue Gwaltney; Methodist.

Attorney, Patterson & Reese; Fairfax County School Bd. 1992-2001; Member: VA State Bar Assn.; Fairfax County Bar Assn.; Fairfax County Republican Committee; Awards: Distinguished Pres., Arlington Optimists 1985-86; VA Congress of PTAs Distinguished Service Award 1992.

Offices 11928 Bennett Road, Oak Hill 20171; 703-476-4505; GA Bldg., Rm. 807, Capitol Sq., Richmond 23219; 804-698-1067.

2004 Committees *Counties, Cities and Towns; Courts of Justice; Education.*

House Key Votes, 2004
Please see Introduction for more information on bills.

1) Budget Bill	AGN	5) Family Life	FOR	9) Morning After	FOR
2) Feticide	FOR	6) Fire Arms	FOR	10) Legal Aid	AGN
3) Marriage	FOR	7) Open Space	FOR		
4) Abortion	FOR	8) Home School	AGN		

Election Results

2001 general	Gary A. Reese	(R)	10,987	60.6%	$60,708

TENTH CONGRESSIONAL DISTRICT
Gayla G. Schoenborn   (D)   7,131   39.3% $10,226

Campaign Contributions 2004 Law $6,321; Realty $5,050; Business/Retail Svs $1,500;Finance $1,500; Energy $1,500; Public Employees $500; Political $500; Health Care $500; Tech/Communications $500; Agriculture $500; Misc $250; Transportation $250.

Economic Interests, 2004 *Sal. & Wages*, $10,000+ ea.: Patterson & Reese, Attorneys at Law, Verizon (son); *Off. & Dir.*, Dulles Area Transit Authority, Honorary Director; *Sec.*, $50,000+ ea.: mutual fund, banks (2), Shueard, Cosco; $10,001-$50,000 MFS Trust; *Bus. Int.*, $50,000+ Patterson & Reese; *Pay. for Rep. & Other Services Generally*, $100,001-$250,000 legal assistance banks; $10,001-$50,000 landlord matters, hotels, atty. gen., etc.; *Real Estate*, commercial offices; Gifts: $200 Washington Gas, Family Center Gala; $236 Access Point, dinner; $62 Dulles, dinner; $203 Dominion Power, two dinners.

SENATE DISTRICT THIRTY-TWO, *Janet D. Howell (D)*

POLITICAL AND LEGISLATIVE BACKGROUND
Senate District 32 consists of the Fairfax County Precincts of Reston #1, Reston #2, Dogwood, Hunters Woods, Reston #3, Glade, South Lakes, Terraset, North Point, Aldrin, Chain Bridge, Chesterbrook, Churchill, Cooper, El Nido, Great Falls, Haycock, Kenmore, Kirby, Langley, Longfellow, Mclean, Pimmit, Salona, Westhampton, Westmoreland, Herndon #1, Herndon #2, Clearview, Forestville, Herndon #3, Hutchison, Stuart, Sugarland, Hickory, Seneca, Marshall, Magarity, and Tysons.

Janet Howell, a former teacher and a Democrat, has represented the district since 1991. Clive DuVal, also a Democrat, had served for 26 years as a delegate and then as a senator and retired in 1991. Howell, a former teacher, had been a legislative assistant to Delegate Kenneth Plum (D-36). It was a close see-saw race in Fairfax County against Republican Frederick Dykes, which she won by 52.5% of the total vote. In 1995, Howell won by 57.3% over Republican Robert M. McDowell, who had been endorsed by the National Rifle Association as the "pro-gun" candidate. In 1999, Howell defeated Republican Whitney Adams with 58.2% of the vote. On of Howell's major accomplishments was the design and passage of Virginia's "Megan's Law", mandated and partially funded by the Federal government to protect children from convicted sex offenders who now live in the community.

During the 2004 session, Howell sponsored twenty-nine bills and resolutions. Twelve bills passed, three failed, two were carried over and three were incorporated into other bills. Eight of nine resolutions passed. Several bills that passed related to family issues: including information reporting requirements for missing children; amended the rules on family abuse and mandatory arrest to require determination of the predominant physical aggressor; required that intake officers provide information on time limits and other legal requirements for the issuance of protective orders. One bill exempted religious organizations from the real estate recordation fees. Another bill change permitted the application of locally adopted employee grievance procedures to social services workers.

Of the bills that failed one would have required ministers, priests or rabbis to report cases of child abuse or neglect; another bill would have prohibited the carrying of a loaded gun in a restaurant with an ABC license; required health insurers to cover the cost of prescription contraceptives.

Sponsored bills that were incorporated into other bills were two relating to the issuance of special license plates and one relating to tobacco taxes and how tobacco tax revenue is used. Sen. Howell's resolutions commending individuals and organizations all passed. One resolution proposing a constitutional amendment relating to the Highway Trust Fund was replaced by a substitute incorporating other related resolutions which then failed to pass.

Senator SD 32

ELEVENTH CONGRESSIONAL DISTRICT

Janet D. Howell (D) Member Senate: 1992-; b. May 7, 1944, Washington, D.C.; home, 11338 Woodbrook Lane, Reston 22094; educ. Oberlin College (BA; Univ. of PA (MA); Unitarian; married, Hunt Howell.

Former Teacher; Pres., Reston Community Assn.; V.Chm., Fairfax Co. Citizen's Comm. on Land Use & Transp.; State Bd. of Soc. Serv. (Chair); Awards: Woman of the Yr. (1993) Netwk. Entrepreneurial Women; Leg. of the Yr. (1995, 1997) Victims & Witnesses of Crime; VA Citizen of Yr. 1991, Natl. Assn. Soc. Workers.

Offices P.O. Box 2608, Reston 20195-0608; 703-709-8283; GA Bldg., Rm. 327, Capitol Sq., Richmond 23219; 804-698-7532.

2004 Committees *Courts of Justice; Education and Health; Finance; Privileges and Elections.*

Senate Key Votes, 2004
Please see Introduction for more information on bills.

1) Budget Bill	FOR	5) Familty Life	FOR	9) Charter School	FOR
2) Feticide	AGN	6) Fire Arms	AGN	10) Legal Aid	FOR
3) Marriage	AGN	7) Open Space	FOR		
4) Child Abuse	FOR	8) Home School	AGN		

Election Results

1999 general	Janet D. Howell	(D)	25,966	58.2%	$314,259
	W. Adams	(R)	18,615	41.7%	$191,415

Campaign Contributions 2000-June 30, 2002 **Realty/Constr.** $33,575; **Medical** $14,600; **Attys.** $14,000; **Tech./Comm.** $10,725; **Individ.** $9,150; **Pub. Empl.** $7,150; **Consult.** $5,950; **Defense** $3,625 (Shipbldg. $750); **Beer/Wine** $3,575; **Electric** $3,500; **Restaur.** $3,250; **Finance** $3,075; **Democrats** $2,750; **Sec./Detective** $2,500; **Kings Dom.** $2,000; **Transp.** $1,650 (Auto Dealers $750); **Retail/Business** $1,125; **Greater Wash. Bd. Trade** $1,000; **Insur.** $1,000; **Oil** $800; **Nat. Gas** $500; **Quarries** $250; **Lumber** $250.

Economic Interests 2004 *Sal. & Wages,* $10,000+ Inter American Development Bank (spouse); *Sec.,* $50,000+ ea.: mutual fund, bonds, money markets (2), stocks in: GE, Minn. Mining, AOL Time Warner, Liberty Media, Proctor & Gamble, Exxon Mobil, Am. Interntl., Citigroup, Federal Natl. Mtg., Johnson & Johnson, Medtronic, financial service funds (4), Merck, Pfizer, Cisco, Intel, Microsoft, Nokia, United Parcel Serv., Duke Energy, Pub. Serv. Ent. Group; $10,001-$50,000 ea.: mutual funds (3), bonds, stocks in: Motanta Co., Dupont, Costco, Genuine Parts, Omnicom Group, Target, AT&T, NY Times, Colgate Pal., Comcast, Transocean Sedco, Anadarko Pete, BP, Assoc. Banc Corp, Chester NY Banc Corp, financial service, Automatic Data Proc., EMS Corp., MDV Resources, Sprint; *Pay. for Talks, Mtgs., & Pub.,* $2,223 state, NCSL Mtg in Salt Lake, conference expenses; *Gifts,* $128 Glaxo Smith Kline, two dinners; $102 Old Dominion Hwy contractors, dinner; $115 VA Auto Dealers Assoc, dinner; $157 Astra Zeneca, dinner;$68 MCI, dinner; $94 Dominion, dinner; $64Dominion, dinner; $103 Wasshington Gas, dinner; $320 VA Bch Hotel-Motel Assoc, weekend in VA Beach.

ELEVENTH CONGRESSIONAL DISTRICT
SENATE DISTRICT THIRTY-FOUR, *Jeanmarie A. Devolites (R)*

POLITICAL AND LEGISLATIVE BACKGROUND

Senate District 34 consists of the City of Fairfax; the Fairfax County Precincts of Olde Creek, Oak Hill, Lake Braddock, Laurel, Villa, Long Branch, Robinson, Olley, Signal Hill, Colvin, Flint Hill, Vienna #1, Vienna #2, Vienna #4, Vienna #6, Westbriar, Wolftrap, Sunrise Valley, Shouse, Hummer, Camelot, Ridgelea, Blake, Freedom Hill, Mantua, Mosby, Price, Walker, Pine Ridge, Stenwood, Thoreau, Oakton, Nottoway, Penderbrook, Oak Marr, Vale, Waples Mill, Woodson Part 1, Woodson Part 2; and Fairfax A.

During the 2004 session, Devolites sponsored twenty-eight bills and resolutions. Twenty-two bills passed, five failed and three were carried over. Five of her six resolutions passed. Of the bills that passed one required that voting equipment always remain in the view of election officials and make provision for the use of portable voting equipment for disabled persons or those over 65; a charter amendment permitted salary increases for members of the Fairfax City council; towns in Fairfax county were given the same authority as the County to regulate the parking of commercial motor vehicles

Several of her bills that passed related to law enforcement and corrections. One bill authorized the Department of Correctional Education to offer pre-release parenting skills training and anger management programs to noncustodial parent offenders; another bill provided for exemption for certain retired law enforcement officers from the fee to obtain a permit to carry a concealed weapon; the membership of the state Criminal Justices Service Board was increased to include one active duty police officer.

Four resolutions commending individuals passed and did one encouraging the Supreme Court of Virginia to amend rules on electronic filing. One resolution to create a subcommittee to study the effect of remote taxation on the Commonwealth failed.

Of the bills that failed one related to criminal history background checks for persons working in adult substance abuse treatment facilities; another dealt with the kinds of newspapers in which legal notices could be published; one would have required the Attorney General to defend local governments against certain private legal actions brought under the Chesapeake Bay Preservation Act.

Senator SD 34

Jean Marie DeVolites (R) Member House: 1998- ; b. February 28, 1956, Swindon, England; home 110 Shephardson Lane Vienna 22124; educ. Univ. VA (B.A.); spouse: Congressman Thomas M. Davies, III; Roman Catholic.

Statistical Consultant. Member: Tysons Corner Rotary (Dir., Comm. Service), Greater Merrifield Bus. Assoc. (Bd. Dir.), Girl Scouts (Troop Leader), Fairfax Co. Repub. Comm. (Chair. Providence Dist.), Oakton HS PTA (Bd.), New Providence Repub. Women's Club (Bd.); Awards: Girl Scout Council of the Nation's Capitol Outstanding Leader Award (1994), Outstanding Volunteer (1997).

Offices   P.O. Box 936, Vienna 22183; 703-938-7972; GA Bldg., Rm. 515, Capitol Sq., Richmond 23219; 804-698-1035.

2004 Committees *General Laws; Privileges and Elections; Rehabilitation and Social Services.*

Senate Key Votes, 2004
Please see Introduction for more information on bills.

1) Budget Bill	AGN	5) Familty Life	FOR	9) Charter School	FOR
2) Feticide	FOR	6) Fire Arms	FOR	10) Legal Aid	FOR
3) Marriage	FOR	7) Open Space	FOR		
4) Child Abuse	AGN	8) Home School	FOR		

Election Results
2003 general   JeanMarie Devolites   (R)   13,719   52.8% $208,407

Campaign Contributions 2000-June 30, 2002   Individuals $2,300; **AFL CIO** $1,500; **Democrats** $1,300; **Consult.** $850; **Tech./Comm.** $700; **Pub. Empl.** $550; **Beer/Wine** $500; **ATI** $400; **Attys.** $250; **Oil** $250; **Env. Eng.** $250; **Realty/Constr.** $200; **CPA** $100; **Misc. Defense** $100; **Forestry/Lumber** $100.

Economic Interests 2004 *Sal. & Wages*, $10,000+ ea.: US House of Representatives; Offices & Directorships: Student Loan Mktg Assoc, Board of Directorsl; sec. more than $50,000: mutual funds, gov't securities; $50,000 or less: mutual funds; Paymts for talks, mtgs and publications: $1,344 Senate, NCSL Fall Forum; for representation and other services generally to $100,000: Technology Training and consulting; Real Estate: Regency Investments; Gifts: $152 Altria, Kraft Days Reception; $157 Astra Zeneca, dinner; $73 Farm Bureau, dinner; $73 Dominion Power, dinner; $52 VA Cable, dinner: $100 Auto Dealers Assoc, dinner.

SENATE DISTRICT THIRTY-FIVE, *Richard L. Saslaw (D)*

POLITICAL AND LEGISLATIVE BACKGROUND
Senate District 35 consists of the Fairfax County Precincts of Bristow, Chapel, Heritage, Kings Park, North Springfield #1, North Springfield #2, North Springfield #3, Ravensworth, Wakefield, Belvedere, Lincolnia, Masonville, Parklawn, Sleepy Hollow, Saint Albans, Westlawn, Weyanoke, Columbia, Brook Hill, Poe, Whittier, Walnut Hill #1, Bren Mar, Edsall, Graham, Greenway, Pine Spring, Shreve, Timber Lane, Woodburn, Merrifield, and Walnut Hill #2; and the City of Alexandria Precincts of Hermitage, Southern Towers-Stratford, James K. Polk School, Patrick Henry School, Landmark Center, Charles E. Beatley Jr. Library, John Adams School, William Ramsay School, and South Port.

Richard L. Saslaw, president of a company of service station operators, and a Democrat, was elected state Senator in 1979 after two terms in the House. The seat was opened by the retirement of Senator Omer L. Hirst, who had served since 1964. Saslaw defeated former Fairfax County Board chair, Jean Packard in the 1979 primary and won over Republican and former Delegate James Tate in the general election.   One of the prominent issues in the campaign was ratification of the Equal Rights Amendment, with Saslaw for it, Tate against it. Saslaw has defeated all opposition since then, running unopposed in 1987. In 1999, Saslaw defeated two challengers, winning with 58% of the vote. Saslaw has been described by some media as an in-your-face legislator.

As Minority Leader in the Senate, Senator Saslaw's influence goes beyond that of his sponsorship of individual bills and resolutions. In 2004 much of his effort was devoted to resolving the state's budget and fiscal problems. He sponsored four bills and one resolution. Three bills passed, as did his one resolution.

Two of the bills that passed related to education. One bill required college Boards of Visitors to designate those projects to be financed by bonds under the Virginia College Building Authority; another bill required the law enforcement officers report the arrest of school students over 18 to the school superintendent for certain crimes, felonies or gang-related activity. A bill relating to applicant fingerprint database management by the State Police passed. A bill to authorize Fairfax County to impose a food and beverage tax failed.

A resolution expressing sorrowing at the death of former Senator Omer Hirst passed.

Senator SD 35

Richard Lawrence Saslaw (D) Member Senate: 1980-; Member House 1976-79; b. Feb. 5, 1940, Washington, D.C.; home, 4418 Randon Ct., Annandale 22003; educ. Univ. MD (B.S. Economics); married Eleanor Barbara Berman; Jewish.

Pres. RTS Associates, Inc., service station operators; Democratic Floor Leader Senate 1996-98; Minority Leader 1998- ; U.S. Army 1958-1960.

Offices P.O. Box 1856, Springfield 22151-0856; 703-978-0200; GA Bldg., Capitol Sq., Rm. 613, Richmond 23219; 804-698-7535.

2004 Committees *Commerce and Labor; Courts of Justice; Education and Health; Finance; Rules.*

Senate Key Votes, 2004
Please see Introduction for more information on bills.

1) Budget Bill	FOR	5) Familty Life	FOR	9) Morning After	FOR
2) Feticide	AGN	6) Fire Arms	AGN	10) Legal Aid	FOR
3) Marriage	AGN	7) Open Space	FOR		
4) Child Abuse	FOR	8) Home School	AGN		

Election Results

2003 general	Richard Saslaw	(D)	11,588	82.9%	$387,338

Campaign Contributions 2000-June 30, 2002 **Realty/Constr.** $33,750; **Medical** $14,850; **Tech./Comm.** $11,500; **Finance** $10,800; **Transp.** $9,000 (Auto Dealers $7,450); **Insur.** $7,500; **Attys.** $7,500; **Democrats** $6,000; **Beer/Wine** $4,500; **Restaur./Hotel/Tour** $3,700; **Electric** $3,500; **GE** $2,500; **Coal** $2,000; **Northrup Grumman** $2,000; **Pub. Empl.** $1,500; **Individ.** $1,200; **Trash** $1,000; **Nat. Gas** $1,000; **Dupont** $1,000; **Kings Dom.** $1,000; **Greater Wash. Bd.**

Trade $1,000; **Honeywell** $500; **Env. Eng.** $500; **Billboards** $500; **Oil** $300; **VA Automat. Merch.** $250.

Economic Interests 2004 *Sal. & Wages*, $10,000+ ea.: RTS Assoc. (self), Fairfax Co. Pub. Sch. (spouse); *Off. & Dir.*, Pres. of: RTS Associates (service station), Great Seneca Corp. (MD serv. stat.), Amerasia (realty), Chantilly Associates (realty); *Pers. Liabil.*, $10,001-$50,000+ banks; *Sec.*, $50,000+ ea.: stocks in: service stations (2), realty co. (2), Community Bank; $10,001-$50,000 stocks in: E Citi Cafe, Microsoft, Given Imaging; *Gifts*, $374 Dominion Resources, Washington Redskin/Giants game; $91 Dominion Resources, dinner; $60 CSX, dinner; $114 VA Sheriffs Assoc, recognition dinner; $130 Altria, dinner; $103 Washington Gas, dinner, Real Estate: condominion.

HOUSE DISTRICT THIRTY-FIVE, *Stephen Shannon* (D)

POLITICAL AND LEGISLATIVE
House District 35 consists of part of Fairfax County comprised of the Flint Hill, Vienna #1, Vienna #2, Vienna #4, Vienna #6, Westbriar, Wolftrap, Blake, Freedom Hill, Oakton, Nottoway, Penderbrook, Oak Marr, Leehigh, and Vale Precincts.

During the 2004 session, newly elected Delegate Shannon sponsored thirteen bills. Four bills passed, three
failed, four were carried over and two were incorporated. Both of his resolutions passed.

Many of the bills related to Shannon's experience as a prosecutor and lawyer as they proposed changes in criminal law. One bill that passed required entering the names of missing children into state and national databases within two hours of reporting; another related to sexual abuse of children under thirteen years of age. Two bills were incorporated into other bills that passed included one on credit card theft and another on jury proceedings after a criminal conviction. One bill related to local regulation of parking of commercial motor vehicles. Two criminal law bills were carried over related to gang activity and the definition of concealed weapons.

Two of the bills that failed involved changes in the state income tax. Another would permit local school boards to provide funds to help employees purchase homes in the locality.

Delegate HD 35

Stephen Shannon (D) Member House: 2004 - ; b. Apr. 5, 1971, educ. Fairfield University, CT (BA 1993), Georgetown University, Washington, DC(MPP 1996), University of Virginia (JD 1999); wife Suzanne Hochberg, children Aidan; Catholic.

Attorney, George Mason Inns of Court, member.

Offices: P.O. Box 1143, Vienna, VA 22183, (703) 281-5200; P.O. Box 406, Richmond, VA 23218, Rm 718, (804) 698-1035, FAX (804) 786-6310.

2004 Committees *Agriculture Chesapeake and Natural Resources,*

Finance.

House Key Votes 2004
Please see Introduction for more information on bills.

1) Budget Bill	AGN	5) Family Life	FOR	9) Morning After	AGN
2) Feticide	FOR	6) Fire Arms	FOR	10) Legal Aid	FOR
3) Marriage	FOR	7) Open Space	FOR		
4) Abortion	AGN	8) Home School	AGN		

Campaign Contributions 2004 Real Estate $18,989; Law $18,271; Political $17,500; Finance $9,500; Business/Retail Svs $9,450; Tech/Communications $8,500; Energy $6,000; Health Care $5,750; Transportation $5,041; Public Employees $3,359; Misc $3,250; Agriculture $2,750Mfg $250; Organized Labor $250.

Economic Interests 2004 *Sal. & Wages*, $10,000+ ea.: RTS Assoc. (self), Fairfax Co. Pub. Sch. (spouse); *Off. & Dir.*, Pres. of: RTS Associates (service station), Great Seneca Corp. (MD serv. stat.), Amerasia (realty), Chantilly Associates (realty); *Pers. Liabil.*, $10,001-$50,000+ banks; *Sec.*, $50,000+ ea.: stocks in: service stations (2), realty co. (2), Community Bank; $10,001-$50,000 stocks in: E Citi Cafe, Microsoft, Given Imaging; *Gifts*, $200 Washington Gas, NOVA Family; $53 Washington Gas, dinner; $ 300 Washington Gas, dinner; $188 Woods Consulting, dinner; $101 Northern VA Tech council, Fall banquet; $115 VA Auto Dealers Assoc, dinner; $59 GlaxoSmithKline, dinner; $88 Reynolds, briefcase; Paymts for representation and other services generally to $50,000: legal services to communications equipment companies; Real Estate: condominium.

HOUSE DISTRICT THIRTY-SIX, *Kenneth R. Plum (D)*

POLITICAL AND LEGISLATIVE BACKGROUND
House District 36 consists of the Fairfax County Precincts of Reston #1, Reston #2, Dogwood, Hunters Woods, Reston #3, Glade, South Lakes, Terraset, Sunrise Valley, Fox Mill, North Point, Aldrin, and Kinross.

Democrat Kenneth R. Plum, the retired director of adult education in the Fairfax County public school system, was first elected to the House in 1977 as part of the five member delegation representing the former 18th District. He was subsequently defeated for re-election in 1979 when Republicans John Rust and John Buckley were elected. In 1981, Plum defeated Republican opposition. He ran unopposed in 1983, and has been successful in every bid for re-election since. In 1999, Plum easily won a three-way race with 62% of the vote. Plum was chair of the Virginia Democratic Party during the 2000 session. In the 2001 election, Plum was unopposed.

During the 2004 session, Delegate Ken Plum sponsored eleven bills and twelve resolutions. Four bills passed, five bills failed and two were carried over. Ten resolutions passed, one proposed constitutional amendment resolution was carried over and one resolution on redistricting failed.

Of the bills that passed one addressed the terms of directors of non-stock corporations (nonprofit corporations) in situations where the corporations articles are silent on the matter; another bill changed the requirement that holders of a conservation easement have a principal office in the state from five to four years; a bill amended the membership of the Small Business Financing Authority to include the Director of the Department of Business Assistance and to clarify voting rights of members. Lastly, a bill exempted hybrid gas-electric motor vehicles that get over 50 miles per gallon from the state emission inspection program.

Several of Delegate Plums resolutions that passed were commending individuals and organizations. One resolution related to the collection of information on infant screening for metabolic disorders; another resolution that passed related to continued state, local and regional cooperation in the effort to achieve a balanced transportation system in Reston.

Three of the failed bills related to transportation: one bill would have increased the motor fuels tax; another would require that the Commonwealth Transportation Board consult with home owners associations with more than 50,000 members in its new transportation construction planning processes; a bill would have established an Integrated Transportation Planning Fund within the Office of the Secretary of Transportation to aid in regional and local transportation planning activities. Another failed bill would have raised the cigarette tax and directed the use of those funds for the state Medicaid Program.

Delegate HD 36

Kenneth Ray Plum (D) Member House 1979-80; 1982-; b. Nov. 3, 1943, Shenandoah; home, 2073 Cobblestone Lane, Reston 22091; educ. Old Dominion Univ. (B.A.), UVA (M.Ed.); married Jane Durham Meacham; Church of Christ.

Retired Dir. Adult Education, Fairfax County Public Schools; Chm. Fairfax Manpower Planning Council; National, VA, & Fairfax Educa. Assns.; VA Lit. Fnd. Bd.; Friends of Fairfax Juvenile Ct. Bd.; Reston Environmental Fndn.

Offices 2073 Cobblestone Lane, Reston 20191; 703-758-9733; GA Bldg., Capitol Sq., Rm. 403, Richmond 23219; 804-698-1036.

2004 Committees *Agriculture, Chesapeake and Natural Resources; Commerce and Labor; Science and Technology*

House Key Votes, 2004
Please see Introduction for more information on bills.

1) Budget Bill	AGN	5) Family Life	FOR	9) Morning After	AGN
2) Feticide	AGN	6) Fire Arms	AGN	10) Legal Aid	FOR
3) Marriage	AGN	7) Open Space	FOR		
4) Abortion	AGN	8) Home School	AGN		

Election Results

2004 general	Kenneth R. Plum	(D)	11,803	99.6%	$101,706

Campaign Contributions 2004 Energy $5,000; Tech/Communications $3,500; Finance $2,750; Health Care $2,749; Business/Retail Svs $2,575; Law $1,750; Realty $1,750; Transportation $1,375; Organized Labor $500; Agriculture $500; Public Employees $125.

Economic Interests, 2004 *Sal. or Wages,* $10,000+ ea.: United Christian Parish (spouse); *Sec.,* $50,000+ bonds; $10,001-$50,000 mutual funds; *Pay. for Talks, Mtgs., & Publ.,* $250 speech University of Richmond; $1,732 VA Delegates, travel expenses; $1,625 Northern VA Regional commission, transportation to Germany, expenses; *Gifts,* $250 Northern VA Bldg Industries Assoc, banquet; $57 Dominion Power, dinner; $62 Washington Airport Authority, dinner; $78 State Farm Ins., dinner; $60 Verizon, dinner; $200 HCA Reston Hospital, banquet; $150 Dulles Area

Transportation Assoc, banquet; $100 Restaurant Assoc of Metro Washington, banquet; $200 Wolf Trap Foundation, ball; $100 NVCC Foundation, banquet; $200 Nortel, banquet; $150 Ads Council of Fairfax, banquet; 150 Medical Care for Children Partnership, banquet; $120 Wolf Trap Foundation, dinner; $75 Committee for Dulles, dinner; $100 Medical Society of Fairfax, dinner; $120 West Group, dinner; $202 Northern VA Tech Council, banquet; $100 VA Society of CPA's , dinner; $90 Jr. League, reception; $130 McGuire Woods, dinner; $500 Gerald Halpin, accommodations; *Real Estate*, One prop. (townhouse) w/spouse.

HOUSE DISTRICT THIRTY-SEVEN, *John Chapman "Chap" Petersen (D)*

POLITICAL AND LEGISLATIVE BACKGROUND
House District 37 consists of all of the City of Fairfax; and part of Fairfax County comprised of the Olde Creek, Sideburn, Villa, Robinson, Bonnie Brae, Camelot, Ridgelea, Mantua, Mosby, Price, Pine Ridge, Woodson Part 1, and Woodson Part 2 Precincts; and Fairfax A.

In a major upset in the November 2001 elections, Democrat "Chap" Petersen defeated Republican incumbent John "Jack" Rust, Jr., winning with 52.2% of the vote. Petersen carried the Fairfax County precincts with 53% and the Fairfax City precincts with 50.7% of the vote. Petersen is an attorney, and served on the Fairfax City Council.

John "Jack" Rust, Jr., a Republican and an attorney, had been the representative for this district since he won a special election in December, 1996 following the death of Robert E. "Bob" Harris from leukemia.

During the 2004 session, Petersen sponsored fifteen bills and nine resolutions. Five bills passed, six failed, three were carried over and one was incorporated into other legislation. Eight of nine resolutions passed; the passed resolutions commended individuals and organizations. The failed resolution was a constitutional amendment relating of public education funding.

One bill that passed made state retail sales tax applicable to telephone calling cards but also exempted calling cards from other utility taxes. A charter amendment for the city of Fairfax would permit compensation of city council members according to state law. A bill to include hazing as a criminal misdemeanor when used as part of a gang ritual or initiation process.

Of the bills that failed one would have allowed counties to impose tobacco taxes; another related to tuition rates and percentage enrollment of in and out of state students at state universities. A bill would have waivered the marriage license fee for couples that had participated in at least four hours of pre-marital counseling.

ELEVENTH CONGRESSIONAL DISTRICT

Delegate HD 37

John Chapman "Chap" Petersen (D) Member House: 2002-; b. March 27, 1968, Washington, D.C.; home, 10616 Moore St., Fairfax 22036; educ. Williams College (B.A.), Univ. VA (J.D.); married Sharon Young Kim; Episcopal.

Attorney; Fairfax City Council 1998-01; Member: Fairfax Noonday Optimist Club; Fairfax Co. Good News Jail Ministry; Northern VA Rugby Football Club.

Offices P.O. Box 887, Fairfax 22030; 703-591-5133; GA Bldg., Rm. 710, Capitol Sq, Richmond 23219; 804-698-1037.

2004 Committees *Militia, Police and Public Safety; Science and Technology.*

House Key Votes, 2004
Please see Introduction for more information on bills.

1) Budget Bill	AGN	5) Family Life	FOR	9) Morning After	AGN
2) Feticide	FOR	6) Fire Arms	FOR	10) Legal Aid	FOR
3) Marriage	FOR	7) Open Space	FOR		
4) Abortion	AGN	8) Home School	AGN		

Election Results

2004 general	J. Chapman Petersen	(D)	9,950	59.1%	$285,827
	John "Jack" Rust, Jr.	(R)	6,765	40.9%	$208,504

Campaign Contributions 2004 Finance $3,250; Energy $3,000; Transportation $2,531; Law $2,500; Tech/Communications $2,500; Realty $2,500; Health Care $2,250; Public Employees $1,300; Organized Labor $750; Agriculture $750; Business/Retail Svs $350; Political $250.

Economic Interests, 2004 *Sal. or Wages,* $10,000+ ea.: Bracewell & Patterson LLP (self), Galloway, Ball & Cossa PLC (spouse); Business Interests $50,000 or less: Locust Grove Farm Corp;*Pay. for Rep. & Other Services Generally,* legal services $1,001-$10,000 electric utilities, banks, legal services to oil or gas companies; *Real Estate,* Interest in farm w/Locust Grove Farm Corp.; Gifts: $100 Le Clair Ryan, dinner; $75 INOVA Health System, dinner.

HOUSE DISTRICT THIRTY-EIGHT, *Robert D. "Bob" Hull (D)*

POLITICAL AND LEGISLATIVE BACKGROUND
House District 38 consists of the Fairfax County Precincts of Barcroft, Belvedere, Lincolnia, Masonville, Parklawn, Ravenwood, Sleepy Hollow, Saint Albans, Westlawn, Weyanoke, Willston, Poe, Whittier, Bren Mar, Edsall, Fort Buffalo, Graham, and Greenway, and parts of Glen Forest and Holmes.

Robert D. Hull, a Democrat and marketing executive, was first elected to the House in a special election on December 15, 1992 to fill the vacancy left by Leslie Byrne's (D) election to Congress. Hull won this one month campaign with 54% of the vote. Hull expressed strong support on gun control and for every woman's reproductive rights. His opponent, Republican A. Strode Brent, who had twice run unsuccessfully against Byrne, favored parental consent on abortion, and was not as strong on gun control. Hull has deep roots in the community and the Democratic Party. Hull won re-election easily

ELEVENTH CONGRESSIONAL DISTRICT

in 1995, defeating Republican Leslie R. Gibson by 61.6%. In 1997, Hull defeated Republican Michael G. Davis, Jr. by 59.4%, and in 1999 defeated Republican Stephen Smith with 59% of the vote. In the 2001 election, Hull won with 58.7% of the vote over three challengers.

Delegate Hull sponsored eight bills and one resolution. Five bills passed, two failed and one was carried over; his resolution passed.

One of the adopted bills amended the income tax law to require professional tax preparers to use electronic filing or barcode capable software for state income taxes. A bill changed the requirements for sanitary districts in Fairfax County to permit the use of notices and geographic descriptions instead of the older and less understood meets and bounds descriptions of district lines. An education bill changed the School Performance Report Card to include information on student Standards of Learning performance. A bill naming a bridge for Stuart Finley in the Lake Barcroft area passed as did a measure to designate the flag of the former South Vietnam as a Vietnamese-American Heritage Flag. A resolution expressing sorrow at the passing of Isaac Fleischmann passed.

A bill proposing the equalization of the taxing authority of cities and counties failed. A bill raising the motor fuel tax and adjusting the allocation formula for highway funding also failed. A requirement to require daytime headlight use on motor vehicles was carried over.

Delegate HD 38

Robert D. "Bob" Hull (D) Member House: 1993- ; b. Dec. 28, 1954, Washington, D.C.; home, 2923 Johnson Rd., Falls Church 22042; educ. VPI & SU (B.S.), married Laura M. Connors Hull; United Methodist.

Marketing Director, Information Dimensions, Inc.; member Greater Falls Church Chamber of Commerce; VA Consumer Council; Falls Church Private/Public Partnership; NAACP; Chesapeake Bay Fndn.; VA Tech Alumni Assn.; VA Crime Prev. Assn.

Offices P.O. Box 2331, Falls Church 22042; 703-573-4855; GA Bldg. Capitol Sq., Rm. 422, Richmond, VA 23219; 804-698-1038.

2004 Committees *Counties, Cities and Towns; Education; Finance.*

House Key Votes, 2004
Please see Introduction for more information on bills.

1) Budget Bill	AGN	5) Family Life	FOR	9) Morning After	AGN
2) Feticide	AGN	6) Fire Arms	AGN	10) Legal Aid	FOR
3) Marriage	NV	7) Open Space	FOR		
4) Abortion	AGN	8) Home School	AGN		

Election Results

2003 general	Robert Hull	(D)	9,674	99.8%	$49,840

Campaign Contributions 2004 Realty/Constr. $3,800; Political $3,051; Finance $2,000; Tech/Communications $1,900; Energy $1,500; Health Care $1,387; Public Employees $1,250; Business/Retail Svs $975; Law $750; Agriculture $750; Transportation $250; Mfg $250.

Economic Interests, 2004 *Sal. or Wages*, $10,000+ McEnearney Assoc, Inc., Creative Cauldron, Inc.; Offices & Directorships: Creative Cauldron, President (wife); *Gifts*: $63 GEICO/State Farm Ins, dinner; $88 Feld Entertainment, circus tkts; $211 Dominion VA Power, Redskins tkts; $211 Dominion VA Power, VA Tech game tkts.

HOUSE DISTRICT THIRTY-NINE, *Vivian E. Watts (D)*

POLITICAL AND LEGISLATIVE BACKGROUND
House District 39 consists of the Fairfax County Precincts of Bristow, Chapel, Heritage, Kings Park, North Springfield #1, North Springfield #2, North Springfield #3, Oak Hill, Ravensworth, Wakefield, Long Branch, Olley, Crestwood, Garfield, Lynbrook, Columbia, Hummer, and Brook Hill.

Democrat Vivian Watts was elected in 1995, returning to serve in the same area she served from 1982-1986. She had resigned the office when appointed Secretary of Transportation and Public Safety by former Governor Gerald Baliles. Democrat Alan Mayer replaced her and served until his retirement in 1995, defeating all challengers, and stressing education, the environment, the needs of the handicapped, and combating drug use in the schools. In making her announcement to run for the seat, Watts said she had always intended to stay in the legislature. Watts has defeated Republican and Independent challenges in every election with comfortable margins. In 2001, Watts won with 53.9% of the vote over two challengers, including a re-match with Republican candidate C. T. Craig.

During the 2004 session, Watts introduced twenty-three bills and four resolutions. Eight bills passed, eleven failed, six were carried over and two were incorporated into other bills. Her bills covered a wide range of topics with several relating to health care and services to seniors and the disabled.

A bill to permit departments of social services to develop multidisciplinary consultation teams was passed as did a bill relating to admissions to Veterans Care Centers. The powers of attorney for incapacitated persons were amended. A proposed change in the regulation of assisted living facilities for mentally retarded, mentally ill or substance abusers was carried over. A proposed change in the sickness and disability program for state employees failed as did a bill to establish staffing standards for nursing homes.

Other bills that passed include amendments for the State Board of Contractors and to the state building code. The development of parenting programs by the Department of Correctional Education passed. Two bills relating to special license plates were incorporated into other bills. Two resolutions on the 50th anniversary of Annandale High School and Garfield Elementary passed.

Bills that failed included proposed changes in the state highway funding allocation, to increase the cigarette tax, and to amend the law relating to persons who may perform marriages.

Delegate HD 39

Vivian E. Watts (D) Member House: 1996-; 1982-1986; Secretary of Transportation 1986; b. June 7, 1940 Detroit, Michigan; home, 8717 Mary Lee Lane, Annandale 22003; educ. Univ. of Michigan (B.A. Cum Laude); married, David A. Watts; Unitarian.

Non-profit Director; former Virginia Secretary of Transportation and Public Safety; PTA Pres.; Pres. Fairfax League of Women Voters; Chair, Fairfax City Fiscal Commission, VA Chamber of Commerce Transp. Comm.; Bd. Mem. VA Community College Child Care; VA Frontier Culture Museum Fndn.; Women Execs. in State Govt.; award Am. Soc. of Civil Engineers, Natl. Capitol Serv.; Network BPW Woman of the Year.

Offices 8717 Mary Lee Lane, Annandale 22003; 703-978-2989; GA Bldg., Capitol Sq., Rm. 406, Richmond 23219; 804-698-1039.

2004 Committees *Finance; Health, Welfare and Institutions; Science and Technology.*

House Key Votes, 2004
Please see Introduction for more information on bills.

1) Budget Bill	AGN	5) Family Life	FOR	9) Morning After	AGN
2) Feticide	AGN	6) Fire Arms	AGN	10) Legal Aid	FOR
3) Marriage	AGN	7) Open Space	FOR		
4) Abortion	AGN	8) Home School	AGN		

Election Results

2003 general	Vivian Watts	(D)	10,724	99.8%	$60,553

Campaign Contributions 2004 Realty $2,650; Law $2,350; Health Care $2,300; Energy $1,750; Finance $1,250; Public Employees $1,200; Business/Retail Svs $725; Transportation $500 Undetermined $450; Misc $450; Mfg $200.

Economic Interests, 2004 *Sec.*, $50,000+ ea.: mutual funds (2), fed. ret. thrift, money market; $10,001-$50,000 ea.: mutual funds (5), bonds; *Gifts*, $62 Metropolitan Washington Airports Authority, dinner; $77 State Farm, dinner; $75 INOVA Health Systems, Gala; $150 Wolf Trap Farm Foundation, dinner and ballet.

HOUSE DISTRICT FORTY-ONE, *James H. "Jim" Dillard II (R)*

POLITICAL AND LEGISLATIVE BACKGROUND
House District 41 consists of part of Fairfax County comprised of the Fairview, Lake Braddock, Laurel, Signal Hill, Burke, Pohick, Orange, Cherry Run, Terra Centre, White Oaks, Burke Centre, and Parkway Precincts, and parts of the Sangster and Woodyard Precincts.

James H. Dillard II, a Republican and retired teacher, has served in the House since 1972, except for one defeat in 1977 in a Republican primary. Dillard sat out the 1977-79 term and won the next

ELEVENTH CONGRESSIONAL DISTRICT

election in 1980. Dillard faced primary challenges from the right wing of the Republican Party - but no Democratic opponent in the general elections until 1989, when he easily won, ran unopposed in 1991 and 1993, and overcame an Independent candidate in 1995. Unopposed in 1997, Dillard won in 1999 over Democrat Eileen Filler-Corn, although outspent. In the 2001 election, Dillard won with 83.9% of the vote over Libertarian candidate Micah C. Gray.

Dillard has a distinguished legislative record that includes getting the first statewide soil erosion control measure passed, establishing a consumer protection agency, and winning authorization for a small claims court in several localities. A strong advocate for education, Dillard chairs the House Education Committee. He supports many women's issues including the Equal Rights Amendment.

During the 2004 session, as Chairman of the Education Committee, Delegate Dillard had responsibility for the development of the Commonwealth's education policy and a number of his bills were education related. Overall, he sponsored eighteen bills and three resolutions.

Education related bills that passed included the creation of a fund for At-Risk Students, changes in the public school Standards of Learning, amendments to family life education to include information on avoiding sexual assault, a provision to provide alternatives to animal dissection, and regarding the methods for rehiring teachers. A bill relating to the boundaries of schools under the Gun Free School Zones Act failed as did a bill to increase the sales tax for educational purposes. A resolution asking JLARC to study the methodology used in Standards of Learning was incorporated into another bill.

Other bills that passed included continuing education for Auctioneers, fees for fishing licenses and for the reduction of nonpoint source pollution. Bills that failed related to obtaining absentee ballots online and for notification of timbering activities by commercial entities to the State Forester. A bill relating to damages for timber cutting encroachment was incorporated into another bill. A resolution to require a study on the need and cost of additional Veteran's Cemeteries failed.

Delegate HD 41

James H. Dillard II (R) Member House: 1972-78, 1980-; b. Nov. 21, 1933, Charlottesville; home, 4709 Briar Patch Lane, Fairfax 22032; educ. Wm. & Mary (B.A.), Am. Univ. (M.A.); married Joyce Woods Butt; Episcopalian.

Retired Teacher; U.S. Navy 1955-57; Fairfax Co. Task Force on Youth Violence (co-chm. 1995-); Inst. for Conflict Analysis & Resolution (bd.); Fairfax Educ. Assn. (past Bd. mem.); VEA; Rosie's Patrol (Bd.); Fairfax Vol. Action (Bd.); Nor. VA Water Study Comm; State Water Study Comm. (Chm. 1980-81); No. VA Mediation Service (pres. & chm.).

Offices 4709 Briar Patch Lane, Fairfax 22032; 703-323-9556; GA Bldg., Capitol Sq., Rm. 702, Richmond 23219; 804-698-1041.

2004 Committees *Education, Chair; Appropriations; Privileges and Elections.*

House Key Votes, 2004
Please see Introduction for more information on bills.

1) Budget Bill	FOR	5) Family Life	FOR	9) Morning After	AGN
2) Feticide	FOR	6) Fire Arms	FOR	10) Legal Aid	FOR
3) Marriage	AGN	7) Open Space	FOR		
4) Abortion	FOR	8) Home School	AGN		

231

Election Results

2003 general	James H. Dillard II	(R)	8,889	63.3%		$64,451
	M.J. Golden	(I)	3,768	27.4%		$14,839
	J.M. Wolfe		(I)	1,294	9.2%	
$ 4,814						

Campaign Contributions 2004 : Health Care $1,000; Agriculture $650; Transportation $500; Tech/Communications $500; Business/Retail Svs $475; Law $250; Realty $250; Candidate Self-Financing $1,000.

Economic Interests, 2004 *Sec.*, $50,000+ ea.: stocks in: Exxon Mobil, Verizon; $10,001-$50,000 ea.: bonds, stocks in: Tri-Cont., CSX; *Pay. for Talks, Mtgs., & Publ.*, $3,036 state (NCSL, SLC, CSG, expenses, per diem); Paymt for talks, mtgs and publications: $650 SREB annual mtg, expenses; $845 NCSL & NCLB, expenses; *Gifts*, $152 Altria, Kraft Days reception; $78 State Farm Ins. Company, dinner; $64 Wyeth Pharmacies, dinner; $82 UVA, dinner; $62 Metro airport Authority, dinner; $100 VPI & State University, football game, food; *Real Estate*, One prop.

HOUSE DISTRICT FIFTY-ONE, *Michele B. McQuigg (R)*

POLITICAL AND LEGISLATIVE BACKGROUND

House District 51 consists of the Prince William County Precincts of McCoart, Springwoods, Westridge, Lake Ridge, Occoquan, Old Bridge, Rockledge, Mohican, Bethel, Chinn, Civic Center, Kerrydale, Lynn, and Kilby.

Michele B. McQuigg, a Republican, was elected to the House following a special election in January, 1998. Governor Gilmore, elected in 1997, appointed Delegate David G. Brickley (D), who had served since 1976, to head the Department of Conservation and Recreation. McQuigg has been active in real estate and in her community. She handily defeated Democrat John Harper, Jr. McQuigg's husband, F. Clancy McQuigg, had unsuccessfully opposed Brickley in 1993 and 1995. In the 1999 election, McQuigg defeated Democrat Virginia Stephens by 55.6% of the vote. In the 2001 election, McQuigg defeated two candidates, winning with 64% of the vote over Democrat Denise Oppenhagen and Libertarian James E. Simpson.

During the 2004 session, McQuigg sponsored fifteen bills and four resolutions. Seven bills passed, two failed, three were incorporated into other bills, and three were carried over. All four of her resolutions passed.

Six of her bills related to transportation and driving. A bill designating the penalty for reckless driving while on a suspended license as a Class 6 felony passed. Speeding fine prepayment costs and the use of community service as an alternative to a fine passed. People who sell or distribute fire equipment, ambulances and funeral vehicles were exempted from the requirement to obtain a license as a motor vehicle dealer. The establishment of a penalty for leaving children unattended in a motor vehicle was carried over. A bill to expand traffic light monitoring to all jurisdictions in the state failed as did a bill on motor vehicle storage charges.

ELEVENTH CONGRESSIONAL DISTRICT

A bill to establish a pilot program for local cooperation in the enforcement of Board for Contractors and the Department of Professional and Occupational Regulation programs passed. An amendment permits the State Fire Marshall to enforce the fire safety code in those jurisdictions that do not enforce the code at the local level. The procedures on the adoption of the FDA Food Safety Code were amended. A bill defining gang related activity was incorporated into another bill as was a bill to abolish the Advisory Committee on Intergovernmental Relations.

Delegate HD 51

Michele B. McQuigg (R) Member House: 1998- ; b. September 2, 1947, NY; home 1415 Admiral Dr., Woodbridge 22192; educ. Mary Washington Col (B.S.), VPI & SU (M.S.); married, F. Clancy McQuigg; Episcopalian.

Former Real Estate agent; Member Lake Ridge Occoquan Coles Civic Assn., Clean Community Council, ACTS, Friends of the Library, Ladies Auxiliary VFW No. 1503, Prince William Co. Regional Chamber of Commerce, VA PTA (lifetime mem.).

Offices 2241-R Tacketts Mill Dr., Woodbridge 22192; 703-491-9870; GA Bldg., Capitol Sq., Rm. 418, Richmond 23219; 804-698-1051.

2004 Committees *Counties, Cities and Towns; Courts of Justice; General Laws; Science and Technology.*

House Key Votes, 2004

Please see Introduction for more information on bills.

1) Budget Bill	FOR	5) Family Life	FOR	9) Morning After	FOR
2) Feticide	FOR	6) Fire Arms	FOR	10) Legal Aid	FOR
3) Marriage	FOR	7) Open Space	FOR		
4) Abortion	FOR	8) Home School	FOR		

Election Results

2004 general	Michele B. McQuigg	(R)	8,128	99.9%	$32,925

Campaign Contributions 2004 Political $5,000; Law $3,975; Finance $2,700; Energy $2,650; Health Care $2,250; Business/Retail Svs $2,100; Tech/Communications $1,000; Realty $750; Public Employees $300; Transportation $250; Mfg $250; Agriculture $250.

ELEVENTH CONGRESSIONAL DISTRICT
Economic Interests, 2004 *Sal. or Wages*, $10,000+ Strategic Financial Planning Systems; *Sec.*, $10,001-$50,000 ea.: mutual funds (2); *Gifts*, $152 Altria, Kraft Days Reception; *Bus. Int.*, $50,000 Strategic Financial Planning Systems (aviation engineering); $50,000/less rental prop.

HOUSE DISTRICT FIFTY-TWO, *Jeffrey M. Frederick (R)*

POLITICAL AND LEGISLATIVE BACKGROUND
House District 52 consists of part of Prince William County comprised of the Dumfries, Potomac, Graham Park, Pattie, Henderson, Montclair, Belmont, Library, Featherstone, Potomac View, and Rippon Precincts, and parts of the Quantico and Washington-Reid Precincts.

Rollison was replaced by Jeffrey M. Frederick. During the 2004 session, Frederick sponsored thirteen bills and three resolutions. One bill passed, nine failed, one was incorporated and two were carried over. Three resolutions, all proposed constitutional amendments, were carried over.

The bill that passed permitted Prince William County to develop alternative real estate tax payment scheduled for elderly and handicapped persons. A bill to permit special license plates for the 275th anniversary of Prince William County was incorporated into another bill.

Two tax related proposals failed including a tax credit for teachers for personal purchases of teaching materials, and a proposed tax credit for employers expenses in enabling employees to telework. A proposal to allocation highway funds according to motor fuel sales reports was rejected.

Delegate HD 52

Jeffrey M. Frederick (R) Member House: 2004- b. Sept. 23, 1975, Fairfax, VA; educ. Emory University, GA (BA Economic & Political Science, 1997); spouse Amy Noone, Christian.

Executive; USNR, 1996-97; Hispanic Business Roundtable, Americas Future Foundation, Council for National Policy, Prince Wm. Taxpayers Alliance, VA Club for Growth.

Offices: P.O. Box 58, Woodbridge, VA 22194, (703) 490-8405, FAX: (703) 783-1310; P.O. Box 406, Richmond, VA 23218, (804) 698-1052; FAX: (804) 786-6310.

2004 Committees: Health Welfare and Institutions, Priveleges and Elections, Education.

House Key Votes, 2004
Please see Introduction for more information on bills.

1) Budget Bill	AGN	5) Family Life	AGN	9) Morning After	FOR
2) Feticide	FOR	6) Fire Arms	FOR	10) Legal Aid	AGN
3) Marriage	FOR	7) Open Space	AGN		
4) Abortion	FOR	8) Home School	FOR		

234

Election Results

2003 general	Jeffrey M. Frederick	(R)	5,384	56.7%	$201,993
	C F Taylor	(D)	4,100	44.2%	$186,253

Campaign Contributions 2004   Tech/Communications $22,342; Business/Retail Svs $13,555; Political $10,680; Realty $10,385; Transportation $9,216; Law $5,960; Finance $5,145; Health Care $4,950; Misc $4,663; Public Employees $3,352; Energy $2,980; Single-Issue Groups $2,315; Agriculture $2,150; Defense $355.

Economic Interests, 2004   *Sal. or Wages*, $10,000+ ea.: GXS Strategies, Inc, 60 Plus Assoc (wife); *Off. & Dir.*, GXS Strategies Inc., CEO, 60 Plus Assoc., Vice President: Sec, $50,000+ stock in GXS; *Pay. for Talks, Mtgs., & Publ.*, $1,160 VA Road & Transp. Blrs. (speaker annual mtg., expenses); *Gifts:* $65 Altria, dinner; $112 Altria, dinner; $315 Kings Dominion, park tkts.

HOUSE DISTRICT FIFTY-THREE, *James M. "Jim" Scott (D)*

POLITICAL AND LEGISLATIVE BACKGROUND
House District 53 includes all of the City of Falls Church; and the Fairfax County Precincts of Haycock, Kirby, Longfellow, Mclean, Pimmit, Westhampton, Westmoreland, Walnut Hill #1, Marshall, Pine Spring, Shreve, Timber Lane, Walker, Woodburn, Stenwood, Thoreau, Merrifield, and Walnut Hill #2.

James M. Scott, assistant Vice President of Community Affairs at Inova Health Systems, and a Democrat, has served since 1991. With his 14 years on the Fairfax County Board of Supervisors, Scott had been expected to win the election handily. But Republican David Sanders led an aggressive campaign and held a 17 vote victory. Scott asked for a recount and won the seat by only one vote when absentee ballots were recounted. Scott's re-election in 1993 was with a vastly more comfortable 53.8% of the vote, and in 1995 increased to 58.3% over Republican challengers. Scott was unopposed in 1997. In the 1999 election, Scott won with 59.6% of the vote against a newcomer, Republican Patrick A. Kelly. Scott trounced Republican opposition in 2001, winning with 60.3% of the vote over Republican David F. Snyder.

During the 2004 session, Scott sponsored twenty-four bills and twelve resolutions. Eight bills passed, four failed, nine were carried over and three were incorporated into other bills. Eleven of his twelve resolutions passed.

One bill that passed expanded the jurisdiction of persons appointed by a Circuit Judge to perform marriage ceremonies from the individual jurisdiction where the person resides to the entire Commonwealth. The financial law involving the use of credit cards was amended to allow credit card purchasers to make certain claims and make certain defenses under the Federal Fair Credit Billing Act. The campaign finance reporting law was changed to raise the reporting requirements for certain contributions by local political party committees from $10,000 to $15,000. An amendment to the Falls Church city charter passed.

ELEVENTH CONGRESSIONAL DISTRICT

A bill to have the Secretary of Technology monitor trends in broadband communications services was incorporated into another bill. DMV provisions were amended to require persons over 80 to have visuals exams under a bill that was incorporated as was provision for vehicle forfeiture for a person convicted of DUI three times in ten years.

Several resolutions commending individuals, expressing sorrow at the deaths of several public-spirited citizens, and recognizing organizations passed. One proposed constitutional amendment on public funding for education was carried over.

The bills that failed covered a range of topics including a bill to change the allocation of federal Electoral College votes; a proposed sales tax increase to fund mass transit, and a bill to prohibit firearm possession by persons convicted of sexual battery or stalking.

Bills carried over included a provision relating to affordable housing by local school board employees; campaign finance reporting disclosure; local emergency management operations plans; and a provision to allow local governments to regulate potentially dangerous dogs.

Delegate HD 53

James M. Scott (D) Member House: 1992-; b. June 11, 1938, Galax, VA; home, 2827 Maple Lane, Fairfax 22031; educ. Univ. of NC (BA, MA), George Mason Univ. (MPA); married Nancy Virginia Cromwell; Methodist.

Assistant Vice-Pres., Community Affairs, INOVA Health System; Fairfax Bd. County Sup., 1971-83; United Way (Exec. Com.); AHOME (bd. dir.); Nor. VA Transp. Comm. (Chmn. 1981); Awards: Greater Merrifield Bus. Assn., Public Servant of the Yr. (1994); Fairfax Co. Citizen of Year, (1990); Public Official of Year VA Housing Coali. (1992); Metro COG Scull Pub. Serv. Award (1984).

Offices P.O. Box 359, Merrifield 22116-0359; 703-560-8338; GA Bldg., Rm. 405, Capitol Sq., Richmond 23219; 804-698-1053.

2004Committees *Commerce and Labor; Militia and Police; Privileges and Elections..*

House Key Votes, 2004
Please see Introduction for more information on bills.

1) Budget Bill	FOR	5) Family Life	FOR	9) Morning After	AGN
2) Feticide	AGN	6) Fire Arms	FOR	10) Legal Aid	FOR
3) Marriage	AGN	7) Open Space	FOR		
4) Abortion	AGN	8) Home School	FOR		

Election Results

2004 general	James M. Scott	(D)	11,588	98.61%	$73,304

236

ELEVENTH CONGRESSIONAL DISTRICT

Campaign Contributions 2004 Realty/Constr. $11,750; Finance $5,700; Health Care $3,500; Energy $3,250; Political $2,250; Tech/Communications $2,000; Law $1,800; Public Employees $1,750; Business/Retail Svs $975; Transportation $750; Misc $670; Mfg $400; Agriculture $250.

Economic Interests, 2004 *Sal. and Wages*, $10,000+ ea.: Inova Health System, Fairfax Co. Public Schools (spouse); *Sec.*, $50,000+ ea.: mutual funds (2), stocks in AOL Time Warner; $10,001-$50,000 ea.: mutual funds (3), stocks in: Fannie Mae, GE, Pepsico, Coca Cola, IBM, Marathon Oil, Wal Mart, investment funds (5); Paymts for Representation by Assoc. INOVA Health System, General Assembly & Executive Agencies; *Gifts* :$89 Altria, food, entertainment; $52 Dominion Resources, food; $1,080 Diageo, Redskins tkts (3); $62 Wash Airport Authority, food; $82 UVA, bus, food, tkts; $266 Dominion Resources, Redskins tkts, food; *Real Estate*, Two residential townhouses.

Agriculture, Conservation and Natural Resources
Chaired by Senator Hawkins, Chichester, Bolling, Ticer, Whipple, Hanger, Watkins, Reynolds, Puckett, Ruff, Obenshain, Rerras, Ruff, Blevins, Deeds, Cuccinelli and Locke.

Commerce and Labor
Chaired by Senator Wampler, Colgan, Saslaw, Chichester, Y.B. Miller, Norment, Stosch, Stolle, Potts, Edwards, Williams, Watkins, Wagner and Rerras.

Courts of Justice
Chaired by Senator Stolle, Saslaw, Marsh, Quayle, Norment, Lucas, Howell, Edwards, Reynolds, Mims, Puller, Rerras, Blevins, Cuccinelli, Obenshain.

Education and Health
Chaired by Senator Potts, Saslaw, Lambert, Houck, Lucas, Howell, Quayle, Martin, Newman, Edwards, Bolling, Ruff, Whipple, Mims, Blevins.

Finance
Chaired by Senator Chichester, Colgan, Lambert, Wampler, Stosch, Houck, Hawkins, Howell, Saslaw, Stolle, Quayle, Norment, Potts, Hanger, and Watkins.

General Laws
Chaired by Senator Stosch, Colgan, Houck, Lambert, Wampler, Y.B. Miller, Hawkins, Locke, Martin, Bolling, Ruff, Bell, Devolites, Davis, Wagner, O'Brien.

Local Government
Chaired by Senator Qualye, Marsh, Lucas, Martin, Hanger, Newman, Ticer, Whipple, Reynolds, Mims, Puckett, Puller, Ruff, Cuccinelli, Obenshain.

Privileges and Elections
Chaired by Senator Martin, Lambert, Hawkins, Bolling, Howell, Potts, Stolle, Deeds, O'Brien, Whipple, Reynolds, Bell, Devolites, Davis, Obenshain, and Puckett.

Rehabilitation and Social Service
Chaired by Senator Hanger, Miller, Marsh, Lucas, Williams, Ticer, Puller, Rerras, Wagner, Cuccinelli, O'Brien, Deeds, Bell, Devolites, Davis, and Locke.

Rules
Chaired by Senator Norment, Colgan, Saslaw, Wampler, Chichester, Stosch, Quayle, Hawkins, Stolle, Hanger, Williams, Houck, Potts, Whipple, Martin, and Mims.

Transportation
Chaired by Senator Williams, Houck, Y.B. Miller, Marsh, Newman, Watkins, Puckett, Mims, Rerras, Wagner, Blevins, Deeds, O'Brien, Bell, Davis and Devolites.

Notes

2005 HOUSE STANDING COMMITTEES

Privileges and Elections
Chaired by Delegate Putney, Dillard, Ingram, Marshall (of Prince William), Hargrove, Jones (of Suffolk), Albo, Black, Rapp, Cole, Cosgrove, Hugo, Frederick, Fralin, Van Landingham, Phillips, Scott (of Fairfax), Brink, Alexander, Joannou, Sickles.

Courts of Justice
Chaired by Delegate Mc Donnell, Albo, Griffith, Kilgore, McQuigg, Black, Weatherholtz, Hurt, Athey, Janis, Bell, Marrs, McDougle, Reese, Johnson, Melvin, Armstrong, Moran, Barlow, Watts, Brink, Ware (of Roanoke City).

Education
Chaired by Delegate Dillard, Tata, Hamilton, Landes, Reid, Black, Rapp, Bell, Linganfelter, Rust, Reese, Carrico, Frederick, Fralin, Council, Van Yahres, Keister, Shuler, Alexander, Ward, Ebbin, Ware (of Roanoke City).

General Laws
Chaired by Delegate Reid, Cox, Albo, Jones (of Suffolk), McQuigg, Suit, Rapp, Wright, Oder, Saxman, Marshall (of Danville), McDougle, Gear, Cosgrove, Phillips, Armstrong, Barlow, Hull, Howell (of Norfolk), BaCote, Abbitt, Ward.

Transportation
Chaired by Delegate Wardrup, May, Black, Welch, Saxman, Carrico, Cosgrove, Gear, Oder, Rust, McDougle, Hugo, Scott (of Madison), Fralin, Stump, Jones (of Richmond City), Moran, Pollard, Ward, Ebbin, BaCote.

Finance
Chaired by Delegate Parrish, Purkey, Orrock, Louderback, Ware (of Powhatan), Welch, Nixon, Byron, Lingamfelter, Cole, O'Bannon, Janis, Hugo, Cline, Johnson, Melvin, Van Yahres, Hull, Watts, Hall, Shannon, Lewis.

Appropriations
Chaired by Delegate Callahan, Putney, Dillard, Morgan, Tata, Hamilton, Ingram, May, Sherwood, Cox, Wardrup, Dudley, Reid, Landes, Jones (of Suffolk), Hogan, Councill, Van Landingham, Phillips, Spruill, Stump, Scott (of Fairfax), Joannou, Miles, Abbitt.

Counties, Cities, and Towns
Chaired by Delegate Ingram, Marshall (of Prince William), Orrock, Dudley, Bryant, McQuigg, Suit, Oder, Marshall (of Danville), Hurt, Reese, Marrs, Cline, Cole, Hall, Stump, Hull, Jones (of Richmond City), Spruill, Amundson, Armstrong, Ware (of Roanoke City).

Commerce and Labor
Chaired by Delegate Morgan, Hargrove,Callahan, Tata, Parrish, Purkey, Kilgore, Bryant, Byron, Ware (of Powhattan), Dudley, Griffith, Nixon, Suit, Plum, Johnson, Jones (of Richmond City), Joannou, Melvin, Keister, Abbitt.

Health Welfare and Institutions
Chaired by Delegate Hamiliton, Purkey, Orrock, McDonnell, Nixon, O'Bannon, Welch, Marrs, Hogan, Bell, Athey, Nutter, Frederick, Janis, Spruill, Moran, Baskerville, Keister, Sickles, Ebbin, Howell (of Norfolk), BaCote.

Agriculture, Chesapeake and Natural Resources
Chaired by Delegate Cox, Morgan, Sherwood, Ware (of Powhattan), Louderback, Wright, Orrock, Weatherholtz, Byron, Saxman, Hogan, Cline, Scott (of Madison), Bryant, Plum, Van Yahres, Amundson, Shuler, Miles, Stump, Eisenberg, Shannon.

Militia, Police and Public Safety
Chaired by Delegate Sherwood, Griffith, Weatherholtz, Kilgore, Louderback, Wright, Carrico, Lingamfelter, Nutter, Athey, Hurt, Hogan, Janis, Cline, Scott (of Fairfax), Pollard, Van Landingham, Barlow, Shuler, Peterson, Lewis, Miller.

Science and Technology
Chaired by Delegate May, Purkey, Marshall (of Prince William), Nixon, Byron, O'Bannon, Rust, Marshall (of Danville), Cosgrove, Nutter, Gear, McQuigg, Louderback, Scott (of Madison), Plum, Baskerville, Watts, Peterson, Alexander, Eisenberg, Howell (of Norfolk), Miller.

Rules
Chaired by Delegate Howell, Putney, Callahan, Parrish, Hargrove, McDonnell, Wardrup, Griffith, Kilgore, Jones (of Suffolk), Landes, Councill, Hall, Joannou, Spruill, Abbitt.

LOCATION, HOUSE AND SENATE COMMITTEE MEETING ROOMS

Rooms 1 and 2 – First Floor, North Corridor, Capitol
Room 4 – First Floor, East Corridor, Capitol

Rooms A, B, C, D – First Floor, General Assembly Building
Appropriations Room – Ninth Floor, General Assembly Building
Speaker's Conference Room – Sixth Floor, General Assembly Building

Capitol Square complex off of 9th Street, Richmond, Virginia

As of December 1, 2002, smoking is not allowed in committee meeting rooms nor is it permitted in the lobbies or hallways. State law already prohibits it in state and local government restrooms among other places.

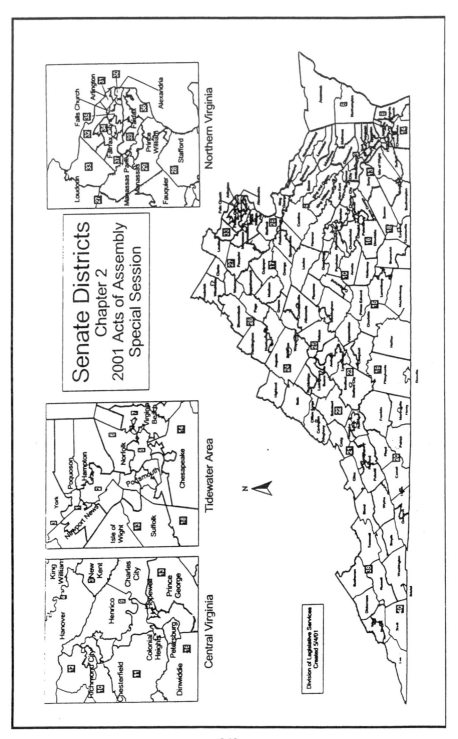

Senate Districts
Chapter 2
2001 Acts of Assembly
Special Session

Northern Virginia

Tidewater Area

Central Virginia

Division of Legislative Services
Created 5/4/01

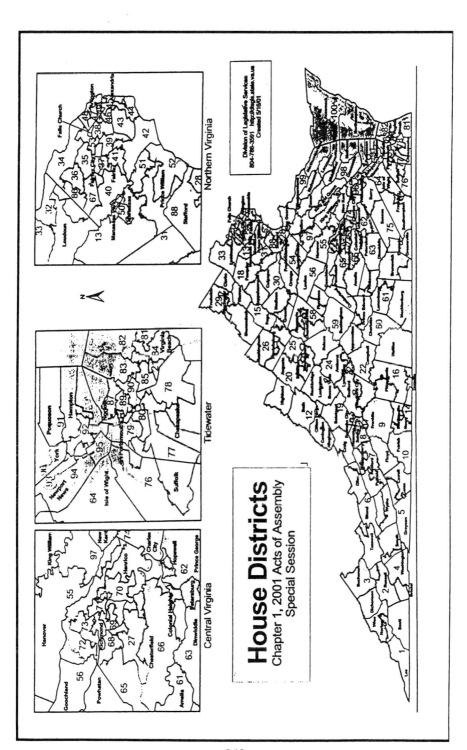

House Districts
Chapter 1, 2001 Acts of Assembly
Special Session

Northern Virginia

Division of Legislative Services
804-786-3591 http://dls.gis.state.va.us
Created 5/16/01

Tidewater

Central Virginia

The 2005 Almanac Of Virginia Politics
Flora Carter • Toni-Michelle C. Travis

Now we offer you the choice of our traditional paperback copy of *The 2005 Almanac of Virginia Politics*, password access to a web edition of the book, or the chance to purchase both! Whatever edition you choose, this is the one book you need to guide you through an understanding of the Virginia legislature, bringing you a summary of the 2004 legislative session and key 2004 votes listed for the delegates and senators. The Governor, Lt. Governor, and Attorney General also are examined.

Professor Larry Sabato, political analyst, said *"The Almanac of Virginia Politics* is an enormously useful volume for any election watcher in the Old Dominion. Its statistical information and descriptive background give both students and political practitioners the flavor of the Virginia assembly and the men and women who serve as members of it."

The Woman Activist Fund, Inc. is a non-profit, tax-exempt research and educational organization. A financial report is on file with the Virginia Department of Consumer Affairs.

PUBLISHED BY THE WOMAN ACTIVIST FUND, INC.   **ISBN 0-918560-39-6**
540-672-9210   **info@almanacvapolitics.org**   **www.almanacvapolitics.org**

ORDER FORM: Almanac of Virginia Politics (please circle appropriate price):

The 2005 Almanac of Virginia Politics	*Price + 5% sales tax*
Book	$34.95 + $1.75 = $36.70
Book and Web Access* 1 user	$54.95 + $2.75 = $57.70
Web Access * 1 user [*Web Access is password protected]	$34.95 + N/A = $34.95
Web Access* 2 or more users	$69.95 + N/A = $69.95
The Wisteria Acres Cookbook by Anne Morrow Donely	$14.95 + $ 0.75 = $15.70
Postage = $3.50 Per Book + $.50 each additional book	$_____
Tax-deductible donation to support the activities of The Woman Activist Fund, Inc.	$_____
TOTAL (enclosed is a check payable to "The Woman Activist Fund, Inc.")	$_____

Name _____

Address _____

City/State _____ Zip Code _____

Telephone _____ Fax _____

Email _____

Orders may be sent to our new publications address: The Woman Activist Fund, Inc., 16480 Trimmers Road Orange, VA 22960. For a discount on ordering larger quantities, please contact The Woman Activist Fund, Inc. at (640) 672-9210 or info@almanacvapolitics.org.